W9-BSZ-725

POLITICAL PARTIES: A BEHAVIORAL ANALYSIS

POLITICAL PARTIES: A BEHAVIORAL ANALYSIS

SAMUEL J. ELDERSVELD
University of Michigan

RAND McNALLY & COMPANY • CHICAGO

RAND McNALLY POLITICAL SCIENCE SERIES

MORTON GRODZINS, *Advisory Editor*

Eldersveld, *Political Parties: A Behavioral Analysis*
Fiser, ed., POLICY BACKGROUND SERIES
Clawson, *Land for Americans*
Clawson, *Land and Water for Recreation*
Sufrin and Buck, *What Price Progress? A Study in Chronic Unemployment*
Froman, *Congressmen and Their Constituencies*
Goldwin, ed., RAND McNALLY PUBLIC AFFAIRS SERIES
America Armed: Essays on United States Military Policy
A Nation of States: Essays on the American Federal System
Why Foreign Aid?
Political Parties, U.S.A.
100 Years of Emancipation
Golembiewski, *Behavior and Organization: O & M and the Small Group*
Hanna, ed., *Independent Black Africa*
Milbrath, *The Washington Lobbyists*
Peabody and Polsby, eds., *New Perspectives on the House of Representatives*
Press, ed., *The Polity: Selected Essays by Norton E. Long*
Schmidhauser, ed., *Constitutional Law in the Political Process*
Schubert, ed., *Judicial Behavior: A Reader in Theory and Research*
Strauss, *The City and Man*
Strauss and Cropsey, eds., *History of Political Philosophy*
Ulmer, ed., *Readings in Political Behavior*
Williams and Press, eds., *Democracy in Urban America: Readings on Government and Politics*

Printed in U.S.A. by Rand McNally & Company
Library of Congress Catalogue Card Number 64:17633

ACKNOWLEDGEMENTS

Modern political analysis of the complexity reported in this study is indebted to the efforts and ideas of many collaborators. The study has relied to a great degree on the scholarly insight of several generations, the financial support of university and foundation, the field work of many students and professional workers, and, above all, on the willingness and frankness of political leaders to speak freely in the interview situation.

I am indebted to the Detroit Area Study of the University of Michigan, initially supported by the Ford Foundation, for the massive and detailed technical work of designing the study and executing the field work necessary for collecting the data during the fall of 1956 and the spring of 1957. Under the direction of Professors Ronald Freedman and Harry Sharp of the Department of Sociology, the idea became reality. I am also grateful for the assistance of the graduate students in the Department of Political Science, particularly Connie Lieder, Archie Singham, John Bochel, and John Gilmore, for much of the interviewing of the top leadership of the two parties in the congressional districts, the county, and the state. Additional grants from the Ford Foundation and the Horace H. Rackham School of Graduate Studies facilitated the early stages of the analysis. The opportunity to spend a year at the Center for Advanced Study in the Behavioral Sciences at Stanford, California, was invaluable for theoretical reflection, review of the literature, and preliminary testing of the proposed analysis with colleagues in the social sciences. The data-processing staff of the Center performed the gigantic task of making the first basic tabulations of the data.

I have consulted many individual scholars in preparing this

study, particularly Heinz Eulau, Morris Janowitz, Henry Valen, James March, Avery Leiserson, Dwaine Marvick, and Warren Miller. But without the ideas and support of my co-investigator, Daniel Katz, the study would never have been completed. In addition, and critical for the completion of the project, was the active interest and unqualified support of the two state party chairmen, Neil Staebler and John Feikens, as well as the many hours granted me and the interviewers by the two Wayne County chairwomen, the six congressional district chairmen for each party, the executive board members in each district, the candidates for Congress, the CIO Political Action Coordinators, the precinct leaders, and the members of the Detroit area public who were interviewed in our cross-section. It is a tribute to these political leaders that they understood the nature of this scientific enterprise and were eager to contribute to it. Dorothy M. Jones painstakingly edited the manuscript. Finally, my wife and children contributed tolerance and patient support which were nothing short of astonishing.

I can only hope that this vast commitment of time, effort, and faith, for the consummation of which the author alone is responsible, has yielded some new understanding of the functional character of the American party system.

TABLE OF CONTENTS

PART III: THE PARTY AS AN ORGANIZATIONAL SYSTEM

PART IV: THE PUBLIC AND THE PARTIES: FUNCTIONAL RELATIONSHIPS

CHAPTER 1

A THEORY OF THE POLITICAL PARTY

The political party is a social group, a system of meaningful and patterned activity within the larger society. It consists of a set of individuals populating specific roles and behaving as member-actors of a boundaried and identifiable social unit. Goals are perceived by these actors, tasks are assigned for and by them, and communication channels are maintained. The party is thus one social organism. But the party is also a polity, a miniature political system. It has an authority structure, although the manner in which authority is graded and legitimated may differ considerably from other social groups. The party has distinctive patterns of power distribution. It has a representative process, an electoral system, and subprocesses for recruiting leaders, defining goals, and resolving internal system conflicts. Above all, the party is a decision-making system, although, again, how "authoritative" the decision-making process is remains a subject of inquiry. The political party, thus, conforms to the common characteristics of social groups. Herbert Simon, for example, has defined a group as a system of "interdependent activity, encompassing at least several primary groups and usually characterized . . . by a high degree of rational direction of behavior towards ends that are objects of common acknowledgement and expectation."[1] The party, as studied here, is such a group. It fulfills, at least minimally, these requirements, although we seek through empirical analysis to determine the degree to which "interdependent activ-

[1] "Comments on the Theory of Organizations," *American Political Science Review*, XLVI, No. 4 (Dec., 1952), 1130.

ity," "rationality," and "common acknowledgement" in fact exist.

In the study of the party as a social group, we are initially concerned with the empirical discovery of structural properties, those characteristic modes of activity which may distinguish the party as a social collectivity. To this end, it is necessary to develop and test empirical theory about the perspectives and behavior of individuals holding positions at all major levels of the hierarchy, their vertical and horizontal relationships with others in the group, and the meaning of this behavior for the subunits (or "primary groups") as well as for the total organization. Structure is people acting in relationship to others, not merely *some* actions and particular relationships, or *some* actors, for then only a segment of the structure will be revealed. The party is more than its executive elite, or campaign workers, or precinct activists, analyzed in isolation. It is a meaningful organizational system of interpersonal relationships. Concentration on those "in power," or the "inner circle," or the "activist cadre," while helpful and suggestive, cannot by itself lead to comprehension of the structure as a whole. Too much party research in America has had to settle for partial images of political reality.

In attempting to delineate the properties of the party, we assume that our knowledge of its tasks and roles in the larger political system will be enhanced. Parties came into existence to perform certain critical functions for the system, and derived their basic form in the process of implementing these functions. If one is interested in understanding the tasks presumably fulfilled by parties, it is necessary to analyze the party as a functioning structural subsystem. This is not to say that all party groups perform the same functions and possess identical structural properties. Social and political environmental conditions vary from one culture to the next. The same is true of "functional priorities." Parties are merely a particular structural response, therefore, to the needs of a social and political system in a particular milieu.

The student of party organization is interested in many of the theoretical propositions and problems which occupy the attention of students of other large-scale social groups. He may be concerned with problems of rule enforcement, morale, task performance, productivity, regulatory mechanisms, and reward systems. But he must also be alert to the probability that the party, as a political-power motivated and instrumental group, is a specific subclass of social organizations, with particular types of substructures and specialized activity patterns. Above all, he must be alert to the probability that party structures have specific group properties, which are basic to understanding the party as a structural organism, and as a functional unit in the socio-political system.

Although other approaches to the study of party structure are feasible, the analysis presented here begins with a specification of the primary structural properties of the party. It then proceeds to the utilization of these theoretical images, after the presentation of empirical evidence attesting to their validity or invalidity, in three ways. First, we are interested in determining the impact of these structural conditions on the ideology, role perception, and motivation of party leaders at different levels of the hierarchy. Second, we are concerned with the patterns of internal organizational relationships as they reflect these structural properties—in what respects is the communication system defective, in what areas does managerial control break down, and to what extent is decisional involvement achieved? Third, we feel that such knowledge of the party as a structure of leadership perspectives and as a structure of interpersonal hierarchical relationships will lead to a better understanding of the quality of the party group as a functional unit. Our major foci are, therefore, the *congruence* of leadership perspectives, the *coherence* of hierarchical relationships, and the *competence* of the group in the fulfillment of social and political functions.

Political party structures have certain common tendencies differentiating them from other groups such as families, churches, labor unions, business firms, lodges. This is a proposition not easily defended. In the long run it can be demonstrated only by the development of probable differentiae and the testing of these through empirical research. In taking the position that there are common structural tendencies, we do not mean to imply that party structures do not vary. They do, both in the same society and in different societies. But, despite such variations which are primarily the product of particular adaptations to special environmental conditions, parties exhibit structural similarities in certain basic respects. We view the party as a specialized system of action in democratic societies, with a special meaning and purpose in the political and social order. It is distinguishable by its primary goal (to occupy at least some of the governmental leadership posts), by its competitive-electoral relationships with similar groups, and by its special pattern of public-support and adaptation strategies. As will be suggested below, certain key structural styles emerge in parties and are inherent in the party type of social organization. Perhaps it can be said that parties are unique structurally because they are groups oriented to the achievement of special goals and functions under unique environmental conditions in the society. Whether these structural properties are maximally conducive to goal and function realization is a major object of our investigation.

In attempting to spell out the relevant structural dimensions of parties as tentative theoretical positions for subsequent analysis, it must be recognized that parties do not possess many of the conventional attributes of the bureaucratic system. In particular, the bureaucratic prerequisites of impermeability, depersonalized human relationships, strict devotion to regulations and rule enforcement, precise allocation of obligations, duties, and roles, discipline, and sanctions, even low circulation of personnel, are found wanting in most party structures. We sense that the Republican and Democratic parties are structurally different from General Motors, the Catholic church, the AFL-CIO, or the Farm Bureau; how they differ is the task of empirical theory and research. We suggest the following four theoretical constructs in a genuinely exploratory sense, conscious that they are indeed "dimensions," with great variation among individual party structures along each dimension, and that they are a mere beginning for theory. Parties may combine these properties differently, emphasizing some more than others. In our opinion, however, it is likely that elements of each of these constructs are not only relevant to all party structures but are also critical for comprehending their essential nature as functioning social and political organisms.

The party must first be understood as a clientele-oriented structure. In contrast to the bureaucratic model, the party is almost by definition an open, informal, personalized system. Roberto Michels wrote long ago of the "omnibus tendency" of parties. He saw party as an "organization ever greedy for new members," adding, "the party no longer seeks to fight its opponents, but simply to outbid them." The result, claimed Michels, was that the party would "sacrifice its political virginity, by entering into promiscuous relationships with the most heterogeneous political elements. . . ."[2] Although Michels was writing particularly about socialist parties a half-century ago, his observations are insightful and have been repeated by many scholars of party politics. The party is always "potential-clientele" conscious. It is open at its base to new recruits for party work as well as to nonactivist supporters. It is often open at the higher levels also, indeed, sometimes at the elite apex, if such a strategy will profit the party's power aspirations. Thus it is permeable and adaptive, even in societies with multiparty systems in which the probability of seducing the small number of "floating voters" is minimal. Singularly reliant on votes as the arithmetic of power, the party reflects structurally an inherent tendency toward joint advantage. The party is a mutually exploitative relationship—it is joined by those who would use it; it mobilizes for the sake of power those who would join it. This porous nature of the party—at its base, sides, and apex—has tremendous consequences for individual perspectives and organizational relationships. Where adaptation is maximal, internal managerial control is difficult, factional pluralism multiplied, operational efficiency likely to be impaired, and goal orientations and ideological consensus highly noncongruent;

[2] See Alfred de Grazia, *Roberto Michels' First Lectures in Political Sociology* (Minneapolis: University of Minnesota Press, 1949), p. 145, and Robert Michels, *Political Parties* (Glencoe, Ill.: Free Press, 1949), pp. 374–76.

where adaptation is minimal, such consequences for internal control and perspectives will doubtless be less severe. This is the first theoretical dilemma the party must face.

The second empirical image follows from the first. The party is a structural system seeking to translate or convert (or be converted by) social and economic interests into political power directly. It consists of a set of socio-economic interests groping for political recognition, articulation, and control. As such the party can be conceptualized as an alliance of substructures or subcoalitions. Many writers have implicitly recognized this character of the party organization. Charles Merriam made the point well 40 years ago:

> Of great significance in the composition of any political party are the numerous types of social groupings. These are fundamental in any scientific study of the political party, and too great emphasis cannot be laid upon them. . . . The practical politician is never guilty of the omission of the study of social groupings, but the students of politics have sometimes proceeded as if parties were working in a social vacuum.[3]

The subcoalitions within the party may be identified variously—in terms of geographical boundaries, on the basis of organizational status, as demographic or social categories, or on the basis of ideological division. In addition, there may be organizational entities almost completely self-reliant, such as the legislative wing of the party (or the congressman with his own "machine"), women and youth auxiliaries, a political club "movement," and affiliated business, labor, or farm suborganizations.

The party, in this image, exists as an intermediary group representing and exploiting multiple interests for the achievement of direct control over the power apparatus of the society. The party becomes inevitably, then, a conflict system. Conflict among the competing interests in the structure can be managed, channeled, avoided—in fact, the structure many times seems constituted to maximize conflict avoidance. But above all, and this is the unique structural characteristic of the party in this regard,

[3] *The American Party System* (New York: Macmillan, 1922), p. 3.

conflict within the party must be tolerated. As a power-aspiring group, "greedy" for new followers, the party does not settle conflict; it defers the resolution of conflict. The party is thus no genuine mediator; it seeks to stabilize subcoalitional relationships and interactions so that these multiple interests will remain committed to the organization, after partial acquiescence to their demands, without permitting intergroup rivalries to collide with the party's grand design for power. Tension between the group goal and subcoalitional demands is, therefore, the second basic structural dilemma of the party.

This theoretical position is similar to, and borrows from, one important stream of current organizational theory—coalitional theory.[4] In adapting this theory to the party structure, each subcoalitional participant can be considered as possessing its own set of demands and goals (or "preference orderings"). The party organization as a single enterprise "bargains" with these subgroups, enters into a coalition agreement with them "for the purposes of the (political) game," and thus develops a "joint preference ordering" of organizational objectives. This, presumably, is the result of "side payments" to the subcoalitions, a subtle calculus of reciprocal strengths, needs, and contributions to the total party structure. Once the "bargain" has been consummated the party is able to move ahead, goal-setting is finalized, and the group can operate as a single "entrepreneur." Variations on this basic model have been advanced, and strong reservations have been suggested. In its applicability to the political party these reservations should certainly be underlined. Yet it is a valuable theoretical formulation with which to work, though the process for determining coalitional objectives, the finality of the agreement, as well as the resultant implication that organizational unity will be attained, are obscure elements in the model. The chief value of the model is that it begins to operationalize insights about the structural properties of parties which have remained

[4] See, for example, Richard M. Cyert and James G. March, "A Behavioral Theory of Organizational Objectives," in Mason Haire, ed., *Modern Organization Theory* (New York: Wiley, 1959), pp. 76–89.

vague and unresearchable for many years. If clarified and systematically utilized, it is a construct which will prove useful in explaining internal organizational relationships as well as leadership perspectives. The nature of decision-making, communicative contacts, consensus, role perceptions, and goal orientations will probably be more strikingly different in a moderately pluralized party structure than in a rigidly pluralized structure of three or four distinct subcoalitions tenaciously clinging to conflicting "preference orderings" and with whom "side payments" are not easily arranged. In the latter context, to say that the party functions with a single entrepreneurial goal may be superficial, as the coalition theorists would be the first to admit. In sum, if the view of the party in coalitional terms is not employed mechanically, and is linked to the view of the party process as joining with, and instrumental for, the social process, it may represent a theoretical image of considerable explanatory power.

A third theoretical position concerning the party's structural properties emerges with the question, What type of hierarchy or structure of power is a party? That the party is a hierarchy is generally not disputed, since certainly a coarchal pattern of perfectly equal power distribution does not exist. Whether the party structure is an "oligarchy," however, has been the subject of speculation since Michels' famous theory of the "iron law of oligarchy." Some insist that a minority inevitably assumes leadership and control of parties, with all the expected oligarchic phenomena which Michels predicted. Others note that even in the most carefully structured American party "machines," a reciprocal pattern of influence and responsibility obtains between the "boss" and his precinct captains.[5] We do not wish to grapple with all the alleged features of oligarchy within the party. Rather, we take issue with the necessity of one crucial assumption in that "iron law," the assumption that control of the party structure is inexorably concentrated in the hands of a single leadership corps, the top, elite, managerial nucleus of the structure. In contrast to

[5] See, for example, Edward C. Banfield, *Political Influence* (New York: Free Press, 1961), pp. 235–62.

this theory we suggest the following alternative image of the pattern of control within the party.

The possibility clearly exists that a special type of hierarchy obtains in parties—one which, to borrow Harold Lasswell and Abraham Kaplan's phrase, we will call *stratarchy*.[6] The general characteristics of stratarchy are the proliferation of the ruling group and the diffusion of power prerogatives and power exercise. Rather than centralized "unity of command," or a general dilution of power throughout the structure, "strata commands" exist which operate with a varying, but considerable degree of, independence. Such allocation of command and control to specified "layer," or "echelon," authorities is a pragmatic necessity. The very heterogeneity of membership, and the subcoalitional system, make centralized control not only difficult but unwise. In the process of adaptation, then, the party develops its own hierarchical pattern of stratified devolution of responsibility for the settlement of conflicts, rather than jeopardize the viability of the total organization by carrying such conflicts to the top command levels of the party. Further, the party must cope with widely varying local milieus of opinion, tradition, and social structure, and this encourages the recognition and acceptance of local leadership, local strategy, local power. In addition, the desperate need in all parties for votes, which are scarcely mobilized at the apex of the hierarchy, results in at least some, if not pronounced, deference to the local structural strata where votes are won or lost. Thus, a kind of "balkanization" of power relations occurs, with variations in the extent of autonomy in middle and lower hierarchical strata from one habitat to the next. While admittedly party systems in different countries will vary in degree of stratarchy, exploratory research suggests the real probability that there is a stratarchical element in all such systems, despite the custom of referring to them in such simple terms as "centralized," monolithic, or unitary.

The political party is thus to be visualized as a "reciprocal deference structure." Contrary to the bureaucratic and authori-

[6] *Power and Society* (New Haven: Yale University Press, 1950), pp. 219–20.

tarian models of social organization, the party is not a precisely ordered system of authority and influence from the top down, though as a "paper" structure it may give this appearance. The organization does not function through the issuance of directives from the top which are obeyed without question. Rather, there is tolerance of autonomy, local initiative, local inertia. The factors contributing to this property of the party are several: sparsity of activists, voluntary nature of recruitment for party work, limited rewards available to activists and irregularity of their loyalty. But, primarily, this "downward deference" stems from the absence of effective sanctions, the strong drive for votes, the instinctively adaptive tactics of success-minded party leaders, and the need for lower-echelon support. More than any other social organization, the critical action locus of the party structure is at its base. And since there is high potential for inefficiency, indifference, and displacement of group (leadership) goals with personal goals among activists at the base, leaders defer. In fact, the basis for the authority of the leadership of party organizations is one of the most puzzling to understand. It does not seem to be a function of expertise, or of role, or of normative expectations. Rather, the party structure appears to be characterized as a "rapport system."[7] Rapport is basic to status. Rapport between the top elite, middle-level cadre, and local activists rests on mutual perspectives concerning the strategy of electoral success, or mutual tolerance of ineptness (and inaction) in the face of sure defeat. The relationship between the executive elite and the "hard-core" activists in the party structure is above all, therefore, one of accommodation—of "centralist" (leadership) drive and strategy for power to "localist" interests, demands, and support. In this structural context the party faces another crucial dilemma—the need for managerial efficiency while maintaining worker morale.

Closely related is a fourth major image which emphasizes the special type of elite careerism patterns found in the party.

[7] For one discussion of this problem, see Robert V. Presthus, "Authority in Organizations," in Sidney Mailick and Edward H. Van Ness, eds., *Concepts and Issues in Administrative Behavior* (Englewood Cliffs, N.J.: Prentice-Hall, 1962), pp. 122–36.

Here, again, we take issue with an important component in the theory of oligarchy, the picture of the party as possessing a single elite cadre, "one directive social group," well-organized, self-conscious, self-perpetuating, congruent, conspiring. In its place we suggest and empirically examine the possibility of another image of the party elite. We see the party elite as consisting of pluralized sets of separable "career classes" or "career categories," with considerable differentiation in congruence, communicative interchange, and self-consciousness. Furthermore, we hypothesize differently the character of "circulation" of the party elite, as well as the basis for the structural stability of the party in the face of such circulation. There is indeed a high turnover in party leadership at all levels of the hierarchy, just as individual mobility for the determined careerist can occur at unbelievable rates. But this is not a *pro forma* turnover, as the oligarchic theorists would contend, a circulation resulting from the "amalgamation" by the old elite of "new elite" elements which are considered "safe." This is not primarily a process of absorption. It is often a process of genuine renovation, adaptation, and reconstitution of the subcoalitional balance of power within the party structure. Or it is often genuine evidence of the loss of power.

The party leader's basis of authority leans heavily on rapport, and yet is essentially quixotic, dependent as it is on an ever changing balance sheet of votes won and lost, as well as on the competitive struggle for power among the organizational subgroups with which he must contend. In addition, although party leadership cadres may indeed have some *esprit de corps,* this is quite different from that of a bureaucratic cadre. In the latter case, *esprit de corps* rests heavily on vocational security, professional associations, expectations of permanency, and a desire to protect the group from its environment. The party, however, is an open structure; tenure is unstable; personal relationships are uncertain. Thus power vanishes easily within a political party, but the saving grace is the existence of career groups of individuals who are not essentially aspiring to power. For many of these the party means "status," not "power," and the continuity of their commitment to party tasks contributes to stability in the face of constant flux and potential disequilibrium. The party structure, thus, has a peculiar career system which, despite insecurity of tenure and high circulation, does result in durability, due primarily to the continuous renewal of those separable career categories so indispensable to the fulfillment of party goals. But the dilemma of the party is clear, for it must accomplish the simultaneous fulfillment of "mobility" and "status" demands and satisfactions in an organization which is heterogeneous in membership, eclectic in ideology, and voluntaristic in motivational orientation.

These four images of the basic properties of the party structure are obviously not mutually exclusive. The argument here is that if the party as a social organization is distinctive from other organizational types, and we postulate that it is, then these tentative constructs may help identify its special character. It is not to be implied that all parties are equally characterized by these theoretical images. They are merely "dimensions," and party structures differ in the degree to which they approximate these properties. The coalitional character of certain party structures may be most relevant in certain locales; in others "reciprocal deference" and stratarchy may be more basic; and certainly parties vary in adaptiveness and clientele-consciousness. The suggestion is that an internal logic about the nature of party structure in a democratic system does exist, which theoretically differentiates it from other social structures. Two common elements in democratic societies contribute to the existence of party groups with these inherently unique structural styles: political power rests on votes; and groups compete for power. Where these components of the democratic system are strong, party groups will manifest their stylistic attributes maximally; where the components are weak, party attributes are also weak.

The specification of these structural properties should not lead to an analysis of the party in an intellectual vacuum, or to complete normative pessimism. In our opinion there are three major clusters of factors responsible for the party structure as it is. One such cluster consists of environmental pressures, both the socio-economic conditions with which the party must contend in a particular area, and the political history and climate of the area. The competitive conditions of political life interact with the social complexion of the area to impress on the party structure certain properties which are in a sense structural responses to environmental demands. Secondly, there is the "internal dynamic" cluster of variables, including the personal orientations and styles of political activism within the power process in a given area. This is the "political subculture" of the area—the normative and operational codes adhered to in the power process, communicated widely to participants in this process, and continually re-enforced by the system itself. The party and its leadership is but one segment of this subculture. Finally, the developmental or chronological component in the analysis of party structure, the factor of time, must be considered. Parties gradually evolve characteristic modes or properties which tend to become accepted and tolerated in a given area and culture. But change can and does occur, and it is possible that at critical points in time party structures do develop reorientations. Thus, although we are rather committed to accepting the basic theory outlined above, as having generalizable validity for modern-day parties in democratic societies, we accept the possibility that these, or their degree of manifestation at this point in time, are not fixed and unalterable. Human institutions do change. Social groups are dynamic. We are not locked into a structural system which is forever imprisoned by identical and constant social pressure.

Throughout this book we will seek to establish the validity of these images for American party structures in the Detroit area. We will then be preoccupied with the derivatives of these images, and the degree to which the empirical evidence of types and patterns of leadership perspectives, organizational relationships, and functional performances suggested, implied and predicted by this set of theoretical propositions are actually found within the Republican and Democratic parties. In the process of making this analysis, specific hypotheses derived from the theoretical positions outlined above will be elaborated.

TRENDS IN SCHOLARLY RESEARCH ON PARTY ORGANIZATION

For at least a half-century, students of politics have been fascinated by the internal conflicts and managerial tactics of the party organization. Early writers such as Michels, Bryce, and Ostrogorski had a deep interest in the formal agencies for action within the party. They also sought to understand the informal struggles for leadership, the nature of ideological conflict, and the manipulative techniques by which the organization was led. Their works provided the landmarks for research in this area, yielded rich insights into the party process, and are, in many aspects, superior to much research in party organization which followed. These men set the tone and pattern for political research, and in two respects we have found it difficult to deviate from their tradition. They were essentially semi-empirical in strategy, relying heavily on description of the statutory and legal status of the organization, the narration of historical background, together with impressionistic, uncontrolled observation and much anecdotal reference. In methodology they were heavily committed to normative concerns. The anti-authoritarian Michels could never conceal his sorrow over the prostitution of the German Social Democratic party organization by its leadership. Bryce claimed the organization "perverts the wishes of the people."[8] And Ostrogorski was so anti-party as to strongly recommend that such organizations be dissolved periodically.

These tendencies and emphases have persisted until very recently. There has been much theory about the party organization, a good deal of it revealing our own normative concerns, but there has been little systematic analysis of the party as an organizational system. The apotheosis of these developments was perhaps reached in 1950 with the edict of the American Political Science Association, again after no systematic study of party organization, that our American parties were not democratic, responsible or effective—that what we needed was "a system that

[8] James Bryce, *The American Commonwealth* (New York: Macmillan, 1916), II, 660.

is accountable to the public, respects and expresses differences of opinion, and is able to cope with the great problems of modern government."[9]

The literature on party leadership and organization at the local level in the United States has improved considerably in the past 25 years. Four early studies of party leadership were published in the year 1935 by Mosher, Kurtzman, Salter, and Peel,[10] followed by Gosnell's excellent study in 1937.[11] These studies examined the social characteristics of local party leaders, their techniques for vote mobilization, and to a limited extent the structure of the party machine. After 1937 a hiatus of some duration occurred. Maurice Duverger's monumental comparative study first appeared in 1951.[12] Only in the past few years, however, have such works as those of Phillips Cutright and Peter Rossi, Renate Mayntz, and Dwaine Marvick and Charles Nixon demonstrated real progress in the systematic analysis of American local party organization.[13] They compare favorably with the two best previous studies by Kurtzman and Gosnell, which for the first time provided fairly reliable data on the activities of precinct leaders and workers at the base of the party structure.

[9] "Toward a More Responsible Two-Party System," *American Political Science Review,* XLIV, No. 3, Part 2 (Sept., 1950), 4, 17.

[10] W. E. Mosher, "Party and Government at the Grass Roots," *National Municipal Review,* XXIV, 15–18; D. H. Kurtzman, *Methods of Controlling Votes in Philadelphia* (Philadelphia: University of Pennsylvania Press); J. T. Salter, *Boss Rule* (New York: McGraw-Hill); Roy V. Peel, *The Political Clubs of New York City* (New York: Putnam).

[11] Harold F. Gosnell, *Machine Politics: Chicago Model* (Chicago: University of Chicago Press).

[12] *Political Parties* (New York: Wiley).

[13] Phillips Cutright and Peter H. Rossi, "Grass Roots Politicians and the Vote," *American Sociological Review,* XXIII, No. 2 (April, 1958), 171–79; Peter H. Rossi and Phillips Cutright, "The Impact of Party Organization in an Industrial Setting," in Morris Janowitz, ed., *Community Political Systems* (Glencoe, Ill.: Free Press, 1961), pp. 81–116; Renate Mayntz, "Oligarchic Problems in a German Party District," in Dwaine Marvick, ed., *Political Decisionmakers: Recruitment and Performance* (New York: Free Press, 1961), pp. 138–92; Dwaine Marvick and Charles R. Nixon, "Recruitment Contrasts in Rival Campaign Groups," *ibid.*, pp. 193–217. See also Robert E. Agger and David Goldrich, "Community Power Structure and Partisanship," *American Sociological Review,* XXIII, No. 4 (Aug., 1958), 383–92.

Certain key observations stand out in any perusal of the literature on party organization. Recent research reminds us again of the importance for understanding the party system of knowledge about the operations of the organization. As Dwaine Marvick and Charles Nixon have said: "active workers are essential components in modern election processes . . . they form the link by which the political process is integrated with other social and community worlds."[14] The importance of organization, and particularly the local organization, has become again a major focus of attention among students of parties. In addition, these recent studies have emphasized the need for systematic, behavioral research attention to the attitudes, perceptions, and perspectives of party leaders, the character of their activities and relationships in the party organization, the nature of decision-making, control, and communicative processes in the party, and the functional linkages between the party structure and the socio-political system. Finally, they have been self-consciously concerned with the careful testing of specific theoretical propositions about party organizational leadership and activity, suggesting an alternative to the tendency to collect data without theory, or to collect theories without data. Although the noncomparability of these individual studies in specialized locales may be momentarily frustrating to the generalist, they are the beginning of precise and systematic knowledge about the party structure and process.

Today we suffer from a mélange of partial, somewhat contradictory, and often polemical images of the party structure and process. Our research has not as yet clarified some of the key questions concerning the nature of party organizational life. Is the party structure in fact an oligarchy or a loose confederation? Are communicative relationships entropic or effective? To what extent is there ideological consensus among the leadership and worker echelons of the hierarchy? How much "irresponsibility" and lack of democracy exists in organizational decision-making? Is the effectiveness of party workers at the precinct level related to organizational morale? These and many other questions

[14] *Op. cit.*, p. 194.

need answers if we are to understand the party. At the local level the lack of empirical support for our images of the party is particularly evident. Traditionally, the American local party organization, in urban centers particularly, is pictured as an efficient, cohesive, vote-getting machine, characterized by a tightly disciplined and controlled hierarchy exploiting political opportunities for personal gain—a machine, in Bryce's terminology, which "enslaves local officials . . ." and which has "in some places set up a tyranny under the forms of democracy."[15] These local parties, to use Duverger's image, derived, no doubt, from a reading of American literature, are really "electoral machines . . . not ideological groups nor class communities . . . teams of men expert in the winning of votes."[16] This traditional image has suffered at times as a result of some observations of later students of American politics, who see a "new style" of local politics and local party structure. On the way out, presumably, is the "old-style" local politics, with its discipline, personal loyalty, spoils system, welfare services, the "deliverable vote," and continuous year-round attention to precinct affairs. On the way in, presumably, are "leaders" instead of "bosses," more visibility in party activity, a looser organization, less discipline, more sporadic vote-getting activity, and more reliance on the mass media. These images of reality are still not firm, however, and much disagreement exists concerning them. Thus V. O. Key saw party organization as having become a "fractionalized system of personal and factional cliques of professionals," and "the doorbell ringers have lost their function of mobilizing the vote to the public relations experts."[17] Avery Leiserson takes a different position in discussing the local party, maintaining that "control of a bloc of votes is still as much coin of the political realm in the modern day of television and the 'educated vote' as it was fifty or a hundred years ago."[18] Until more studies in depth of the party organ-

[15] *Loc. cit.*
[16] *Op. cit.*, pp. 21–22.
[17] *Politics, Parties, and Pressure Groups* (4th ed.; New York: Crowell, 1958), pp. 375–76.
[18] *Parties and Politics* (New York: Knopf, 1958), p. 189.

ization are completed, these images will remain partial and pure conjecture.

Research into the organizational life of the party has been delayed by a series of factors, one of which may be a restricted definition of the "organization." We are inclined to view the party as the top leadership elite within a constituency, a particular leadership segment, or those manifestly "in power." Further, the fluidity, or poorly articulated character, of the American party hierarchy leads to pessimism in our efforts to specify the relationships between the strata of party leaders. Problems of "accessibility" to political leadership also compound research difficulties. Finally, the absence of neatly tailored organizational concepts applicable to this group we call the party has resulted in a failure to place our information and data into a coherent organizational theory context. As a consequence, much of our material relevant to understanding the party as an organization exists in disparate units, not theoretically aggregated. We then retreat to generalization about leadership characteristics or activities, impressionistic discussion about campaign techniques, or anecdotal accounts of activity within the party structure. We have thus been unable to generalize about the party as an organizational subsystem within the polity and society, differentially structured from other social groups, and differentially effective or functional in the community arena in which authoritative decision-making and conflict resolution are taking place.

One unfortunate consequence of the unsystematic and partial character of research on party structure is the existence of a fundamental tension in modern democratic societies between the abstract, idealized notion of "party," and the empirical realities of party life. To democrats, the political party is a specialized subsystem of group action indispensable for the working of the political system. Its legitimacy is uncontested even when other groups may be condemned as "outside the regime."[19] We may indict parties for being internally weak and organizationally irresponsible, but the symbol "party" is inviolable. And therein lies the tension for, while philosophically committed, we have prac-

[19] Lasswell and Kaplan, *op. cit.*, p. 170.

tical doubts—doubts that political parties can really function effectively as intermediary groups in the democratic political system the way we feel they ought to function.

The extent to which the ordinary citizen in modern democracies accepts "party" as an article of his political faith is striking. The results of public opinion surveys in several countries, though varying considerably in quality, generally re-enforce the finding from a previous Detroit survey, that over 70 per cent of adults approve the party system.[20] People think that parties are necessary, especially at the state and national levels of the system. Further, they observe with a consuming curiosity the personality conflicts, factional battles, and competition for power inevitable in the party process, whether it occurs in the halls of legislatures, regional party arenas, or in the arguments of hometown politicians. The public recognizes and accepts the party battle as central to government in a democratic society.

The studies of political involvement, on the other hand, consistently corroborate the finding that only a small percentage of adults are willing to be party activists. In both 1952 and 1956 one national survey organization in the United States found only 3 per cent of the adults engaged in party work, although a somewhat larger percentage contributed money or attended party rallies.[21] In the Detroit metropolitan area the figure was 4 per cent in 1956, and a total of 13 per cent of the sample said they had done some party work in the past.[22] There is evidence to suggest that in foreign countries the extent of party "militancy" is similar, although variations exist by country and by type of party.[23] From the few studies conducted, it is clear that a rather small

[20] S. J. Eldersveld, *Political Affiliation in Metropolitan Detroit* (Ann Arbor: University of Michigan, Bureau of Government, 1957), pp. 127–29.
[21] See Angus Campbell *et al.*, *The Voter Decides* (Evanston: Row, Peterson, 1954), pp. 29–30; *The American Voter* (New York: Wiley, 1960), p. 91. In addition to the percentage reported here, 2 to 3 per cent reported belonging to a political club.
[22] From the study whose findings are presented in the following pages.
[23] See, for example, Duverger, *op. cit.*, p. 111; S. M. Lipset, *Political Man* (Garden City: Doubleday, 1960), p. 102; *De Nederlandse Kiezer* (The Dutch Voter) (The Hague: Staatsdrukkerij en Uitgeverijbedrijf, 1956), pp. 29–30, 89; Hadley Cantril, ed., *Public Opinion 1935–1946* (Princeton: Princeton University Press, 1951), pp. 573, 581.

proportion of adults demonstrate a real interest in party work.

The responses to queries about this matter provide some explanation.

"political parties are too narrow an interest—they are mostly interested in getting into power, in getting people into office . . ."

"parties aren't really interested in local problems and in issues . . ."

"politics is unpleasant, dirty and dishonest"

"parties are weak compared to other groups—there's a better chance for success in other groups—there's less criticism and opposition in other groups"

"it is difficult for an individual to have much say in a party what with bosses running the show"

"politics is complicated and difficult for a newcomer to understand"

"I wouldn't want to commit myself to any one party—once you do you're stuck—it might be a dead end"

"party work is tedious, uninspiring, and it takes too much time"

"both parties are pretty much the same—there's no difference in what they stand for"

A large segment of adults believe that a citizen should do more than just vote (42 per cent in our Detroit study in 1956), but the majority would prefer to work outside the party structures. Many people have deep stereotyped perceptions of political parties. They are suspicious of party leadership and internal organization, they have difficulty in perceiving the party's goals, they question the propriety of party techniques and tactics, and they anticipate both tedium and tension if drawn into party activity. These empirical images of the party are held by the same individuals who will stoutly defend the abstract role of the political party in modern democratic society. This may mean for some that their perceptions of reality are compartmentalized—they see no conflict between their democratic values and their empirical image. For others it may lead to a tension between these values and their understanding of the realities of party life.

This same conflict finds its parallel in scholarly circles. Intellectually, we have become committed to the position in the twentieth century that parties are central to our system, the primary "lubricants" and "moving forces" of the governmental process, that "party is king."[24] We are inclined to echo Graham Wallas' statement of 1908: "The party is, in fact, the most effective political entity in the modern national state."[25] More recently V. O. Key said, "Political parties constitute a basic element of democratic institutional apparatus."[26] Avery Leiserson in his recent book adds to this:

> The political party is a strategically critical concept . . . . the political party, or party system, provides the major connective linkage between people and government, between separate, formal agencies and officials of government, and between official and non official (extragovernmental) holders of power.[27]

Sigmund Neumann asserted in sweeping fashion: "The viability of a party system becomes a test for the stability of a social and political order."[28] It is accepted as incontrovertible truth that the historical development of democracy would have been impossible without the concomitant appearance of political parties. Representative, popular government could not have been implemented without intervening political groups to support legislative leadership, mobilize voters, and agitate for alternative programs and policies. We have come to accept the basic idea, as E. E. Schattschneider has put it, "that the only kind of organization that can translate into fact the idea of majority rule is the political party."[29] By the same token, when democracy is considered to be under crisis, a considerable portion of the blame is assigned to political parties. Stephen K. Bailey's recent discussion of the weaknesses of the American system of government led him to conclude:

[24] James Bryce, *op. cit.*, p. 3; Herman Finer, *The Theory and Practice of Modern Government* (New York: Holt, 1949).
[25] *Human Nature in Politics* (New York: Knopf, 1921), p. 103.
[26] *Op. cit.*, p. 12.
[27] *Op. cit.*, p. 35.
[28] *Modern Political Parties* (Chicago: University of Chicago Press, 1956), p. 396.
[29] *The Struggle for Party Government* (College Park: University of Maryland, 1948), p. 10.

the real problem is *political*. . . . It is time for a stringent look at the national politics we have had, the kind of national politics we want, and the reasons for believing that our traditional party system, like a vast glacier, may now have reached the edge of the sea.[30]

In recent years there has been an accentuation of interest in the "functional properties" of party systems in general and the American system in particular. This discussion is but an extension of an identical interest among scholars in the past. Charles Merriam, for example, concluded his *The American Party System* in 1922 with a brilliant theoretical analysis of the functions of party. To many today, as Avery Leiserson has put it, "the distinguishing quality of politics consists in its *function*."[31] Although argument persists as to the type of parties we need, it is generally agreed that democracy requires groups such as parties to perform critical functions—to recruit leadership, formulate policy, organize decision-making, communicate upward and downward between leaders and public, promote consensus, enforce responsibility, and thus move the society toward the effective and expeditious resolution of its conflicts. It is significant that Maurice Duverger concludes his comparative study of parties with the observation that "Democracy is not threatened by the party regime but by present-day trends in party internal organization . . . ."[32] This epitomizes well the philosophical commitment to parties among scholars; parties are focal institutions of democracy, the internal functioning of which is critically related to the functioning of the political system.

The disparity between our firm philosophical belief in party organization and our imperfect and uncertain knowledge about party organization can only be resolved by persistent, systematic, behavioral research into the party structure. We have, in many ways, an illustrious heritage of intellectual and scholarly concern with the nature of the internal workings of the party. But the basic queries still confront us: What really is the "party

[30] *The Condition of Our National Political Parties* (New York: Fund for the Republic, 1959), pp. 4, 6.
[31] *Op. cit.*, p. 8.
[32] *Op. cit.*, p. 426.

organization"? What is the nature of its internal structure? What activities does it actually pursue? Why is it differentially effective in varying locales? What is the basis of the public's image? What, therefore, must be done if one is bent on reform? This study assumes that these questions can be answered by an orderly, empirical analysis of the party as an organized system of action, beginning at the lowest levels of the democratic system. New data are presented from an investigation of American local party organization, leadership, and process in one major metropolitan area. Characteristics of the actors in the local party, their perspectives, behavior, activities, and organizational relationships are also explored. Through such an analysis the study hopes to arrive at a better understanding of the types of functions the party performs as one social group in the larger society, as well as the quality of that functional performance. Some students of the American party today feel that the party system is adequate, effective, viable. Others claim that atrophy, incoherence, and dysfunction predominate. If so, certain clues should be manifest in the operations of our two great parties at the local level. To discover such evidence, and to relate it to the primary theoretical concerns developed in the Introduction, is the hope and plan of this intensive case analysis.

CHAPTER 2

THE RESEARCH DESIGN, SOCIAL CONTEXT, AND POLITICAL CLIMATE

THE STUDY DESIGN

The research for this study focused on an investigation of the structure and activity of the Democratic and Republican parties of Wayne County, Michigan, within which the city of Detroit is located, in the presidential campaign of 1956. In one sense, the study is concerned with two vast county political machines. Within each county party, however, are six huge district party organizations (the Michigan 1st, 13th, 14th, 15th, 16th, and 17th Congressional Districts), and 2,007 precinct subdivisions. The analysis presented here will deal with each of the following organizational levels of the party: county, district, and precinct. Our interest is as much in how the precinct level of party leadership and activity fits into the district subsystem, as it is in how the six district subsystems articulate within the county system. Finally, we will relate the perceptions, attitudes, and behavior of the adult citizen public to the party structure at each level of party organization.

The intent of this design, therefore, is to study different types of "party organizations" and levels of leadership, in relation to certain key dimensions of political behavior. To implement the design, interviews were conducted with the primary and secondary leadership nuclei of the Republican and Democratic parties in Wayne County (county chairmen, congressional district chairmen, a sample of members of the executive boards of each congressional district, and the candidates for Congress). A random sample of precinct chairmen, and a representative cross-section of 600 adults, selected from the precincts in the study and stratified by congressional district and precinct type, were also canvassed. With interview data for the top echelons of the party, the precinct activists, as well as the public, analysis of "vertical" relationships between party and public was greatly facilitated.

The specific universe for this study was Wayne County, but the aim of the study was to understand the nature of the American party process in a wide range of political and social climates. The great social and political diversity of the Detroit area was especially helpful in this purpose. On the one hand were the *natural* differences of the six congressional districts themselves. Thus, the 1st District is split about 40–60 between Negroes and Poles; the 13th is heavily Negro; the 14th has a large contingent of Italians, as well as a sizeable German population, and is heavily Catholic, etc. In addition, the party strength of the districts reveals a great range, from 52 per cent Democratic in 1954 in Congresswoman Martha Griffiths' 17th District, to 88 per cent Democratic in Congressman Machrowitz's 1st District in the same year. On the other hand, the *design* of the study was formulated to permit a wide range in community or neighborhood character at the precinct level. Thus, we stratified in the selection of the precinct sample in order to obtain socially "homogeneous" (overwhelmingly Negro, or Catholic, or working-class, or Polish, or Protestant, etc.) precincts, as well as "heterogeneous" precincts with no single predominant population or social structure characteristic. In political complexion our precincts ranged from 63 to 94 per cent turnout for eligible citizens in 1956, and from 7 to 88 per cent Democratic strength in the presidential vote. The research setting, therefore, permitted the study of the party process and political behavior in a variety of socio-political "cultural contexts." Whether Wayne County was typical of other urban areas was not the important question. The questions were, first, what patterns of party leadership and organizational activity are found in specific types of socio-political environment; and second, how does the political behavior of the American public vary in terms of environmental conditions?

Although years of observational experience with Michigan party politics underlie this research, the body of data concerned in this study was secured from standardized interviews at all the population levels of the analysis. The 70 top leadership interviews for Republicans and Democrats were secured following the 1956 election and emphasize both depth and breadth of inquiry. Many of these required five or more hours with the respondent, often over two or three days. Information received from these leadership interviews, using a standardized schedule of questions, was very rich and in considerable detail. The primary sampling unit of the study was the precinct, of which 87 were selected through a random, stratified procedure. Two series of interviews were conducted within these 87 precincts, one with each party's precinct leader, or "delegate," the other with individuals from a cross-section of the population. In all, 77 Republican and 72 Democratic precinct leaders were interviewed prior to the 1956 elections, a total smaller than expected, but not all of the precincts had representatives from both political parties. Precinct leaders had been previously contacted through a letter signed by the respective state party chairmen, urging the leaders to cooperate with the study. Although these interviews were shorter, from one to two hours, again they provided a valuable body of data for comparison with the top leadership. The 596 cross-section interviews were conducted after the election by the Detroit Area Study, with the help of professional interviewers of the Survey Research Center of the University of Michigan. The procedures in designing, pretesting, and implementing this part of the study were similar to techniques used by the Survey Research Center in national studies, and by the Detroit Area Study at the University of Michigan each year since 1951. Most of the interviewing at all levels was completed by February, 1957, except for a follow-up of top party leaders who had previously been inaccessible.

Our study of party organization in the Detroit area is not designed to settle all theoretical differences of opinion concerning the nature and trends of local party politics. Nor are we in a position to trace and discuss in detail the historical pattern of change in precinct leadership, although inquiry was made in 1956 about the characteristics of previous district leadership and organizational process. Some of our data permit trend analyses of leadership careers, but, in the main, we can only try to answer questions about what the local party *has become*, not what it was. This is, essentially, a "comparative" study of a series of specific precinct and district party organizations as they operated in 1956. Our examination is directed toward an understanding of "styles" of party leadership and organization in different socio-political contexts, the kinds of tasks and functions they perform, and their impact on the system.

WAYNE COUNTY AND THE DETROIT AREA AS A RESEARCH LABORATORY

Certain social and political characteristics of the population of Wayne County should be kept in mind. Wayne is one of three counties (the others are Macomb and Oakland) comprising the Detroit Standard Metropolitan Area. Its population of 2,435,235 in 1950 (and 18 per cent increase over 1940), is 97 per cent urban. Within the county are located the cities of Detroit (population in 1950: 1,849,568), Hamtramck, and Highland Park, which are "island cities" within Detroit (each with over 40,000 population in 1950), and many suburban cities.

The Greater Detroit Area is characterized by considerable residential mobility. Of the 10 largest Standard Metropolitan Areas in 1950, Detroit, with 15.4 per cent of its population moving from one dwelling place to another in the preceding year, ranked third behind Los Angeles (24.1 per cent) and San Francisco (21.0 per cent). A special study of mobility in the Detroit area has estimated that between 1950 and 1956 there was a 61 per cent increase in the population of the area outside Detroit, while the city grew by 3 per cent. This should not lead to the inference that population movement has been single-directional, from central city to suburbs, nor that the central city population has not been mobile. In fact, intracommunity migration analysis revealed that in 1956 only 0.6 per cent of the adult residents of the Detroit area had lived all their lives in the same dwelling unit, and one-half moved less than 4½ years previously. In 1956, 35 per cent of the "inner city" population (within six miles of the central business district) were planning to move, while 22 per cent of those in the "outer city" perimeter and 20 per cent of the suburban residents had similar plans. There are several patterns of population movement discernible from the 1956 study: "centrifugal" (movement from the center outward), 46 per cent; "lateral" (movement in which the addresses of origin and destination are of equal distance from the center), 34 per cent; "centripetal" (movement from within the area to the center), 12 per cent; and migration from outside of the area, 8 per cent. These patterns suggest the complexity as well as magnitude of the residential flow and counterflow characterizing the area of this study.[1]

The social heterogeneity of Wayne County must also be noted. Our sample study of adults revealed the following population distributions in 1956:

Race:	
Negroes	16%
Education:	
College	16%
High school	46
Less than high school	37
Religion:	
Roman Catholic	31%
Jewish	3
Protestant	57

[1] See "A Social Profile of Detroit, 1956," A Report of the Detroit Area Study of the University of Michigan, Bureau of Government (Ann Arbor, 1956), pp. 76–82.

Where lived most of life before coming to Detroit:

Southern U.S.	24%
North East U.S.	11
North Central U.S. (not Michigan)	14
Michigan (not Detroit)	10
Foreign	12
Native Detroiters	28

Size of place lived before coming to Detroit (excluding foreign origins and natives):

Farm	19%
Under 10,000 population	14
10,000–100,000	10
Over 100,000	14

Occupation of family head:

Professional, technical, etc.	8%
Managers, officials, proprietors	13
Clerical and sales	10
Craftsmen and foremen, etc.	29
Operatives, domestic service	33
Housewives	3

Industry of occupation of head of household:

Manufacturing: auto	32%
Manufacturing: other	19
Wholesale or retail trade	9
Profession, public administration	11
Construction	5
Transportation, communication, utilities	5

Family income 1956:

Under $4,000	18%
$ 4–$5,000	15
$ 5– 6,000	13
$ 6– 7,000	12
$ 7– 8,000	10
$ 8– 9,000	11
$10,000 plus	16

Nationality (on father's side):	
English	9%
Scottish	4
Irish	7
French	4
Other northwestern European	11
German	13
Polish	8
Other central or eastern European	10
Italian	3

From these statistics one can see the great range in income and occupation among families in the area, the size of the racial, nationality, and religious subgroups, and the diverse geographical origins of the population. Although there was considerable stability in these proportions in the period from 1951 to 1956, in the area of socio-economic status rather interesting changes occurred, as the data on family income for 1951 and 1955 for the Greater Detroit Area reveal:[2]

	1951	*1955*
Under $3,000	16%	14%
$ 3–$4,999	42	27
$ 5– 6,999	25	24
$ 7– 9,999	10	22
$10,000 plus	7	13

These population characteristics and trends are important in understanding the social milieu within which the two parties must function.

What has been the pattern of electoral behavior in Wayne County and the Greater Detroit Area during this period of social mobility for a heterogeneous metropolitan population? The three-county area increased over 130 per cent in potential voting population from 1920 to 1950, and in 1950 included 47 per cent of the state's electorate. In 1952 and 1956 this area cast nearly 50 per

[2] *Ibid.*, pp. 27–31.

cent of the state's presidential vote. Voting activity in Detroit has been on the rise from 60 per cent in 1940 to 67 per cent in 1952, but the turnout in the suburban fringe in 1952 raised the three-county total to 76 per cent. As Table 2.1 indicates, this

TABLE 2.1

DEMOCRATIC STRENGTH, PRESIDENTIAL ELECTIONS

	1920	*1928*	*1936*	*1940*	*1944*	*1948*	*1952*	*1956*
Detroit City	15.4%	37.6%	65.4%	62.4%	64.7%	59.3%	60.2%	61.7%
Wayne County	–	36.8	64.5	61.6	63.4	57.9	57.4	57.9
3-county metropolitan area	18.2	34.7	66.0	60.0	60.8	56.2	54.3	54.3
State	22.1	29.0	56.3	49.5	50.2	47.6	44.0	44.1

area, overwhelmingly Republican in the twenties, was a bulwark of support for Roosevelt and almost as strong for Truman, and has continued its Democratic strength in 1952 and 1956, despite the Eisenhower landslide. The gross Democratic pluralities of close to a quarter-million in this metropolitan area were decisive in presidential elections during the Roosevelt period, as well as for Governor Williams since 1948.

Detroit Area Surveys since 1951 document the continuance of Democratic strength, but they have also shown some interesting fluctuations in party affiliation in the area (Table 2.2). More people have tended to call themselves Republicans and Democrats

TABLE 2.2

DETROIT AREA SURVEYS—RESPONSES TO TRADITIONAL QUESTION: WHAT DO YOU CONSIDER YOURSELF TO BE?

	1952	*1954*	*1956*	*1958*	*1959*
Republican	20%	23%	26%	23%	27%
Democrat	48	56	58	52	59
Independent	28	19	12	20	8
No preference, no interest	4	2	4	5	6
Number of cases	371	737	793	650	774

from 1952 to 1959, with the Democrats, however, maintaining a better than two-to-one superiority.

An impression of considerable homogeneity in political behavior is conveyed in such statistics, yet the actual breakdown of party strength within the area reveals great diversity. For example, in recent years the city of Hamtramck traditionally has been over 80 per cent Democratic, Grosse Pointe 85 per cent Republican, Dearborn 48 per cent Democratic. Detroit increased its Democratic strength in the two recent presidential elections, while the suburban and subrural segment of the metropolitan area contributed more than 14 per cent of the state's Republican pluralities of over 300,000.

These different patterns in electoral trends in constituencies within Wayne County are noted when the trends in the six congressional districts, the basic units in our investigation, are compared (Table 2.3).

TABLE 2.3

POSTWAR HISTORY OF VOTING BEHAVIOR—
SIX WAYNE COUNTY CONGRESSIONAL DISTRICTS
(Percentage Democratic, Congressional Elections)

Congressional District and Congressman	*1946*	*1948*	*1950*	*1952*	*1954*	*1956*	*1946*
1st—Machrowitz	65.9%	83.4%	82.2%	84.2%	88.3%	86.1%	90.4%
13th—Diggs	46.9	62.5	61.4	64.8	65.8	69.8	72.7
15th—Dingill	51.9	65.0	64.1	66.7	72.7	74.1	78.5
16th—Lesinski	51.9	62.5	60.7	60.7	67.9	64.1	71.8
14th—Rabaut	46.3	56.9	51.5	53.2	58.2	56.8	64.2
17th—Griffiths*				47.0	52.2	53.3	60.3

* Boundaries before 1952 were considerably different.

The 14th and 17th are districts less Democratic than the other four, districts which Moos designates as "marginal" (the 17th) and "critical marginal" (the 14th) in his study of congressional elections.[3] Further, one notices in Table 2.3 that although there are

[3] Malcolm Moos, *Politics, Presidents, and Coattails* (Baltimore: The Johns Hopkins Press, 1952), p. 53.

Democratic "low points" for each of these districts, a continuous rise of Democratic strength occurred in each during the postwar period. The two marginal districts have remained in Democratic control in all recent elections. If one compares the vote in 1948 with the vote in 1956, only the 14th has seen no change; all the others are more Democratic. Again, a comparison of off-year elections 1946 and 1954 (or 1958) reveals a phenomenal increase in Democratic strength in each district. Thus, from 1946 on, while the population of the county increased, while great intra-community migration occurred, and while some flux in political affiliation perceptions took place, the area maintained and increased its support for the presidential and congressional candidates of the Democratic party. To identify the forces responsible for this stabilization of the party's electoral power position is an extremely difficult though implicit objective in our study of party operation in these districts.

This variation in electoral behavior by area becomes more pronounced as one analyzes and compares the precincts themselves. Precincts vary in (1) the extent of party strength, (2) the size of voting turnout and (3) the variability of these two factors over time (Table 2.4).

Examination of this random sample reveals differing patterns of voting change. Two-thirds of the precincts increased their Democratic strength from 1948 to 1956. Even the most Republican precincts have become more Democratic in terms of such a comparison. On the other hand, one-half of these precincts were less Democratic in 1956 than in 1952. Thus the findings are (a) precincts consistently increasing the Democratic vote, (b) precincts consistently decreasing the Democratic vote, and (c) precincts fluctuating mildly, or greatly, in the size of the Democratic vote. The same three patterns can be seen in voting activity, although there are few instances of a decline in turnout since 1948. In the long run, more Democratic support and increased turnout is seen, but the great trend variation in these factors for precincts, and their great range in party strength, excite concern as to the basic explanatory forces at work.

TABLE 2.4

VARIATIONS IN PRECINCT ELECTORAL BEHAVIOR, WAYNE COUNTY
(For Illustrative Purposes 15 Precincts Were Selected at Random)

	Percentage Democratic			*Percentage of voter turnout*		
	1948	*1952*	*1956*	*1948*	*1952*	*1956*
"Republican" precincts						
Highland Park, P3	38.9%	36.6%	38.5%	69.9%	87.4%	85.2%
Detroit, W21, P225	17.6	18.0	21.0	87.9	89.3	87.5
Grosse Pointe Township, P1	–	10.2	6.7	–	91.5	88.2
Dearborn, P101	10.1	14.0	11.8	84.1	86.6	91.0
Detroit, W22, P202	11.0	11.4	14.7	72.4	92.0	89.4
"Marginal precincts						
Detroit, W4, P24	25.0	32.8	52.2	77.6	83.3	80.5
Detroit, W16, P68	51.6	46.5	47.3	79.9	87.0	85.0
Mongnagon Township, P8	35.2	19.5	45.0	77.3	94.6	88.8
Detroit, W22, P68	44.4	47.5	46.5	85.2	88.9	85.6
*Detroit, W22, P242	52.8	47.3	43.1	78.7	89.6	88.0
"Democratic" precincts						
*Detroit, W6, P7	72.6	–	84.3	71.8	–	83.2
Dearborn, P1	68.2	75.2	71.1	77.7	78.3	77.0
Detroit, W22, P1	67.2	69.3	66.0	80.7	90.7	87.8
*Detroit, W15, P8	55.5	61.1	63.4	80.4	83.8	83.1
*Detroit, W12, P17	74.2	83.7	78.0	86.4	81.7	81.7

* Precinct boundaries changed during this period. If the precinct included other precincts previously, the statistics are summations of the vote in those precincts. Precincts without an asterisk included essentially the same territory in 1956 as previously.

PARTY STRUCTURE

The general structure of the two parties in Wayne County and its six congressional districts can be fairly easily described in formal terms. Michigan election laws have provided for some time that "in all counties having . . . two or more congressional districts or parts of congressional districts within the boundaries of the county, such congressional districts or a part of any congressional district . . . shall each be considered a county . . . ."

Further, the election laws specify that the district party convention shall be held "in lieu of county conventions, in such cases," and shall elect delegates directly to the state convention. Similarly, delegates "shall be elected by townships and in cities by precincts" to a district convention in the same manner as to county conventions elsewhere. Finally, "at the fall congressional convention (in even numbered years) . . . there shall also be elected for each political party a district chairman, secretary, treasurer, and committee of fifteen members to serve for two-year terms or until their successors are duly elected and qualified."[4] Although the parties have augmented and modified this structure in practice, it is the skeletal statutory form of the party organization.

In Part III we analyze the formal and informal aspects of party structure in considerable detail. Here it is important for the setting of the study to grasp a few key aspects of Wayne County party organization. Based on interviews with state, county, and district party leaders, as well as our own observations over the years, these features stand out:

1. The county chairmen's job is essentially one of "coordinating" the party work. Both county chairmen are women. They work with the district chairmen, with whom they have conflicts from time to time. They are also frequently in contact with the state chairmen. Each has permanent headquarters in Detroit, but very little staff. They feel responsible to their county executive committees. Feelings range from despair to great optimism over the potential of the job.
2. The six district chairmen are the kingpins of the organization, feeling generally independent of the county and in sole control, with their executive boards, of their own district organizations. They convene as a group at the call of the state chairmen (two to four times monthly for one party) or at the request of the county chairmen, to discuss joint patronage and strategy matters. The district chairmen consider themselves fairly autonomous centers

[4] Michigan Statutes Annotated, 6.1592, 6.1600.

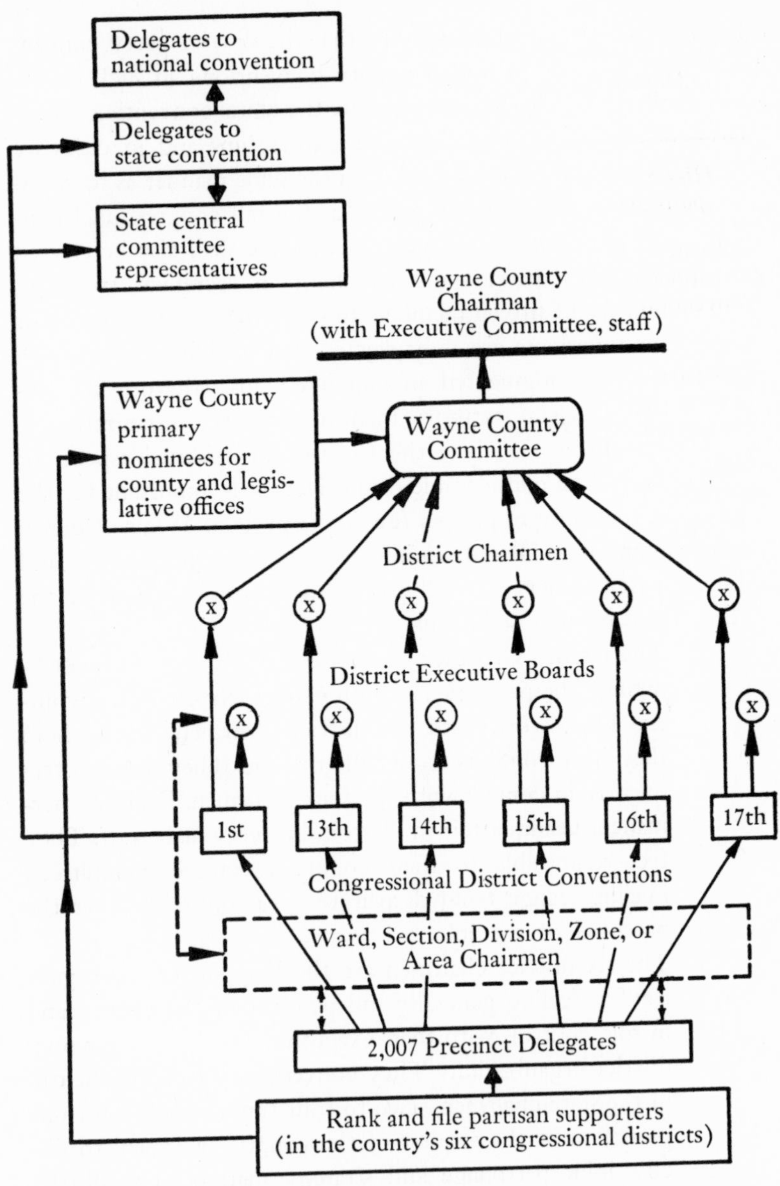

Note: Arrows indicate the direction of the selection process. Dotted lines indicate possible relationships and components not clearly specified nor uniform throughout the structure.

FIGURE 2.1. Diagram of Wayne County Formal Party Organization.

TABLE 2.5

DESCRIPTION OF WAYNE COUNTY ORGANIZATIONAL ROLES AND RELATIONSHIPS

Hierarchy positions	*Organizational conditions and practices*	*"Functions" or "roles"*
Delegates to national convention	Technically picked in district caucus of district delegates to state convention; ratified by convention.	"Ambassadors" of the district organization at the national and state levels.
Delegates to state convention	Elected by district conventions, directly before each state convention.	
State central committee representatives	Two-year term. Two men and two women from each congressional district. Formally selected by state convention, in the spring of odd years. Actually picked by district caucus or convention.	
County chairman	Selected by county committee.	"Moderator" of district organization; coordinator of election campaigns.
County committee	State statutes and party rules define composition of county committee. District executive board members and others may sit on it. District chairmen *always* sit on it. Primary nominees entitled to seats by statute.	County-wide policy-makers; candidate selection, patronage.
District chairmen	Interim selection of chairmen by executive board. Ordinarily by district convention (statute).	"Top executive power elite."
District executive boards	18 statutory members of boards—but usually larger by district party rule.	Secondary consultative, managerial and representative cadre; leadership reservoir.

Congressional district conventions	Two-year terms for convention delegates. Convention meets at statutorily specified times.	Policy deliberation; select district leadership.
Ward, section, division, zone, or area chairmen	Not required by statute. Practice varies—may be appointed or elected; nonexistent in some districts. May sit on executive boards.	Intermediate administrators and coordinators.
Precinct delegates	Nominated by petition—elected August primary even-numbered years. Not all precinct posts are filled.	Immediate planning and direction of all grass roots activities.
Rank and file partisan supporters	Michigan has "open" primary—no party affiliation tests.	Worker and opinion reservoir.

of power, the "prime movers" of Wayne politics. They are reluctant to delegate power, and tend to be overwhelmed by the multiplication of their responsibilities.

3. Most districts are attempting, or have attempted, with a great range in success, to set up subordinate "sectional" or "zone" or "area" chairmen to coordinate the work of a bloc of precinct leaders and workers. It is difficult to assess the effectiveness of this devolution of responsibility.
4. District factions are found in both parties. For the Republicans the most recently prominent are the Republican Voters Associated (RVA), described by one Republican leader as a "disruptive group with a reactionary bent, consisting of young men and women whose parents have been well blessed financially," and the Republican Precinct Organization (RPO), which is apparently more liberal and has been in existence for a longer period of time. The influence of certain business leaders, especially

from the auto industry, apparently played a significant role in the forging of a new "automotive alliance" which had ramifications for these factional struggles. The factionalism in the Democratic party varies from district to district, as it does for the Republicans. It has perhaps been manifested most recently in the fight between the CIO-Liberals and the "old guard" for control of district conventions since 1948. The Teamsters Union officials represented one sizeable fragment of the "old guard" which was routed during this conflict.[5]

5. Precinct delegates elected once every two years to the six congressional district conventions are uniformly considered the "hard core" of the organizational base, due to their legal position and actual leadership functions, although variations by district are reported in role and importance. Some districts have not been able to fill all these precinct delegate posts; in others, they are fiercely contested positions. Most precinct delegates are considered to be effective cogs in the machine; but some district chairmen report the need for appointing precinct "captains" of their own, if the legal delegates are "sleeping" delegates and do no work. In at least one district the party club organizations play a more important role in "working" certain sections of the district than do the precinct delegates. The relationship between the precinct delegate and the district chairmen varies considerably—from tight control or frequent personal interaction, to very loose control and virtually no personal contact.
6. District executive boards range in size, from the 18-member groups designated by law, to more than twice that number in certain districts. The board fulfills a variety of functions, again depending on the district. It may be a nominal consultative group for the chairman, or it may

[5] For an interesting account of these aspects of party history, see Stephen B. Sarasohn and Vera H. Sarasohn, *Political Party Patterns in Michigan*, Wayne State University Studies (Detroit: Wayne State University Press, 1957).

assume major directive work in the campaign, setting up its own functional type of campaign committees dealing with publicity, nationalities, organization, finance, etc. It is usually perceived as a group representing the different geographical parts of the district and its factions, and in fact is purposely constituted, in some districts, of ward or zone chairmen to fulfill this objective. On the other hand, it is possible, as in one district, for the chairmen representing one faction to be forced to work with an executive board representing another faction.

7. The district delegate convention is generally considered the democratic, deliberative base of the organization. It has legal plenary powers of great importance; it selects the district chairmen, delegates to state conventions, district officers, and the statutorily provided executive board. The convention may also make policy and strategy decisions which can influence the district's operations considerably. It is here that factional fights for control of the organization are most visible and, in a sense, most crucial.

THE BACKGROUND OF PARTY COMPETITION

A brief explanation of the trends in political development in the state of Michigan from 1948 to 1956 is necessary in order to have clearly in mind the state-wide political context within which these organizational and electoral elements have meaning. It must be remembered that since 1948, when Mennen Williams upset the Republicans and instituted his unparalleled gubernatorial supremacy of Michigan government, both parties have undergone major "revolutions" in leadership, structure, and program. Wayne County has been focal in this period, since it controlled slightly less than half of the state convention delegate strength in the Democratic party, and approximately 30 per cent in the Republican party. The basic question has two parts: How did Wayne influence state party changes, and how did it reflect these changes in its own local organization?

The year 1956 was in a sense the midpoint of a period of great political transition in Michigan. Personalized party politics was always on the scene, but it seemed to be modified by a greater emphasis on organizational politics. An "old-style" factionalism, based on a combination of personalities, geographical differences, and patronage, seemed to be gradually replaced with a "new-style" factionalism. The latter, while still personality-oriented, was more ideological in content, at least in appearance, and pitted significant interest groups, vitally concerned with the issues of state politics, against the remnants of the old alliances in both parties. The state CIO-PAC, in 1948, announced its decision that the best way to support liberalism "is to join the Democratic party," and that its objective was "to remold the Democratic party into a real liberal and progressive political party," advising "CIO members to become active precinct, ward, county, and congressional district workers, and to attempt to become delegates to Democratic conventions."[6] According to Sarasohn, "By the fall of 1950 the CIO-Liberal faction [was] in control of the incumbent district committees in four of the six districts . . .," producing much bitterness on the part of anti-alliance elements.[7]

At the same time the old McKay-Barnard-McKeighan Republican machine in Michigan was losing control to an insurgent alliance of newcomers. The automobile companies played an important part in this new development. Although they had been active in the forties, it was in 1952 that they asserted greater control. In the Detroit area and Wayne County, working with the Republican Precinct Organization (RPO), the automobile companies were in charge of five of the six congressional districts, according to Sarasohn, and "control over the Republican party on a state-wide basis was . . . apparently firmly established by the new faction.[8]

During this period of complicated internal party turmoil, both the Democrats and Republicans had "liberal" party leader-

[6] *Ibid.*, pp. 54–55.
[7] *Ibid.*, pp. 56, 60.
[8] *Ibid.*, p. 37.

ship at the state level. Neil Staebler, liberal businessman of Ann Arbor, assumed the state Democratic chairmanship in 1950 and has retained it since that time. John Feikens, a Detroit attorney and Eisenhower backer since late 1951 was selected, in 1953, to lead the Republican party and continued in that position, despite opposition from the conservatives until the spring of 1957. Thus the liberals won out at the state leadership levels in each party during this period. Both chairmen advocated fairly similar tactics in their attempts at party rejuvenation. They sought to play down factionalism and promote party harmony. They both saw the need for "issue-oriented" parties, though not ignoring the need for personality candidates. They tried to build parties which would attract ideologically motivated people, with patronage de-emphasized. One chairman said that "patronage should be abolished as a reward for party service," and the other claimed in 1956, "patronage has now only a symbolic effect."[9] This "voluntarism" in precinct work was accompanied by an emphasis on the importance of the job of the precinct worker, in a conscious effort to improve his morale and reward his work with recognition. This tendency was well described by Staebler in 1955: "We believe in the principle that everybody is a precinct worker first . . . everybody works on the firing line."[10] While building into their systems all degrees of prestige recognition for the precinct volunteer, neither chairman, however, neglected the need for professionalization of party activity. They maximized the opportunity afforded by television and exploited this medium to the fullest extent. In addition, field workers were hired, finance operations systematized, salaried publicity men provided, and communication techniques and directive responsibilities carefully defined and regularized. Both party leaders sought to develop organizations which would be more unified, programmatic, systematically

[9] From our interviews with the state chairmen.

[10] From a speech by Staebler of April 18, 1955, quoted in Robert L. Sawyer, Jr., *The Democratic State Central Committee in Michigan. 1949–1959; A Study in the Rise of the New Politics and the New Political Leadership* (Ann Arbor: University of Michigan, Institute of Public Administration, 1960), p. 215.

structured, and supported by a massive body of volunteer precinct workers with ideological commitment and high morale.

Such was the organizational strategy of both parties during the years 1950–56, a time of tremendous leadership and issue controversy in Michigan politics. This was the period during which Mennen Williams, by ever increasing margins of victory, defeated Kim Sigler, Harry Kelly, Fred Alger, Donald Leonard, and Albert Cobo. It was the period of state party conflict over a host of issues, including income taxation, hospital construction, prison reform, the Straits bridge, unemployment benefits, FEPC (finally adopted by the legislature in October, 1955), educational appropriations, administrative reorganization, legislative reapportionment, highway construction, and many others. It was a period of numerous primary battles within the Republican party, and a few within the Democratic.

To conclude this brief inspection of social and political conditions and trends in Michigan and the Detroit area for the period preceding our investigation, perhaps the relevance of the perspective can best be highlighted by suggesting a few critical questions pertinent to our study. In a sense this survey of Wayne parties and politics asks: (1) How have the parties functioned in the context of great population change in the Detroit area, and, specifically, has the increase in Democratic success resulted from a greater capacity of the Democratic party to appeal to, recruit from, and establish contact with this changing population? (2) Has there been a reflection of the "new" factional politics (more heavily economic-interest-oriented in 1956), in the organizational character and control relationships, within the Wayne parties, at the district and precinct level? (3) Concerning the political perspectives of state leaders like Feikens and Staebler—perspectives which emphasized professionalism, voluntarism, factional harmony, internal organizational morale, and liberal ideology—is there any evidence that these perspectives pervaded the local parties in Wayne County? (4) What has been the nature of the activity of the local precinct worker at a time when television was being utilized to the fullest in both state and national campaign strategy?

These and other key queries must be kept in mind while studying the nature of the local party effort. For, in seeking to generalize about the different levels of competence of local party activists and the factors relating thereto, it is always necessary to see the local parties as units of action within a larger organizational system and within a broader context of political competition. The local party is a system of action to be studied by itself as an organizational collectivity, and as a unit influencing the behavior of the citizen public. But it must also be understood as a subunit within the larger state and national party. In this perspective, while we are interested in correlating party activity with public behavior, we are also concerned with the significance of the workings of the local party for the more inclusive system of party politics.

PART I

FOUR IMAGES OF THE PARTY STRUCTURE

CHAPTER 3

THE "OPEN ACCORDION"

A political party is constantly plagued by the need to reconcile two divergent essentials: group solidarity (conscious selection of members) and broad social representation (unrestricted entry into the organization). If success-oriented, the legal tender of the party is, after all, votes. A major query thus confronting any investigation of party structure is: How undiscriminating in its social recruitment does a party become as a result of power-expansionist drives? Does the leadership recruit workers and supporters at wide range, seeking to maximize its vote potential, or does it consciously restrict itself to the need for congruence in social and political perspectives? This is a dilemma of a party in a democratic society, not shared to the same degree by nonparty groups which are less vote-motivated. The dysfunctional by-products of a calculated policy of selective recruitment as against a policy of "natural selection," for internal control and external power, need careful assessment.

Roberto Michels is famous for his "accordion theory" of party recruitment, in which he described the calculating manner of the elite party in authoritarian societies as it periodically opens, and then closes, membership in the party to the masses.[1] This is a rhythmic strategy, presumably shrewd for both symbolic and operational reasons. In a competitive, democratic party system, however, the pendulum policy supposedly does not exist. Rather, our parties are committed to the conflict for power, and membership theoretically is "open."

Nevertheless, some limits on indiscriminate recruitment of support might be logical, even for a democratic party, for two

[1] See Alfred de Grazia, *op. cit.*, pp. 153–54.

reasons: the maintenance of group solidarity, and the evolution of organizational efficiency. In a geographical area where the opposition is passive, indiscriminate recruitment might be considered unnecessary by the party in power, or even perceived as a threat to the controlling leadership of the majority party organization. On the basis of this assumption, certain local machines, particularly in America, may be considered "closed," monolithic machines of handpicked ward heelers, precinct captains, and congenial, dependent workers. Under certain circumstances, then, exclusive recruitment makes sense. Ambivalence, even overt permissiveness in recruitment strategy, on the other hand, would be plausible in areas where the population is heterogeneous and the two (or more) parties well matched, or in areas where a minority party is constantly and aggressively broadening its base of support. Yet it is conceivable that even in these areas one might argue for limits on the mobilization of clienteles, particularly if the party is to retain its distinctiveness as a policy-oriented group, and if it is to work in collaboration as a team of workers and leaders. The basic factor here is the political orientation of those concerned with making the critical decision on the best way to stabilize or improve the party's chances for power. Finally, these expectations must include the possibility that, despite the decision, the "natural selection" of like-minded people as workers would assuredly mean that the party was not "wide open." Variations in three factors, then, probably condition the degree of open clientelism in a party: its political-competitive status, natural interpersonal relationships and affiliations of those in the party structure, and the particular social and demographic complexion of the geographical area. One can not, in other words, expect our parties to be completely expanded accordions. What do the data reveal?

SOCIAL DIVERSITY AMONG THE LOCAL PARTY EXECUTIVE ELITE

We look first at the 12 district chairmen who have fought their way to top managerial positions in the local Republican and Democratic organizations. As members of the party elite, they hold considerable power, direct party activities in their districts, and are responsible for the performance of the organization. They distribute patronage and are consulted by state and county chairmen before appointments are made. In district conventions they generally wield considerable control and are the basic organizational link between the state chairman and the precinct militants. District chairmen are reputed to have an important voice in candidate selection, party policy, and strategy. As a group they are caucused and heeded at state conventions before formal action is taken.

Diversity in the top district leadership is evident in each party. Among the Republican chairmen were two Baptists, one Greek Orthodox, one Anglican, and a Catholic. One was a Czech who was born in Greece, two had English nationality (one was Canadian by birth), another was of German nationality, and one was born in Detroit of Austrian immigrant parents. These men differed considerably in present occupation: a court clerk, the owner of a wholesale drug firm, a machine-shop supervisor, a public relations specialist, and a former acrobat in Mexico who was, in 1956, a division head in the city department of public works.

The top Democratic leaders also showed a great range in family origin and occupation. Their nationalities were Polish, Irish, Scotch-Irish, Russian. The chairman of one district was a Negro. Three were Catholics, one Methodist, one Jewish. In contrast to the Republicans, all were born in the United States, though the fathers of two were born abroad. Their occupations were quite different from the Republicans: a secretary to a congressman, an International Ladies' Garment Workers Union official, a deputy sheriff, two teachers of social studies. In addition, the Democrats showed a greater age range, from 33 to 63; the Republicans varied from 52 to 65 years in age.

Personal data of this kind suggest, at the outset, the complexity of human experience one encounters in attempting to understand the leadership of our parties. The social perspectives of an assemblyline worker from South Dakota are quite different from those of a native Detroit social science teacher; the perspectives of a Bay City acrobat turned safety engineer probably have very little in common with those of a Macedonian-born Czech, self-educated to become a court clerk.

In analyzing the backgrounds of these men, three observations are clear. First, obvious differences existed between the Republican and Democratic elite cadres. The Republicans tended to be middle-aged, white, high-school educated, English, German, Austrian, Czech. The major gaps are perhaps the absence of younger adults, Negroes, the college-educated, and Poles. The Democrats were younger, included a Negro, were more highly educated, and had different nationality backgrounds. Thus, the two cadres seemed drawn, partially at least, from distinctive social subpopulations; nor was the top leadership of either party representative of certain important elements in the population (particularly the lower occupational strata, those with farm background, and migrants from the South).

Secondly, these top executive groups are not completely "closed" social cliques. One did find among the Republicans a skilled worker, a Catholic, a Czech, and at least two with labor union backgrounds. The Republicans were not all white-collar, native-born Protestants. Similarly, the Democratic top elite had no one with a high income, but the occupational range was considerable, as was geographical origin and nationality. They came from radically diverse social backgrounds. Though the upper echelons of the party structure might be expected to be more socially exclusive than the middle-level cadre of precinct activists, individuals from "unexpected" social groups do not find top leadership positions totally inaccessible.

Third, the elite in each party gave evidence of invading (or recruiting, or admitting, from) the "social territory" of the other. In addition, each group had the same general social-class orientation as seen in the following descriptive findings about the 12 chairmen:

None were wealthy, only two had incomes over $10,000.

None held top-level directive, managerial, or professional occupational positions.
All had more than elementary-school education.
With possibly one exception, all had an occupational history of upward economic mobility from father, through first occupation while in politics, to present occupation.
With possibly one exception, all owned their home or were buying a home.
Only one had extensive farm experience.

These data suggest that both parties have a top leadership group which is "middle class" in its present status, but whose background suggests considerable familiarity with lower economic class conditions. Their fathers were factory workers, truck drivers, mill-hands, machinists, saloon-keepers. The group consisted of northern urbanites, moderately cosmopolitan in experience outside the area, though they had lived in Detroit long enough to be considered virtual "natives" (over 30 years, except one Democrat who, by 1956, had lived there only 19 years). Finally, they had all moved upward in politics during a period in which they experienced moderate personal economic progress, achieving the status of "white collar and a little better." Party politics did not benefit them phenomenally as to economic status. In fact, one wonders whether this group had sufficient economic independence to permit it to devote the necessary time and energy to the tasks of directing the complex political operation of a congressional district organization. Here, then, are two parties led by individuals from the middle sector of the social-status spectrum, in some cases representing identical subpopulations, in others revealing distinctive social and demographic origin. But there is no rigid and complete compartmentalization, socially, of the discrete leadership cadres.

CLASS STATUS AND MOBILITY OF THE SECONDARY CADRE AND PRECINCT ACTIVISTS

Party leaders at the lower levels of the structure were even more diverse in social origins and status, and thus a better cross-section of the great variety of population subgroups. Viewed here as county-wide leadership aggregates, the data suggest a recruitment which penetrates more deeply into social strata than is the case for the powerful district chairmen. Whereas the latter tended to be middle class, the lower echelons were more "open" to both upper-class and lower working-class elements. The parties do not recruit from identical social bases. They differ in signifi-

TABLE 3.1

INCOME, OCCUPATION, AND EDUCATION FOR MIDDLE AND LOWER-LEVEL PARTY LEADERS

	Republicans		*Democrats*	
	Executive board	*Precinct leaders*	*Executive Board*	*Precinct Leaders*
Income				
Under $4,000	0%	15%	0%	7%
$4–5,000	10	10	0	16
$5–10,000	52	35	100	53
Over $10,000	38	35	0	17
Not ascertainable	0	5	0	6
Education				
Only elementary	9	11	0	14
High school	30	38	75	60
College (other than business college)	61	51	25	26
Completed college	52	22	18	14
Occupation (of head of household)*				
Professionals	43	19	18	16
Managers, proprietors	17	36	29	10
Clerical and sales	9	14	6	17
Blue collar (craftsmen, foremen)	30	16	41	35
Blue collar (semi- and unskilled)	0	15	6	22
Number of cases	23	143	18	138

* In this table there are five precinct leaders who have been handled as follows: those "not in the labor force" (primarily housewives) have been coded by head of household's occupation, and the one "farmer" has been left out.

cant respects in the proportions of certain social groups represented among the leaders, and thus in the statistical opportunities of these groups for access to the two parties. Yet, while such representational imbalances can be found, there is also great recruitment overlap.

The economic status data illustrate these observations well. The lower one stands in the hierarchy in either party, the more likely one is to have a family income under $4,000, an elementary-school education, and hold a semi- or unskilled blue-collar job. On the basis of income, about one-fourth of the precinct leaders were low status, compared to less than 10 per cent of the executive board members, and one out of 12 district chairmen. On the other hand, a fairly large number of leaders employed in the professions (especially in the Republican party) and college-educated leaders were found at these lower levels. It is interesting in this connection that, although none of the top Republican leaders had a college education, over half of the Republican lower-level leaders had been to college, and a considerable proportion had finished college. This distinction is not as marked among the Democrats although here, too, over one-fourth had been to college.

Obviously, there is much more "spread" in economic status at the lower reaches of the party hierarchy. And equally obvious is the "organizational level" to which the different social groups rise. The evidence indicates limited involvement and opportunity for the less skilled blue-collar workers. They were found primarily at the precinct level. The same is true for those with only an elementary education. In contrast, the self-employed businessman, proprietor, or manager of a business firm was found in sizeable numbers among both the executive board members and precinct activists. Clerical and sales people were fewer in number, but were also found at all levels in the Democratic party, but not in the Republican party. Skilled blue collar were rather large in number at the lower party-hierarchy echelons (especially in the Democratic party), but did not seem to be able to take over the top managerial positions in the party. The "wealthy" (over

$10,000 income) populated the lower reaches of the hierarchy (even one-fourth of the Democratic precinct leaders are in this income category), but were not found in the top leadership nucleus in either party.

The occupational mobility of lower-level precinct leadership was considerable, although not as striking as for top leadership. In Table 3.2 we look at intergenerational occupation from father's "usual occupation" to respondent's first occupation (i.e., when he first became active in politics), and present occupation.

It is difficult from this table to determine exactly the extent of occupational status change, particularly when the leader's first occupation is taken into consideration. The 30 per cent of Republicans and 17 per cent of Democrats whose own first occupations were that of student or housewife, or not ascertainable, complicate the analysis. Also, the large percentage of fathers who were farmers, of which there are many status varieties, requires

TABLE 3.2

INTERGENERATIONAL OCCUPATIONAL MOBILITY: THREE POINTS IN TIME (Precinct Leaders)

	Republicans			*Democrats*		
	Father's position	*Leader's first position*	*Leader's present position*	*Father's position*	*Leader's first position*	*Leader's present position*
Professional	17%	13%	15%	9%	12%	15%
Managers	17	22	33	12	1	10
Clerical, sales	7	6	11	1	14	16
Craftsmen	20	15	15	33	29	30
Blue collar (semi- and unskilled)	24	14	15	38	27	22
Farmer	14	0	1	7	0	0
Not in labor force	0	18	8	0	12	7
Not ascertainable	1	12	3	1	5	0
Number of cases		143			138	

caution in analysis. Despite this, it is interesting to note the gradual increase of professionals and those in the clerical-sales category among the Democrats, and the gradual increase of managers (including proprietors) among Republicans. More significant is the fact that 38 and 45 per cent of the fathers of these Republican and Democratic leaders were semi- and unskilled workers or farmers, while 34 and 21 per cent, respectively, were in the professional-managerial group. The first occupations of leaders, however, indicate a considerable drop in semi- and unskilled occupations for both parties, although the drop in the higher-status occupations is much smaller. This is testimony again to the breadth of occupational backgrounds among party leaders.

Upward economic mobility occurs at the lower levels of the party hierarchy. This is clear when we compare fathers' primary occupation with present occupation of precinct leader for an analysis of "net mobility." From one-fifth to one-fourth of precinct leaders in both parties improved their occupational position, although the change takes a different pattern in each party.

For the Republicans, change occurred in business-managerial positions, while for the Democrats there was actually a decline in such positions, and the great change in economic status is manifest in the larger proportions of professional and clerical-sales people in precinct party work at the time of the survey. Further, there were still fewer high occupational-status Democrats than Republicans in 1956, as was the case when occupations of the father were compared—about two-fifths of the Democrats in 1956, in contrast to two-thirds of the Republicans.

A summation of *net occupational mobility* at the three levels of the party is presented in Table 3.3.

By all measurements, the top leadership nucleus in each party was the most mobile in socio-economic terms. But while mobility was directly related to level of party position among the Democrats, it was not clearly related for Republicans. A larger percentage of Republican precinct leaders appeared to be moving upward than middle-level board members. Party organization politics, then, seems to attract some of the upward-oriented in

TABLE 3.3

UPWARD OCCUPATIONAL MOBILITY (FATHER AND PRESENT OCCUPATIONS) THREE PARTY HIERARCHY LEVELS

	Republicans	*Democrats*
Top leadership	40%	40%
Middle cadre	9	33
Precinct actives	19	18

Note: The percentages are net, gross shifts between "white-collar" and "blue-collar" categories for all leaders as a group. The farmer fathers are excluded in this table.

the general population, who may be drawn to party work because they feel it will be economically rewarding, or who happen to be simultaneously ambitious in both directions, or because they are thrust into party work as a consequence of achieving a higher occupational status.

VARIATIONS IN SOCIAL BACKGROUND WITHIN THE HIERARCHY

Both parties attract, in considerable number, individuals with southern, central, and eastern European (exclusive of Germany) backgrounds. While the proportion of this group in the adult population was 21 per cent, about 37 per cent of the precinct leadership came from these nationalities. A smaller number was found in the secondary cadre—23 per cent (R) and 32 per cent (D). This influx included a fairly equal number of Italians and Poles in both parties. At the same time, the Irish were still dominant in the Democratic structure at the two top levels (about 35 per cent), but had a much smaller group in the precinct cadre—only 13 per cent. In the Republican structure the English, Germans, and Scots were still prevailing, also at the two top levels (60 per cent at the top and 38 per cent in the middle cadre), but they were less numerous among precinct activists—about 20 per cent. In both parties Negroes have penetrated the two lower levels in almost equal proportion (18 per cent middle,

16 per cent precinct for the Republicans; 19 per cent middle, 23 per cent precinct for the Democrats), but only one of the 12 top leaders was a Negro.

Other social-status characteristics at different levels of hierarchy are documented in Table 3.4. The Democrats included more Catholics; two-fifths or more of the middle and lower echelons were of that faith (60 per cent of the top elite). The Democrats also included larger proportions of foreign-born, although it is interesting to note the small percentages (less than 10 per cent at the precinct level) in both parties. The Democrats had no great margin in leaders with a southern background, suggesting that some reversal in party affiliation occurs among these migrants. Contrary to expectation, perhaps, those with a farm background tended to be Democratic, especially among the middle cadre. Despite the tremendous population mobility in the Detroit area, both parties tended to recruit or attract people who

TABLE 3.4

Social Backgrounds Within the Hierarchies

	Republicans		*Democrats*	
	Executive board	*Precinct*	*Executive board*	*Precinct*
Catholic	26%	24%	38%	47%
Foreign-born	9	3	18	9
Southern origin	17	19	13	26
Farm origin	14	10	29	13
Born in Detroit	43	36	19	22
Lived over 20 years in area	83	80	80	80
Traveled abroad	50	30	50	43
Age				
Under 30	9	17	0	5
30–40	13	14	22	29
Over 60	8	20	17	14
Women	22	20	17	15
Government employees*	22	9	18	16
Number of cases	23	143	18	138

* Based on occupation of "head of household."

had been residents of the Detroit area for some time. Party leaders appear to have been well-established and acclimated to the geographical area before assuming party work. This does not mean they were necessarily parochial in viewpoint, however, since from 30 to 50 per cent had traveled abroad. The small percentage of very young people in leadership positions, particularly at the middle level, indicates again that the party leader was well-integrated in his community. In further support of this interpretation is the fact that 80 per cent of the leaders were married, though they did not have large families—38 per cent of the precinct leaders had no children living at home, 22 per cent had only one child, less than 15 per cent had three or more children at home. There seem to be certain adult age-brackets and marital time-periods, or family situations, which are conducive to taking on party organizational positions.

A few tentative reflections on these data may be in order. It is clear that this party leadership subculture was not primarily Anglo-Saxon or upper economic status. As one moves down the hierarchies of both parties, great heterogeneity can be seen in social backgrounds. Nor does there seem to be a "flight" of the middle class from party organizational life. In fact, the opposite might be more easily demonstrated. There are indeed recruitment gaps in relation to certain populational subgroups—the very young, the unskilled workers, those with an elementary-school education, and some of the smaller nationality groups. Each party was predominant in particular demographic and social categories—for example, professional-managerial white-collar people in the Republican party (55 per cent of the precinct leaders), and skilled craftsmen in the Democratic party (35 per cent of the precinct leaders): the importance of these differences will be examined in a subsequent analysis. But, although the parties tended to be controlled by white, middle- and upper-income males, a close inspection of the characteristics of these leaders reveals that they were a very unlike group in occupation, race, religion, and national origin. Perhaps of greater importance are the intrahierarchical differences in these social status distributions, and the dysfunctional probabilities which these differences suggest. Potential conflict existed, for example, between the Irish, Poles, and Negroes in the Democratic organization, with the Irish predominating at the top, but other groups beginning to replace them at the bottom. Similarly, in the Republican structure, there was conflict between the young college-educated and more wealthy leaders at the precinct level and the top elite who were older and less well off economically. In both structures a great range of life experiences is represented. How the organization contained these conflicting social pressures, if it did in fact contain them, and what the impact of intrahierarchical diversity was on the functioning of the party, will be referred to throughout our report.

PROMISCUITY IN SOCIAL RECRUITMENT

We return to the question of how "open" and "potential-clientele-oriented" the party is in attracting personnel. Our analysis in the Detroit area indicates that when the party seeks out and accepts precinct leaders it behaves as a very eclectic recruiter. The Democratic and Republican organizations seemed almost desperate in their efforts to induce those from "the other side" to take a grass-roots party position with them (Table 3.5).

TABLE 3.5

COMPETITIVE RECRUITMENT OF "DEVIANT" SOCIAL CATEGORIES (Precinct Leaders)

Percentage of Republicans from "Democratic" Social Categories		*Percentage of Democrats from "Republican" Social Categories*	
Catholic	24%	Protestants	44%
Negro	16	Business-managerial	10
Union members	30	Clerical-sales	17
Irish	6	German	8
Poles	7	English	7
Semi- and unskilled	15	Professionals	16
Income under $4,000	15	Income over $10,000	17
		Income over $15,000	7

Within the Republican party precinct cadre were large proportions of Catholics, Negroes, union members, low-income workers, even Irish and Poles. A similar picture exists on the Democratic side. The Democrats had invaded such traditional "Republican" social groups as the upper occupational and income classes, those with a German or English background, whether Catholic or Protestant. Social counterinfiltration is evident when one realizes, for example, that 8 per cent of Republican precinct leaders were semi- and unskilled Catholic workers, and that 5 per cent of the Democrats were upper-occupational Protestants with a northwestern European (non-Irish) background.

The percentages of some of these "deviant" groups are small, to be sure, but the range is great. The accordion seems, indeed, open, but not wide open, since we found, for example, no Jews, no Negro Catholics, no very low-income Negroes in the Republican sample, and no extremely wealthy Protestant businessmen in the Democratic sample. One cannot be sure whether this says anything significant about party recruitment, or about the capacity of such categories to be mobilized. With these exceptions, however, both parties seemed to recruit with abandon from the most remote sectors of the population.

This is not just a recent tendency, the product of an increasingly heterogeneous metropolitan population or of an accentuation of party conflict in recent years. As Table 3.6 reveals, both parties have been appealing to these "deviant" social groups for leadership for over 30 years, and during the period of Republican ascendancy in the area. The Republicans have not become interested in Catholics or union members or Negroes or Poles only recently. Nor have the Democrats suddenly developed a concern for proprietors, Germans, English, and those with high income. Before the depression, in pre-World War II years, as well as in the postwar era, both parties demonstrated promiscuous recruitment patterns. It is indeed somewhat remarkable that in the thirties, when class-consciousness in American politics was presumably at its peak, the Republicans attracted 50 per cent of those union members in precinct leadership posts

TABLE 3.6

YEAR OF RECRUITMENT OF "DEVIANT" SOCIAL GROUPS
(Precinct Leaders)

Era began party work	*Republicans*					*Democrats*				
	Catholics	*Negroes*	*Union members*	*Income under $4,000*	*Poles*	*Protestants*	*Business managerials*	*Professionals*	*Germans and English*	*Income over $10,000*
1956	10%	43%	12%	24%	0%	28%	0%	24%	11%	42%
1952–55	50	4	16	5	60	15	29	29	58	30
1944–51	12	4	23	38	0	21	43	14	26	15
1932–43	3	30	35	10	0	18	29	0	0	3
Before 1932	26	17	14	24	40	18	0	33	5	10
Number of cases	34	23	43	21	10	61	14	21	19	33

in 1956. And the Democrats, during this same period, attracted 30 per cent of the leaders with upper occupational status who were in precinct roles in 1956. This phenomenon of competitive recruitment thus appears to have historical validity. Despite social "centers of gravity," both parties have for a long time, wittingly or otherwise, represented a wide social spectrum of interest and background in the hierarchy.

Conscious party effort and informal social, extra-party, pressures were responsible for this recruitment product, as Table 3.7 reveals. When we asked, "What first led you to become active as a party worker?" we found a high proportion of "indirect recruiters" in the friends, relatives, and neighbors of these actives, as well as in the formal racial, ethnic, religious, and civic groups to which the actives belonged. All told, 54 per cent of the Republican Catholics, Negroes, and union members were induced into the party fold in this indirect way, and 26 per cent of the

TABLE 3.7

STYLE OF INDUCTION OF PRECINCT LEADERS FROM "DEVIANT" SOCIAL GROUPS

	Source of Attraction to Party Work:					
	Party leaders	*Popular candi-dates*	*Other Formal groups*	*Rela-tives and friends*	*Other sources**	*Number of cases*
Republicans						
Catholics	9%	15%	3%	35%	38%	34
Negroes	30	17	22	22	9	23
Union members	9	0	18	53	20	43
Democrats						
Income over $10,000	30	24	27	0	19	33
Professional and managerial occupations	29	11	17	9	34	35

* These individuals gave particular issues or social conditions as explanations of entry into party work and did not cite the influence of particular individuals or groups.

Democrats who came from upper occupational and income groups gave similar explanations. This suggests that both parties had penetrated the social structure of Detroit long before World War II; otherwise this type of indirect recruitment probably could not have occurred. Some individuals in these "deviant" social groups seem to have made up their minds independently and to have come into the party because of particular candidates, issues, or conditions, or from feelings of civic duty. Nine per cent of these deviant Republicans said their entrance was "accidental"; 3 per cent of the deviant Democrats had the same perception. But party leaders, clubs, and auxiliary political organizations played a direct role, too, especially in the Democratic recruitment of those from upper-class social strata, and in the Republican recruitment of Negroes. The induction of individuals from these remote, and somewhat unexpected, social sectors is, thus, a product of a complex interaction of the party with a wide range of social structural components in the community.

The two top echelons of both parties, though more homogeneous, also reveal the consequences of open clientelism. Thus, 18 per cent of the Democratic executive board members were college graduates, and 29 per cent occupied business-managerial positions. On the other side, 26 per cent of the Republican executive board members were Catholics, 18 per cent Negroes, and 23 per cent blue-collar workers. In this connection, it is interesting to note that 30 per cent of the two upper echelons of the Republican party were blue collar when they entered their party positions, while 10 per cent of the Democrats were white collar when they entered. Combining these data, we find, then, a correlation between economic and political career mobility (see Table 3.3), and continuance in an upper hierarchical party status despite a "deviant" social or economic status.

One basic question to be raised at this point is whether the party is an "open accordion" because of the conscious recruitment practices of the district chairmen or his subordinates. Since precinct leaders hold the position of delegate to the district convention, to which they are elected every two years, one wonders about the influence and interest of the chairman in encouraging these people to run. It is clear from our interviews that one or two chairmen took a positive interest. It is equally true that most chairmen felt it unwise or impossible to control rigidly the recruitment of precinct leaders. Quotations illustrative of explanations of their role are:

> "Most of the time we find people not interested at the precinct level. They want to get into the upper levels. I am interested in getting young people into politics and to keep the union members in the party. Labor's only place is in the liberal wing of the Democratic party. But we have relatively little to do with the choice of precinct delegates. We are often happy to see any people run for that office." (Democrat)

> "Precinct delegates are chosen by the people and I do not interfere. I have no patience with ethnic group representatives and I dislike appeals on this basis. But I am a minority on this question as far as my party is concerned." (Republican)

> "Ward chairmen are asked to get a candidate for delegate running in each precinct in their ward. I encourage young Democrats to run. But I leave most of the responsibility to ward chairmen, although I will give unofficial support to a candidate I especially want to see elected." (Democrat)

There seems to be a subtle attempt to influence the recruitment of precinct leaders, plus a great deal of devolution of responsibility to subordinates, with opportunities for self-starters always present. Some of the analysis of individual districts indicates there may have been more studied attempts at careful selection than chairmen would admit. Interesting "coincidences" can be found—for example, a district chaired by an Irish Catholic, 70 per cent of whose precinct leaders were Catholic, 71 per cent from northwestern Europe, and 25 per cent Irish; or a Czech chairman with a very small percentage of precinct leaders from northwestern Europe; or the only woman chairman who turned out to have the largest proportion of women workers. But these tendencies are counterbalanced, both by the overt desire for social representativeness, and by the absence of control over the process in a gigantic party structure. Social homogeneity among leaders is impossible to demonstrate, even in those districts where the chairman claimed the greatest interest in the process. Rather, it seems that interpersonal associations, friendship relationships, as well as self-generating initiatives, were responsible for the appearance of individuals on the scene who might be classified as "congruent" or "deviant" members of the party hierarchy.

The individual contact of those already in the party with potential activists is the important factor in the desperate struggle to fill precinct leadership positions. These positions are in a constant state of attrition if our experience is at all indicative—22 per cent of precinct positions were filled in 1956 by new persons, and from 5 to 11 per cent of the precinct positions in our sample were not filled by anyone at the time of our study. In addition, for those precincts in which interviews were possible and in which precinct leaders existed, 16 per cent of the Democratic precincts and 39 per cent of the Republican precincts had leaders with no helpers at all. Several reasons account for this state of affairs, but the unavailability of willing helpers is primary. The party cannot afford to be exclusive to any great degree, unless it is purely status-maintaining. Cajolery in place of careful screening for hierarchical positions, laissez faire instead of control, is necessary in those areas where the party is in a competitive situation.

The evidence indicates, therefore, that much induction to party activism occurs in a context of "self-starting," after informal interpersonal influence "softens up" the individual for the decision to accept or seek a party position. This process is difficult to document precisely and directly, but some interesting and highly relevant data are available. Since so much induction is at the precinct level, it is important to know the extent to which the associational relationships of precinct leaders are socially "closed" or "open." Do precinct leaders interact politically with deviant group types and thus possibly involve them gradually? We have already seen that 14 to 30 per cent of precinct leaders from deviant groups certified that they became interested in party work because of the efforts of political leaders and organizations. A sociometric analysis of the political associates of precinct leaders will indicate the extent to which they can be conceived as a medium for inducting into the hierarchy. We asked the precinct leaders to inform us of "three people you have worked with most closely in politics." In checking the occupations of these associates an interesting picture emerges (Table 3.8). One-third or more Republican white-collar precinct leaders had political associates from other occupational classes, and 60 per cent of Democratic blue-collar leaders had

TABLE 3.8

OCCUPATIONAL DIVERSITY IN THE POLITICAL ASSOCIATES OF PRECINCT LEADERS

	Democratic leaders		*Republican leaders*	
	White collar	*Blue collar*	*White collar*	*Blue collar*
Percentage with political associates from another class	53%	60%	36%	80%
1 associate	35	27	36	18
2 associates	9	22	0	8
3 associates	9	11	0	54
Number of cases	56	67	78	40

white-collar political associates. The "cross-occupational" recruitment potential implicit in the data is obvious. In addition, the extreme openness or vulnerability of the party to those social groups least *expected* to be represented is attested to by the precise occupations of the persons with whom their leaders associated. A detailed analysis of these data revealed, for example, that 34 per cent of the Democratic blue-collar leaders associated with businessmen and proprietors of businesses, while 18 per cent of white-collar Republican leaders maintained political connections with skilled, semiskilled, and unskilled workers. Neither party showed rigid occupational barriers to political intercourse, though the Democrats appeared somewhat more fluid.

Thus, in addition to 31 per cent of the Republican leaders

themselves coming from blue-collar ranks (of whom about 40 per cent maintained blue-collar contacts), another 20 per cent of Republican leaders had blue-collar political associations. Over 30 per cent of Republican leaders avowed that at least one of their political associates was blue collar—one out of four of whom was a semi- or unskilled worker.

On the Democratic side, about 42 per cent of the leaders came from the white-collar strata (of whom 80 per cent retained white-collar contacts politically). To this percentage can be added another 29 per cent of the Democratic leaders who had white-collar contacts. Thus, 62 per cent of all Democratic precinct leaders had some white-collar associations—one out of two of whom were in business-managerial occupations.

This highly permissive recruitment context is paralleled by the emergence of loyal "support" groups in the electorate which were also socially heterogeneous.[2] The loyal partisans, designated by self-perception of party affiliation and voting behavior as a reservoir of support, were drawn from diverse and "deviant" social categories (Table 3.9). The Republican loyalists were 26 per cent blue collar, 13 per cent Catholic, and 32 per cent of central, southern, and eastern European nationality backgrounds. The Democratic loyalists included 24 per cent who were white collar, 23 per cent from northwestern Europe (exclusive of the Irish), and, for example, 11 per cent with a northern farm background. The extreme "deviant" groups which one would expect in one or the other party appeared in these support units—for the Republicans the semi- and unskilled (8 per cent), Irish (8 per cent), Jews (1 per cent); for the Democrats, those with a business-managerial profession (10 per cent). Thus, again, an open system is suggested. Republicans were successfully attracting into a very close personal affiliation with

[2] The bases on which these "loyal partisans" in the adult cross-section were identified were: self-classification as "loyal" Democrats and Republicans *and* voting behavior in the presidential and gubernatorial elections of 1956. Democrats were not considered "loyal" if they defected to Eisenhower; Republicans did not qualify if they voted for Governor G. Mennen Williams.

TABLE 3.9

DEVIANT SOCIAL ORIGINS OF REPUBLICAN AND DEMOCRATIC LOYAL PARTISANS

Republicans		*Democrats*	
Occupation*			
Skilled	8%	Professional	4%
Semi- and unskilled	8	Managerial	10
Service	10	Clerical	8
		Sales	2
Education		Some college	8
Less than elementary	7	Completed college	2
Only elementary	12		
Nationality			
Central, southern, or eastern European	32	Northwestern Europe (excluding Irish)	23
Irish	8	Farm background	
Race		North	11
Negro	8		
Religion			
Catholic	13		
Jewish	1		
Father's politics			
Democratic	23	Republican	11
Number of cases			
Total	90		183
In the labor force	59		126

* Based on those in the labor force only.

the party groups presumed to be Democratic, and vice versa. This reserve cadre of supporters was under constant pressure from friends, already in party work, to assume more responsibility. They are thus a vital liaison cadre between the precinct leader and his public.

There is a curious finding here concerning the interrelatedness of the deviant social origins and backgrounds of loyal partisans and precinct leaders. The analysis shows that the party appears to be so clientele-oriented that it actually includes larger percentages of deviant social groups in the hierarchy than it has induced into loyal partisanship. Thus, Table 3.10 reveals larger

TABLE 3.10

COMPARISON OF LOYAL SUPPORTERS AND PRECINCT LEADERS BY SELECTED TYPES OF "DEVIANT" SOCIAL CHARACTERISTICS

Republican			*Democratic*		
	Loyalists	*Precinct leaders*		*Loyalists*	*Precinct leaders*
Catholic	13%	24%	Professional	4%	16%
Negroes	8	16	Managerial	10	10
Irish	8	6	Clerical and sales	10	16
Semi- and unskilled	8	15	Farm background	11	13
Skilled	8	16	Northwestern European origin	23	20

percentages of Catholics, Negroes, and semi- and unskilled workers in the Republican precinct cadre than were actually represented in its loyal support group. And the Democrats had pulled into precinct leadership posts higher percentages of those with professional, clerical, and sales occupations, as well as those with a farm background, than were found in the Democratic loyal support group. Rather than lag behind its constituent groups in this respect, the lower reaches of the party structure seemed unduly anxious or unwittingly promiscuous in the recruitment of those with alien social backgrounds. Thus the two parties penetrated each other's territory more deeply in their hierarchical composition than in the attraction of consistent followers.

An understanding of the environmental context of the party battle is basic to a grasp of this image of the party structure. One theory which seeks to explain these recruitment data stipulates that open clientelism is a reciprocal response of a party structure to the opposition's expansionist recruitment tactics. After a careful look at the competitive status of the individual precincts in our sample and correlating our recruitment data with this factor, we found considerable support for this hypothesis (Table 3.11). The deviant precinct leader was found in two

TABLE 3.11

SOCIAL DEVIANCY OF PRECINCT LEADERS BY COMPETITIVE STATUS OF THE PRECINCT*

Proportions "deviant"	*Sure Democratic precincts*	*Doubtful precincts*	*Sure Republican precincts*
Democratic leaders	15%	83%	66%
Republican leaders	68	57	23
Number of cases			
Democratic	79	30	29
Republican	69	39	35

* Competitive precincts had an average Democratic percentage in 1948–1956 in presidential elections of between 45.0% and 54.9%; sure Democratic precincts, over 55%; sure Republican precincts, under 45%.

types of precincts, as the table strikingly demonstrates. Deviant Republican leaders were found in precincts apparently lost to the Republicans. On the other hand, over 50 per cent of the Republican leaders in doubtful precincts were also deviant, as were the overwhelming number of Democrats in doubtful precincts (83 per cent). Neither party seemed to recruit deviant types in precincts where it was most sure of victory (15 per cent of the Democratic leaders, 23 per cent of the Republicans). There is no need for a porous structure and expansionist leadership recruitment tactics in the "sure" areas. But both parties were "open" structures in marginal areas, and in areas where they were greatly outnumbered currently. There seems to be no point to selectivity in these areas, and the traditional social backgrounds of the party leadership have much less appeal here. Thus, both parties adapted, and allowed socially deviant leadership where the power-winning requirements of the situation demanded or permitted it.

In summing up the meaning of this analysis, certain facts are clear. The so-called "omnibus" tendency which Michels noted long ago in parties is largely confirmed in a democratic and competitive milieu. Through a variety of processes, the parties revealed in their structures very diverse and indeed "deviant" social groups contributing sizeable proportions of the leadership. And this had been going on for a long time. It is true for the precinct cadre, the upper hierarchical elite, and the loyal partisan supporters. Although the evidence indicates that party leaders were conscious of the need for a permissive and open recruitment strategy, many leaders came into the party after an interest was generated in other social groups, or in interpersonal associations with party activists. This suggests a reciprocal relationship between the party structure's needs and strategy, on the one hand, and the desire of certain social categories to secure access to both parties. Once in the party, individuals in the precinct cadre maintained political associations with individuals with "deviant" social backgrounds; thus the openness of the structure was reenforced. Not all substructures and precinct organizations were equally promiscuous, however. The data indicate that where parties are competing on fairly equal terms, they vie with each other in open social recruitment practices. In addition, they are prone to be very tolerant and least exclusive where their status is that of the minority.

This picture of eclecticism in recruitment should not lead to the conclusion that the deviant social categories are taking over the party structure. There is no evidence of the "flight of the middle classes" from party hierarchical positions. At least 45 per cent of our precinct leaders, for example, were in the middle income brackets—from $4,000 to $8,000—and close to 50 per cent were in clerical, sales, professional, and skilled crafts occupations. Nevertheless, the emphasis is not on the traditionally safe groups but on the "deviant potential." Michels' accordion is expanded, especially in marginal constituencies, and poised to play many types of political music! For it is highly improbable that an interest solidarity can be expressed under these conditions, or a maximally efficient structure maintained. The party is forced to solve its dilemma, therefore, by ignoring social congruence in the leadership group and opting for profit maximization through organizational social expansionism. This may be dysfunctional to efficiency but it *is* functional to power, and tends certainly to the emergence of social subsystems within the party structure with varying degrees of leadership autonomy, differential electoral tactics, and conflicting perceptions of party goals. Subsequent sections of this theory of party organization are concerned with these kinds of strains and stresses.

CHAPTER 4

ALLIANCE OF SUBCOALITIONS

Great theorists of parties, past and present, have been ever alert to the probability that the political party is basically an institution through which the social interests of the masses are both implemented and controlled. This was Charles Merriam's emphasis:

> The broad basis of the party is the interests, individual or group, usually group interests, which struggle to translate themselves into types of social control acting through the political process of government.[1]

And Max Weber's:

> But "parties" live in a house of "power." Their action is oriented toward the acquisition of social "power," that is to say, toward influencing a communal action no matter what its content may be . . . . parties may represent interests determined through "class situation" or "status situation," and they may recruit their following respectively from one or the other . . . in most cases they are partly class parties and partly status parties, but sometimes they are neither. . . . Parties differ according to whether or not the community is stratified by status or by classes.[2]

This theoretical image has been echoed many times. Franz Neumann claimed, "The single most important instrument for the translation of social power into political power is the political party."[3] E. P. Herring asserted, "The task of the party is to

[1] *Op. cit.*, p. 2.
[2] "Class, Status and Party," in R. Bendix and S. M. Lipset, eds., *Class, Status, and Power* (Glencoe, Ill.: Free Press, 1953), p. 74.
[3] *The Democratic and the Authoritarian State* (Glencoe, Ill.: Free Press, 1957), p. 12.

achieve a working combination of sections, of interests, and also of the liberals and conservatives within its own ranks."[4] Avery Leiserson contends that "the modern political party is therefore an agency of informal, indirect representation of social groups and classes. . . ."[5] And V. O. Key, whose classic study of southern factional politics laid the groundwork for empirical testing of this theoretical orientation elsewhere, said: "Social structures that develop leadership and bring together like-minded citizens lay the basis for the effectuation of the majority will."[6] Our literature is thus replete with insights encouraging an empirical assault on the conceptual implications of the party structure as a collectivity of social interests which are aggregated by, as well as transform, the party as an organizational process. We will attempt to identify the subunit "interests" in the party's structural system and to assess their viability, autonomy, and system loyalty.

Politicians who lead political parties, and thus have a broad experience and perspective as actors in the system, naturally think in these subcoalitional terms. This is particularly so if they have contact with the lower echelons. In our interviews with the top state and county Democratic and Republican leaders, we found they were very aware of the existence of subgroups, were, in fact, plagued by the problem of "coordination" of subgroups and by the need to "harmonize" group interests with party goals. The component elements of the coalitional theory of party structure emerge clearly from these interviews.

First, party leaders could describe in some detail the number and identities of the subgroups:

> "Let's take this district here. There are two major racial groups, the Negroes and the Jews. But it is not only nationality groups, but also political groups—for example, we have the Young Democrats and the CIO. We do not have a right wing faction, but we have small businessmen's interests and labor interests. Our trade unions are split into two separate units, even though

[4] *The Politics of Democracy* (New York: Norton, 1940), p. 133.
[5] *Op. cit.*, p. 73.
[6] *Southern Politics* (New York: Knopf, 1949), p. 304.

they are externally united. The AFL is conservative, the CIO is the liberal group . . ."

"One of my colleagues has told me he thinks I hold together 11 factions in this district. They are . . ."

"There are 26 clubs in my district. Mine is a continuing job to maintain harmony."

"I got my job after a struggle with those in power. There are factions here among nationality groups, clubs, and personal differences also. General Motors and the Detroit papers might also have some influence."

There was a recurring emphasis on the autonomy and cohesiveness of these subgroups in the structure:

"The whole organization is a mess. When I came in everyone hated each other. We don't have many meetings because of these factions. Tonight I will take you to two factions. They operate independently and hence we don't have the loyalty of the people."

Most leaders when pressed had some theory stating why such factions exist, although their discussions of this were not particularly lucid. Here is one attempt at explanation:

"The Democratic party is a party of different factions. Some are in the party to use it. . . . Others are in it because they are being used by other people."

The dynamic and continuing character of the subgroup composition and conflict in the structure is implicit in much that these leaders said. One of the most explicit discussions is this:

"The district chairman has to be a Sherlock Holmes in the Republican party. We have, as you know, many splits in our party, and there is a constant battle of wits as to who is for whom. You have to be flexible—to meet these people on their own level, talk shop, pat them on the back, and get the work out of them."

And another, which emphasizes patterns of uniformity:

"You have to realize that politics is give and take. There is always one faction trying to keep control and another to take it away. There are forces against me here. I'm not sure of being re-elected in August. The older people have underestimated the

> youngsters who are the hope of the future. They have a very powerful group."

The party leader above all did not wish to have his structure perceived as dominated by one group. He wanted to convey a picture of great freedom of interaction among subgroups and much reciprocal influence. For example:

> "We have been attacked in Wayne for being too prolabor. But I think we are proud of labor's support. But it is not true that the CIO runs our party. We often influence the CIO as much as they influence us. I try to involve all the people in decisions."

Without exception, party leaders were conscious of the effect of such subcoalitions on the party structure. Examples are:

> "There are many factions and fights for control of the districts. I am sorry about the part played by the RPO. One member of my committee, a member of the RPO, has not attended one meeting of the Executive Committee, even during the campaign . . ."

> "Party organization has been a diffused and complicated structure. We have on the one hand the official organization and on the other hand we have 101 clubs and associations. . . . At the moment the party has no control over candidates. . . . Factions mean loss of elections."

One of the major preoccupations of the party leaders was how to keep everybody happy as part of this supra-entity the "party" —that is, how to provide motivational satisfaction and loyalty to the organization at the same time:

> "In our district we have a Polish section, a Negro section, a Jewish section, and any number of smaller groups. I have to be a jack of all trades. My job is to get as many people in these groups happy as I can and see that they get the votes out."

This responsibility placed the leader in a very paradoxical position, in effect neutralizing him in the struggle among groups:

> "The job of the district chairman is to keep all the groups in the party. For example, we have the Republican precinct workers' organization in Detroit whose major function was to throw out the old bosses in the Republican party and make it a liberal party as it should be. The 'Old Guard' still want to live in the

> eighteenth century and we have either to bring them along or leave them. My job, however, is to keep all these people together and thus win elections."

This, then, is the theory of factionalism as seen through the eyes of the party organizational elite. Some of these leaders saw the existence of such subgroups as inevitable and not necessarily harmful: "These factions in my opinion are not necessarily dangerous or disadvantageous to the party." Others bitterly denounced them: "We have simply got to do away with factions. The party must be united to win." But despite such conflicting evaluations, almost all of these leaders were conscious that subgroups existed, that they posed a threat to structural viability, and that one of the major tasks of the party was to satisfy these groups and, at the same time, cope with them.

To demonstrate that the subcoalitional conceptualization of the party structure is reality-oriented, and not an alien subject for discourse with the practicing politician, is not difficult. But the precise identification and operationalization of subcoalitions within the structure is a more elusive and complicated exercise. In selecting those substructures within each party which we would utilize in our research, we relied on two criteria: the "subjective" recognition of the substructures by the party leaders, and the "objective" appearance of these substructures in our data. Further, in both cases we wished to test for those substructures of most concern in our theoretical perspectives. We assiduously "pumped" the top leaders in both parties for information on which "factions" were important in the individual districts and in the county-wide organization. From the standpoint of data, analysis, and theory, certain problems arose which required attention. For one thing, the size of some of the groups mentioned was too small for analysis with our data—individual clubs (such as the Old Hickory Club in the 14th District, or the Workmen's Circle in the 13th), or certain social categories (such as the Jews or young Democrats in an individual district). Another problem concerned the overlapping nature of the subgroups—young versus old, liberal versus conservative, in addition to nationality and economic-interest-oriented subgroups. Clearly, a decision had to be made if our analyses were not to continue indefinitely. There were also considerable variations by district, and in the end we had to adopt a subcoalitional model for the county party, since the data were too sparse for individual district coalitional analysis. Finally, there were differences of opinion among our leader informants which had to be reconciled.

Despite these operational problems, and after carefully assessing all possibilities, we arrived at the subcoalitional models used below. In presenting these, certain cautionary observations are in order. First, it must be understood that this subcoalitional "picture" of reality derives from our major theoretical assumption that a party must first be viewed as an aggregate of *social and economic interests*, and subsequently as a set of ideological subgroups. In the tradition of Merriam and others, therefore, we do not define subgroups initially in ideological terms, but rather characterize social and economic substructures in terms of their ideological characteristics. Second, we do not maintain that the subcoalitions used here in each party constitute an inclusive set. There are many organizational subsystems, varying from almost independent leadership machines (such as candidate organizations), to more permanent groups which parallel party structure, merging at certain vertical points with the structure (such as the UAW-PAC subsystem in some districts in 1956). These types of subsystems, including the women's auxiliary, or fairly autonomous clubs, or special affiliates, are not utilized here. Third, it must not be assumed that all members or supporters of an organization are necessarily identifiable as associated with a subcoalition. In fact, as our analysis suggests, there is an "organizational residue" which we find difficult to classify in subcoalitional terms. This may be a fault of our model, or it may be a measure of reality. Finally, we were interested in locating substructures in the party which, on the basis of leadership reports and our own observations, would reveal evidence of at least a minimal degree of substructural interaction, self-consciousness, and similarity of subunit interest and outlook. These were "secondary" or "dependent" research concerns, however, and their actuality must emerge from the data. Our initial design was to identify one set of party subcoalitions defined in terms of the social and economic interests which they articulated and presumably did represent.

Using the dominant groups identified by the top leadership of the Democratic party in the Detroit area, we constructed the coalitional image found in Table 4.1, basing the calculations on our data from a cross-section of the adult population of the area. Most of the socio-economic categories considered to be components of the Democratic coalition are self-explanatory, but a few comments are in order. We attempted to isolate distinguishable and unitary socio-economic interests in each case: thus CIO Negroes were used separately from AFL Negroes and the nonlabor Negroes. The same was done for the Poles and Irish. One group which many observers and leaders had been aware of for some time in Detroit was the low-status whites from the South. Again we separated those with labor union memberships from the others. A large group of whites who belonged to labor unions, but were not distinguishable in terms of particular social or economic status in large enough numbers for analysis, were grouped together as "other labor whites," CIO and AFL again separated. Another group strongly emphasized currently in the Democratic party is the "business and professional Democrats," which the party has organized into luncheon clubs and societies. Finally, the "residue" which we could not conceive as fitting into the coalitional model, and which are assumed not to be affiliates of a particular subgroup, were set aside as "other nonlabor blue-collar whites" and "unemployed." We assume here a positive socio-economic interest, as well as some possibility of informal, if not formal, personal interaction in the political context of some members in these subcategories. There is also the likelihood of similarity of political perspectives stemming from their strongly homogeneous social status or class position.

The distributions in Table 4.1 suggest the coalitional complexity of a major party. If we look only at the loyal party supporters, the first column in the table, we can see the number and

TABLE 4.1

A SUBCOALITIONAL IMAGE OF THE PUBLIC SECTOR OF THE DEMOCRATIC PARTY

Subgroups	*Loyal supporters*	*Weak supporters*
Negroes		
CIO	8%	8%
AFL, etc.*	5	2
Nonlabor	15	6
Poles		
CIO	6	4
AFL, etc.	4	3
Nonlabor	1	2
Irish		
CIO	2	4
AFL, etc.	2	2
Nonlabor	5	6
Blue-collar southern† migrants (whites)		
CIO	3	2
AFL, etc.	2	2
Nonlabor	3	3
Other labor (whites)		
CIO	21	20
AFL, etc.	8	15
Business-professional and White-collar group (whites)	9	12
Organizational residue		
Other nonlabor Blue-collar whites	5	7
Unemployed (no one in the labor force)	0	2
Totals		
All CIO	39	39
All AFL, etc.	22	24
Number of cases	185	240

* Includes a few independent unions.

† This category does not include 21 Irish who also had Southern origins, 14% of whom were loyal.

proportionate size of the groups with which the party theoretically is concerned. True, the Negroes as a group represented 28 per cent of all loyal supporters, but only 8 per cent were CIO. The Poles, in all, constituted only 11 per cent, and just barely half of these were CIO. The tremendous diversity of the Democratic structure is reflected in the presence, in contrast to the Negroes and Poles, of almost 10 per cent of the loyal supporters who were in the "Business-professional" category, and another 8 per cent who were blue-collar southern migrants (there were actually 16 per cent, if Irish southern migrants were added to this group). This was the basic character of the aggregate of socio-economic interests in the party, then, which admitted to loyalty and, in turn, sought consideration and a party response to its demands. Though indeed, in one sense, the CIO was the largest subcoalitional entity, it was broken up into, and overlapped with, other status groupings. At its peak the CIO represented no more than two-fifths of the loyal support cadre, which in turn consisted of a wide-ranging spectrum of social subgroups.

We present the same type of distribution for the Republican party in Table 4.2. Again a word of explanation about the categories used is in order. We were interested in achieving as "pure" categories as possible. The "Business-managerial subcoalition" had, of course, been identified by several Republican leaders as well as being, in the minds of many observers, a key segment of the party. We decided to use occupation and nationality jointly in placing the remainder of the nonlabor whites into coalitional categories. Thus, we isolated the other white-collar Germans and English, as well as the nonlabor blue-collar Germans and English. The labor union whites were hypothesized as a viable unit, as well as the Negroes, although the Negroes were divided into labor and nonlabor. This left us with a "residue" of roughly one-fifth whom we could not place in any particular coalitional scheme based on class and nationality (or racial) status.

The tremendous diversity in the social-group substructure of the Republican party is again demonstrated by Table 4.2. If we look at the loyal supporters alone, the largest single segment was

TABLE 4.2

A Subcoalitional Image of the Public Sector of the Republican Party

Subgroups	*Loyal supporters*	*Weak supporters*
Business-managerial, whites	22%	7%
Other white collar (nonlabor whites)		
Germans	10	4
English (Scottish, Welsh)	9	7
Other northwestern Europeans (not Irish)	5	5
Nonlabor blue-collar (whites)		
Germans	3	4
English (Scottish, Welsh)	4	9
Other northwestern Europeans (not Irish)	3	9
Labor (whites)	12	15
Negroes		
Labor	2	4
Nonlabor	7	10
Organizational residue		
White-collar nationality deviants*	12	11
Blue-collar nationality deviants*	9	15
Unemployed	2	2
Totals		
All Germans	19	9
All English (Welsh and Scottish)	26	15
Number of cases	90	163

* "Nationality deviant" means in this case coming from central, southern, or eastern European nationality backgrounds (excluding the Germans), and including the Irish. A few cases of individuals whose nationality was not ascertained were also included here.

the business-managerial subgroup, with over 20 per cent. The other white-collar Republicans who were nationality "regulars" added up to 24 per cent of the loyal supporters, true, but these were divided between German, English, and other nationality subgroups. The spread is considerable. Over 10 per cent were whites who are labor union members, another 9 per cent were Negroes, and another fifth were deviants in nationality and/or occupational terms. In one sense the heart of the Republican party consisted of the 46 per cent white-collar nationality "regulars"; in another sense it consisted of the 45 per cent who were German, English, Welsh, or Scottish. But the great variation in class and social status is again apparent.

Before proceeding further with tests of the theory of subcoalitions by examining the orientations to politics of individuals in each substructure, it is interesting to note the extent to which these subgroups were represented at different levels of the party hierarchy. In a sense, one test of the meaningfulness of a coalitional segment is its status in the hierarchy. Table 4.3 presents these data.

Only two subcoalitions identified did not have representation in the party's leadership structure—the southern blue-collar migrants (Democratic party), and the blue-collar Germans (Republican party). There were other subgroups, however, whose representation was slight—for example the Negro nonlabor subgroup in the Democratic party, and the blue-collar nationality "deviants" in the Republican party. It is interesting to note how close the percentages of Democratic loyal supporters (Table 4.1) were to the percentages of precinct leaders—almost a perfect mirror except for the nonlabor Negroes and southern migrants. On the other hand, the elite structure of the Democratic party was top-heavy with three elements: Irish, business-professional, and CIO Democrats.

The Republican hierarchy, in contrast, revealed no close congruence between loyal supporters (Table 4.2) and the precinct leaders in Table 4.3. Paradoxically, both ends of the social spectrum were over-represented—the business-managerial group and the two lower-status subgroups of "Labor whites" and Negroes. Several of the subgroups were greatly under-represented at the precinct level, notably white-collar Germans and the entire nonlabor blue-collar set of subgroups. In the Republican top elite we found, however, no top-heavy clusters of certain factions. Only the nonlabor blue-collar nationality regulars seemed deprived of hierarchical status. This was contrary to expectation, and has significant implications for mobility within the Republican party structure, fluidity in the Republican top echelons, and managerial control within the Republican party.

This picture of both parties, as an aggregate of subcoalitions in socio-economic terms, is presented at the "loyal follower" level, and at different hierarchical levels of the structure. The next step is an analysis of the attitudes, interactions, and perspectives of these coalitional subgroups. The aim of this analysis is to determine the extent of subcoalitional homogeneity, similarity in outlook, and loyalty to the party as the supravening political structural entity within which these subgroups exist.

A basic question is: to what extent do the subgroup categories in each party exhibit political self-consciousness as subgroups? Three kinds of tests of data were used to measure this phenomenon: evidence of political discussion (and thus inter-

TABLE 4.3

REPRESENTATION OF SUBCOALITIONS IN THE PARTY HIERARCHIES*

Democrats			*Republicans*		
Subgroup	*Top elites†*	*Precinct leaders*	*Subgroup*	*Top elites†*	*Precinct leaders*
Negroes			Business-managerial whites	18%	32%
Labor‡	14%	19%			
Nonlabor	5	4			
Poles			Other white-collar Germans	11	1
Labor	10	10			
Nonlabor	5	1			
Irish			English (Welsh, Scottish)	14	8
Labor	23	4			
Nonlabor	9	9			
Blue-collar southerners			Other northwestern Europeans§	4	3
Labor	0	3‖			
Nonlabor	0	0			
Other labor	19	40			
Business and professional whites	18	10	Nonlabor blue-collar Germans	0	0

TABLE 4.3—*Continued*

REPRESENTATION OF SUBCOALITIONS IN THE PARTY HIERARCHIES*

Democrats			*Republicans*		
"Residue"	0	2	Nonlabor—*Continued*		
			English (Welsh, Scottish)	4	1
			Other northwestern Europeans§	0	0
			Labor		
			whites	18	24
			Negroes		
			Labor	11	6
			Nonlabor	4	10
			"Residue"		
			White-collar	14	13#
			Blue-collar	4	3
Totals			Totals		
All labor‡	70	73	All Germans	14	17
All CIO	60		All English (Welsh and Scottish)	25	24
Number of cases	22	138	Number of cases	28	143

* Percentages are of those from a particular social category who have representation in a particular echelon indicated.
† Includes the district chairmen and executive board members.
‡ CIO and AFL were not separated because the precinct leadership data were not adequate for this purpose.
§ Includes all others with a northwestern European background, excluding the Irish.
|| These were all Irish, and are also included under Irish labor.
Three % of this 13% are Irish "deviants."

action) among subgroup members, convictions that the subgroup should take positions on political questions, and the frequency with which members felt that their subgroup leaders' opinions on political matters were important. The Democratic party's subcoalitions revealed considerable political self-consciousness, although the range in the scores of cohesion suggests great variability in subgroup autonomy. A high percentage of the CIO Negroes, for example, discussed politics (79 per cent); Irish labor union members were low (21 per cent), and nonlabor Negroes were also relatively low (47 per cent). Nonlabor Negroes, however, were very high in the proportion believing that Negro groups should take political positions on issues (88 per cent), while Polish labor union members were low (46 per cent). On the third test of cohesion, the southern labor migrants generally did not rank their union leaders' opinions as important (only 25 per cent), whereas Irish labor was high (59 per cent), as were the nonlabor Negroes (53 per cent).

The summary index for Democratic groups (Table 4.4) indicates considerable subcoalitional integrity and self-consciousness within all groups, and the index score for all exceeds that of the organizational "residue." But, where the Polish CIO members and the CIO Negroes were on the average 21 per cent and 18 per cent above the adult norm, the nonlabor Negroes were only 8 per cent above the adult norm. A further striking fact is that those who claimed to be "loyal" Democrats generally were much more self-conscious and, presumably, attached to their own coalitional subgroups, than those who were only lukewarm party enthusiasts. So far as we can determine from these data, the more one is attached perceptually to his party, the more likely also that he will be aware of his subcoalitional loyalties. He will exhibit more tendencies to discuss politics with subgroup members, to feel the subgroup should articulate political positions, and have more confidence in the importance of the opinions of the leaders of his union, race, nationality, or business group.

The viability of Republican subcoalitions is, however, much more suspect for, although the data reveal similar degrees of political conversational interaction among subgroup members in both parties, much smaller percentages of Republicans felt their own subgroup should take political positions. With few excep-

TABLE 4.4

SCALE POSITION OF DEMOCRATIC SUBGROUPS ON THE DIMENSIONS OF POLITICAL COHESION (COMPARED TO ALL ADULTS)

	All partisans	*Only loyal partisans*
Negroes		
CIO	+18	+38
All labor	+17	+30
Nonlabor	+ 8	*
All Negroes	+13	+17
Polish		
CIO	+21	*
All labor	+ 7	*
All Polish	+14	+23
Irish		
Labor	+11	*
Nonlabor	+10	*
All Irish	+11	+28
Southern blue-collar migrants	+10	+ 4
Business and professional whites	+10	+23
Other labor		
CIO	+14	+21
AFL	+16	+30
"Residue"	− 6	− 3

* Too few cases for comparable analysis.

tions, they had a lower estimate of the importance of the opinions of their subgroup leaders. An interesting contrast is provided, for example, between the Irish (Democrats) and the German (Republicans): over 60 per cent of the former, but less than 10 per cent of the latter, believed their own group should take political positions. Similarly, the subgroup of labor union whites in the Republican party was far below the adult norm, only 9 per cent ranking their group's leaders' opinions as important, while both the AFL and CIO members in the Democratic party, whether as aggregates or by nationality and racial groups, had much more subcoalitional self-confidence and viability.

The net result of these data, if one calculates an index score for Republican subgroups (in comparison with adult norms)

(Table 4.5), is that most of the Republican subgroups appeared at the negative end of the cohesion scale. Only the business-managerial subgroup of the Republican party and the white-collar English (Scottish and Welsh), had cohesion scores comparable to those of the Democratic party's subgroups. These two "factions" exhibited considerable integrity and autonomy. Contrary to Democratic substructural tendencies, however, the "loyal" members of these Republican subgroups seemed less attached to the group than the moderately enthusiastic party members in the subgroups.

The Republican party may be characterized as a loose aggregation of social categories with two substructural components, the business-managerial class and the white-collar English, sufficiently articulated and politically self-conscious to exhibit some measure of stability and autonomy. The Democratic party was more a collection of seven to nine major subgroups, with consid-

TABLE 4.5

SCALE POSITION OF REPUBLICAN SUBGROUPS ON THE DIMENSIONS OF POLITICAL COHESION (COMPARED TO ALL ADULTS)

	All partisans	*Only loyal partisans*
Business-managerial whites	+17	+ 7
Other white collar		
Germans	−16	*
English (Welsh and Scottish)	+16	*
Total group	+ 3	+ 4
Nonlabor blue-collar whites		
Germans	−12	*
English (Welsh and Scottish)	− 5	*
Total group	− 8	*
Labor whites	−14	−22
Negroes		
Nonlabor	−14	*
All Negroes	− 7	*
"Residue"	− 2	− 6

* Too few cases for comparable analysis.

erable evidence of substructural identity and integrity. The persistence of substructural identifications, among even the "loyal" Democrats, is particularly striking. If our data begin to approach reality, they document the theory that the party is a coalitional system, and not just a heterogeneous collectivity of individuals with great diversity in social background. Though the subcoalitional styles of the two parties diverge, the concept of subcommunities within the party structure seems to be tenable.

Thus far we have utilized data only from partisan supporters in the adult population not involved in party work. Exploration of the extent of subcoalitional cohesion and identification in each party hierarchy—precinct leaders in the first instance—will reveal subcoalitional self-consciousness intensified. It is difficult to secure comparable, meaningful data in this area for those in the hierarchy. But if, for example, we consider one of the measures used with adult partisans—whether the individual considered the political opinion of the leaders of his own social interest group of importance—we see a greater persistence of subgroup identification among precinct leaders. Table 4.6 documents this comparison. The Democratic precinct leaders demonstrated a high degree of subgroup involvement. Of the Poles, 100 per cent said that their Polish leaders had political opinions which were important, 66 per cent of all the Negro precinct leaders felt the same way about their group's leaders, 71 per cent of the Irish, and the same percentage of the business-professional Democrats asserted business leaders' opinions were important. Other types of analyses were made of the extent of precinct leaders' commitments to their own social groups, with interesting corroborating results. For example, we asked the precinct leader to tell us who he considered to be the party's leaders in Wayne County. It was significant to find, in reply to this question, 89 per cent of the Irish leaders mentioned Irish Democrats, 54 per cent of the Negroes mentioned Negro Democrats, and 38 per cent of the Polish leaders mentioned Polish Democrats. Great variations existed among these groups of course, but these and other questions provided "telltale clues" confirming theoretical expectations.

TABLE 4.6

COMPARISON OF SUBCOALITIONAL COHESION OF PRECINCT LEADERS AND PARTISAN SUPPORTERS (ON RANKING OF THE IMPORTANCE OF THE POLITICAL OPINIONS OF SUBGROUP LEADERS)

	Democrats		*Republicans*	
	Partisan supporters	*Precinct leaders*	*Partisan supporters*	*Precinct leaders*
Percentage ranking subgroup leaders' opinions as important*				
High	59%	100%	56%	87%
Low	22	62	0	41
Index score (in comparison with the adult norms)*				
Highest	+19	+78	+19	+43
Lowest	+ 5	+42	−16	+36

* The highest and lowest percentages or scores for any of the subcoalitional categories.

It is also meaningful to find, in the Republican party *hierarchy*, more support for a theory of subcoalitions than among the Republican loyal partisans. The contrast is striking. Two-thirds of Republican Negro precinct leaders related themselves to their racial subgroup connections, while only one-third of the Republican partisan Negroes did. Again, labor union whites in the Republican precinct leadership cadre had a high regard for labor union leaders' opinions (68 per cent) while those who were partisan supporters had a very low regard for labor union leaders (9 per cent). Even for the Republican party, then, the leadership structure of the party can be conceptualized in subcoalitional terms. In a sense the Republican party structure differs from its mass of supporters, while the Democratic party structure is similar, in this respect, to its mass of supporters.

A final question to be answered in a subcoalitional theory of the party structure is: to what extent has subgroup loyalty displaced party loyalty? If it is true, as the data seem to indicate, that identifiable subgroups exist within which there is considerable group commitment, what force binds these subgroup members to the supravening entity called the "party"? To answer the question five measures of party loyalty for adult partisan supporters, and three measures for precinct leaders, were utilized. In general we found, with a few exceptions, a degree of loyalty to the party which exceeded the adult norm. The exceptions in the Democratic party, for partisan supporters, and based on an overall index, were the Irish (but not Irish labor), and AFL members, with the southern blue-collar migrants ranking rather low. Among Republican loyal partisans those subgroups revealing low party loyalty were nonlabor blue-collar Germans and English and nonlabor Negroes.

From the maze of data available to test the extent of party loyalty, a few may be selected as illustrative. For example, we asked our cross-section of adults whether, if they were to become more active in politics, they would prefer to work through political parties or other groups. For all adults, 23 per cent said

TABLE 4.7

EVIDENCES OF SUBCOALITIONAL PARTY LOYALTY: DEMOCRATS AND REPUBLICANS

	Democrats		*Republicans*		*Adult norm*
	Partisan supporters	*Precinct leaders*	*Partisan supporters*	*Precinct leaders*	
Rank party leaders' opinions most important*					
High	32%	50%	33%	39%	
Low	0	12	9	12	19%
Consider parties as standing for different things*					
High	94	88	60	82	
Low	51	63	40	48	59

* The highest and lowest percentages for any of the subcoalitional categories.

they would prefer to work through parties. If this is the "adult norm," only two Democratic groups may be classified as subnormal in terms of commitment to parties: the Irish (but not Irish labor) and the southern blue-collar migrants, both of whom were below the norm. The business-professional Democrats had a proportion of exactly 23 per cent. The highest percentage, 44, was CIO Negroes who preferred to work through parties. On the Republican side, only the Negroes and the white labor union members fell above the norm. The business-managerial whites were slightly below the 23 per cent norm with 19 per cent, none of the English partisans preferred to work through parties, and less than 10 per cent of the Germans. This conveys a picture of low party loyalty among Republicans, that is, low commitment to the party as an ongoing structure for the realization of social goals.

When other criteria of party loyalty were utilized, however, Republican subgroups demonstrated greater party loyalty. For example, only 48 per cent of the adult population called themselves "loyal" to a party, but these partisans, with the exception of the nonlabor blue-collar whites, and the labor whites, exceeded 48 per cent. Thus, 80 per cent of the Republican Negro supporters and 71 per cent of the business-managerial class called themselves "loyal." The Democrats were even more loyal to their party, with no subgroups falling below the 48 per cent norm, except the AFL members (43 per cent).

Another criterion was ranking the opinions of party leaders as "most important" (that is, more important than the opinions of any other set of group leaders). Here we found great variation among subgroups. Among Democrats, in comparison with an adult norm of 19 per cent, the Negroes were low in party loyalty (14 per cent), Negroes in the CIO very low (3 per cent), southern migrants also (3 per cent), Poles moderately loyal though still below the norm (15 per cent of the Polish CIO), while the Irish stood high (29 per cent) along with the business-professional whites (28 per cent). Republican leaders tended to be more impressed with the opinions of party leaders.

Only the English and Negro Republicans fell below the adult norm of 19 per cent. On this dimension, therefore, the Republicans exceeded the Democrats in evidences of loyalty to the party.

If one examines the data on the dimensions used for these subgroups and computes a score based on all five (Table 4.8),

TABLE 4.8

INDEX SCORES OF SUBCOALITIONAL PARTY LOYALTY
(Partisan Supporters Only)

Democrats	*Index score*	*Republicans*	*Index score*
CIO Negroes	14	Business-managerial whites	14
All Negroes	12	Other white collar	
CIO Polish	12	Germans	12
All Polish	8	English (Welsh and Scottish)	6
Irish labor	12	Nonlabor blue collar	
All Irish	−5	Germans	− 5
Southern labor	1	English (Welsh and Scottish)	−19
All southern	4	Labor whites	8
Other labor		Nonlabor Negroes	− 1
CIO	7	All Negroes	11
AFL	−1		
Business and professional whites	6		

Adult norm = 0

the general picture becomes clear. Only a few groups, when all factors were considered, fell below the adult norm on party loyalty. They may have deviated considerably on individual measures, but in summary were inclined to reveal more loyalty than those who had not declared themselves partisan supporters. This would indicate that while there was a certain degree of subcoalitional commitment and self-perception, the members were still bound to the party and desired to achieve their subgroup aims through the instrumentality of the party as an organization of action.

The precinct leaders who were in a sense representatives of these subcoalitions, tended to be more loyal to their respective parties than partisan supporters (Table 4.9). Three tests of party loyalty were used for precinct leaders: the extent of their approval of split ballots, whether they perceived the parties as standing for different ideals, and whether they ranked the opinions of party leaders as *most* important (that is, more important

TABLE 4.9

EVIDENCES OF PARTY LOYALTY IN HIERARCHICAL SUBCOALITIONS
(Based on Precinct Leaders Only)

Subgroups	*Rank party leaders' opinions as* MOST *important*	*Parties stand for different things*	*Disapprove of splitting the ballot*	*Index score*
Democratic				
Negroes				
Labor	19%	88%	54%	+12
All Negroes	16	81	56	+ 9
Poles—total	50	63	87	+21
Irish—total	12	78	39	+ 1
Other labor	42	82	33	+10
Business and professional whites	14	86	79	+18
Republican				
Business-managerial whites	20	57	11	−13
Other white collar				
Northwestern Europeans (whites)	35	82	35	+ 9
Labor				
whites	12	56	35	− 8
Negroes	39	48	27	− 4
All Germans	4	43	39	−13
All English (Welsh and Scottish)	18	86	22	0
Norms for adults	19	59	48*	0

* In the absence of data directly related to "splitting" from the cross-section, we have used here the 48% who considered themselves "loyal" to a party.

than their own group's leaders' opinions). The variations by these measures were great, some ranking above the adult norms, some below. Thus, 50 per cent of the Poles ranked party leaders' opinions as "most important," but only 12 per cent of the Irish and 4 per cent of the Germans had the same opinion. Again, 88 per cent of the Democratic Negro labor union members felt parties had different objectives, but only 56 per cent of the Republicans who were "labor whites" felt the same way, and only 48 per cent of Republican Negroes. On the third measure, ballot-splitting, the high on party loyalty occurred again among the Poles (87 per cent), while the lows were Irish (39 per cent), "other labor" members of the Democratic party (33 per cent), the "business-managerial class" of the Republican party (an extremely low percentage of disapproval—11 per cent), and Republican Negroes (27 per cent).

As the index score indicates (last column of Table 4.9), Democrats were on the average more loyal than Republican precinct leaders. Serious question can be raised about the degree of party loyalty of certain Republican subgroups (the business-managerial class, the Negroes, and the labor whites), as well as that of the Democratic Irish. But for only two of these groups (the Irish Democrats and the Republican labor whites) did we find precinct leaders less loyal to the party than the cross-section of partisan supporters (using the two measures for which we have directly comparable data).

Thus, an analysis of the party loyalty of Democratic precinct leaders, as hierarchical representatives of subgroups, indicates that while manifesting significant self-consciousness as members of a subcoalition, they were, at the same time, revealing above-normal party loyalty. The Republican precinct leaders, however, who were previously demonstrated as exhibiting marked subgroup cohesion (Table 4.6), fell considerably below the Democrats on party loyalty. The data on Republican precinct leaders, in fact, forces one to wonder whether possibly these leaders were not much more subcoalition-oriented than party-oriented.

The question of the relative strengths of subcoalitional unity and party loyalty can be discussed by noting that theoretically seven possible patterns are conceivable: high party loyalty but no subgroup cohesion, clear evidence of subcoalitional cohesion but no party loyalty, neither subgroup nor party loyalty, a high degree of both subgroup and party loyalty, a low but positive degree of both subgroup and party loyalty, a balance in favor of the subgroup, and, finally, a balance in favor of party loyalty. If we summarize our data on group and party identifications of the precinct leaders in both parties, we discover that, since there is strong evidence of subgroup self-consciousness, two of these alternatives are not found in the data. Two patterns emerged in the Republican party: three subgroups with strong subgroup cohesion but subnormal party loyalty (the business-managerial class, the labor union whites, and the Negroes); a second pattern exists for the other white-collar Republicans with a northwestern European background who revealed both subgroup and party loyalty with some indication of balance in favor of the party.

The Democratic precinct leaders manifested four patterns. First, the Poles were very high in subgroup self-consciousness *and* in party loyalty. Second, the business-professional Democrats also had plus scores on both dimensions, but did not place as high on either dimension as the Poles. Third, the Irish pattern was one of plus scores on both measures but with a definite balance in favor of the nationality subgroup. And, fourth, the "other labor" group of CIO and AFL members with plus scores also revealed a decided balance in favor of the dimension of party loyalty.

The following observations conclude this exploratory investigation of subcoalitional tendencies in the parties. The theory of subcoalitions does seem reality-oriented and meaningful in the empirical analysis of the party structure. The insights of practicing politicians, their suspicion that a focal problem of organizational dynamics is the harmonizing of "factions" and subgroups, are supported by the data. Subgroups existed within the party, both at the level of the public supporter cadre, and the precinct leadership cadre; they had substantial, though variable, subunity cohesiveness and integrity. For some of these "factions" the data suggest that party loyalty had become minimal, particularly in the Republican party. For others, a balance in favor of the subgroup developed. For still others, a high degree of party loyalty was found side by side with commitment to factional objectives. The task of the Republican managerial elite seemed to be much more one of developing loyalty to the party as the instrument for factional goal-achievement than was the case for the Democrats. But the managerial leadership nucleus of both parties apparently must deal constantly with the containment of subcoalitional divisiveness and autonomy, as well as with the possible displacement of party goals by subgroup goals. In a later chapter we will examine the ideological character of these subcoalitions. Here we have begun the delineation, as Merriam suggested long ago, of the phenomenon of the party structure as "group interests, which struggle to translate themselves into types of social control. . . ."[7] As Maurice Duverger has nicely described it, "A party is not a community but a collection of communities, a union of small groups."[8]

[7] *Loc. cit.*
[8] *Op. cit.*, p. 17.

CHAPTER 5

THE PARTY "STRATARCHY"

A social organization is generally conceived as structured like a pyramid in authority and power, with the top elite nucleus involved in the processes of control, and with control relationships articulated, understood, and followed at the lower echelons. This image of a social organization assumes an effective communication circuit from top to bottom, and bottom to top, indivisible authority and control, and a predominantly upward deference system. In contrast to the traditional pyramid, one could postulate entropic communication, formal separation of authority and control, and reciprocity in deference. It is the second type of image that we hypothesize for the party structure, and which we seek to explore empirically in this chapter.

Many writers, particularly observers of the American political scene, have advanced interpretations which approach the theory of "stratarchy" as outlined in our introductory chapter. Thus, E. E. Schattschneider, noting the "decentralization of power" in American parties, maintains: "The strongest and most stable organization within a city may be a ward organization rather than a city-wide machine."[1] And, again, "Local party machines, like local public utilities, are natural monopolies."[2] Similarly, E. P. Herring contended long ago that "our political parties are temporary alliances of local leaders. . . . These men know the temper of their supporters and they can guess shrewdly as to how far they can compromise with fellow politicians from other sections without endangering their own local follow-

[1] *Party Government* (New York: Rinehart, 1942), p. 147.
[2] *Ibid.*, p. 149.

ing."[3] Long before this, Charles Merriam noted the "wide range of power" which ward and precinct organizations assumed, as well as the centrifugal tendencies of "independency" and "counter-organization."[4] These observations begin to make operational for political parties the conditions implicit in the general notion of "stratarchy" as used by Lasswell and Kaplan:[5] the enlargement of the ruling group of an organization, its power stratification, the involvement of large numbers of people in group decision-making, and, thus, the diffusion and proliferation of control throughout the structure.

This conceptual position is naturally concerned with the relevance of certain components of the oligarchic model of parties. This model asserts the inevitability that a "handful" of individuals will assume control and power in the organization, that these individuals will not represent, nor be representatives of, the rank and file of the organization, that they will exhibit congruence in organizational perspectives and perpetuate themselves in power, particularly through careful recruitment into the ruling group, and that this elite becomes in effect a new managerial class. "As a result . . . every party . . . becomes divided into a minority of directors and a majority of directed."[6] Without engaging in a discussion of the elements in this model, we will merely point out that our analysis of stratarchy in this chapter deals with one crucial aspect of the theory of oligarchy —the extent to which the top ruling group in an organization, such as a party, *does in actuality control or direct* the activities of subordinates. It is our position, without questioning directly the validity of other alleged oligarchic phenomena, that the theory of elite control of the organization, which the oligarchic model assumes, is empirically incorrect. In lieu of the doctrine of elite control, we suggest that, although authority to speak for the organization may remain in the hands of the top elite nucleus, there is great autonomy in operations at the lower "strata" or

[3] *Op. cit.*, p. 121.
[4] *Op. cit.*, see pp. 60–101.
[5] *Op. cit.*, pp. 219–20.
[6] Roberto Michels, *op. cit.*, especially p. 32.

echelons of the hierarchy, and that control from the top is minimal and formal. We shall utilize a variety of criteria to develop this position.

One of the first questions in the empirical investigation of a social organization is: How clear are the structural images of those who have leadership positions in the organization? A well-defined picture of the "paper organization" of the party exists, either nationally or locally, but one wonders whether this matches reality. Theoretically, the positions, roles, and tasks of individuals in the party structure are defined, distributed, differentiated, and integrated into a meaningful structural system. If this is true, one becomes concerned with coherence as a system property of the party, that is, the precision and clarity with which organizational roles and relationships become articulated. In the investigation of this property of coherence, we are interested in both the "paper" structural units and relationships, and the nature of the perceptual awareness of the hierarchy toward the organization. Do those who hold positions in the organization have an accurate and generally similar understanding of the structure, or are there contrasting and conflicting images? The "meaning" of an organization is in one sense, after all, in the minds of those who hold positions in the organization. And the image a person holds of the structure may condition in large part his relationship to it and his behavior within it.

When we asked the chairman of a district organization to describe the "concrete parts" of his "empire," he usually did so with great pride in detail. Our interview schedules are filled with careful diagrams and precise statements about relationships, methods of selection, terms of office, jurisdictions, powers, functions, tasks. There is the usual description of executive boards, district conventions, ward and precinct chairmen—their size, selection, responsibilities and importance. In addition, the chairman usually outlines his own task expansively, and his relationship to other concrete parts of the hierarchy—the state chairman, county committee, the congressional candidate and his organization.

Several aspects of this mass of information provided by the top elite are worthy of note. Since state statutes prescribe certain organizational parts and procedures, the structural skeleton was remarkably similar for each district. But each chairman took pride in detailing certain nuances, or innovations in structure, in his district. One man pointed out that his ward chairmen were selected democratically by the precinct workers, in contrast, he said, to other districts. Another man claimed that he had subdivided precincts into areas presided over by "block captains." A third pointed with pride to the fact that his district was a four-layer structure, with two echelons, instead of one, between the precinct and the executive board. A fourth described carefully the existence of a functional structure, rather than a geographical one, controlled through a district level "steering committee," each of whose five members chaired a functional committee for the entire district. Another chairman put great stock in an executive board which was double the statutory size of 15 members. A colleague carefully explained how each of the major factional groups in the district (the CIO, the Poles, the "club movement," etc.) had been placated by providing each with its own headquarters. Finally, there was the chairman who disdained organizational charts and claimed to carry on operations through informal and personal contacts with leaders at all levels in the hierarchy.

The party chairmen were convinced they knew their own organizations thoroughly and were exceedingly frank in discussing particular organizational strategies, as well as problems in developing integrated structures. They openly discussed the secret caucuses in which decisions were made in advance of regular board or convention meetings; admitted their desire to develop working relationships with certain dominant groups (the CIO, the Negroes, the conservatives, etc.); appeared to be aware of certain structural problems and inadequacies. At times the party chairman could also be very critical of his own organization. But the striking fact above all is that the chairman was certain he understood the state of the organization. Only one chairman, a Republican, admitted that he was out of touch with his precinct delegates. The ordinary chairman might have had reservations about his control over the structure, but insisted that his picture of the nature and condition of the structure was clear and accurate.

This assumption by the chairman that he is in command in an organization which he "knows" is not justified by other data. Our interviews with the chairmen, compared with information received from executive board members and precinct leaders, gave evidence of limits to the chairman's "instrumental" knowledge. These interviews revealed differential and conflicting perceptions of key aspects in organizational relationships, as well as incomplete information on the state of the organization at the lower echelons. First, there were descriptive inaccuracies. In at least three districts we found chairmen who described incorrectly the method for selecting county chairmen, did not know whether there were ward chairmen, or how ward chairmen were chosen. Second, it became obvious when pressed that some chairmen were ill informed about certain key areas of decision. The Republican chairmen knew relatively little about the financial organization of the party in their districts and the county. In both parties, the chairman's knowledge about the selection of candidates was most inadequate. Third, some chairmen revealed interpretive ambiguity over the rationale for certain organizational units and processes. "How are ward chairmen integrated with the executive board?" generally evoked weak and inconclusive explanations. Finally, in marked contrast to the CIO-PAC district coordinators (who had very precise knowledge about their structures), the district chairmen many times could not tell us who their precinct leaders were, which precincts did not have leaders at the moment, and above all, the duties of the job. Often, when urged for detail, the chairman responded: "Well, I really don't take an active part in (nominations)," or "I leave that pretty much up to the section chairmen," etc. In the case of at least half of the chairmen one had the impression of a "skeletal" body of information, plus some sense of what might be "going on," and specific knowledge about only certain matters. Too often the district chairman had decidedly limited and superficial knowledge about personnel and process aspects of the organization with which he should have been very familiar in order to direct properly the structure to the achievement of its basic goals.

This conclusion is substantiated by interviews with district board members. Here one found contradictory information about the organization as well as conflicting judgments. Board members in the same district would contradict the chairman, as well as each other, on such matters as how the "slate" was prepared, what the powers of the board were, how often it met, even the method for selecting the chairman. Part of this was the result of outright confusion about the operation of the district. For example, in two out of every three districts for both parties, board members differed about the degree of power actually held by the board. Misinformation was also evident, and the net impression was an organizational image disputed and unclear even among the chairman's top-echelon colleagues.

This point can be demonstrated systematically and in greater depth by examining carefully the conditions of organizational life and awareness at the precinct level. First, to what extent was hierarchy fully realized? Certain chairmen mentioned the existence of gaps and difficulty in securing personnel, but one cannot comprehend the extent of incompleteness from interviews with the chairmen. What do the data reveal? To begin with, there were no Democratic precinct leaders in 11 per cent of the sample precincts and no Republican leaders in 5 per cent. Beyond this there were the following evidences of organizational inadequacy:

	Democrats	*Republicans*
No precinct helpers	19%	40%
Helpers, but no meetings or other types of direction	26%	22%

(These are percentages of precincts in which there were leaders who were interviewed.)

These figures are rather startling and suggest, even for the majority (Democratic) party, deficient hierarchical articulation in 45 per cent of the party's manned precincts during the 1956 campaign. In three-fifths of the minority-party precincts there was minimal articulation. Thus we found, in total perspective, a viable Democratic organization in less than half the precincts, and a working Republican organization in about one-third of the precincts.

Individual districts varied greatly in degree of incomplete precinct organization. The percentage of leaders who reported no helpers, or no direction of helpers varied, from 21 per cent in a Democratic district, to 88 per cent in a Republican district. The Republicans showed the poorest organizational development in three very strong Democratic districts; the Democrats were weakest (62 and 70 per cent of the precinct leaders admitting a poor precinct operation) in the two most "marginal" districts. In three Republican and two Democratic districts there was virtually only a shell of organization, with over 60 per cent of the precinct leaders performing a "lone-wolf" type of holding operation. This is a very revealing insight into the state of party organization in a metropolitan area presumably well-organized, at least by the Democrats. It is a picture which would not emerge from interviews with the chairmen, however, for despite expressions of occasional concern, none admitted the parlous state of his own organization. There seems little doubt that the actual condition of health of the precinct cadre and its strata operations differed from the structural image held by the elite nucleus, suggesting that intelligence reports from the grass roots were distorted, or never arrived.

This analysis of the completeness of hierarchy, though significant, is not definitive. More must be discovered about the perceptions of the organization held by leaders at all levels. To systematically rate precinct leaders on the extent and accuracy of their knowledge and perceptions about the organization, we constructed an "Index of Organizational Awareness." From among many items available, six were selected as the best tests: knowledge of the existence of a ward level between the precinct and the executive board; ability to identify party leaders in the area; clarity of their own role perceptions; preciseness of knowledge about precinct leaders' meetings in the district; the extent to which they were familiar with party strategy in the campaign; and knowledge of between-election activities of the district party. These are not esoteric criteria. The index does not require awareness of remote elements of the structure but tests the precinct leaders' knowledge and perception of party structure and processes most proximate to them and about which they should be informed. If the index has bias, it is in the direction of producing high awareness scores.

At least half of the precinct leaders were unaware or ignorant of some aspect of the organization critical to their own performance (Table 5.1), and from 11 to 24 per cent were extremely ignorant of the state of party structure and process.

TABLE 5.1

ORGANIZATIONAL UNAWARENESS OF PRECINCT LEADERS
(Percentage of All Leaders)

	Democrats	*Republicans*
Specific items of organization		
Uninformed about precinct leader meetings in the district	4%	9%
Ignorant of between-elections activities	4	1
Unable to articulate own role	9	12
Unclear on campaign strategy	9	26
Cannot identify party leaders	19	17
Incorrect or uninformed about the organizational level between precinct and district	22	40
*Distributions of organizational awareness**		
Very aware (Score 0)	50	36
Doubtful (Score 1–3)	39	40
Ignorant (Scores 4–8)	11	24

* The maximum score possible, indicating the greatest organizational unawareness, was 10. Knowledge of precinct leader meetings in the district and between election activities were scored 1, the other items being rated more relevant and given a score of 2.

Perhaps the most revealing evidence of ignorance was the 39 Republican leaders (27 per cent) and 25 Democratic leaders (18 per cent) who were aware of no ward organization, even though our interviews with district chairmen and board members (many of them ward leaders) established clearly the existence of a ward substructure. The significance of these findings does not disparage the precinct leader, but rather questions the extent to which the organization was articulated, thus enabling the precinct cadre to have accurate images. Ignorance and misperception of the structure by precinct leaders are merely a reciprocal of the state of the system.

District variations in organizational awareness were again pronounced (Table 5.2).

TABLE 5.2
ORGANIZATIONAL AWARENESS BY DISTRICTS
(Precinct Leaders—Percentage Very Aware)

Districts	*Democrats*	*Republicans*
1st	35%	25%
13th	26	0
14th	25	63
15th	83	18
16th	63	41
17th	48	48

Two of the three Republican districts showing a high degree of organizational incompleteness were also low on organizational awareness—the 13th and 15th. There was some parallelism for the Democrats in the 14th District, but the first and 13th, which had fairly complete precinct organizations, showed a relatively low level of awareness among Democratic leaders. This suggests that the two phenomena are not necessarily part of the same pattern. On the one hand, the organization may appear well articulated, with many positions filled; on the other, these men may be quite unaware of significant aspects of party structure. Indeed, this becomes clear when we combine the two dimensions

(Table 5.3). It is true that precinct leaders who developed and directed their own organization carefully were likely to be more aware of the total structure in which they were operating; but degrees of extreme ignorance and misperception were still found in precincts which were fairly complete. This suggests that the most vigorous organizational elaborators in the precinct might not be those with a clear view of the total hierarchy. It also implies that in many cases the precinct leader and his associates might be operating, so far as their own perceptions are concerned, a rather isolated, self-contained, and semi-autonomous substructure.

TABLE 5.3

ORGANIZATIONAL COMPLETENESS AND AWARENESS OF PRECINCT LEADERS

Organizational awareness level	*Incomplete precinct structure*		*Fairly complete precinct structure*	
	Democrats	*Republicans*	*Democrats*	*Republicans*
Very aware	42%	27%	55%	52%
Doubtful	47	48	33	24
Ignorant	11	25	12	24
Number of cases	60	93	78	50

The same type of analysis for executive board members revealed that organizational awareness did not necessarily improve as one moved upward. In fact, the data indicate that a larger percentage of precinct leaders than board members were aware of relevant aspects of organizational life. Many board members replied, frankly, "Don't know" when asked to explain board duties, the powers of the board, the manner in which strategy was elaborated, how finances were managed, etc. When more difficult questions were raised concerning the influence of the chairman, the board, and precinct leaders, the responses were extremely vague. Thirty-eight board members, scored on the same basis and with the same type of items as the precinct leaders, are distributed as follows:

	Democrats	*Republicans*
Very aware	6%	10%
Doubtful	65	57
Ignorant	29	33

It appears that as the career leader moves into middle- and upper-echelon positions, he is cut off from the precinct job with its fairly straightforward delineation of responsibilities. In this new middle-hierarchy position, he enters a confusing maze of relationships, undefined tasks, and unclear perceptions. This is no doubt related to the length of time the board member has served in his new position, as well as the amount of time he gives to the job. But his own place in the hierarchy is not clear to him, and particularly noticeable are the conflicting perceptions among board colleagues *in the same district*. One finds disagreement on specific operational procedures, such as how often the board met, what was discussed in board meetings, whether candidate nominations were discussed in board meetings, how important ward and precinct organization leaders were, whether ethnic and racial groups were self-consciously included on board "slates," and the ideological position of the party in the district. On the latter point, for example, in five of six Republican, and in three of six Democratic organizations, the board members split on their interpretations.

The perceptions of board members contrasted sharply sometimes, as in their descriptions of the county chairman's job. Democratic district chairmen tended to de-emphasize the county chairman, while Democratic board members, with only one exception, considered the county chairman quite important. Republican board members and their district chairmen split almost equally on evaluations of the importance of the county chairman. Similarly, in discussions of the district chairman's job, board members took quite different views—about 50 per cent of Democratic board members stressed the "coordinating task," others failed to mention this but saw the chairman as a patronage provider, a candidate selector, a precinct leader recruiter or trainer, and a factional harmonizer. Except for the last responsibility, district chairmen themselves did not emphasize these other roles for themselves. Directly opposing views were advanced by board members in three Democratic and four Republican districts concerning the extent of the power of the executive board. Interviews from the same district boards informed us that the board "really controls" the chairman and district operations, or that the board has "no power" or "very little power." From this it is seen that, although there was admittedly a minority of executive board members who were keenly aware of what was going on, the majority had only a limited grasp of organizational detail, or "instrumental" knowledge, not necessarily compensated for by any great "substantive" or general "evaluative" insights.

One meaningful test of a hierarchical system is congruence, as well as convergence, in role perception. A party organization is in theory a role system. As in any social organization, those holding positions throughout the structure should have a clear understanding of the requirements of their own position and also a clear perception of the responsibilities adhering to the positions of others. Thus, a certain reciprocity in perception is necessary if the organization is to conform ideally to the viability needs of the system.

Applying this theory to the party, it is interesting first to find that precinct leaders, executive board members, district chairmen, and county chairmen ordinarily did have perceptions about their positions. Only about 10 per cent of precinct leaders had no perception at all as to their role, and 9 per cent (Republican) to 18 per cent (Democratic) executive board members did not. District chairmen and county chairmen conveyed the impression that they knew quite well what their position entailed. Thus, holding a position in a party organization usually meant that one secured some understanding of the roles.

These role explanations varied, however, for the same type of position,[7] and lack of convergence was demonstrable at all levels of the hierarchy. District chairmen were agreed, generally, on

[7] See Chapter 10 for a more detailed analysis of roles. Here we merely present some data relating role perceptions to the theory of "stratarchy."

many aspects of their role—almost all felt heavy responsibility for coordinating the campaign, "getting out the vote," perfecting the organization, and promoting factional harmony. Beyond this, however, there was wide disagreement on secondary tasks—screening candidates, securing patronage, recruiting workers, directing financial drives, sponsoring social activities, keeping party workers informed on policy and program, promoting the social and economic welfare of constituents, controlling elected representatives, conducting public relations drives, providing community leadership, and maintaining effective liaison with the state party leadership. All of these tasks were mentioned, but not by all chairmen. A considerable range existed in conceivable interpretation of role.

The same observation held for executive board members and precinct leaders (Table 5.4). There was no great unanimity

TABLE 5.4

VARIATION IN PRIMARY ROLE PERCEPTIONS—PRECINCT LEADERS AND EXECUTIVE BOARD MEMBERS

	(Percentage holding primary role perception)	
Executive board members	*Democrats*	*Republicans*
Coordinating several precincts	24%	20%
Representative link between board and precinct	14	16
Special skills (organizational, legal, financial, etc.)	14	25
Geographical representative on the board	5	3
Functional or interest-group representative	19	25
Elite appointee	5	3
No role articulated	18	9
Precinct leaders		
Vote mobilizers	45	45
Ideological mentors	24	23
Socio-economic welfare promoters	22	14
No role articulated	9	12

about the job of the board member whether his responsibilities were directive or representative or the primary task of the precinct leader.

Of more importance, in comparing one echelon with another, is the lack of mutuality in role perception about the same position. The basic question is, for example, to what extent did precinct leaders actually assume the roles expected of them by state chairmen, county chairmen, district chairmen, and executive board members? A meticulous cross-check of this problem of role-convergence for precinct leaders and executive board members gives results as summarized in Table 5.5.

From these limited data it is clear that precinct leaders and executive board members disagreed with district chairmen as to *whether* a role should be assumed, and in the *extent of concurrence* for a particular role. For example, one role for precinct leaders, emphasized by a majority of the district chairmen, was that of discussing the party program in the neighborhoods and communicating this program to the public. Yet less than a fourth of the precinct leaders accepted this role. About one-fifth of the precinct leaders did emphasize, however, working for community projects and demonstrating community leadership (not necessarily linked to party objectives), a role mentioned by no district chairman. Similarly, executive board members seemed to view their jobs in a perspective different from that of the chairman. They claimed more of a participating role in district decision-making (75 per cent compared to 36 per cent of the district chairmen), but did not see themselves as involved in "getting out the vote" or in solving factional strife, as did the chairmen.

No neat overlap was found between role perceptions. This divergence and lack of unanimity suggests no clear understanding or expectation in the party hierarchy as to specific tasks of those in precinct and executive board positions, either as perceptions by others or among themselves. There seemed to be great freedom and autonomy in the leader's own role specification, attesting again to the nonbureaucratic character of the party

TABLE 5.5

DIVERGENCE AND DISAGREEMENT IN ROLE PERCEPTIONS

District chairmen's perceptions of precinct leaders roles	*Percentage of all district chairmen emphasizing the role*	*Percentage of all precinct leaders accepting the role*
Service to constituents	25%	40%
Discussing and communicating to the public the party program	58	23
Getting out the vote (including precinct organizational work)	58	44
Representing major social groups or the public in party affairs	19	1
Controlling upper-echelon party leaders	36	0
Passing on patronage	9	0
Community leadership	0	18
District chairmen's perceptions of executive board members' roles	*Percentage of all district chairmen emphasizing the role*	*Percentage of all executive board members accepting the role*
Participating in decisions on broad organizational policy matters	36%	75%
Liaison with, and general oversight of, precinct operations (including training and recruiting precinct workers)	45	35
Participating in patronage decisions	45	68
Getting out the vote	19	5
Ideological leadership	19	33
Participating in selection of candidates	27	28
Providing support for chairman as elite appointee	0	5
Solving factional controversies	19	0
Representing factions	0	23

organization. If the precinct leader wished to de-emphasize his vote-mobilizing function and act as a community leader, there was no one to object. And if the executive board member wished to de-emphasize his supervisory responsibility as coordinator of precincts, and play instead the role of factional representative in determining district policy, this seemed perfectly realistic. The individual leader was thus not only isolated in terms of over-all knowledge of the party structure, or in his development of an organization for his own subunit as he saw fit, but also in defining his tasks in terms of his own preferences. He appeared more and more, therefore, as a free-lancer, sharing some hierarchical expectations but also permitted considerable operational autonomy and originality.

Implicit in this picture of "stratarchy" is the question of communication patterns in the party structure. To what extent did precinct leaders have communication contact with those in the upper echelons and what were the consequences for the specification of tasks and operational styles? This matter will be discussed in greater detail in the chapters on organizational processes, although a few relevant findings may be presented here. Precinct leaders were asked how often they met with district leaders and what they discussed in these conferences. Thirty per cent of the Republican leaders and 51 per cent of the Democratic leaders saw their district leaders "often," that is, throughout the year. In addition, another 31 per cent Republican leaders and 22 per cent Democratic leaders saw district-level leaders fairly frequently, but during the campaign only. Thus large percentages did have some communication link to the top elite nucleus of the party. When asked, "What sorts of things did you discuss?" approximately two-thirds of the precinct leaders mentioned topics that dealt with various aspects of precinct operation, but these were primarily presentations about campaign tactics and getting the voters to the polls. Less than 10 per cent said that the long-range duties and organizational responsibilities of the precinct leaders were the focus of attention. Nevertheless, it is safe to assume that in the course of discussing the vote-mobilization problem much might be said concerning the direction of the precinct. The empirical question is then: Were those precinct leaders who manifested most autonomy in their operation, individuals who were cut off from the top elite? The answer to this question is No, as found in Table 5.6. In this table we have contrasted the "lone operator" (without helpers, at a minimal level of performance) with the "enterpriser" (the leader with an effective precinct organization, many helpers, and some direction of precinct activities). As the table reveals, 60 per cent of

TABLE 5.6

COMMUNICATION FREQUENCY BETWEEN PRECINCT LEADERS AND THE TOP ELITE

Contact with district elite	*"Lone operator" precinct leaders*		*"Enterprising" precinct leaders*	
	Republican	*Democrat*	*Republican*	*Democrat*
No contact	40%	41%	32%	20%
Frequent campaign contact	27	22	27	31
Contact often throughout the year	33	37	41	49
Number of cases	67	27	22	51

those precinct leaders who displayed most inefficiency and/or autonomy had some contact with district leaders, and about one-third of them had fairly constant contact with district leaders. In fact there was very little variation in the amount of communication between the lone operator type of precinct leader and the enterpriser. The conclusion is inescapable that the amount of contact with the top elite seems to be irrelevant to the particular type of precinct operation carried out. Either the district leader was not vitally concerned with how the local precinct leader operated, or he sanctioned organizational inertia of which he was aware, or he was concerned and attempted to lay down guide lines for perfecting the organization, but was unable to implement his specifications for change effectively.

This preliminary analysis of communicative relationships in the party structure suggests three conclusions: (1) one-third of all precinct leaders had no contact with district leaders; (2) much of the discussion in conferences between district and precinct leaders seemed oriented less to the "direction" of the precinct operation than to the "suggestion" of ways in which the precinct *might* improve in getting out the vote; and (3) precinct leaders acted as autonomous agents irrespective of the frequency or content of communication with district leaders.

Two basic problems underlying any movement toward less "stratarchy" and more management are control over recruitment of precinct leaders and discipline within the organization. Of these problems the chairmen were well aware. Only one chairman did not consider precinct leaders the most important cog in the organization; and 70 per cent of the executive board members agreed. The following quotation from one chairman recurred constantly: "The precinct delegate is the key man. He can deliver the vote and also controls the whole convention." Yet, though chairmen were conscious of his importance, they lamented their inability to control him on the job, either through initial selection or later. Recruitment of precinct leaders appeared to go by default—only three chairmen indicated that they personally took a hand in the recruitment process. This seemed to be a result of scarcity of available candidates, the time-cost factor, an emphasis on local prerogatives, and a feeling that it just wasn't part of the chairman's job. As one Democratic chairman put it: "as far as precinct delegates are concerned, we have relatively little to do with their choice. We are often happy to see people run for office." Once the precinct leader was in office the chairmen seemed handcuffed; they all claimed to have no effective sanctions against the leader who failed to perform his tasks. Typical was this statement: "I can replace section chairmen and put an additional worker in a precinct if these people do not do their jobs properly. This does not often happen and I have no other ways of ensuring that section and precinct leaders do their jobs." Replacement was indeed rare. One reason:

"Precinct leaders are elected and so cannot be replaced." Another reason: "Voluntary organizations have a very difficult time keeping their members, let alone disciplining them. We cannot punish them for we will lose them to our opponents." A final reason: "The precinct delegate has the votes behind him." Thus, although sanctions were available, that is, replacements could be sent into a precinct, the chairman did not act. Most chairmen finally asserted, therefore: "Precinct delegates can be controlled only during the time they get elected and there is no other way." The majority (all but four chairmen) would have liked more discipline in the organizations, as would 40 per cent of the executive board members. They were, with one exception, eager for more patronage as a means of building up the structure and controlling subordinates; but in the absence of these palliatives, their control was limited.

This is a picture of plaintive rationalization, with a complex set of reasons involved in the diffusion of control. The independent status of the precinct leader stemmed no doubt in part from his elective position, and Detroit is certainly not unique in this respect. The stratarchical character of the organization was more profound than this, however. The chairman, after all, theoretically had considerable opportunity to exert influence on precinct leaders if he wished. The fact of the matter was that he did not. Only one Democratic and one Republican chairman admitted that they saw their precinct chairmen regularly during the campaign. Nor did the chairman ordinarily choose to hand pick new precinct delegates. The reason was partly that he was too busy acting out his authority as district leader and asserting his representational responsibility upward in the hierarchy. But, more than this, the chairman was caught in a reciprocal deference system, and a system of factions or subcoalitions struggling for control in the organization. He needed the support of the precinct people more than they needed him; moreover, he was virtually neutralized in the conflict among the subgroups he sought to immobilize. To challenge his precinct leaders and organize his own substitute for them from a lean reservoir of potential workers would jeopardize his status in the top elite. Thus he maintained authority by relinquishing, or not vigorously asserting, control. This, in large measure, is the essence of "stratarchy."

We have presented, in a preliminary fashion, evidence testing the theory of stratarchy. An attempt was made to determine how clear the organizational image was in the minds of the party leader, how complete and coherent elements and relationships in that organization were articulated, how aware party leaders were of the basic structure within which they worked, how congruent and convergent role-perceptions were and certain over-all communicative relationships. In subsequent chapters we will examine the manifestations of stratarchy in leadership motivation, perspective, activity, and function. It is our thesis that the proliferation of control and the reciprocity in deference found in the party structure have a significant impact on the internal and external functioning of the leadership system.

CHAPTER 6

MULTIPLE PARTY ELITES: CAREER ORIGINS

Only one major theory of party leadership has emerged from decades of research and scholarship in the field of political parties. This is surprising, since the great party theorists have been aware that any theory of human groups is heavily conditioned by the image of the leaders—their social characteristics, motivations and attitudes, power ascension patterns, interpersonal interactions, and tactics of control. Charles Merriam, for example, was vitally interested in "all leaders from the smallest voting unit to the largest."[1] Yet recent theorizing about party leadership has been, with few exceptions, unimaginative and empirically barren. We have ignored the need for theory and turned instead to anecdotal accounts of the "boss" and his "machine," collections of irrelevant demographic data about leadership groups, and discussions about the "model" leader. Or, if really concerned with the development of a testable theory of party leadership, we have taken refuge in Michels. It is amazing how heavily we have relied on the "iron law of oligarchy" from 1915 to the present. Thus, in Duverger we come full circle in 1951: "In consequence the leadership of political parties . . . is democratic in appearance and oligarchic in reality."[2]

Several components of this fashionable theory will be examined in the present chapter. In the previous chapter we discussed the theory of leadership control; here we are concerned with the

[1] *Op. cit.*, p. 33.
[2] *Op. cit.*, p. 133.

meaning of the leadership "group concept" as utilized in elite and oligarchic thought. One of the major emphases, for example, is on the party leaders as constituting a single, viable group. We are inclined to speak, as did Michels, of *the* "bureaucracy," *the* "organization," *the* "elite," *the* "leadership." The assumption is that the leaders of the party are not merely an aggregate, but a "group," a single, directive, managerial "class" which perceives itself as a meaningful collective unit, and is perceived thus by others. In spite of a stratification among these leaders, they are all seen as hierarchically ranked within an "elite system." We like to hypothesize, as a consequence of this basic position, that the leadership develops its own patterns of communication, interests and goals, techniques for self-perpetuation and socializing of newcomers, bureaucratic *esprit de corps.* Above all, the elite is supposed to be socially congruent and unrepresentative of the rank and file. The elite, as a single self-conscious group, thus develops its own self-interest orientation, becomes an "interest group" or a "social class" in its own right, and uses a variety of clever "tricks" to exploit the party and keep the rank and file at bay.

This theory has never been satisfactorily and systematically substantiated through empirical research. There are grave doubts that, for the majority of parties in democratic societies, it ever could be. Alternative theoretical positions should at least be articulated and tested concurrently. One such theory which may accord more closely to reality begins with an opposite theoretical proposition—that a political party's leadership is pluralized, consisting of separate career groups or categories which, in no genuine sense, are incorporated into a single elite managerial class. Not only are these career classes distinct with individual members severely isolated, but the level of personal interaction is minimal. Furthermore, we would see these career categories as socially heterogeneous, the product of the subcoalitional balance of forces within the party at any point in time. Although there is no doubt of a response lag, in the long run leadership can be seen as an adaptation to internal structural conditions. In addition to the factors of pluralism, low interaction, and social heterogeneity, we would hypothesize that much of the movement into leadership positions is "self-generating." That is, in contrast to the oligarchic dogma that those in power perpetuate themselves through assimilation, amalgamation, and careful selection of new leaders, we would suggest that those "in power" have a difficult time excluding the politically ambitious from populating at least the lower reaches of the hierarchy which are critical to the survival of the organization. The scarcity of talent and lack of intensive and sanctioned control make it unlikely that those "in power" can or will deny entrance to those with ability, drive, and/or local support. This is not to say that there is no interest in careful screening, or that there is no socialization of these people once they arrive on the scene. Rather, calculated policies of inclusion and exclusion, of selection and rejection, which are intrinsic to oligarchic theory, collide with reality. Above all, we would question the theoretical position which implies that the party leadership has great security and low turnover, in personal or categoric social terms *because of* the ingenuity of those "in power." We see party leadership groups as much more fluid, and self-consciously insecure. Leadership replacement occurs more frequently than oligarchic theorists would have us believe, and, fortunately, less often than it might. But any security which leaders have is not the result of cohesion and cleverness in the invulnerable "elite." It derives, rather, from the effective neutralization of top leadership by the subcoalitional interests constituting the structure, and the maintenance of effective control over activities by party personnel at the lower reaches of the hierarchy. In effect, revolution becomes unnecessary, unless a new equation of social interests, dominating the lower reaches of the structure, perceives an "old guard" as threatening the new equilibrium. This seldom occurs. Rather, people move in and out of the various career classes of the structure, climbing the ladder as the result of a variety of personal mobility or status pressures, descending the ladder or leaving the party as the result of a variety of motivational discontents. Yet no one single elite class dominates the structure, exploits it, or determines its organizational destiny.

The group concept as postulated by the devotees of oligarchy, thus, emphasized (1) a single, viable elite class, which has (2) a high rate of interpersonal communication, which (3) carefully controls the entrance of individuals into political careers, which (4) therefore is socially congruent though unrepresentative of the party "mass," and which (5) is highly congruent in terms of elite class goals, attitudes, and motivations. In this chapter we shall be particularly concerned with the first four of these components. In the process of analyzing career origins, communication, social characteristics, and career developmental patterns we shall seek to determine whether the elite structure of the party is monolithic or pluralized, and whether those who enter party careers are directly or indirectly solicited and co-opted, or whether they become interested in assuming party position because of nonelite and self-generating impulses and circumstances.

Related to this theory is a basic recognition that the political culture within which the party must operate creates career problems of a special kind. The party inevitably attracts people who see in party work opportunities for achieving different kinds of personal objectives. The legitimacy of these various perceptions, and their utility for party work, must usually remain unchallenged by party leaders, even though the latter may rank these objectives quite differently. The party organization must seek to satisfy the entering perspectives in party work, and, at the same time, strive for group goals with broad appeals. Second, the party needs to maintain continuity of personnel in the precincts, while also continuously inviting new workers into its ranks, particularly in areas of great population mobility and interparty competition. Third, though a modicum of cohesion is necessary, the party must have great tolerance for personal conflict and factional disagreement, if it is to retain those workers whose career perspectives may clash with others, but who are skilled and thus indispensable for party success. Fourth, while rewarding the effective worker, the party must also keep in the organization individuals who are less skilled, less self-conscious about a career in politics, but who represent significant social and opinion sectors of the public.

Fundamentally, this poses a unique careerist dilemma: the party needs power-aspiring careerists because it is a power-seeking and power-converting group; but it cannot afford too many power aspirants because of resulting threats to structural viability. Substitutes for power must be found, such as "prestige," "status," "recognition," "social gratification." Yet these, if overplayed, may well transform the group into something other than a political party. Thus, the party structure must be an arena in which large numbers of workers satisfy individual needs and demands without subverting the party's power goals. While keeping lower-level careerists at menial tasks in the precincts, the upward-mobile aspirants with ability must be channeled into managerial tasks. In addition to accommodating the subcoalitional social interests which comprise the structure, the top directors must work out an adjustment and maintain sound organizational relationships with the nonaspiring "hard core" in the precincts.

CAREER ORIGINS

Precise data on how people become involved and active is a primary key to understanding the operation of the party structure. Exact information on the circumstances surrounding the beginning of a party career will tell us much about control in the induction process as well as help in understanding subsequent attitudes and behavior of the individual activist.

Party leaders were most eager to recall the circumstances of their entry into a political career. True, the recall of salient factors might have been to some extent camouflage and rationalization, but it does provide clues to prominent historic conditions in their lives which may be relevant. Often the spontaneity and frankness of the explanation pointed strongly in the direction of authenticity; at other times, more indirect probing was required to approximate the "real" factors responsible. In any event, the implication in the responses is that these party leaders felt early circumstances had great impact on their views about party work in 1956.

The period in history at which the political career began differs by hierarchical level within the organization, and in some respects also by party (see Table 6.1). Almost 50 per cent of the precinct leaders, less than 10 per cent of the executive board members, and none of the top-level chairmen began work after 1952. At the other extreme, only 15 per cent of the precinct leaders, 30 per cent of the executive board members, and approximately 40 per cent of the top elite began work before 1932. This is to be expected because of the time and experience needed to

TABLE 6.1

ERAS IN WHICH PARTY CAREERS ORIGINATED

Years	*Top chairmen*		*Executive boards*		*Precinct leaders*	
	R	*D*	*R*	*D*	*R*	*D*
1956 on	0%	0%	0%	0%	22%	23%
1952–55	0	0	13	6	25	21
1948–51	33	40	18	33	18	11
1940–47	0	20	18	0	9	11
1932–39	16	20	22	28	10	20
Before 1932	50	20	29	33	16	14
Number of cases	6	5	23	18	143	138

move up the political ladder, but these hierarchical differences do suggest significant intra-party differences in personal perspective. This means, for example, that the great bulk of the Democratic precinct leaders were Mennen Williams era supporters (1948 on), while most of the district chairmen were of an earlier era. And the three Republican district chairmen who antedated the New Deal might have been "old guard" to the 65 per cent majority among Republican precinct leaders who came in during the post-war and Eisenhower party eras. On the other hand, these data suggest the recruitment of leaders over a great range of "political generations," an overlapping of value for maintaining the grass-roots durability of the two parties. Al Smith, Roosevelt, Truman, and Stevenson Democrats worked side by side to forge a winning combination (at the state level it is Comstock, Murphy, Van Waggoner, and Williams Democrats). Hoover, Willkie, Dewey, Taft, and Eisenhower Republicans maintained, through concerted action, the continuity of the Republican tradition. These were grass-roots organizations, therefore, not exclusively dedicated to the ideology, policies, and traditions of a single political era or dominant political elite.

The explanations offered by political leaders for becoming active have a rich and diversified content. The following are excerpts from interviews with upper-echelon leaders:

1. "At the time I became active in politics the best people in Michigan politics were in the Republican party, and I wanted the best. So I became stuck with the Republican party, as some people are with a religion. Also, FDR's hostile attitude to small business crystallized my Republicanism."
2. "I became a party worker because of my respect for FDR and what he had done for the people. I wanted to see his work continued (this was in 1940). In 1936 I was fired from my job in a store because I took a day off to see FDR when he came to Detroit."
3. "Al Smith appealed to me as a kid. He was a Catholic as I was, and my family thought a lot of him too. Anyway, Irish are generally Democrats and we were.
4. "We were the only Republican family in our block and one day a ward chairman who was a friend of mine asked me whether I would like to be a precinct worker. He told me the job of the precinct worker was simple—to sell the candidate and get out the votes—not so simple! My parents were immigrants from Austria and they came over to escape tyranny and build a new life. Therefore, they were what you might call rugged individualists. They were you might say conservatives, but conservatives in the tradition of McKinley, Teddy Roosevelt, and Howard Taft."
5. "My father was a saloon-keeper in Detroit and quite a politician, a lot of politics went on in the back room of the saloon. I heard a lot as a child. I was brought up in a political atmosphere and having had a taste of politics I wanted to know something about what went on on the inside. So I

started to work for the party when I was first able to vote. I then ran for precinct delegate. Now I have a good civil service job."

6. "I was drafted into being a precinct delegate. A friend in my company was the person most responsible for getting me in. I was disturbed by people in public office like Judge Murphy whose motives and activities were not always clean. I have no desire for power and do not intend to stay in politics all the time. In fact I might like to miss all the headaches of this job."
7. "I was active in the UAW as a shop steward. One night at a local educational meeting I heard Gov. Williams speak. I don't remember what he said, but a state senator pointed out to me the position of the parties in Lansing. He pointed out the division of votes in Highland Park and I saw that it wasn't impossible for the Dems there. I wanted to find someone else to run, but couldn't. The usual candidate was associated with the Communists so everybody was for me when I said I would run."
8. "When I was a kid I carried papers and worked for Cox, the Democratic presidential candidate. Cox was a newspaper man and I always liked him. I also believed in the League of Nations. My family have always been Democrats and interested in politics."
9. "In 1930 my father ran for office, and I helped my father. I also have two brothers in legislative jobs. I have a political job too—traffic court referee. In 1936 I decided that we were going through a period of growing political importance. I wanted to be a judge so I think the best way is by remaining in politics."
10. "The question is a little personal. I have always favored the Republicans. In 1944 I had a heart attack. The doctor told me to widen my interests. I had a friend in the RPO (Republican Precinct Organization) and I asked him to introduce me. My father was always active—as a liberal Democrat. Political work has helped me with my job—as attorney for the DSR (Detroit Municipal Transportation System)."
11. "My family had always been Democrats. I had heard Hoover was responsible for the depression and the Democrats were for the little man. I had organized a strike at Ford's. Then while in the service I read a lot and studied

politics and found a lot I had been told wasn't true. In 1950 I met the Republican candidate for Congress and found much in common. So I went to work for him."

12. "A friend of mine was section leader in this district. He worked at a store and in front of his store I caught the bus for work. He called me in one day and asked me to run in the precinct. I liked the people I met and what I heard, and decided this is for me."
13. "I began immediately after FDR packed the Supreme Court in 1936. Many things were involved, but largely it was FDR's blatant disregard of judicial process."

There is evidence of considerable "motivational pluralism" in these explanations. Each party leader seemed to be recalling his own personal circumstances at the time as well as the special historical conditions of American political life at the moment he entered the party. Despite this diversity, certain uniformities emerge when we ask specific questions of the data. If we concentrate on the *source* of initial involvement, we can ask whether the individual indicated that he deliberately sought out a party career, or whether he appeared to have been drafted by others. We asked the following open-ended questions in this connection:

"What first led you to become active as a party worker?

"How was it you became active at that time?"

"How did you happen to run for precinct delegate?"

After coding the responses, we found the distributions presented in Table 6.2.

There is very little conclusive evidence here to support the theory that "an elite" co-opts precinct leaders to fortify and perpetuate a "machine." One-third of all precinct leaders indicated strongly, in their first reasons, that they made the decision themselves to enter party work; and 80 per cent of all leaders gave some indication (in all three explanations we coded) that there were "self-generating" reasons for entering politics. On the other hand, it is true that over 50 per cent of precinct leaders were primarily "drafted" into politics: 56 per cent began party work as a result of outside influences, and 52 per cent became precinct delegates in the same manner. But the crucial question is, "Who

TABLE 6.2

SOURCE OF INITIAL INVOLVEMENT IN PARTY WORK
(Precinct Leaders)

Source	*As a party worker*		*As a precinct delegate*	
	Percentage mentioning source first	*Percentage mentioning source at all*	*Percentage mentioning source first*	*Percentage mentioning source at all*
Outside influences				
Political clubs, organizations, and leaders	23%	27%	29%	33%
Relatives in politics	6	9	5	5
Formal groups (union, business, racial, ethnic, etc.)	11	20	7	10
Relatives *not* in politics	7	7	0	1
"Friends" (other than political leaders)	9	17	11	12
Self-generating forces				
Attraction to popular candidates	9	13	1	1
Concern for social or economic problems and issues	7	23	3	6
Ideological commitment to party	6	14	4	5
Interest in civic affairs	10	22	8	12
"Accidental involvement"	5	8	22	27
Not ascertained	7		10	
	100%		100%	

did the drafting?" There seem to have been three major sources for solicitation of party personnel: political group life and political leaders' persuasions, friends and relatives who were *not* in politics, and politically interested groups or leaders with which the respondent had associations. At most, 38 per cent of the precinct leaders were co-opted by "elite" politicians (if "relatives who are in politics" are combined with "political clubs and leaders"). Possibly another 20 per cent were induced by relatives and friends, and a final 20 per cent maximum were involved as a result of aroused interest in ethnic, union, business, or social groups. In addition, one interesting statistic should be noted: the 22 per cent (or 27 per cent) who claim they became precinct delegates "accidentally." They meant by this, usually, that "no one else would run" for the position, and they were cajoled into becoming the candidate in the absence of competition and against their will.

One does not emerge, therefore, with clear evidence of a calculating elite recruiting a select corps of like-minded precinct leaders who are committed to maintaining "the elite" in power. The extent of self-generating circumstances, the competitive social environment within which recruitment took place, as well as the haphazard involvement of a large minority of precinct leaders suggests, rather, that here was a fairly open, unstructured, and fluid recruitment system. In conjunction with the subcoalitional image of the party hierarchy presented in Chapter 4, and the devolution of responsibility for recruitment discussed in Chapter 5, these data confirm the pluralistic and centrifugal state of the party structure.

The theory of oligarchy implies that those who are drafted to precinct work by party leaders will rise more rapidly in the organization yet our data do not reveal this to be the case. At least two-thirds of the district chairmen indicated that the initial "push" into party work was their own decision; the same held true for 55 per cent of executive board members. This confirms a previous finding that these top-elite leaders were economically and politically mobile and ambitious. Further, a careful analysis was made of those precinct leaders who were "upward mobile," that is, had demonstrated continuity in party work, aspiration for higher status, as well as selection for upper-echelon positions at the ward, district, city, or county level (to be discussed in greater detail subsequently in this chapter). Here again we found (Table 6.3) that those who were co-opted by party people had no better chance of being selected for upper-echelon positions than those recruited as a result of other forces. In fact, those who were influenced by relatives and friends *not* in political work turned out to be the most mobile. This lack of correlation of career mobility to the role of the party in the original recruitment process demonstrates again the absence of personnel control by the top elite. Career mobility seems clearly the consequence of other forces—self determination, local support, and subgroup affiliations.

The socialization context within which party work was launched is basic for understanding the beginning of a political party career. A social "amalgamation" took place. For the majority this indoctrination and exposure process seemed to be of long duration; for a small minority a sudden occurrence or chance incident may have resulted in involvement, although this is "social-

TABLE 6.3

MOBILITY SUCCESS BY SOURCE OF INVOLVEMENT IN PARTY WORK (Precinct Leaders)

*Source of involvement**	*Percentage who had become "organizational mobiles"*	*Number of cases*
Political organizations, leaders, and relatives in politics	10%	82
Formal nonparty groups, and group leaders	10	31
Relatives and friends *not* in politics	38	45
Self-generating forces	17	90
"Accidental" involvement	27	14

* Based on "What first led you to become active as a party worker?"

ization" of a different character. The socialization process seemed to proceed differently in the two parties. The question was asked: "Before you actually got into party work, how did you develop an interest in political matters?" A variety of explanations were given by precinct leaders (Table 6.4) with at least 50 per cent referring to primary- or secondary-group influences. The Republicans were more inclined to refer to family, friends, and employers; the Democrats seemed to be more susceptible to union influences, but the differences were not great.

Socialization for politics in the family was prominent in the case histories of approximately 20 per cent of all leaders—precinct, secondary cadre, and top elite. One striking difference emerges in the contrast between Republicans and Democrats: exposure to politically active fathers resulted in a significantly earlier entrance into Democratic party work (Table 6.5). The data on age at entrance into party activity reveals generally small differences, although upper-echelon Democrats were more likely to begin careers early, even before the age of 30, than were the Republicans—65 per cent as compared to 45 per cent. But when one combines family socialization and age at entrance, great dif-

TABLE 6.4

Self Explanations for the Arousal of Political Interest (Precinct Leaders)

"How did you first develop an interest in political matters?"	*Republicans*	*Democrats*
Issues created an interest	10%	15%
Desire to elect someone	6	2
Family influences	20	15
Friends' influences	7	4
School, reading	14	21
Employer influence	6	1
Union influences	0	13
Citizen responsibility	17	14
Don't know	15	13
Not ascertained	5	2
	100	100

TABLE 6.5

Career Entrance Age of Leaders Whose Fathers Were Politically Active

Age of entrance into politics	*Republicans*		*Democrats*	
	Two upper echelons	*Precinct leaders*	*Two upper echelons*	*Precinct leaders*
Under 21	0%	3%	25%	3%
21–30	37	33	50	55
Total under 30	37	36	75	58

ferences are found. There was a peculiar career gap for many Republicans; two-thirds waited to enter party work until after the age of 30, while only one-fourth to two-fifths of the Democrats delayed that long. Democrats made earlier career decisions, particularly those who subsequently became very mobile. Republicans, under similar guidance and the influence of active fathers, waited until later to implement party career decisions.

The isolation of the one most important motivational orientation for active party participation is extremely difficult. We asked each of our respondents to rate 11 common motivations as "very important," "important," or "unimportant," in terms of his own personal involvement. In addition, we asked the leaders to indicate which reason was "most important." Neither technique is completely satisfactory, but together they do indicate the most salient reasons recalled for entering the party (Table 6.6). The distributions for top-echelon leaders and precinct leaders showed remarkable similarity. Close to 60 per cent mentioned a community obligation and a desire to influence governmental policies as very important. Social gratification needs were emphasized by 56 per cent. Less than half of the leadership groups rated other factors as very important, but the range of acceptance of these reasons as relevant to their own decision to enter politics is great. When they were asked to indicate which reason on the list was most important, again, all 11 reasons received some support with

TABLE 6.6

RATINGS OF REASONS FOR BECOMING ACTIVE
(Precinct Leaders)

	Rated as very important reason	*Rated as best reason*
Personal friendship for a candidate	23%	12%
Political work part of my way of life	43	11
Strong attachment to the party	47	13
Social contacts and friendships	56	5
Fun and excitement of politics	34	7
Trying for a personal position in politics	11	2
Influence governmental policy	58	21
Like being close to influential people	34	3
Party work helps in business contacts	6	*
Helps fulfill my community obligation	65	20
Gives me a feeling of recognition in my community	20	2

* Not quite 1%.

four or five predominating: community obligation, desire to influence policy, party attachment, and friendship for a candidate.

The impression one might deduce from these data is that entrance motivations were idealistic, ideological, and impersonally-oriented. It is true that heavy emphasis was placed on such career orientations by these ratings, yet, a careful inspection of the data discloses at least 19 per cent of these leaders committing themselves overtly to highly personalized explanations—social contacts, desire for recognition, personal excitement, etc. A further detailed analysis of responses was made to discover, in *all* their ratings of reasons for getting into politics, what percentage recognized the importance of personalized motivations, whether or not they finally ranked such motivation as highest (Table 6.7). When we arrange the data thus, it is evident that most party leaders did see politics in terms of personal need fulfillment, although this might not have ranked at the top of their motiva-

TABLE 6.7

PERSONAL AMBITION AND NEED FULFILLMENT AS AN IMPORTANT MOTIVATION FOR BECOMING POLITICALLY ACTIVE*

Reason	*Executive board members*	*Precinct leaders*
	Percentage who ranked the reason as very important or important	
Trying for a personal position in politics	26%	17%
Party work helps with business contacts	10	7
Desire for personal recognition	24	36
Desire to be close to important people	10	16
Like the fun and excitement of politics	15	12
Want social contacts and friendships	10	5
Total	95%	93%

* These percentages are based on *any* reference to personalized motivation; they are *not* to be construed as *the most important* reason for entrance into party work.

tional scale of values. From one-sixth to one-fourth were frankly personally ambitious; another 7 to 10 per cent wished to exploit politics for business purposes; one-third admitted that there was some interest in personal recognition; and another third admitted the importance of being close to influential people, fun and excitement, and social contacts.

For most party leaders there was a double component to reasons for entering party work. Thus, 99 per cent of our precinct leaders rated certain impersonal orientations as important, and yet 93 per cent gave some evidence that personal need fulfillment was also important. For a minority, an overt desire for personal power was manifest; for many it was not personal power which motivated, rather it was social status, social mobility, or social friendships. But whether it be an overt craving for power, or striving for social status, or some other personal need, most party leaders saw politics as personally instrumental,—at the same time claiming involvement for other reasons. This is true whether the individual was "drafted" for politics or sought a party career deliberately. If we can trust his recall of entrance motivations, the party leader was revealing that a heavily emphasized component in socialization is the service to one's personal satisfactions, ambitions, and needs, which a party career may provide. However, simple explanations of career motivations are not supported in the data. Rather, it is evident that for most party leaders motivations were diverse, multiple, and represented a synthesis of personal and impersonal interests. Above all, it is apparent that a party structure consists, at all levels, of a balance sheet of leaders with different career origins and entrance motivations. These salient career predispositions, as well as the particular developmental pattern at the start of the leader's career, are basic to understanding his behavior, as well as the party structure within which he functions.

CHAPTER 7

MULTIPLE PARTY ELITES: CAREER DEVELOPMENT

The developing party career passes through many stages of transformation, with observable differences in terms of extent of career continuity, modes of ascent (and descent), mobility speed rates, and height of position achieved. These diverse developmental patterns result in differential exposure to skill experiences with bearing on attitudes toward party work and capacity for effective performance. In addition the developmental process is highly relevant to understanding the different types of career classes which emerge in a party structure.

The movement of party activists in and out of the group seems inevitable in American parties. It is, indeed, a phenomenon to be tolerated, but with important consequences for the type of party career which evolves in our society, and for the role of the individual activist. The "in-and-out-er" poses a real problem for the party organization at the grass roots, requiring a constant recruiting and training effort which may attract new people but produces organizational instabilities at the very level where the party's status, image, and performance are most vital. For the individual, interrupted involvement in party work means loss of contact with the organization and the subtle processes by which the party changes and adapts over time, as well as interference with his training and career opportunities. For the upwardly mobile worker, particularly, discontinuity may be personally traumatic, and his drive for status under these circumstances produce dysfunctional organizational relationships within the party.

There is, of course, greater continuity in party work at the top and middle levels of leadership than in the precincts. All the party's top executives had worked continuously, while only three-fifths of the precinct leaders had careers without interruption. Executive board members were intermediate between these two proportions, a sizeable minority moving upward despite interruption. The number of years of continuous occupation in a particular position varied greatly, however, for chairmen and executive board members. The former ranged from two to 10 years in experience; the latter ranged similarly, with 45 per cent having served in the position for one year or less, and only 15 per cent (Republican) and 26 per cent (Democrat) having served for over eight years. Few top leaders were able, or interested, in maintaining their positions over long periods of time—"the elite" tires, or it appears to be easily replaceable.

TABLE 7.1
CONTINUITY BY ERA OF ENTRANCE INTO PARTY WORK
(Precinct Leaders Only)

Era	*Republicans*			*Democrats*		
	Continuous	*Not continuous*	*Number of cases*	*Continuous*	*Not continuous*	*Number of cases*
1952–55	70%	30%	36	93%	7%	29
1940–51	85	15	39	80	20	30
1932–39	67	33	15	55	45	27
Before 1932	90	10	21	75	25	20

The historic era of entrance into party work may be an important factor linked to continuity of service. For our sample of precinct leaders, those who began careers prior to 1932 were more likely to have served continuously than those who entered after 1932 and prior to World War II. Those who began work after the war had the best Democratic record, but not necessarily the best Republican record. Discounting these "new" arrivals in both parties, however, more continuous service had been rendered by those who were committed in the pre-New Deal period, indicating, again, a considerable intergenerational overlap among the hard-core activists.

The data (Table 7.2) give some indication of the types of people who worked continuously for their party. Women had a much better record than men, Negroes might have been as faithful as whites, Republican Catholics were less sporadic than Protestants, and those from lower income classes had a relatively good record. The variations in continuity for the structural subcoalitions (identified in Chapter 4) are also revealing. All the Republican subcoalitions had excellent records of work continuity, with the Negro and German subgroups least impressive. It is significant, also, that over 40 per cent of the Republican Negroes joined at the time of the 1956 campaign. The Democratic subgroups

TABLE 7.2

CONTINUITY OF PARTY WORK FOR SOCIAL CATEGORIES AND SUBCOALITIONS

(Precinct Leaders)

	Republicans		*Democrats*	
Social categories	*Continuously Active**	*Number of cases*	*Continuously Active**	*Number of Cases*
Race				
Negroes	100%	13	73%	22
Whites	75	98	77	84
Sex				
Women	100	14	94	17
Men	75	97	73	89
Religion				
Catholics	84	31	70	50
Protestants	78	72	78	45
Income				
Under $5,000	81	26	79	24
$5–7,000	60	25	87	31
$7–10,000	86	14	72	32
Over $10,000	85	40	70	10

TABLE 7.2—*Continued*

CONTINUITY OF PARTY WORK FOR SOCIAL CATEGORIES AND SUBCOALITIONS

(Precinct Leaders)

Subcoalitions	*Republicans*				*Democrats*		
	Continuously active	*Joined in 1956*	*Number of cases*		*Continuously active*	*Joined in 1956*	*Number of cases*
Business-managerial whites	72%	15%	46	Negroes	50%	31%	32
Other white collar (North-western European)	65	18	17	Poles	38	0	16
Labor union whites	62	12	34	Irish	61	28	18
Negroes	57	43	23	Business and professional whites	78	14	14
All Germans	52	26	23	All labor	58	22	100
All English (Welsh and Scottish)	64	14	28				
Nationality deviants	65	35	20				

* Based on those who began party work before the 1956 campaign.

revealed more intermittent party careers, particularly the Poles, who had been in the party for some length of time, but less than 40 per cent had worked continuously. It is also significant that the "business-professional whites" in the Democratic party, with a 78 per cent record, were much higher in continuity than labor union precinct leaders. The white-collar subgroups in both party structures appeared most loyal in this respect. Generally, however, the data indicate that all status and class groups recognized the importance of continuity for a party career, and sizeable numbers of hierarchical representatives had accumulated considerable party experience as a result of continuous service.

Two additional factors discriminated among party workers in respect to continuity—political activity by father, and the nature of the motivation for entrance into politics. Among Democrats, particularly, those whose socialization context included a politically active father were more likely to serve continuously (93 per cent compared to 68 per cent for those with inactive fathers). The distinction held true to a lesser degree for Republicans (85 per cent, compared to 75 per cent). Correlation of responses to the question, "What was the most important reason for your becoming active?" with continuity of service, revealed interesting findings (Table 7.3) among precinct leaders. Those who admitted to a personal drive for influence or status, or declared party loyalty as basic, or expressed interest in influencing the policies of government, were least likely to be sporadic performers in the party. These data are important for two reasons. First, they demonstrate that different motivations can induce consistency in party work. Not only the personal drive-oriented individual worked consistently; the self-conscious ideologist also has an excellent record. Second these data suggest the surprisingly large percentage of people who continue with uninterrupted party careers, despite seemingly low motivational involvement. That these people remained in party work attests either to the capacity of politics for satisfying a diversity of personal interests and needs, or to the tendency of people, once involved in politics, to become diverted to other motivations and goals. This is a question to which we shall return in a later analysis.

A second element in career development concerns change of position, or mobility. Party workers varied considerably in degree and modes of career mobility, as one considers the types of position held besides precinct leader. All of the district chairmen and all of the district executive board members were, at one time, precinct leaders. Moving upward from this bottom rung on the ladder, they differed in career development and in the types of organizational experiences to which they were exposed. The posi-

TABLE 7.3

CONTINUITY OF PARTY SERVICE BY CAREER ENTRANCE MOTIVATION

Entrance motivation	*Republicans*		*Democrats*		*Percentage both parties*	
	Continuously active	*Number of cases*	*Continuously active*	*Number of cases*	*Continuously active*	*Number of cases*
Personal ambition						
Desire to be close to important people, interest in business contacts, seeking recognition	100%	14	87%	8	95%	22
Party attachment	83	18	100	5	87	23
Influence policies of government	92	24	96	26	94	50
Personal friendship for candidate	72	18	75	8	73	26
Community obligation	64	22	67	12	65	34
Enjoy friendship, social contacts, fun and excitement of politics	56	9	60	21	60	30
Politics part of my way of life	60	5	57	21	58	26

tion held by most workers was that of state convention delegate. Yet not all executive board members had this opportunity, and only half of the precinct leaders. The most highly prized positions were probably those in the state party (state central committee, or some administrative role in the state organization), and that of national convention delegate or alternate, apart from the district executive position itself. Only a small minority of precinct leaders (3–6 per cent) were able to achieve state or national positions, while up to a third of the upper echelon leaders attained this status.

From the data we see diverse career achievement patterns, and if we look at all party leaders in the Wayne County sample, at all echelons, a stratification picture in terms of mobility success and present status emerges:

Top mobile executive elite—all district chairmen
Highly mobile executive board members—57 per cent of all executive boards
Highly mobile and influential precinct leaders—20 per cent of all precinct leaders
Low mobility executive board members—43 per cent of executive boards
Nonmobile precinct leaders—80 per cent of all precinct leaders

There seem to be no significant differences between the two parties generally, although in certain specifics differences did occur. (Thus, Democratic precinct chairmen were less likely to be picked as delegates to state conventions—35 per cent, compared to 64 per cent for Republicans.) Of course, several graduations in upward mobility success did exist which the general picture may blur, but the kinds of difference noted above are perhaps most helpful as an introduction to the analysis of career development patterns.

Rates of speed in career mobility differed tremendously. A careful study of the most mobile executive board members reveals that slow, plodding persistence is by no means a *sine qua non* for advancement. There was the Republican, for example, who entered the party as precinct worker in 1954, ran for the state legislature and lost, but in two years found himself on the district executive board. The time required in the Democratic party may be longer, yet one Democrat entered the party at the grass roots in 1952, won the race for state representative, and was soon on the district executive board. Another Republican leader started party work in 1946, by 1947 was on the executive board, and three years later appeared on the state central committee—perhaps an unparalleled case of rapid upward movement through the hierarchy. On the other hand, there were cases at the opposite extreme of long and continuous work in the precincts before movement upward began. One of the Democratic leaders joined the party in 1911 and worked for 29 years before running for the state legislature. He lost, but moved to the district executive board in 1942, to the state central committee in 1945, and was selected as a national convention delegate in 1948 and 1952. It is apparent, therefore, that mobility may be fast or slow, achieved within two years or require 40. The mean number of years required for the most highly mobile executive board members to achieve that position was 14. This, of course, obscures the extremes, as illustrated above, and also fails to take into consideration other positions within the hierarchy, elective or appointive, which can be secured earlier by the more energetic entrepreneurs.

Three general patterns for upward mobility are suggested by the modes of ascent for leaders holding positions in the upper echelons. First were those who began their careers in the precinct, distributing literature, canvassing, working at the polls, and performing menial services for the party. A small minority of these competed early for election to the post of precinct delegate to the district convention—24 per cent of the Republicans, and 14 per cent of the Democrats. However, the common pattern for this group was to run for the precinct delegate post subsequently, and win, although not always on the first attempt. A second group also began at the grass roots, but in women's groups of the party, youth organizations, political clubs, or the unions. All of these, without exception, very soon made successful races for the precinct delegate position. The third group, much smaller in size, ran for some public office first and at the same time, or soon thereafter, won election to the precinct delegate position. Thus, the way in which they started may have varied, but all seemed to realize that the road to advancement lay through the gateway of precinct delegate. No one rose

TABLE 7.4

MODES OF ASCENT: ENTRANCE PATTERNS

(Upper Echelon Sample)

	Republicans	*Democrats*
Began with precinct work and in regular precinct organization		
Precinct delegate position	27%	14%
Nonleadership position	27	37
Began in auxiliary party agencies		
Young Republicans (Democrats)	15	5
Women's groups	4	10
Political clubs	15	10
Union organization	0	19
Began by running for public office	12	5
Number of cases	26	21

within the hierarchy, no matter how high the position achieved, without conforming to this common mobility pattern or expectation. The importance of precinct leadership status seems to have been universally recognized, and soon, by the mobiles.

The sequential pattern, then, for all those who moved upward, involved early occupancy of the precinct leadership position. No one started at the top, at the district level or county level, nor did he arrive there if he failed to establish a grass-roots connection in the precinct organization. The normal pattern for the upward-mobile party worker included assumption of some type of ward, area, or divisional responsibility, coordinating the work of several precincts, and, almost simultaneously, selection as a delegate to the state party convention. Subsequent to this the pattern varied greatly—some moved to district and/or county committee positions, others later ran for public office (14 per cent of the Republicans, 23 per cent of the Democrats), some occupied city party positions, a few took on additional state commitments (18 per cent of Republicans and 6 per cent of Democrats), about a fourth went to national conventions. Those who had become involved through clubs, unions, or youth and women's organizations often maintained these connections, but they constituted in no real sense the organizational avenue to higher position in the regular party structure.

The data provide very little evidence of downward mobility, since our interviews were with those holding important party positions. Evidence does exist indicating this may be an important phenomenon to examine with another sample. Among Republican and Democratic executive board members, for example, we found 23 per cent and 12 per cent respectively who were "demoted" in the sense that they at one time had held more important posts—district chairmanship, state central committee positions, or county responsibilities. Several had gone to the national convention as a delegate earlier, but had been passed over or replaced in 1952 and 1956. On the other hand, only 1 to 4 per cent of the precinct leaders had at one time held such higher position. This data must be used with caution, because the conditions under which alleged "demotion" occurred were not always clear. It is plausible to suggest, however, that the downward mobile may cling to a reduced power status, such as membership on an executive board, but loss of prestige and influence is not accompanied by a willingness, or the possibility, of remaining in the relatively lowly position of precinct leader. Gradual loss of organizational status no doubt occurs, but relatively few continue activity at the lower levels of the hierarchy, and precipitate downward mobility probably results in severance of all organizational connection.

Aspiration toward a career, as well as continuity and mobility, is a third important component differentiating party activists. When asked whether they would take a more responsible job in the party "if you had the opportunity," some of the leaders of the sample vowed this was their last campaign, others indicated having a possible interest in a higher position, and still others knew exactly what positions they wanted and why. The distribution of "aspirers" was as follows:

District chairmen	67%
Executive board members	64%
Precinct leaders	57%

The only difference between Democrats and Republicans was among precinct leaders—Republicans more frequently aspired to higher positions (62 per cent compared to the Democrats' 51 per cent). This was particularly true among those who began their careers in 1956—81 per cent of the Republicans were "aspirers," 50 per cent of the Democrats.

The jobs aspired to were both public (elective and appointive) and party. Party positions desired most often were the district chairmanship, the state central committee, and a delegate post at the national convention. Public positions sought included congressmen, state legislature, county clerk, state board of education, United States marshal, and judgeships. One executive board member aspired to a key leadership position in the union.

Which social classes and status groups tend to have a high aspiration level within the party hierarchies? In general, one might expect those social subgroups which have recently become interested in party careers, and for whom upper-echelon positions might have greater social prestige and influence value to reveal the greatest aspiration, but important differences existed between the two parties in this respect. The following specific findings emerged:

1. Those groups with only an elementary-school education, or less, had high Republican, but low Democratic aspirations. The highest Democratic percentage was among the college-educated.

2. Similarly, the low-income Republican leaders (below $5,000) aspired more frequently than all other groups except those in the income bracket of $7,000 to $10,000. There was very little difference among Democratic leaders in income, except for the most wealthy, who were the least likely to aspire to career success.
3. Negroes exceeded whites in both parties.
4. Women exceeded men among Republicans, but the opposite was true among Democrats.
5. Nationality background made no difference among Democrats, but there was a definite tendency for those with a northwestern European background to aspire more frequently among Republicans.
6. Protestants exceeded Catholics in both parties.
7. Young people, under 35, showed no greater evidence of career aspiration than did the middle-aged and older. In fact, among Democrats the most aspiring were those 60 or older.

Perhaps more striking than these general relations between social status and party aspiration are the high percentages of certain "minority" groups who desired to move upward, par-

TABLE 7.5

PARTY CAREER ASPIRATION AMONG SOCIAL GROUPS
(Precinct Leaders Only)

	Republicans		*Democrats*	
	Percentage aspiring	*Number of cases*	*Percentage aspiring*	*Number of cases*
Protestants	61%	97	60%	62
Catholics	56	34	48	65
Education				
Elementary	70	16	40	20
High school	57	53	51	81
College	65	74	57	37

TABLE 7.5—*Continued*

PARTY CAREER ASPIRATION AMONG SOCIAL GROUPS
(Precinct Leaders Only)

	Republicans		*Democrats*	
	Percentage aspiring	*Number of cases*	*Percentage aspiring*	*Number of cases*
Negroes	74	23	63	32
Whites	60	120	47	106
Women	68	28	43	21
Men	61	115	52	117
Age				
Under 30	68	25	(14)*	7*
30–60	60	89	50	112
60 and over	66	29	69	19
Nationality				
Northwestern European	60	45	49	45
Central, eastern, and southern European	44	52	49	53
Central European alone	50	34	41	41
Income (Family)				
Under $5,000	70	33	56	27
$5–7,000	44	32	59	39
$7–10,000	89	18	53	34
Over $10,000	62	50	27	33
Number of groups belonged to				
0–2	54	35	41	22
3–5	55	66	36	47
6 plus	81	42	64	69
Labor union membership				
Yes	56	43	53	100
No	65	100	45	38
Campaign era entered politics				
1956	81	32	50	32
1952–55	56	36	31	29
1940–51	48	39	53	30
1932–39	73	15	63	27
Before 1932	62	21	60	20

* Too few cases for any reliable analysis.

ticularly in the Republican party. Consider these facts: 70 per cent of elementary-school-educated persons in the Republican precinct leadership group aspired to higher positions, 56 per cent of Catholics, 74 per cent of Negroes, 44 per cent of those from central, eastern, and southern European backgrounds, 56 per cent of those with a labor union background. The pressures on the party generated by aspirations from these social strata can have considerable implications. On the one hand, they demonstrate potential clienteles for the Republican party, if it wishes to expand its social bases. On the other hand, the managerial structure of the Republican party might be revised if such pressures were successful. This picture of aspirations of social groups forces the Republican party into a dilemma of "implementation."

The Democrats seemed to be in no such aspiration-pressure situation. The Negroes, indeed, were pressing, as were the Protestants, particularly those in the age bracket over 60. But there was less aspiration pressure among these groups in the Democratic party, particularly among the traditional "out-groups."

Party career aspiration is often merely a political manifestation, in a special context, of a socialized orientation. Just as "power begets power," activity breeds more activity, and mobility triggers an aspiration for more mobility. The gregarious person who belongs to and is active in several groups is much more likely to aspire to political position. He has tested his capacities, grown to like collectivistic approaches to action, and sees the opportunities and techniques for political mobility. Both Republican and Democratic precinct leaders who belonged to six or more groups revealed high aspiration. Similarly, particularly among Republican leaders, the precinct leader who had already tasted some career success as a congressional district executive committee member was interested in more.

It is probably significant that these data reveal that within a minority party (such as the Republicans in the Detroit area), there exist high percentages of aspirers in certain social subgroups of leadership. The picture here is not one of disillusionment, but rather of a leadership anxious to assume party office and responsibilities, despite defeat, and an aspiring leadership from several of the same social groups reputedly well integrated within the Democratic party—Negroes, Catholics, Italians, labor union members, and the working class. This attests, also, to the heterogeneity of party appeal and leadership support—to the "open accordion." There exists, no doubt, a higher level of aspirational "tension" among Republicans than Democrats; whether this can jeopardize the functioning of the Republican machine is open to question. Certainly many leadership social categories within the Democratic party, especially the less well-educated, low-income, Catholic, young, and female leadership contingents, appeared relatively blasé about career advancement compared to their counterparts in the Republican organization.

An interesting problem posed by this analysis is, Who are the people, active in party work for some time, who have and do aspire to higher position, but are nonmobile? Is their lack of career success attributable to their mode of recruitment? What happens to their morale, motivations, and orientation toward party work? By isolating the 34 cases of nonmobile and noninfluential aspirers among precinct leaders who had been continuously active, we were able to examine certain characteristics of this group.[1] In both parties these aspiring but perpetual precinct captains were in the older age groups (50 per cent over 60), in the lower income and educational groups (48 per cent had incomes under $6,000, compared to 31 per cent having such income status among all precinct leaders), white-collar workers (60 per cent), and relatively recent entrants in the party (62 per cent since 1944, 32 per cent since 1952). There were also certain interesting concentrations for each party. Republican women (35 per cent of this Republican group) and Catholics (48 per cent) had particular difficulty in rising in the hierarchy. There was also a large concentration of labor union actives (75 per cent) among this Democratic group of nonmobiles.

Many of these leaders seemed to be people who had not

[1] In selecting these cases we eliminated those who had joined the party only in 1956.

been in party work long enough to realistically expect advancement, or individuals in lower economic-status positions from which it may be difficult to rise, an explanation particularly relevant for the Democrats. Yet, there was a sizeable minority (38 per cent) who had been continuously active as far back as the twenties, were not in the lower economic-status categories, and yet were nonmobile aspirers. What impact did this have on their motivation and morale? The number of cases for analysis are few, but comparisons presented in Table 7.6 suggest certain possible differences. First of all, the orientations of these people were somewhat unique. Seventy-four per cent had come into politics because of urging by others (politicians, family, and friends), compared to 56 per cent for other precinct leaders. The majority contend that they became involved in politics either because of a desire to work for policies in which they believed, or to build a personal position in politics, in these respects exceeding the normal distributions for precinct leaders. Their career in party politics apparently accentuated their issue orientation, although social contacts became much more important to the majority. Despite evidence that new personal needs were being met by party activity, the morale of these people seemed lower than usual: about 76 per cent wanted to be consulted more by party leaders, a desire of only 48 per cent normally.

Now, these data raise serious questions about the so-called phenomenon of oligarchy. Exactly 50 per cent of the nonmobile aspirers were originally drafted by party leaders and by relatives already in party work. Though reluctant, they joined the party out of political and social pressure, were apparently led to believe that careers awaited them, developed clear motivations, yet did not move upward in the hierarchy. Nevertheless they stayed on, but became much more than ordinarily critical of the internal party process. There is clear evidence here that those in "the party elite" either lost interest in the future careers of these draftees or, more probably, were powerless to promote their careers. If an "amalgamation" process was initiated, it was certainly short-lived and abortive, leaving a minority of able leaders to become malcontents.

The grass-roots party precinct activist who works for the party and does not have his mobility aspirations realized represents about one-third of all workers at a given time (36 per cent in the sample), although many of these are latecomers and irregulars. A third of them (12 per cent of the sample) are regulars who persist in party work year in and year out; approximately one-half of these (5 per cent in the sample) have had from 16 to 30 years of party service. This latter group, though small in size, may be the real heroes of the grass-roots operation —dedicated, committed, ideologically motivated, as well as personally ambitious. They have loyalty, personal drive, and a consciousness of the issues for which one works in politics. But they are also the most frequent critics of the inadequacies of the

TABLE 7.6

CAREER ORIENTATIONS OF NONMOBILE CONTINUOUSLY ACTIVE ASPIRERS (Precinct Leaders)

	Nonmobile aspirers ($N = 34$)	*All precinct leaders* ($N = 281$)
Early interest in politics result of		
Family and friends	47%	23%
Issue involvement	18	12
First activity in politics		
Primarily result of social pressures	74	56
Recruited by politicians	50	29
Specific reasons for first activity		
Issues interest	**21**	21
Fun and excitement feelings	6	7
Social contacts desire	18	5
Personal ambition	12	2
Party attachment	18	13
Satisfactions missed most if had to drop out of politics now		
Work for issues believe in	26	10
Social contacts	56	55
Fun and excitement	6	6
Nothing would be missed	10	61
Low morale—want more say in internal party affairs	76	48

party operation. They reflect, therefore, a paradoxical blend of functional and dysfunctional conditions in the local party system. The problem is greater for the Republicans, as the minority party in Wayne County, than for the Democrats. At least twice as many nonmobile aspirers appear among Republicans as Democrats.

Half of the district chairmen and over 60 per cent of the executive board members joined the party before 1940, attesting to the value of early entrance and continuity in party work. One-half of the early careerists (among precinct leaders) were nonmobile, it is true, but 50 per cent of these were not regulars. The greater number (80 per cent) of nonmobile regulars among early careerists were Republicans. Actually, early embarkation on a party career, plus continuity and aspiration, proved to be of considerable advantage for the large majority of ambitious precinct leaders.

These interrelationships can also be seen by returning to the analysis of all our precinct leaders. Those with continuous activity tended to have the best chances for upward organizational career movement. (Table 7.7). The percentage of the continu-

TABLE 7.7

MOBILITY AND ASPIRATIONS BY CONTINUITY OF PARTY WORK
(Precinct Leaders)

	Pre-1956 continuously actives		*Pre-1956 irregulars*		*Began party work in 1956—last campaign*	
	R	*D*	*R*	*D*	*R*	*D*
Organizational mobiles moved to some congressional district position	28%	28%	21%	4%	0%	3%
Nonmobiles	72	72	79	96	100	97
Aspired to higher position	61	49	42	55	81	50
Did not aspire	39	51	58	45	19	50
Number of cases	87	81	24	25	32	32

ously active who aspired to higher positions may be no higher, or only slightly higher, than the irregulars or late entrants, but it was continuity of work which distinguished the organizational mobiles. As Table 7.8 shows, the Democratic nonaspiring workers were as mobile as the Democratic aspirers. This was not true of the Republicans, for here aspiration seems to have had returns in mobility, but the factor of continuity was much more important. Democrats and Republicans who showed continuous activity outdistanced their irregular co-workers, whether or not they aspired to higher office. This does not mean that aspiration is irrelevant—it appears to have more relevance (1) for the Republican party than for the Democratic party, and (2) for the irregulars than for the persistent workers. In both parties the aspiring but irregular worker is more likely to move upward in the hierarchy than is the nonaspiring irregular.

A SUMMARY TYPOLOGY OF PARTY CAREERISM

The preceding discussion of three important components of the party career—continuity, aspiration, and mobility—will be of assistance in distinguishing party leaders by career group. The following factors were considered in constructing a typology of career classes: era of career origin, continuity of career, evidence of formal organizational mobility, evidence of "informal mobility" (i.e., extent of influence and contact with upper hierarchy leadership even though not holding formal position in the upper echelon), and aspiration for higher position. The types which emerged are shown in Table 7.9.

This stratification picture of the activists is not only operationally meaningful but theoretically useful. The party distributions reveal a certain balance. True, there were more "professionals" and more noncareerists among the Democrats. There were more nonmobile regulars and potential careerists among the Republican leaders. Yet both parties seemed to have a sizeable number of developing careerists to whom they could turn in the future. If there was any imbalance here, it was in the Democratic party

TABLE 7.8
MOBILITY BY CONTINUITY AND ASPIRATIONS
(Precinct Leaders)

	Pre-1956, continuously active				*Pre-1956 irregular actives*				*All irregulars*	
	Aspire		*Do not aspire*		*Aspire*		*Do not aspire*		*Aspire*	*Do not aspire*
	D	*R*	*R*	*D*	*R*	*D*	*R*	*D*	*R*	*D*
Organizational mobiles	73%	57%	38%	76%	50%	7%	29%	0%	25%	16%
Nonmobiles	27	43	62	24	50	93	71	100	75	84
Number of cases	40	53	34	41	10	14	14	11	24	25

TABLE 7.9

TYPES OF PARTY LEADERS DISTINGUISHED BY CAREER GROUPS

Type	*Description*	*Percentage of precinct leaders* R	D
Top mobile regulars			
Formal organization mobiles	Pre-1956 entrance, continuously active, achieved at least district position	17%	17%
Informal mobiles	Pre-1956 entrance, continuously active, evidence of frequent contact with upper hierarchy leadership	13	27
Nonmobile regulars	Pre-1956 entrance, continuously active but remained at precinct level; some aspire to higher positions	31	15
Potential careerists	(1) Pre-1956 entrants with irregular record of service; (2) 1956 entrants. Both groups reveal aspiration to higher positions, or evidence of some formal or informal upward mobility, but record of service is sporadic.	28	23
Noncareerists	Not continuously active; no evidence of aspiration or mobility.	11	18
		100%	100%
Number of cases		143	138

with three times as many top-level "regulars" as nonmobile regulars. On the other hand, there was possibly less tension and pressure among the Democratic middle-level activists than one might find among the Republicans. Above all, in the light of our career dimensions, these groups appear distinctive as to career status.

There were important differences in the social characteristics of these leadership career subgroups (Table 7.10). The "top organization mobiles" of the Democrats and Republicans were contrasted in the following respects:

- three times as many women among the Democrats
- three times as many Catholics among the Democrats
- one-fourth of the Democrats were Irish and Scottish, not found among the Republicans
- three times as many English among the Republicans
- Democrats had many more young leaders under 40 in age
- Republicans had almost twice as many in the professional-managerial classes as the Democrats
- one-sixth of the Democrats were unskilled workers; there were no unskilled Republicans
- 78 per cent of the Democrats had union affiliation (one-half of whom were union leaders); this was twice as many labor union members as among Republicans.

There were no very significant differences in income, education, or race. The lower income and education groups were only minimally represented among these top mobiles in both parties. There was, however, much greater occupational diversity among the Democrats than the Republicans. The Democrats showed greater balance, also, by including more women, and in a wider nationality representation. The most striking differences are reflected in the heavy union orientation of the Democratic group, its youth, the relative prominence of Catholics and Scotch-Irish, and the presence of a sizeable proportion of unskilled workers. The Catholics had not given way to the Protestants, nor the Irish to the Poles; but the union blue-collar worker had established a sizeable foothold in the Democratic hierarchy. The Republican top mobiles were still predominantly male, professional-managerial in occupation, middle-aged, Protestant. Skilled workers and the central, eastern, and southern European nationality groups seemed to be securing access to higher organiza-

TABLE 7.10

SOCIAL HETEROGENEITY OF PRECINCT CAREER GROUPS

	Top organization mobiles		*Informal mobiles*		*Potential careerists*		*Nonmobile regulars*		*Noncareerists*		*All precinct leaders*	
	D	R	D	R	D	R	D	R	D	R	D	R
Negroes	17%	13%	16%	32%	34%	25%	29%	9%	20%	0%	23%	16%
Catholics	48	17	46	5	47	10	33	48	60	25	47	24
Northwestern European	35	17	43	21	13	50	29	34	44	12	20	31
Age over 60	0	13	26	37	6	15	29	28	4	0	14	20
Blue collar	47	33	51	26	69	28	48	25	40	25	57	31
Union member	78	38	70	58	79	16	66	20	68	50	72	30
Number of cases	23	24	37	19	32	40	21	44	25	16	138	143

tional positions in the Republican party, yet the Republicans reflected considerably less social diversity.

One test of the adequacy of a party structure is in the types of people in reserve, beyond those already upward mobile in the organization. There were three such "reserve" groups among the precinct leaders—the "nonorganization influentials," the "nonmobile and noninfluential regulars," and the "developing careerists." Our data indicate that these shock troops did, indeed, include greater proportions of certain social categories than are found among the top mobile precinct leaders. Negroes, for example, were more likely to be found in both parties among these three reserve groups, consisting of 34 per cent (D) and 25 per cent (R) of the aspiring potential careerists. Republicans had few women in the top category or among the influentials, but included 20–25 per cent women among the nonmobile regulars and potential careerists. The English and Germans had somewhat better representation in this secondary cadre, as did those with only an elementary education and those in the lower income brackets. The Republicans, particularly, had many more young people, those with low incomes, unskilled workers, and union members in the lower echelons. Older Democrats were found in the reserve groups rather than among the top mobile elite. College-educated workers appeared with fair consistency in all career categories of both parties. Thus both parties had somewhat different and more comprehensive social concentrations upon which to draw for organizational tasks. While the Republicans appeared to be a more exclusive social elite upon examination of the top mobiles only, this was not true for the secondary cadre. For example, almost half of the Republican nonmobile regulars were Catholics, 29 per cent are in lower income brackets, and 18 per cent were unskilled workers.

The "potential careerists," who are presumably the top mobile elite of the future, may hold some key to developmental tendencies in the party. On the Democratic side they seemed to be a group with heavy proportions of Negroes (34 per cent), Catholics (47 per cent), from central, eastern and southern

Europe (50 per cent), with a high-school education only (72 per cent), relatively low income status, heavily blue collar (69 per cent), and union affiliates (79 per cent). This certainly appeared to be a low-status group, both socially and economically. The Republican potential careerists were heavily Protestant (90 per cent), more from northwestern Europe (50 per cent), younger in age (33 per cent under 30), college-educated (62 per cent), also relatively low in income at present, still predominantly professional-managerial in occupation (43 per cent), and few union affiliates (16 per cent). The Republican "top mobiles of the future," therefore, were more diverse in social and economic background and might compete more effectively due to the higher proportions of college-educated and young people. Yet, the nationality, occupation, and religious characteristics of this aspiring Republican group might suggest a partial reversion to the relative exclusiveness of the present top Republican precinct leadership elite.

The noncareerists, irregular in party work and nonaspiring, were revealing in terms of social characteristics. On the one hand, no Democratic women were found in this group, no Republican Negroes, and few Republicans with a northwestern European background. Very few older people were noncareerist in either party, and none with very low incomes. These data suggest that, for certain social aggregates or strata, depending possibly on the political party, individuals either work with the clear idea of career mobility or regularity, or do not work at all, even irregularly. On the other hand, the high percentages of union-affiliated, professional-managerial-clerical workers, and high-income people in the noncareerist groups of both parties, and of college-educated people in the Republican party, indicate that sporadic party work with no aspiration for personal advancement is a luxury which certain middle and upper social-status groups can and will afford. These intermittent and occasional activists were not in lower status positions in the society, for such people probably seek to equate political activity with social and economic status improvement. Rather, the intermittent activist is the person who can only work now and then, does not particularly seek economic advancement through politics, but will work, if continuity of service is not required.

Other characteristics of these career groups should be mentioned. Few if any of the Democratic top careerists had Republican fathers, while one-third of the Republicans were reared under Democratic fathers. In both parties those with politically active fathers were more likely to be in the group of top mobiles—65 per cent of the Democratic top organization mobiles and 46 per cent of the Republicans. There was a greater tendency for the potential careerists and noncareerists to have joined the party in the period from 1948 on, while the top mobiles included larger proportions who had been active before World War II. Two exceptions to this were the 41 per cent Democratic potential careerists who joined before 1940, worked irregularly, but still aspired to higher position; and the 40 per cent Republican nonmobile regulars who joined before 1940, worked continuously for the party, but had not moved upward. The greatest historic "spread," however, was found among the top mobile leadership—one-third joined before 1940 (13 per cent of the Democrats before 1932), while from 40 to 50 per cent joined during the 1952–55 period. Those who were moving upward in the hierarchies of both parties thus represented a wide historic time span.

CAREER CLASSES AND THE THEORY OF OLIGARCHY

Submitted here, as an alternative to the concept of a single, viable party elite, is empirical evidence of a plurality of career "categories" or classes, based on the three criteria of continuity of party work, mobility, and aspiration. The evidence points up the fact that party leadership is indeed fragmented, consisting of at least five distinguishable groups of leadership with differentiated career status. It is now necessary, however, to return to the basic components of oligarchic theory, to test whether, despite findings of pluralization of leadership, there is evidence that one elite group is, nevertheless, dominant and directive in the organizational life of the party. In testing this theory it is particularly important to scrutinize closely one career class, the "top organizational mobiles," in contrast to the "nonmobile regulars" and the "noncareerists." The problem will be to determine whether these top careerists exhibited characteristics and perspectives suggesting a close affinity to those of the chairmen and executive board members, who constituted the elite nucleus in the county.

One elitist hypothesis is that "the elite" will be socially exclusive and increasingly unrepresentative. If this were so, one might expect our "top organizational mobiles" to reveal personal characteristics similar to those of the elite nucleus and different from the nonmobile regulars or noncareerists. On careful examination of Table 7.11, however, it is difficult to demonstrate that this was in fact true. Very small differences appeared, for example, in percentage of union members in the Democratic party career groups, or in those drawn from central, southern, and eastern European nationality backgrounds. There was also a fairly even balance of Catholics and Protestants in the Democratic party at all levels. True, there were larger proportions of Negroes among Democratic "nonmobile regulars," but to claim this is great enough to suggest that these precinct careerists have been excluded is highly speculative. Above all, it is quite clear that the Poles surpassed the Irish in co-opting large numbers into the top precinct career group. And in addition, the white-collar Democrats, who constituted three-fourths of the top Democratic nucleus, had drawn close to 50 per cent of the precinct mobiles from blue-collar classes, a percentage similar to that of the nonmobile regulars. There is no striking evidence here that the top elite nucleus was able to recruit at will, or that those fortunate precinct leaders who moved upward were a distinct social set, or that the elite groups were considerably unrepresentative.

The same appears true for the Republicans, who showed slightly more elite exclusiveness, yet the top elite did not under-

TABLE 7.11

SOCIAL CONGRUENCE OF TOP ELITE, PRECINCT MOBILES, PRECINCT REGULARS, AND LOYAL SUPPORTERS (IN THE PUBLIC)

(Note: each percentage is a proportion of the career group indicated)

	Democrats				*Republicans*			
	*Top elite nucleus**	*Precinct mobiles*	*Precinct non-mobile regulars*	*Loyal followers*	*Top elite nucleus**	*Precinct mobiles*	*Precinct non-mobile regulars*	*Loyal followers*
Negroes	17%	17%	29%	30%	14%	13%	9%	8%
Catholics	43	48	33	38	25	17	48	13
Central, southern and eastern European	48	39	29	51	50	38	45	32
Blue collar	26	47	48	76	18	33	25	26
Union members	68	78	66	61	27	38	20	14
Irish	27	9	24	9	3	0	2	8
Poles	14	22	0	11	7	17	11	1
German	5	17	24	5	14	4	14	19
English, native, Welsh, etc.	18	21	0	10	38	17	21	26

* District chairmen and executive board members.

represent the rank and file seriously. In fact, the percentages between the "loyal partisan" and top precinct mobiles are remarkably similar, except for the over-representation of union members. The precinct mobiles did not seem to be a hand-picked group. Compared to the elite nucleus, 38 per cent were union members, (as against 27 per cent of the elite), 33 per cent were blue collar (18 per cent elite), and 17 per cent were Poles (7 per cent elite). Further, the nonmobile Republican regulars were not a group consisting largely of those held down in the Republican party; this was true only of the Catholics who constitute 48 per cent of the nonmobile regulars. Yet, up to 25 per cent of the top elite groups were Catholic. Just as the Irish Democrats did not seem able to control the career chances in their party, so the Germans and English "recruited" relatively small percentages of their stock into the Republican precinct mobiles. The conclusion seems inescapable that, with few exceptions, we have very little support for a theory of party structure controlled by an elite which guarantees mobility priority to socially acceptable precinct leaders. They may desire to do so, but they have not been able to follow through on this recruitment goal with any measure of success. Social categories which one would not expect to be mobile in either party, in terms of the characteristics of the top elite nucleus, have been achieving their aspirations for a party career. The imbalances in the social congruence of the different leadership categories were not so great as to lend credibility to the doctrine of top elite control over the mobility of precinct subordinates.

Before leaving this discussion, it is useful to recall the "subcoalitional" theory of the party structure and apply it to the social composition of career classes. As seen in Table 7.12, there was a fairly even balance in the representation of the subcoalitions in the precinct category of "organizational mobiles." In the Democratic party the Irish had the smallest representation (11 per cent) and the Poles were high (31 per cent). But all coalitions, except southern migrants, were represented in all career classes. On the Republican side, although one might ex-

TABLE 7.12

SUBCOALITIONAL CHARACTER OF PRECINCT CAREER CLASSES

Subgroups	*Organizational mobiles*	*Nonmobile regulars*	*Noncareerists*	*Number of cases*
Democrats				
Negroes	13%	19%	16%	32%
Poles	31	0	25	16
Irish	11	28	28	18
Business-professional whites	14	43	7	14
Other labor	16	7	16	55
All labor	18	14	17	100
All labor officers	39	13	17	23
Republicans				
Business-managerial whites	13	39	13	46
Other white collar (Northwestern European)	18	35	0	17
Labor (whites)	24	24	24	34
Negroes	13	17	0	23
All Germans	4	26	39	23
All English	14	43	4	28

pect a predominance of the business-managerial subcoalition, it was actually at the same level as the Negroes in representation among the "organizational mobiles." No Negro and few English "noncareerists" appeared, yet again there was considerable spread, as in the Democratic party. In a sense, therefore, the mobiles as well as the nonmobile regulars constituted an alliance of subcoalitional interests, with all subgroups having representation and no one subgroup predominating.

In the light of the elite hypothesis of "amalgamation" of new and aspiring lower-echelon workers into the hierarchy, it is interesting and useful to look at the recruitment context for career classes (Table 7.13). Highly significant is the finding that the

TABLE 7.13

RECRUITMENT CONTEXT FOR POLITICAL ACTIVITY—CAREER CLASSES

Recruitment source	*Organization mobiles*		*Nonmobile regulars*		*Non-careerists*	
	D	*R*	*D*	*R*	*D*	*R*
Political clubs, political leaders, relatives in politics	4%	29%	38%	32%	36%	19%
Nonparty groups and leaders	9	0	19	14	36	0
Relatives and friends *not* in politics	26	50	0	14	8	50
Self-generating forces	61	4	43	30	0	31
"Accidental involvement"	0	17	0	10	20	0

influence of political leaders or organizations was not responsible for the entrance of the top mobiles into politics, an extension of the finding mentioned earlier in the discussion of career origins. Instead, it seems almost a liability to have been induced by politicians to begin party work, for much higher percentages (at least among Democrats) of noncareerists and nonmobiles admitted their initial stimulus came from a political leader or in a political group. One cannot dismiss the implications of these data. Only a small minority of the top precinct mobiles claimed they were recruited by party workers or leaders, and in detailing reasons for joining, two-fifths said that they were initially motivated by a desire to affect governmental policies. In a later chapter we shall see what happened to these motivations as their party careers evolved.

Aside from the lack of elite social congruence and the limited nature of effective elite recruitment, a variety of other data can be assembled which may relate to the validity of the theory of oligarchy (Table 7.14). For example, the frequency of contacts of the top mobiles with district leaders was high in both parties—100 per cent for the Democrats and 83 per cent for the Republicans. Once these leaders entered the party structure and began their career ascents, therefore, they had much more contact with the top elite nucleus than did nonmobile precinct lead-

TABLE 7.14

CONTRASTING PATTERNS OF BEHAVIOR AND PERSPECTIVES FOR PRECINCT CAREER CLASSES*

	Democrats			*Republicans*		
	Top mobiles	*Non-mobile regulars*	*Non-careerists*	*Top mobiles*	*Non-mobile regulars*	*Non-careerists*
Have contacts with district-level leaders	100%	29%	20%	83%	41%	56%
Political associates *both* white and blue collar	65	57	24	25	43	70
Began party career after 1952	52	38	68	37	36	94
Unaware of organizational relationships	0	10	20	8	34	13
Feel they have very little to say about how the organization is run	22	35	96	29	74	6
Have ineffective precinct organizations under their direction	30	53	60	42	68	75
Low party loyalty: feel splitting the ballot is ok	43	38	80	87	70	56

* Each figure is a proportion of the total number in each career class.

ers. The opportunities for elite influence on their attitudes and views might be considerable, a matter we shall examine in a subsequent chapter. Concurrently, however, we also find that only for the Democrats were the top mobiles more socially heterogeneous in political associations (item 2 in Table 7.14). In fact, on the Republican side the top mobiles appeared to be much more class-bound in their selection of political friendships.

The relatively high turnover, and consequent insecurity, of even the top mobiles is indicated by item 3 in the table. At least half the top precinct mobiles in the Democratic party, and two-fifths in the Republican party, had brief political careers. On tenure, the data suggest that one can move upward in precinct leadership fairly fast, or one can remain a precinct leader, despite much aspiration and some mobility, for a long period of time. One-third of the top mobiles in both parties had been in the party continuously for at least 16 years.

Among these precinct mobiles, therefore, one finds great variation in mobility rates as well as intergenerational differences in career origin. It was not a uniformly mobile group with similar historical perspectives. There were, in addition, variations among the top mobiles in morale, effectiveness in organizing precincts, and party loyalty. Though their record was usually better than that of nonmobile regulars and noncareerists, it was by no means an example of consistency and efficiency. Over 20 per cent of the top mobiles felt they had little to say about the operation of the party organization; from 30 to 40 per cent admitted their own precincts were run without any systematic direction; and high percentages (43 per cent Democratic and 87 per cent Republican) gave some indication that their party loyalty was limited. In fact, the nonmobile regulars in both parties seemed to be more loyal than were the top precinct mobiles.

Only a few of the implications of these findings can be presented here. It is fairly clear, first, that the career classes of precinct leaders were distinctive categories of leadership—in communicative patterns, political work attitudes and capabilities, and political group perspectives, as well as in mobility and aspiration characteristics. Second, it seems clear also that the top precinct mobiles were not a tightly congruent, cohesive, happy, and uniformly effective group of leaders. They differed greatly in the way they began their party careers, in their personal characteristics, and in their views about politics and political effectiveness.

There can be no doubt that they were a relatively alert and knowledgeable group of leaders, stemming no doubt from their mobility status and consequent interaction with district and county leaders. But the data do not support the image of the party structure as one in which a top elite nucleus carefully screens certain aspiring precinct leaders for organizational posts, leaders congruent to the social composition and group perspectives of the top elite, and thus perpetuates itself as the single directive elite of the party structure. Not only was the total leadership component fragmented into district career groups, but there was pluralization of the top elite nucleus and the top precinct mobiles into subcategories of leadership based on career origins, career motivations, and career perspectives.

"SYSTEM" IMPLICATIONS OF PARTY CAREERISM

American parties face a strange paradox: they are "open" structures at the base, theoretically accessible to the many social groups from which the party must draw support; but they are "closed" in the sense that the public seeks to divert its political energy and activity into primarily nonparty efforts and channels. Only 13 per cent of our adult respondents said they would encourage sons who were "thinking of going into politics," 28 per cent said they would discourage them, 55 per cent said they would make no suggestion. From the reasons they gave, it seems that many people feel party politics is a parasitic occupation. In the face of such negative and neutral public attitudes about a party career, it is clear that only a minority of people can be socialized positively for politics during the years of development into adulthood. They are more likely to be protected from party careers than urged to consider them. This may account for the small proportion of party activists, the types of individuals who do become active, their reasons for making a decision to join the party, as well as their attitudes toward leadership positions. In evaluating the careerists who do become involved in one of our American parties, then, it is necessary to realize that these people are behaving contrary to prevailing public mores.

Has the "anti-party" climate of public opinion in reality deterred the fulfillment of the party's personnel needs? In answering this basic question, it is necessary to relate the data on careerism to certain basic structural requisites for a political party. The first such requisite is *durability*, the need for personnel with enough continuity in service to maintain the stability of party operation over time. Political parties are not *ad hoc*, campaign leadership and worker groups with a majority of new activists at each election. This is refuted by our data on era of career origin and proportions of leaders with uninterrupted careers. Top-echelon leaders had been in the party longer and more continuously, it is true, but from one-fourth to one-third of our precinct leaders dated back at least 20 years, and of these far more than half had been continuously active.

In contrast to durability is the requisite of *dynamism*. If the parties were static groups with very little movement of personnel upward in the hierarchy, stagnation would set in and innovation become unlikely. The two components of careerism investigated in this connection were aspiration and mobility. The data suggest that over half of the leadership was aspiring, with 57 per cent of the precinct leaders interested in higher positions. Further, we find that over one-fourth of the precinct leaders who had worked continuously, and over one-half of those who aspired *and* were continuously active, had already begun to move upward in the hierarchy. We would estimate that probably 25 per cent of the precinct leaders and 55 per cent of the upper-echelon elites were clearly "entrepreneurs," perceiving their political careers in "instrumental" terms at the time of entrance into politics. Analysis of their career development indicates that these motivations had been to some extent facilitated. In both parties there was considerable upward movement—less in the Republican than in the Democratic party, despite the higher percentage of aspirers within the former—enough to justify the conclusion that intraparty personnel mobility patterns had indeed been dynamic.

A third personnel requisite is skill *diversity* and experience. The party needs intelligent and experienced leaders if it is to be an efficient group operation, particularly in all the special tasks connected with vote-mobilization. It needs "menials," both perennial and intermittent, and "managers," middle level and top level, who are acquainted with their jobs and willing to perform in them. Important in this connection is the finding that all the top party officials in the congressional districts, including executive board members, started at the bottom in precinct posts and worked up to the positions they held at the top in 1956. Yet, by no means were all acquainted only with the "regular" organization. Analysis of modes of ascent reveals that from one-third to one-half were acquainted with the "auxiliary" party agencies—women's groups, clubs, youth organizations, and labor union political action groups. This suggests that there was thorough exposure to the operational procedures of the precincts as well as diversity of training in affiliated party enterprises. The data concerning types of positions held at the top and bottom of the hierarchy indicate that district chairmen and executive board members must have had, collectively, an adequate knowledge of party needs at different levels in the state and nation—at national conventions, in state central committees, county party administration, ward, and precinct. Their career paths had been sufficiently different to guarantee considerable diversity in perspective, much more than for precinct leaders. But even among the precinct leaders small percentages had already known work on district executive boards and in ward, county, and state representative or administrative capacities. Fifty per cent had attended state conventions.

The educational background of these leadership groups leads, furthermore, to the conclusion that if education is a "skill indicator," the party hierarchies were not in dire difficulty. Among precinct leaders the "top mobiles" had less than 10 per cent with only an elementary education. The "perennial menials" (nonmobile regulars) had higher percentages of those with an elementary education, but from one-fourth to almost one-half were college-educated, and the percentage of college-educated among the "sporadic menials" (noncareerists) was even higher. The

Republicans were certainly at an advantage among all career groups in this respect, yet the proportion of college-educated workers in both parties was considerable. Thus, although there was a tendency for grass-roots politics to be the politics of the high-school graduate, it does not appear that negative public attitude made party careers attractive only to the less educated. Probably not enough college-trained adults were involved, but among party actives, the college-trained constituted a very sizeable group.

It is when one assesses the *adaptability* of the local parties, as manifested in the characteristics of career groups, that more serious questions can perhaps be raised. There may not be significant implications in the small proportions of low-income groups and younger age groups found in the top organization mobiles. But the small percentages, relatively, among the Republican top mobiles of women, Catholics, and unskilled workers, for example, may indicate the difficulty which such groups have had in moving to higher career positions. They seemed more likely to be consigned to the position of perennial menials or occasional activists. This might not be construed as serious if there were not evidence of considerable aspiration for upward mobility among such groups in the Republican party. But there *was* such evidence—68 per cent of the women, 56 per cent of the Catholics, 56 per cent of the labor union membership, as well as 74 per cent of the Negroes, and 70 per cent of those with an elementary-school education, did aspire. And the proportions of women, Catholics, and unskilled among Republican "potential careerists" gave no promise that the mobility chances of these social categories would be improved in the future. Although the Democrats also "excluded" certain social categories, and had by no means implemented their aspirations fully, the data suggest much closer integration with the social structure on the part of the Democratic top mobiles. Democratic women, Catholics, and Negroes showed less faithfulness in continuity of service than their Republican counterparts, yet the mobility chances of at least the first and second of these social categories had been greater in the Democratic party. This implies a greater adaptability of the Democrats to the social milieux within which vote mobilization must be maximized.

This brings us back to the question of *cohesiveness* as a requisite of the party operation. On the surface, the Republicans seemed to be a more cohesive "machine" in terms of the personal characteristics of the top precinct mobiles, because of the high percentages of Protestants (80 per cent), males (87 per cent), well-to-do (38 per cent over $10,000 in income) and those with professional and managerial occupations (58 per cent). The Democrats seemed to have greater diversification in religion, sex, have more young people, and better occupational representation.

One cannot ignore, however, the "deviant" social groupings which had made their way into the top mobile cadre of the Republican party—Negroes who were 13 per cent of the top mobiles, Poles (17 per cent), all those from central, southern, and eastern European backgrounds (38 per cent), those with very low incomes (8 per cent with incomes under $6,000, compared to 4 per cent of the Democratic top mobiles), and the skilled blue collar (33 per cent).

Both parties had within their structures considerable "conflict potential"—the probability that the newly "arrived" social groups will clash with those in the top elite nucleus—as well as "frustration potential"—the probability that those who aspire but have not been able to move upward in the hierarchy will become disgruntled. And in both parties these potentials can be disruptive of harmony and effective team effort in the organization.

Finally, a party structure must be judged in terms of its *competitiveness*. The greatest assets for the Republicans were the educational level of their top and potential careerists, and the great evidence of upward aspiration among Republican precinct leaders. Though there was a viability problem here, the Republicans did have more leaders from social-status groups eager to develop careers in the Republican party. The significance of this for the expansion of Republican efforts among groups assumed to be predisposed to the Democrats—Negroes, Catholics, unskilled workers, Poles, even labor union members—was great. On the other hand, the Democrats appeared to be somewhat more adaptable to the environment and, though possibly less cohesive socially, to suffer fewer internal strains in the implementation of career perspectives.

The distribution of the five party career groups in terms of the competitive character of the congressional districts is suggestive of the different concentrations of career talent for the two parties (Table 7.15). Three observations are clear. (1) The Democrats had more top mobiles in both types of district than the Republicans. Both parties had their smallest percentages of aspiring and mobile precinct leaders where they most needed them—in the competitive districts. (This was true also if the "informal mobiles" were included.) (2) The Democrats had a much smaller percentage of type II (leaders who had served continuously but had not moved upward) than the Republicans.

TABLE 7.15

PRECINCT CAREER GROUPS BY COMPETITIVENESS OF DISTRICTS
(Percentage of all Precinct Leaders in the Districts which are Found in Specific Career Categories)

	Democrats						*Republicans*					
	IA	*IB*	*II*	*III*	*IV*	*N*	*IA*	*IB*	*II*	*III*	*IV*	*N*
Three overwhelmingly Democratic districts	19%	37%	15%	13%	16%	54%	22%	15%	35%	27%	1%	55%
Three more competitive districts	15	20	15	30	20	84	14	14	28	28	16	88

Legend: IA–organization mobiles
IB–informal influentials
II–nonmobile regulars
III–potential careerists
IV–noncareerists

Although some of these leaders might have been frustrated party "menials," they were a cadre of experienced workers faithful to the Republican operation in both types of district. (3) The Republicans had only 1 per cent of noncareerists among their precinct leaders in the sure Democratic districts. This attests to the difficulty a minority party has in such districts in attracting those only marginally interested in party work. Those who do work for the minority party are career motivated, aspiring, and continuously active.

It seems from these data that the distribution of career types in the two kinds of electoral areas—sure Democratic and more competitive—favored the Democratic party slightly on balance. The latter had larger proportions of experienced, mobile leaders as well as potential careerists (though less than half as many of these in the sure Democratic areas), and noncareerists. Though disadvantaged in some respects, the Republicans were not short on able and experienced careerists, actual or potential, in the one-party areas. It may, in fact, be somewhat remarkable that in congressional districts which had recently gone from 65 per cent to 85 per cent Democratic, the Republicans were still able to muster a sizeable cadre of able and upward-aspiring precinct leaders.

The characteristics, motivations, and career development patterns of precinct and upper-echelon leaders revealed here document the existence of a diversified body of party activists, in both the managerial nucleus and in the ranks. There was longevity of service, and exposure to party work, from the precinct and auxiliary agencies to the top. There was also a great range in the contexts and motivations for initial involvement. No major social strata had been completely excluded, although there were marked differences in the social composition of the most mobile groups of party leadership cadres. We have noted certain potentially dysfunctional aspects of party careerism in this chapter, particularly the possibilities of motivational disjunction between the top and lower ranks of the hierarchy and the pressure for mobility among those aspiring for more status. Continuity, mobility, and aspiration—three components of careerism to be singled out as important for the development of a party career corps—existed in abundance among those already active. Sizeable minorities of the precinct cadre were intermittent in service, unfamiliar with the organization, or had low morale, yet, the career structure was one of considerable dynamism. Whether leadership motivations and activities were of adequate form and pattern to realize party personnel needs, as well as the needs of the political system, is difficult to say until organizational relationships and performance records are collated with careerism data. The problems of structural viability, integration of career groups into the party machine, and functional effectiveness—the maximizing of career group activities in the achievement of the party's primary power acquisition tasks—are critical problems which will be examined in subsequent chapters.

PART II

THE POLITICAL PERSPECTIVES OF PARTY LEADERS

INTRODUCTION

Party leaders, like all elites, are constantly concerned with the orientations and perspectives of group activists at all echelons, toward group goals, tasks, and tactics. This is, on the one hand, a problem related to the recruitment of individuals into the organization; on the other, it concerns the indoctrination of members after involvement with the group. To maintain an effective congruence in perspectives is a matter especially acute for a political party machine. The "open base" which must necessarily characterize a political party, its relative fluidity of active workers, its "potential clientelism," and its adaptive relationships with the public in the process of mobilizing political support—all these accentuate the problem of developing a meaningful, collaborative structure of leadership and membership political perspectives.

There are five basic attitude content areas which are important in this context and which together constitute the individual leader's political perspective. The first of these is his perception and evaluation of the party's primary *goal*, perhaps the most relevant single query being whether he recognizes and accepts the objective of winning power, or retaining power, directly and legitimately, with all other objectives being secondary. Second is his *ideology*, the structure of his attitudinal positions on the critical public-policy questions of the day, and the extent to which his position coincides with the group's position, insofar as this is clearly definable and explicit. Next is the content of his personal *motivational* perspectives, the rewards and gratifications he seeks in active party work, the important query being whether these are more than personally instrumental. Related to this but separable is his *role-perception*, or his own understanding and definition of his particular task in the organization. Finally, there are his general orientations toward the *political environment* in which he as a party activist performs—his view of the party system, the election system, the organization and process of governmental decision-making, and particularly his view of the importance of the political party as an agency of political and social action. Related to this is his concern, both perceptual and evaluative, about party *tactics*, particularly about the manner in which the group must and does press toward its primary objective, whether he approves and can (will) implement the basic strategy and types of appeals. His feelings about the organizational style and operational code of the party structure in which he has a position also help to define his "morale" status within the organization. These perspectivist attitude clusters are not completely autonomous, and there is considerable overlap. But together they represent an orientation "state" of the individual activist which is important in understanding his behavior. And when the "states" of all those holding positions within the organization are considered, they become critical in understanding the total group, its character, mode of activity, and the effectiveness of its performance.

These perspectives can be theoretically operationalized, and analyzed from different vantage points. Here we are primarily interested in the competition-maximization problem, and seek to interpret the data in terms of the probabilities and actualities of the success of the party as an action group. This implies that we view the party group as a "competitive" structure, seeking to operate efficiently as a unit, and also as an "adaptive structure," continuously integrative with the social environment within which it must function. The party, in one sense, is what it believes—its attitudes and perspectives, at all echelons. And what the party leaders believe may certainly determine in large part the image it communicates to the public, and the success with which it mobilizes public support. We are asking, then, two types of general question in this analysis: (1) How much additional congruence is present, at the same leadership level, and between leadership levels, and what type of dissensus is in evidence, and at what level? (2) To what extent is congruence, or dissensus, important in the party's "public relations"—does it assist or seriously impair the party's functional performance? It is possible that these attitude and perspective patterns are completely irrelevant. On the other hand, it is more probable that they are very relevant, both to party internal effectiveness and unity, and to the maximization of the party's competitive status in the political arena. The exploration of the validity of these positions constitutes the aim of this section.

A reading of the literature on American party politics does not provide the basis for a theoretical expectation about leadership perspectives. The work which has been done suggests that certain big-city party machines may be well-regulated, even monolithic, structures of action, wherein one might expect to find considerable congruence in goal and tactical orientations. On the other hand, the literature indicates considerable attitudinal inconsistency concerning public-policy questions among party leaders, and possibly noncongruence between the upper and lower echelons of party leadership. The implications of certain studies differ, however, as to the perspectivist conditions under which the party can best maximize success—whether under conditions of ideological unity, consensus, clarity, and distinctiveness in relation to the opposition party, or whether these conditions are irrelevant. Indeed, there are some exponents of the argument that ideological "moderation" is most productive of party success on the American scene. In sum, the importance of leadership orientation and attitude has not been emphasized in empirical party research. In the absence of reliable data, one receives the impression from the writing that, to a great extent, there is incoherence in party leadership orientation, that this is naturally to be expected because of the character of the American party system, and that such incoherence may not be dysfunctional in the calculus of party success. American parties, after all, it is said, are structures of action, not structures of ideology.

Our primary interest in this section of the analysis is to test certain specific propositions about leadership perspectives for the Republican and Democratic leaders at all echelons of the hierarchy, and to compare them when possible with the attitudes of the adult public. We shall be building on the four theoretical images of the party empirically explored in the preceding pages.

CHAPTER 8

THE IDEOLOGICAL STRUCTURE OF THE PARTY

American politics has for some time been characterized as "nonprogrammatic." The "end of ideology" for the American political scene has often been proclaimed. Yet, every practitioner of politics knows the ideologue in party activity, the militant who fervently holds definite political views and is involved in party work solely for the purpose of implementing those convictions. A set of important empirical questions confronts us in the study of party ideology. Has the alleged hushing of ideological warfare discouraged the ideologue from joining the party, muted the issue enthusiasm of those already in the party, and produced a leadership organizationally conscious but indifferent to issue controversies? Or is the American party a structure which comprehends ideologues as well as those apathetic on the issues of the day, and is thus a sound balance of idealistic fervor and realism? And what is the pattern of ideological conviction in the party structure—are there significant differences by echelon, by subcoalitional interest groups, and by career status? Is the party clearly fractionated ideologically according to internal structural differences—by hierarchical level or by socio-political interests, or is the party a melange of ideological divergencies which are not neatly structured and highly irregular? A survey of the ideological *direction* of party leaders, the *intensity* of their issue positions, and the *congruence* of ideology within the hierarchies of the parties will suggest answers to these questions.

In determining ideological direction at all leadership levels, we used in our interviews a series of questions touching on significant policy matters. The three areas most frequently used were: aid to foreign countries "even if they are not as much against communism as we are," civil rights, and governmental assistance in helping people "get doctors and hospital care at low cost." We probed to discover whether the respondent had an opinion, whether he thought the government should act, and whether the level of governmental action at present was adequate or not. There were other questions concerning campaign issues and the issue differences between the parties which were designed, however, and here utilized, for different analytical objectives.

HIERARCHICAL VARIATIONS IN IDEOLOGY

At the apex of the local party machines, the Republican chairmen were consistently more conservative on these issues than the Democrats. Only one Republican district chairman was a thoroughgoing liberal on all three issues, while five of the six Democratic chairmen showed this attitude. There was somewhat more liberalism in the Republican top leadership on the civil rights question, and somewhat less Democratic liberalism, but differences at this level of the party, in the elite nucleus, were striking and consistent. This is not to say that the district chairmen were rabid ideologues. A minority of one-third in each party was quite outspoken and articulate about issue positions and the need of the party to fight its battles in ideological terms. The majority, however, were by no means forceful and forthright crusaders. But when the interviewer pushed beyond the generalities about "rugged individualism," "free enterprise," "government for the common man" and pressed for specific opinion on controversial issues, it was clear that they had opinions, and fairly consistent ones in an ideological sense. These chairmen, holding considerable influence and control over their respective organizations, were not operating in an ideological vacuum. The

Republican elite consisted of committed conservatives; the Democratic elite were committed liberals.

Among the secondary leadership cadre in each party, the executive board members, there was somewhat less consistency and uniformity in outlook, but the ideological direction was the same (Table 8.1). One-fifth of the Republicans and three-fifths of the Democrats were consistent liberals on domestic policy questions. The important difference appeared in the issue of foreign aid. Here the Republicans showed much more liberalism

TABLE 8.1

IDEOLOGICAL DIRECTION BY HIERARCHY LEVEL

	Republicans (percentage liberal)		*Democrats (percentage liberal)*		*Party difference*	
	Executive board	*Precinct*	*Executive board*	*Precinct*	*Executive board*	*Precinct*
Civil rights	36%	41%	61%	57%	25%	16%
Foreign aid	54	37	74	59	20	22
Medical aid	22	28	69	76	47	48

in the middle ranks than at the top, with over half of the executive board members supporting foreign aid. There was more Democratic liberalism on this issue also, three out of four secondary-level leaders giving their support. The medical aid question received the least Republican support among executive board members, while civil rights received the lowest Democratic support.

On all issues the Democratic executive board was considerably more liberal than the Republican group, with a marked contrast on the question of medical aid—only 22 per cent of the Republicans in support, but 69 per cent of the Democrats in support, a 47 percentage-point differential. Yet, it appeared that the middle cadre of Republicans was definitely more liberal than the top level; for the Democrats, if any difference was discernible, it was that the middle-level Democratic leader was inclined to be somewhat less liberal than the top echelon of the organization. These differences were not great for the Democrats, however, and one must be cautious about developing a thesis of hierarchical retrogression in liberalism until the precinct leadership data are seen.

A sizeable number of ideological dissenters appeared within each party at the middle level of leadership. About one in four Republican executive board members was a consistent liberal, and about 10 per cent of the Democrats were conservative, especially on domestic issues. The split in Republican ranks was more in

TABLE 8.2

Attitudes Within the Hierarchy on Two Issues, Domestic and Foreign Policy

	Republicans		*Democrats*	
	Executive board	*Precinct*	*Executive board*	*Precinct*
"The U.S. should give help to foreign countries, even if they are not as much against communism as we are."				
Agree strongly	33%	5%	61%	12%
Agree	21	32	13	47
Unsure	18	8	4	4
Disagree	28	27	4	12
Disagree strongly	0	8	0	10
No opinion and not ascertained	0	20	18	15
"The government ought to help people get doctors and hospital care at low cost."				
Agree strongly	11	11	65	51
Agree	11	17	4	25
Unsure	18	11	4	4
Disagree	61	31	9	11
Disagree strongly	0	22	0	4
No opinion and not ascertained	0	8	18	5

terms of domestic versus foreign policy issues. The vast majority of Republican leaders were decidedly against governmental aid in the medical and public housing fields, but less opposed to foreign aid to countries, even though they might be in the communist orbit of influence, or tending in that direction, or neutralist. Yet, despite this sharp contrast with Democratic leaders, ideological factionalism existed in each party. This was no monolithic ideological party structure.

These observations of party differences and hierarchical diversity are re-enforced by the attitudes of precinct leaders. Fewer precinct leaders than middle-level cadres, in both parties, had strong, positive liberal views on foreign aid and medical assistance. Thus, only 12 per cent of the Democratic precinct leaders agreed strongly on the foreign aid question, compared to 61 per cent of the executive board members; the parallel Republican percentages are 5 and 33 per cent. The Republicans were a relatively nonliberal group at the precinct level, especially on the medical aid question. Apparent, too, was the wide range and diversity in attitudes among precinct leaders of both parties, particularly in the Republican party. No Republican executive board members disagreed strongly on either the foreign aid or medical aid issues, but extreme conservatism was found among Republican *precinct* leaders. (See, for example, the distribution of opinion on the medical aid issue.) The same tendency, to a lesser degree, was found among the Democrats, suggesting that the upper echelons of the two parties were more homogeneous in ideology.

An intensive analysis such as this reveals striking differences within the local party structures on critical policy issues. Democrats were indeed much more liberal, significantly so, than were Republicans, at all echelons of the hierarchy, even in a city like Detroit, where since 1950 there had been a movement away from conservative policy positions in both parties, encouraged by liberal state chairmen. And precinct leaders re-enforced this condition of ideological distinctiveness, rather than diluted it. As a consequence, although a certain amount of ideological factionalism existed in both parties, particularly at the precinct level, there was remarkable like-mindedness in both hierarchies, from top to bottom.

Precinct leaders in these two structures were, thus, not the most liberal contingent. In fact, the middle-level cadre was most liberal on the Republican side, and the middle and top levels appeared most liberal on the Democratic side. This raises questions about the thesis proposed by Herbert McCloskey to the effect that lower-echelon Republican leadership is more liberal than the upper echelons, and practically as liberal as the Democrats.[1] The McCloskey thesis is not completely refuted by these data, since the top Republican leadership was, indeed, the most conservative element of either party. But there is no evidence here that the Republican party became more liberal as one proceeds down the hierarchy, nor that Republican party leadership at the grass roots was essentially as liberal as the Democratic. The rank order of party leadership in descending order of liberalism suggested by our data is:

Most liberal	Democratic chairman
	Democratic secondary cadre
	Democratic precinct
	Republican secondary cadre
	Republican precinct
Least liberal	Republican chairmen

Two other aspects of leadership ideology can be measured with these data. One is homogeneity of leadership attitudes at any hierarchical level; the other is congruence of attitudes between levels (see Table 8.3). Our indices measure homogeneity in three ways. First, in terms of *range of opinion* on the three issues we used, the index shows considerable similarity in outlook, with the exception of the middle-level Republican cadre, where relatively great diversity existed. Otherwise the scores were low. Second, the *amount of extremism* (in *content* of

[1] "Issue Conflict and Consensus Among Party Leaders and Followers," *American Political Science Review*, LIV, No. 2 (June, 1960), 406–27.

TABLE 8.3

INDICES OF IDEOLOGICAL CONSENSUS

	Republicans			*Democrats*		
	Chairman	*Executive board*	*Precinct*	*Chairman*	*Executive board*	*Precinct*
Ideological direction*						
Liberalism (means)						
All respondents	28%	37%	35%	89%	68%	64%
Those with opinions	28%	40%	39%	89%	79%	71%
Conservatism (means)						
All respondents	67%	49%	47%	11%	13%	27%
Those with opinions	67%	52%	53%	11%	16%	26%
Homogeneity						
Range in percentages of liberalism on three issues	17	39	16	17	13	18
Amount of extremism						
Percentage with 2 extreme positions (medical aid)	34%	9%	37%	83%	72%	58%
Factionalism—percentage deviating from majority on medical aid	17%	22%	30%	0%	14%	15%
Congruence between levels (percentage-point difference on liberal mean)						
Between chairmen and executive board		9			21	
Between executive board and precinct		2			4	
Between chairmen and precinct		7			25	

* These percentages are averages of the proportions which are liberal or conservative.

opinion, not intensity, or affect) was measured. Our data indicate that the Democratic chairmen were highest in this respect (all but one were ultra-liberals), while the Republican executive board was lowest (less than 10 per cent extremism). There was considerably more extremism in Democratic leadership groups than in Republican. Thus, the Democratic precinct leaders included 58 per cent who held extreme positions, compared to 37 per cent of the Republican precinct leaders. Third, the *factionalism score* indicates more homogeneity in Democratic ranks. Smaller percentages of Democrats at each leadership level deviated from the majority ideological position at that level than among the Republicans. In sum, Democrats and Republicans revealed about the same range in opinion, but the Democrats took more extreme (liberal) positions on issues, while the Republicans revealed more factionalism in the distribution of opinion.

The congruence indices show that the two lower echelons of the party structure were extremely close in ideological viewpoints. The district chairmen were more distant ideologically from the middle-level cadre than the middle was distant from the precinct level. But there was much more congruence in the Republican structure—in fact, relatively, the latter gave the appearance of a tightly-knit group in issue positions as compared to the Democrats. It is particularly interesting that the Republican chairmen were closer to the precinct leaders than were the Democratic chairmen. There was a great gap between the positions of the Democratic top nucleus and both the middle cadre and the precinct. Although there was some distinctiveness of the same order for the Republicans, the latter had a more unified, essentially conservative, state of organizational consensus.

IDEOLOGICAL CONGRUENCE—LEADERS AND FOLLOWERS

Significant findings emerge when the condition of public opinion in the Detroit area on the issues of medical assistance, foreign aid, and civil rights is examined. The "public" was divided into the following sectors:

Loyal Republicans Loyal Democrats	(self-identified partisans who had consistently voted for their party) 33 per cent
Other Republicans Other Democrats	(self-identified partisans who had not, however, consistently voted or voted for their party) 47 per cent
Independents and others	(did not consider themselves partisans and revealed no consistent voting behavior) 20 per cent

The total population varied in the extent of its "liberalism" on these issues, ranging from 33 per cent supporting foreign aid programs, through 54 per cent liberal in the civil rights controversy, to a high of 62 per cent agreeing that the government should provide aid in securing low-cost hospital and medical care programs.

Most critical in the study of party leadership is the analysis of the division of opinion within the five sectors, and the relation of sector opinion to the issue positions of the party leadership. How close to, or removed from, public opinion is a party's leadership structure?

The answer certainly depends on the type of public policy question involved. In the Republican party, for example (see Table 8.4), on the question of foreign aid, the leadership (with the exception of the executive board) was very close to the incidence of "liberalism" among its own loyal supporters, other Republicans who were not too loyal, the independents, and the population generally. But the reaction to the question of medical aid under government sponsorship is quite different, with a great deal more acceptance of the idea appearing among the public sectors than among the Republican leaders. The Republican precinct leaders were only 28 per cent "liberal" on this issue, while the loyal Republican voters were 40 per cent, other

Republicans 48 per cent, independents 55 per cent, and the general population as a whole 62 per cent. Similarly, the Democratic leadership was close to the public sectors in its opinion on civil rights, but far removed ideologically on the issue of foreign aid.

Despite these differences in relationships in terms of the type of issue, a composite analysis reveals certain uniform relationships between party leadership and its publics. If the leaders are viewed as a single category, our data reveal the Republicans to be a more like-minded group than the Democrats, but the leadership tended to be more conservative than the followers. The "mean" or "average" liberalism scores are as follows:

	All leaders	*Loyalists*	*Others*	*All followers*
Republicans	33%	44%	48%	46%
Democrats	74%	56%	51%	54%

The only Republican leadership group which surpassed the Republican followers in liberalism was the executive board contingent, on the issue of foreign aid. The opposite is true for the Democrats: only one instance occurred of "followers" surpassing the Democratic leaders in liberalism, and this was the Democratic loyalist group, on the question of medical aid. The Republicans, thus, were fairly like-minded, with a leadership lagging behind the liberal opinion movement in its supporter ranks. The Democrats were less well-knit, but the leadership group, together with party supporters, were moving in more liberal directions.

A second concern is the precise leadership level most representative of the party rank and file. Is it true that precinct leaders are closest, while district chairmen, entrenched over time in their power positions, are more distant? Our data suggest that the latter is indeed clearly true, while at the same time noting that the top elite is not necessarily the most conservative. The Republican precinct leaders were on balance closer than their Democratic counterparts to the rank and file. The Democratic district chairmen were the most unrepresentative

TABLE 8.4

CONGRUENCE OF LEADERSHIP OPINION WITH PUBLIC OPINION
(Percentage "Liberal" on Each of Three Issues)

	Republicans					*Democrats*						
	Chairman	*Executive board*	*Precinct*	*Loyalists*	*Others**	*Chairman*	*Executive board*	*Precinct*	*Loyalists*	*Others**	*Independents*	*Population*
Medical aid	17%	22%	28%	40%	48%	100%	69%	76%	87%	67%	55%	62%
Foreign aid	34	54	37	39	37	100	74	59	26	35	31	33
Civil rights	34	36	41	53	59	67	61	57	55	51	51	54

* "Other" Republicans or Democrats who claimed to be partisans but did not vote consistently for their party.

and ideologically removed. Table 8.5 indicates these differences in relationship.

TABLE 8.5

IDEOLOGICAL GAPS BETWEEN LEADERSHIP LEVELS AND FOLLOWERS
(Average of Differences on Three Issues*)

	Chairmen and		*Executive board and*		*Precinct and*	
	Loyal-ists	*Others*	*Loyal-ists*	*Others*	*Loyal-ists*	*Others*
Republicans	16	20	17	23	9	13
Democrats	33	38	24	17	15	13

* Two computations are possible here. The one used is the average of differences on each issue, whatever the ideological direction of the difference. Another measure, the "average size of the liberal gap," not used in this table, would slightly alter the figures, since pluses and minuses on liberal direction would cancel each other out. Using such a measure would make the Democratic precinct leaders slightly closer to the party loyalists.

The ideological distance of Democratic chairmen from the loyalists on this liberalism index is more than twice as great as the distance of precinct leaders, while executive board members are only moderately distant. The Democratic party thus exhibits a neat descending order of ideological relationships, while the Republican party reveals small gaps and less hierarchical orderliness in attitude structures. The Republican leadership appears, therefore, to be more "representative" of the attitudes of its loyal and consistent supporters than the Democratic leadership. The evidence is not as clear that the Republican leadership is more representative of the "other Republicans" who are less loyal to the party in terms of self-perception and voting behavior. The theory of oligarchy holds that the top elite nucleus of the organization will be unrepresentative of the rank and file, *and* more conservative. Although these data tend to confirm the unrepresentativeness of the so-called oligarchs, an increasing conservatism is not demonstrable in our data. The Democratic top elite is much more liberal than the party's rank and file, and, even in the Republican party, the precinct leadership is clearly very conservative and highly congruent ideologically with the Republican top elite.

A third problem and type of analysis is thereby suggested. In the study of the party we are interested in the ideological relationship between the leadership (and party structure proper) and those to whom the party must appeal for support—the irregular partisans and the independents. How congruent are the attitudes of leadership with the "floating voters"? In a metropolitan area such as Detroit this is an especially critical problem for the Republicans, as the minority party. But with 20 per cent of the adult population classifiable as "independents," probably a minimal figure, this is a concern of the majority party as well.

The independents in the Detroit area tended to be less liberal than the population generally on these three issues, and less liberal than the Republican followers on all issues except medical aid. Yet the greatest ideological gap between Republican leaders and independents occurred on the issue of medical aid. The Republican leadership was actually more liberal than the independents on the foreign aid issue, although remote and more conservative on the other two issues, the extreme case being medical aid.

The Democratic organization, on the other hand, from chairmen down to loyal supporters, was generally more liberal than the independents, the gap widening as one moves up the Democratic hierarchy. The closest congruence existed on the civil rights question, and the least on the foreign aid question.

Though a minority party, the Republican leadership was not competing ideologically for the independent vote as realistically as the Democratic leadership. This was true particularly on domestic issues. Although it is apparent that the Democratic machine's top nucleus was far too liberal for the independents, the grass-roots leadership of the Democratic party was closer to, and more representative of, the attitude directions of independents on domestic issues. Their support potential among the independents was, thus, greater, even though they needed such support less urgently than did the Republican leadership. The latter, a fairly like-minded conservative hierarchy, despite differentials in conservatism within leadership ranks, not only lagged slightly behind the liberals in its own loyalist ranks, and among those predisposed to be Republican supporters, but lagged behind the liberal tendencies of independents as well. The Republican leadership thus tended to live in relative ideological isolation.

SALIENCY OF IDEOLOGY

So far we have dealt with the *direction* of ideology (defined as particular or patterned attitudes toward public policy questions). Since party leaders differ also in the *saliency* of ideology (the extent to which they think in terms of party ideology, and the importance they attach to attitude differences in political perceptions), it is also necessary to examine the echelons of the party hierarchies in this respect. In which party and at which hierarchical level does ideology seem to be most salient?

Different measures of the phenomenon of "saliency" were used: perception of differences between the parties, motivations for political activity, basis of interest in politics, and perception of own role in the party. For illustrative purposes, we will use only the first of these approaches (Table 8.6).

In both parties the precinct leaders seemed less ideologically conscious than the upper echelons. This is particularly true for Democratic precinct leaders, who typically explained the differences between the two parties in terms of the constituency they

TABLE 8.6

IDEOLOGICAL SALIENCY OF PARTY LEADERS AND THEIR PUBLICS (Percentage Perceiving Party Differences in Issue Terms)

	Chairman	*Executive board*	*Precinct*	*Loyalists*	*Others*	*Independents*
Republicans	33%	69%	29%	26%	17%	14%
Democrats	83	76	17	8	7	

represented: "The Republicans are the party of the rich," "The Republicans represent the business people," "The Democratic party is the party of the working man." Though more liberal, lower-echelon Democrats were less inclined to articulate issue difference, while the conservative Republican grass-roots activists were more articulate. These differences corresponded also to the extent of saliency found in the immediate support groups of the parties. The Republican loyalists differed considerably from the Democrats, and were only slightly less ideologically conscious than the Republican precinct activists. The "other," less loyal, Republicans also exceeded the Democratic irregular party followers. The latter were certainly less ideologically involved, and there was less pressure on the party leadership to emphasize its issue image in competing with the Republicans.

This resulted in a strange paradox for the Democrats. The top and middle-level leadership was very "salient" on ideological differences. Though not rabid ideologues, as pointed out above, the top Democrat leaders were articulate and conscious of issue positions. Having a follower base with negligible ideological saliency means that it was difficult to maximize support primarily by issue appeals. It may also mean that moving upward in the Democratic party hierarchy was an educational experience so far as exposure to public policy positions of the party were concerned. Those at the lower reaches of the Democratic structure had little ideological intensity. In fact, the independents showed as much saliency as the Democratic precinct workers, and more than the Democratic loyal supporters. It may be that in both parties, but particularly the Democratic, career continuity and mobility could result in more awareness of party issue differences.

The two top leadership groups presented a study in contrasts, the Republicans conservative, and not ideologically involved, the Democrats quite liberal, and heavily involved with the issue differences between the parties. Only at the top echelon of the Democratic party and in the middle-level cadre of both parties did we find substantial ideological awareness. The basic direction of ideology was different in each party, but there was a great range in the extent to which the party's position on policy issues was of first importance in the thinking of the leaders.

IDEOLOGICAL DIFFERENCES IN LOCAL PARTY ORGANIZATIONS

In the description of the parties as ideological structures, we have suggested by implication that the direction of a party leader's (or follower's) thinking on public-policy questions, as well as the importance of ideological differences to him, is partly a product of the party to which he belongs, and the echelon at which he is working. This is, of course, only part of the story; other major types of explanations require investigation. One of these is the internal characteristics of the particular party structure and certain conditions of party life, especially conditions of party competition, which are relevant to the development of ideological conviction in the party leader.

District organizations within the same political party varied remarkably in the ideological relationships between leadership and followers. This emerges clearly from Tables 8.7 and 8.8.

TABLE 8.7

IDEOLOGICAL GAPS AND CONGRUENCE—THREE DISTRICTS
(Percentage Liberal on the Civil Rights Issue)

	District X		*District Y*		*District Z*	
	Republican	*Democratic*	*Republican*	*Democratic*	*Republican*	*Democratic*
Chairman	*Con**	*Pro**	*Pro**	*Pro**	*Unsure*	*Con**
Precinct	11%	89%	35%	62%	46%	40%
Loyalists	66†	70†	41	61	58	42
Irregulars			53	61	39	54
Independents	59		59		46	

* Con = conservative; Pro = liberal.
† The loyal and irregular supporters were combined because there were too few cases for separate analysis.

TABLE 8.8

IDEOLOGICAL GAPS AND CONGRUENCE—THREE DISTRICTS
(Percentage Liberal on the Medical Aid Issue)

	District A		*District B*		*District C*	
	Republican	*Democratic*	*Republican*	*Democratic*	*Republican*	*Democratic*
Chairman	*Con**	*Pro**	*Unsure*	*Pro**	*Con**	*Pro**
Precinct	6%	53%	55%	47%	27%	98%
Loyalists	72†	77†	78†	75†	50	95
Irregulars					47	75
Independents	71		71		62	

* Con = conservative; Pro = liberal.
† The loyal and irregular supporters were combined because there were too few cases for separate analysis.

Leaders were not always more conservative, or more liberal, than the supporters. As a matter of fact, three distinct types of relationships for each party may be observed.

There was the district (X and A, for the Republicans) in which the leadership was very conservative and unrepresentative of the followers, with extreme cases showing for the Republicans on both the civil rights and medical aid issues. The majority of Republican followers, two-thirds or more, were liberal, while the chairman was a conservative, and the precinct leadership was overwhelmingly conservative. This occurred in less extreme form on the Democratic side (districts A, and B).

The second type occurred in the district where the leadership was much more liberal than the followers. Sometimes only the chairman was a liberal, while the precinct leaders were conservative (Republicans, District Y). In other cases there was a split in the follower group, although the differences in this respect were not usually great. An example of this may be found in the overwhelming support of medical aid by the Democratic leadership and loyal supporters in District C, with somewhat less liberalism among the irregular Democrats.

The third basic type was the district organization in which there was fairly close congruence between the opinions of the leadership and the followers. In one case the chairman might be ambivalent on the issue in the face of a decided split within the ranks (Republicans, District Z). In another case the chairman might take a conservative position in the face of a split in the ranks (Democrats, District Z; Republicans, District C). In this case the ideological position of the precinct leadership might be the controlling factor for the chairman, or vice versa.

The striking fact which emerges from a district-by-district analysis of the data is that a political party is a composite of significantly varying ideological types. Each district structure may be characterized as an ideological entity. The Republican precinct leaders in District A were extremely different in their attitudes on medical aid from those in District B—the one group was only 6 per cent liberal on this question, the second group 55 per cent liberal—while both the precinct leadership cadres, Republican and Democratic, differed radically in Districts X and Z. There did not appear to be as much difference, however, in the attitude distributions of the "loyalists" and irregular supporters of the parties by district, although differences did exist. The range in liberalism for all of the six congressional districts in our study is shown in Table 8.9, revealing that, on each issue, the precinct leaders as groups were more dispersed and the

TABLE 8.9

Range of Liberalism Within Six District Party Structures
(Percentage-Point Spread in Liberal Positions from the Lowest Percentage of Liberalism in a District to the Highest)

	Precinct leaders		*All followers*		
	Repub-lican	*Demo-cratic*	*Repub-lican*	*Demo-cratic*	*Independents*
Civil rights	59	49	35	26	18
Medical aid	64	51	59	15	34
Foreign aid	38	41	16	14	20

followers more homogeneous from district to district. There is a strong suggestion here that rank and file partisan supporters and independents were relatively stable throughout the metropolitan area in their political opinions, but activists varied greatly in their attitudes from one party structure to the next. One primary reason for this is that the party as a group influences and conditions ideological position, making the activist more conservative in the Republican case, or more liberal (though there are exceptions to this, too) in the Democratic case. A second reason with some probability is that the party attracts (or recruits) as activists from its support group individuals who were ideologically predisposed to follow the attitude positions of those already in the hierarchy, at the same time discouraging those perceived to be too liberal or conservative, as the case might be. No doubt both factors operated together; the evidence is too clear and the variations too striking to indicate otherwise. A party structure is constantly struggling, in its subtle relationships with the environment, to maintain itself as a viable ideological entity. The potential supporters of the party structure are constantly evaluating the ideological position of the party machine, and if inclined to political activity, calculating their chances for ideological survival and career mobility if they assume activist responsibilities.

In this two-way flow of contacts between the party leadership and its publics, the Democrats seemed to have developed a more successful set of relationships. The job of the Democrats had been abetted, of course, by the existence of a majority liberalism among its followers in these districts. With the exception of perhaps two districts, there was less range in the extent of liberal support among Democrats, and, too, they seemed to have done a better job of inducting liberals in the constituent groups into precinct work. The exception was District B. The Republicans in some districts had done fairly well in this respect also, notably Districts Y and Z, thus maintaining a proper equilibrium in ideological position between leaders and followers. But generally the Republican leadership had inducted conservatives into the hierarchy, leaving a follower remnant at odds, in attitude, with the leadership. Third, the Democrats in four of the districts had developed a leadership structure conforming more closely to the ideology of independents than had the Republican party.

PARTY COMPETITION AND THE IDEOLOGY OF THE ACTIVISTS

The competitive context and status of the two parties differed greatly among districts. There were three basic types:

1. Conservative Republican leaders faced relatively conservative Democratic leaders (Districts Z and B)
2. Conservative Republicans faced liberal Democrats (Districts X, Y, and A)
3. Liberal Democrats and Republicans faced each other in the same district (a district not included in the above tables, where, for example, 70 per cent of the Republican precinct leaders were liberal on civil rights and medical aid issues, and 89 and 78 per cent of the Democratic leaders were liberal, respectively, on each of these issues).

Now, three of these districts were overwhelmingly Democratic, and three were somewhat more competitive, though still voting Democratic. In the "sure Democratic" districts the Republican leadership was of all three types noted above, while in the more "marginal" districts were only Republican conservatives, opposing either Democratic liberals or moderate conservatives.

Clear-cut ideological struggles, therefore, appeared in three of the districts, with liberals opposing conservatives on most issues. This conflict occurred primarily in marginal districts; in fact, in the most marginal district in the area one found the most highly conservative Republicans arrayed against the most liberal Democrats. The Republicans and Democrats had diversified their organizational "battle plans," but moderation in ideological position did not characterize those areas with the greatest potential in party competition. The Republicans did not appear to be making much progress in those sure Democratic districts where they were either as conservative as the Democrats, or almost as liberal as the Democrats. And, in a sense, Republican liberalism was wasted in the sure Democratic district where this held, but they had waged battle in marginal areas by remaining conservative in the face of Democratic liberalism. Whether this was wise in the long run, in the face of considerable liberalism among their followers and the independents, is a difficult question to answer. These marginal districts were becoming less marginal over time, and more Democratic. Witness the 17th District, which was only 52 per cent Democratic in the congressional election of 1954, but in 1958 was 60 per cent Democratic. This was apparently the manner in which the Republicans sought to battle in marginal districts, by maintaining a distinctive ideological position in the hierarchy, in contrast to their diversified approaches in sure Democratic areas. This technique was probably not sufficiently adaptive to the types of constituency to which they must appeal, for example, barely 10 per cent of the Republican precinct leaders were liberal on the civil rights issue in a Negro congressional district organization. But, realistic or not, it produced party conflict situations which were more clear-cut than one would expect in a two-party system under which both parties were seeking *presumably* to maximize their appeal to "potential clienteles" in a metropolitan electorate.

There is evidence here, then, of three organizational conditions which influence the ideological character of the leadership structure of the party. One is the tendency for the leadership to maintain itself as a viable ideological structure. Another is the tendency of certain types of people to be attracted to party leadership. The third is the character of the competitive struggle in the district, with marginal competitive conditions finding conservatives in the Republican organization, and liberals in the Democratic. Thus, with district party structures varying greatly in ideological composition, the type of district organization to which the activist is recruited may have a great deal to do with his subsequent ideology. He may be conservative or liberal at the time he is recruited, but certainly the indoctrination process commences as soon as he has joined the party machine.

Confirmation of this last finding is found by detailed analysis of the ideological position of precinct leaders in relation to the competitive status of the 87 precincts included in the study (Table 8.10). Of the Republican leaders, 80 per cent were opposed to medical aid in the marginal precincts, while 60 per cent were opposed in the sure Republican precincts, and only 35 per cent were opposed in the sure Democratic precincts. In contrast, none of the Democratic precinct leaders in the marginal

TABLE 8.10

IDEOLOGICAL DIFFERENCES OF PRECINCT LEADERS BY PRECINCT TYPE

	Sure Democratic precincts		*Marginal precincts*		*Sure Republican precincts*	
	Republican	*Democratic*	*Republican*	*Democratic*	*Republican*	*Democratic*
Medical aid						
Liberal	39%	67%	18%	100%	20%	76%
Conservative	35%	20%	80%	0%	60%	13%
Index*	43		162		103	
Civil Rights						
Liberal	48%	58%	31%	53%	40%	62%
Conservative	49%	33%	69%	47%	51%	34%
Index*	26		44		39	
Foreign aid						
Liberal	29%	48%	36%	80%	54%	62%
Conservative	28%	23%	53%	20%	28%	24%
Index*	24		77		12	

* The index score is a computation of party differences, including both the liberal and conservative percentages. Unless indicated otherwise, it represents the extent to which the Democrats were more liberal than the Republicans.

precincts was opposed to medical aid, while 13 per cent and 20 per cent were opposed in the sure Republican and sure Democratic precincts, respectively. The opinions on the other issues bear out this finding that the party leadership structures were strikingly opposed to each other ideologically in marginal districts. Index scores also indicate that the greatest ideological distance between Republican and Democratic leaders was found in these marginal precincts.

While the Republicans competed as conservatives in marginal precincts, they tended to be more liberal in sure Democratic precincts. Not a majority, to be true, and not extremists, but this was where they appeared to be concentrated. Since the lowest Democratic liberal tendencies appeared in the sure Democratic precincts, it may be that the Republicans saw this as the best tactic to win back some support from the complacent, and less liberal, Democrats. The rationale may also have been that these were precincts where the Republicans could afford to be relatively liberal, and precincts in which liberal Republicans could infiltrate as activists without too much competition.

The most fundamental observation from these data is that where there was the most intense party competition, conservatives sought, or were selected, for Republican precinct leadership posts, and liberals sought, or were selected for, the Democratic posts. This, of course, contradicts much impressionistic observation about American politics, particularly the view that the parties moderate and mute ideological differences in order to maximize their votes in the most competitive areas. So far as the precinct leaders were concerned, the battle forces in highly competitive areas were ideologically distinctive.

SOCIAL STRUCTURE AND LEADERSHIP IDEOLOGY

The three social factors of race, religion, and nationality affect the interrelationship between ideology and the social stratum of the individual party leader. These differences cut across party lines and in each case Negro precinct leaders tended to be more liberal than whites, Protestants than Catholics, and those with eastern and southern European nationality backgrounds more liberal than those from northwestern or central Europe. These elements in positions of leadership constitute an ideological continuum undergirding the party organization and provide an ideological integration for the party system.

This was not true of the ideological tendencies of income groups, educational groups, or age groups. The lower-income groups were the most liberal on the Republican side; the higher income groups liberal for Democrats (very liberal on civil rights, moderately liberal on medical aid). The college-educated Republican precinct leader was the least liberal, while the college-educated Democratic leader was rather liberal. Nor did union affiliation relate to more liberalism among Democratic party leaders, although it did seem to be associated with liberalism among Republicans.

Two striking results from this analysis are the differences between parties in the ideology of women and Catholics. Less than 10 per cent of female Republican precinct leaders, but over 70 per cent of female Democrats, were consistent liberals. Democratic Catholic party leaders were considerably more liberal than Republican.

The ideological differences between the parties, as a matter of fact, for these different demographic groups were very consistent. In Table 7.11 out of 36 comparisons which could be made between the liberalism of Democratic and Republican party leaders for these personal characteristics, only three instances emerged in which the Republican subgroup exceeded the Democratic subgroup in liberalism. These were all on the civil rights issue for the lowest social-status groups—those with an elementary-school education, and the two lowest income groups—otherwise the Democrats were invariably more liberal. We checked this finding on the foreign aid issue and for other demographic categories, and found that in 88 per cent of the comparisons the Democratic leadership subgroups were more liberal.

This suggests strongly that ideology is a party-related phe-

TABLE 8.11

IDEOLOGICAL DIRECTION BY PERSONAL CHARACTERISTICS
(Precinct Leaders Only—Percentage of Demographic Category Liberal on Each Issue)

	Republicans		*Democrats*	
	Civil rights	*Medical aid*	*Civil rights*	*Medical Aid*
Race				
White	36%	23%	52%	78%
Negro	70	61	78	72
Sex				
Male	50	33	54	77
Female	4	11	81	71
Religion				
Catholic	21	24	48	66
Protestant	52	29	63	82
Education				
Elementary or less	70	31	45	08
High school	47	49	54	80
College	31	14	73	65
Nationality				
Northwestern European	36	22	51	78
Central European	29	18	41	76
Eastern and southern European	50	33	100*	90
Income				
Under $5,000	58	50	41	88
$5–7,000	47	19	44	74
$7–10,000	22	39	79	82
Over $10,000	36	20	70	61
Union affiliation				
Yes	53	49	58	77
No	36	20	58	74

* Too few cases for reliable analysis.

nomenon on the leadership level, even though there seem to be consistent differences in terms of race, religion, and nationality which cut across party lines. The liberal ideologues were Democrats, whatever their social stratum. The Republicans could increase their liberalism by recruiting more Negroes, and perhaps also by attracting certain nationality groups, Protestants, and certain lower social-status groups. These people eventually proved to be less liberal than their counterparts in the Democratic party, the product again, no doubt, of the two-way interaction between party and potential clientele groups. The party selectively recruits, the potential activists selectively choose sides.

Analysis of the personal characteristics of liberals and conservatives on the executive boards of the two parties (though the number of cases for each demographic and social subgroup is, of course, small) suggests certain distinctions in the precinct leadership. Thus, the Republicans had slightly more female, Catholic, college-educated liberals on the executive boards than in the precincts. The Democrats had fewer female, Negro, college-educated liberals on their executive boards. In both parties uniformly, Catholics were less conservative and Protestants more conservative on the executive boards than in the precincts. It may be that the parties could, or must, tolerate more liberalism, or conservatism, in the upper echelons. The Republicans found themselves with more liberal Catholics on executive boards, for example, while the Democrats encountered a rather conservative-minded group of women on their boards. This tendency may have been the product of recruitment deficiencies at the precinct level or an indication that individuals change ideologically as they move up the party hierarchy. In any case, both parties faced ideological factionalism among the same social-group memberships at two different levels of the organization.

THE IDEOLOGY OF THE SUBCOALITIONS

Party subcoalitions can vary widely in ideological direction. If we look at the ideological position of those structural subgroups described in Chapter 4, party differences existed, clearly, but subcoalitional differences also appeared (Table 8.12). The medical aid and foreign aid issues were selected as illustrative, although other issues revealed the same tendencies. In both party

TABLE 8.12

THE IDEOLOGY OF THE SUBCOALITIONS AND THE "DEVIANTS"
(Percentage of Subgroup Liberal on Each Issue)

Subcoalitions	Democrats: Medical aid, Precinct leaders	Democrats: Medical aid, Loyal followers	Democrats: Foreign aid, Precinct leaders	Democrats: Foreign aid, Loyal followers
Negroes	69%	88%	50%	21%
Poles	94	100	56	19
Irish	67	88	39	41
Other labor	76	81	62	21
Business and Professional whites	86	71	79	35
Southern blue collar	*	100	*	6
All CIO	*	95	*	30
All AFL	*	73	*	13
"Deviants"				
Germans	55	53†	100	26†
English	91	78†	91	27†
Business-managerial group	74	69†	84	31†

Subcoalitions	Republicans: Medical aid, Precinct leaders	Republicans: Medical aid, Loyal followers	Republicans: Foreign aid, Precinct leaders	Republicans: Foreign aid, Loyal followers
Business-managerial whites	11%	30%	50%	35%
Other white collar (northwestern European)	35	27	53	50
Nonlabor blue-collar whites	*	38†	*	33†
Labor (whites)	44	53†	18	34†
Negroes	61	93†	17	13†
All Germans	22	24	30	59
All English, Welsh, and Scottish	29	35	36	39
"Deviants"				
Irish and Poles	11	62†	39	29†
Other southern, central, and eastern Europeans	32	74†	84	42†
Semi- and unskilled	43	58†	43	25†

* Too few cases, or analysis was not possible.
† Based on *all* followers, since there were too few cases of "loyal" followers.

structures the degree of liberalism or conservatism varied by subcoalitional issue orientation. Among Democratic subgroups the least conflict appeared on medical aid (all were over 60 per cent liberal); yet subcoalitional precinct representatives varied from two-thirds to almost 100 per cent support. On foreign aid there was much more difference in ideological conviction in the Democratic structure: only 39 per cent of the Irish precinct leaders were liberal, 50 per cent of the Negroes, while 79 per cent of the "business-professional whites" were liberal. In the Republican party there was extreme subcoalitional variation in ideology. On medical aid, 61 per cent of the Negro Republican precinct leaders were liberal, but only 11 per cent of the business-managerial class, and 22 per cent of the Germans. Conversely, 50–53 per cent of the white-collar and business-managerial precinct leaders were liberal in foreign aid, but only 17 per cent of the Negro leaders (and 18 per cent of the "labor whites").

Ideological disagreement by subcoalitions among precinct leaders was greater among the loyal followers. The Republican party was a structure which had to reconcile a subgroup of Negro supporters (93 per cent of whom were liberal) with a subgroup of upper-status businessmen who were 30 per cent (or 32 per cent if all followers were used) liberal. The "ideological spread" in the Democratic structure was not as great, but on the issue of civil rights, for example, the variation shown in Table 8.13 appeared among loyal Democratic supporters.

The ideological distance between Negro loyal Democrats and the rest of the party, particularly the business-professional group, is obvious. One wonders, indeed, whether a serious effort at compromising these groups at the top level of the party structure could even be attempted!

We have included in Table 8.12 some of the "deviant" social categories for each party used in Chapter 3. The purpose here is twofold—to reveal the party differences for each "deviant" group, and to test the proposition that open recruitment can result in ideological disjunction in the party structure. Although Negroes have an ideology which tends to be homogeneous re-

TABLE 8.13

VARIATION AMONG DEMOCRATIC LOYAL FOLLOWERS ON CIVIL RIGHTS ISSUE

Loyal followers subcoalition	*Percentage liberal on civil rights issue*	*Number of cases*
Negroes	85%	52
Poles	43	21
Irish	47	17
Business and professional whites	29	17
Southern blue-collar migrants	44	16
All CIO	42	73
All AFL	45	40

gardless of party, the same cannot be said for other categories. Irish and Polish precinct leaders in the Republican party, for example, were overwhelmingly conservative, while in the Democratic party they were generally liberal. The same finding, in reverse, exists for the German and English Democratic precinct leaders, who were very liberal contrasted to the Republican Germans and English, only one-fifth to one-third of whom were liberal. Similarly the "business-managerial" class in the Democratic party was over 70 per cent liberal, while the same class in the Republican party was very conservative on medical aid, and 50 per cent liberal on foreign aid. Here is clear evidence again of the probability that a precinct leader in the Democratic party, rather than the Republican party, was *either* a liberal at the beginning, *or* that the party had a real influence on his ideology after he joined. In fact, the hypothesis that recruitment of "deviants," as precinct leaders or as followers, attracts people at ideological odds with the rest of the party, is not generally supported by data on the Democratic party. Only the German Democrats pose a problem as a conservative force. The hypothesis does seem to be true for the Republican party's socially "deviant" followers, however, though not for their "deviant" precinct leaders. The "deviant" precinct leaders were not particularly liberal, but 62 per cent of the Irish and Polish followers and 58 per cent of the semi- and unskilled laborers *were* liberal on the issue of medical aid. While Democratic "deviants" seemed to have relinquished their conservative leanings, Republican "deviants" still clung to liberal attitudes.

CAREER STATUS AND IDEOLOGY

The question of the role of career background and status in ideological perspective deserves special analysis since ideology appears strongly related to selection of party. Is there evidence that career pattern variables are related to the ideological structure of the party? Or does party career origin and process have nothing to do with ideology?

The time of origin of political career is a related factor to ideology in both parties (Table 8.14). The latecomers in the Republican party, and those who began their careers before 1932, were the most conservative (though the latecomers were relatively liberal on civil rights). Among Republican precinct leaders, therefore, the ideological conflict arrayed the newest members and the oldest members against those who entered the party in the thirties and the forties.

It is interesting that recent Democratic entrants were also quite conservative, and in sharp contrast to the liberalism of those who began Democratic careers prior to 1932. These findings suggest that there may have been a movement toward ideological moderation in both parties in 1956.

The family political context in which the individual was "socialized" for politics also bears some relationship to ideological direction among activists. Democratic fathers sired more conservative Republican activists than liberals; Republican fathers produced more Democratic liberal activists than conservatives, *and* a larger proportion of liberals than did Democratic fathers! A "rebel reaction" seems to be indicated here. It is indeed significant that 86 per cent of the offspring of Republican fathers who served as Democratic precinct leaders in 1956 favored medical aid programs, but only 40 per cent of the offspring of

TABLE 8.14

CAREER BACKGROUND AND STATUS AS RELATED TO IDEOLOGY
(Precinct Leaders Only)
(Percentage of Career Category Liberal on Each of Three Issues)

	Republicans			*Democrats*		
	*CR**	*MA**	*FA**	*CR**	*MA**	*FA**
Career origin						
1956	49%	22%	22%	59%	38%	31%
1952–55	50	22	72	69	83	83
1940–51	41	38	30	43	97	77
1932–39	40	47	40	41	78	59
Before 1932	24	19	14	85	90	35
Father's preference						
Democratic	40	40	40	53	81	58
Republican	45	27	28	79	86	57
Father politically active						
Yes	36	24	23	53	87	67
No	44	32	36	60	70	54
Father's preference and activity						
Republican						
Active	32	27	47	‡	‡	‡
Inactive	49	27	29	80†	90†	50†
Democratic						
Active	45†	18†	45†	46	85	65
Inactive	38	50	38	56	79	54

* CR–civil rights; MA–medical aid; FA–foreign aid.
† Small number of cases: R, 11; D, 10.
‡ Too few cases for analysis.

Democratic fathers who were in the Republican camp in 1956 favored medical aid programs. The data reveal that the political activity of the father is also an important variable—Republicans with active fathers were more conservative, while Democrats with active fathers were generally more liberal. Yet, a combined analysis (though the cases are few) indicates that there may be some validity in the "rebel reaction" theory. Active Democratic fathers produced a preponderance of conservative Republicans, though greater conservatism resulted from having an active Republican father. And active Republican fathers contributed liberals to the Democratic camp. This finding emphasizes again the fluidity of the American party affiliation structure, and hints at an alienation tendency at home combined with an indoctrination process in the party, which together may have much to do with the ideological position of the activist.

On the question of career status, and using the same career categories employed in Chapter 6, we are able to see whether position in the party hierarchy is related to ideology (Table 8.15).

There is an obvious and clear connection between career continuity, mobility, and aspiration on the one hand, and ideological direction on the other. The "top organization mobiles" and the "regulars" (who had been in the organization a long time even though nonmobile) were fairly distinctive groups. They were the most conservative in the Republican organization, and the most liberal in the Democratic. Only one-fifth of these took a liberal position on medical aid and civil rights questions in the Republican party, while from 60 to 90 per cent did in the

TABLE 8.15
CAREER STATUS AND IDEOLOGICAL DIRECTION
(Precinct Leaders)
(Percentage of Career Category Liberal on Each Issue)

	Republicans				*Democrats*			
	*CR**	*FA**	*MA**	*Index*†	*CR**	*FA**	*MA**	*Index*†
Top mobiles	21%	46%	21%	29	65%	80%	83%	76
Informal influentials	53	26	63	47	60	57	90	69
Nonmobile regulars	23	28	16	22	57	71	90	73
Potentials	60	33	35	43	56	25	78	53
Noncareerists	63	75	25	54	52	60	36	49

* CR–civil rights; MA–medical aid; FA–foreign aid.
† The index score is a simple mean of the three percentages.

Democratic party. The "potential careerists" (who aspired but had not served long or continuously) tended to be more liberal in the Republican party (particularly on foreign aid). This may have resulted from basic differences with the hierarchy, or misperceptions as to the ideological conditions under which one moved upward, or evidence that they had not been subjected to the indoctrination process of the party. In any event, they constituted an ideological challenge in both parties, much more so than the "noncareerists" (the irregular activists who come and go and have no organizational aspirations). The latter were also rather liberal in the Republican party, and somewhat conservative in the Democratic party (particularly on the question of medical aid).

Three major observations emerge from this analysis of career status. One is that there is clear evidence that length of tenure in the party machine and movement upward, combined with aspiration to be influential, inclined the party activist to an ideology which is conformist. He was less likely to be a liberal in the Republican party machine under such conditions, and less likely to be a conservative in the Democratic party. (The only exception to this was the group of Republican "informal influentials" who had held no formal position beside precinct leader, but who seemed to have many contacts in the hierarchy. This group tended to be rather liberal in the Republican party, just as it did in the Democratic party.)

A second basic observation is that the nonmobile and irregular activists, who constituted 40 per cent of the precinct leadership cadre, were least conformist—more liberal in the Republican party, and more conservative in the Democratic party. The party relied heavily on these newcomers and irregulars, not all of whom aspired to position in the party, and there was a latent dysfunctional aspect in their relationship to the party. The party might have to capitulate to them or modify its position on key policy issues if it wished to maximize the support and efforts of these precinct leaders.

Third, although the top mobiles in the precinct cadre were

inclined to be congruent attitudinally with the top executive nucleus (the chairmen and executive board members), one-fourth of them were noncongruent. And they were no more congruent than the nonmobile regulars, a finding which raises questions again as to the acceptability of the theory of oligarchy.

CONCLUSIONS

This chapter has discussed party leadership as a structure of ideological perspectives, presumably shared within the hierarchy. We have been interested in the ideological basis of party organization and the ideological conditions under which the parties compete in the precincts. We examined the extent of ideological dissensus and unity in the party machine, and how monolithic, incoherent, or balanced ideologically the party structure was. We sought to assemble and study the available evidence concerning the problem of ideological indoctrination and the role of the party structure in determining the attitudes of its leadership on public policy questions.

Some observers assert that it is ideological homogeneity which makes a party structure viable, but examination of party structures discloses, in fact, considerable ideological diversity, by echelon, by subcoalition, by career status.

We found that the Republican and Democratic hierarchies varied considerably in ideological direction, at all echelons—the Republicans conservative, the Democrats much more liberal. These differences were striking at the top leadership level, but were significant at the precinct level as well. Yet, there were sizeable dissenting groups in each party—from 10 to 25 per cent of the leadership, depending on the leadership echelon. In neither party was the precinct leadership the most liberal, a finding which is possibly at odds with general impressions and other research.

Our indices of the amount of extremism in attitudes, the extent of factionism, intraparty attitudinal congruence, and the relationship between leadership and followers reveal a lack of homogeneity in both parties. Republican leadership tended to lag considerably behind the Republican rank-and-file in liberalism; Democratic leaders were also ideologically distant from their follower base. It seems clear that the Republicans were not competing realistically for independent voters, who were much more liberal than the Republican leadership groups. These descriptive differences seem most important in ideological direction, even though in both parties there was a low level of ideological awareness and saliency, particularly at the precinct level.

In probing for explanations and relationships, certain factors seemed to be working together to produce these differences. The type of party organization in which the leader is active seemed of considerable importance. District organizations developed, over time, their own distinctive ideological directions, and the activists seemed to vary from one district to another, even though the follower groups and the public generally were rather consistent and stable in their opinion directions. Another factor, the competitive character of the district and precinct (whether it be sure or doubtful) revealed ideological differences in leadership. This was particularly noticeable for marginal districts, where the Republican leadership fought as conservatives, while the Democrats fought as liberals.

Thirdly, there were differences in ideology by the personal and social backgrounds of the leaders, religion, race, and nationality appearing to have the greatest cross-cutting relevance. Within each party, also, there were certain social backgrounds which correlated with liberal or conservative ideology. The subcoalitional differences were particularly significant, revealing a 40 per cent difference for Democratic precinct leaders from its subgroups, and a 50 per cent Republican subcoalitional difference. Finally, career background and career status were factors related to differences in ideological direction. Those with career origins prior to 1932, as well as the more recent entrants, seemed to be most distinctive in ideology. Father's political preference and activity were also relevant, with considerable "rebel reaction" in evidence.

A prominent and consistent finding, with explanatory power,

is that ideology is a phenomenon related to party organization. There were major differences between the two parties' leadership structures, at all leadership levels. The type of district organization in which the activist was recruited or found himself, the competitive nature of the precinct, and the career status of the individual activist in the party—all made important contributions, it appears, to the ideology of the leader. This configuration of factors operated with a variety of processes for which one might be tempted to accept simply this explanatory image: The would-be activist has a perception of the leadership ideological structure, makes the decision to join, or is involuntarily "recruited." The party, on the other hand, endeavors to recruit a selective leadership. Subsequently, the party socializes this leadership in terms of its own ideological position, indoctrinates the party "line" through overt or informal and indirect processes, and "promotes" a majority of those with conformist tendencies to upper-echelon tasks and responsibilities. Thus, in this image, induction into the party structure and indoctrination following induction are twin re-enforcing processes with great potential for ideological control.

Countervailing forces and evidence reveal, however, that there are serious limits to ideological control, particularly by the top elite nucleus. It is quite apparent that large minorities of leaders at the executive board level did not know or follow the "party line"—from 20 to 40 per cent. It is also obvious that even the top executives were not all liberals or conservatives. Further, sizeable numbers of precinct leaders continued in their posts even though, theoretically, their ideological position must have been anathema to top leadership—from 30 to 40 per cent. Again, though conformity to the party line may seem to have had value, the "deviants" were tolerated and nonconformists promoted. Approximately 30 per cent of the Republican "top mobiles" in the precinct cadre were liberals and 25 per cent of the Democratic "top mobiles" were conservatives. Apparently, the top elite nucleus could not obstruct their mobility aspirations despite ideological nonconformity. Above all, the subcoalitional diversity in ideology which the party must and did tolerate is obvious. We have here, then, concomitant with evidence that ideology is influenced by party associations, evidence also of great ideological diversity, autonomy, nonsocialization, dilution, and dissent. The party machine is no monolith, co-opting and coercing a homogeneous and unique ideological leadership. Pressure to conform exists. But the party gladly embraces, and freely associates with, a most ideologically conglomerate set of potential supporters and activists. From the bottom to the top, the party welcomes, and rewards, the ideological deviant.

CHAPTER 9

GOAL PERSPECTIVES OF PARTY LEADERS AND FOLLOWERS

Students of the political system universally view the party as a "power group," aspiring to the acquisition, exercise, and retention of power in the community. This is to be accomplished, basically, through successful competition for, or control over, the top decisional positions of the polity. Other goals may also be recognized: public education, social service, ideological clarification, leadership training, individual or group representation, or group compromise. But while such goals may be important, to most students of parties they do not supersede the capture of power in the name of the party group. Thus, Max Weber wrote, "But 'parties' live in a house of 'power'. Their action is oriented toward . . . influencing a communal action. . . ."[1]

James Bryce's famous description of the party "machine" placed heavy emphasis on this unique goal of the party:

> But the reader will ask, How is the Machine run? What are the inner springs that move it? What is the source of the power the committees wield? What force of cohesion keeps leaders and followers together? . . . The source of power and the cohesive force is the desire for office, and for office as a means of gain. This one cause is sufficient to account for everything, when it acts, as it does in these cities, under the condition of the suffrage of a host of ignorant and pliable voters.[2]

This theoretical position is amazingly akin to the "self-interest" axiom of the Anthony Downs model: "From the self-interest

[1] See R. Bendix, *et al.*, *op. cit.*, p. 74.
[2] *Op. cit.*, Vol. II, p. 111.

axiom springs our view of what motivates the political actions of party members. We assume that they act solely to attain the income, prestige, and power which come from being in office."[3]

Although writers differ in their views of the purposes for which the "party" wishes power and the strategies employed for achieving power, the goal of power is a widespread conceptual orientation of most writers. The primacy of the party as a group with power-winning perspectives will be examined in this chapter. We wish to determine the extent to which there is an empirical basis for the theory that the party leadership accepts as its *primary* goal the winning of power by all the direct and legitimate means at the group's disposal. We will identify and characterize those leaders who do perceive the party as a power enterprise, in contrast to those who may perceive it as some other kind of enterprise, and follow with an analysis of the conditions and forces which help explain the genesis and development of such goal perceptions. Many key questions about the party as a political system group hinge on such an analysis. To what extent do parties fulfill the self-interest requirements which are so crucial to the entire Bryce–Downs model? Where, within the party structure, does one find the greatest congruence on goal perspectives? At what echelons, in what subgroups, and in which career classes is found minimal power-consciousness? And what is the impact of power saliency, or power unawareness, on individual leadership behavior and relationships in the party structure? This is a second, basic, perspectivist analysis, necessary for assessing the character and competence of the political party. The "power function" may not, in fact, outrank other "functions," such as "representation," "education," or "compromise," in importance. It is, however, a function so widely acclaimed that some empirical verification, even in exploratory fashion, should be attempted.

At the outset it must be admitted that to operationalize the concept of "power-winning" as a goal orientation of leadership is difficult. The development of a research technique which

[3] *An Economic Theory of Democracy* (New York: Harper, 1957), p. 28.

properly "discovers" those leaders who perceive the party in specific goal terms is also difficult. Our experience showed that many leaders did not intellectualize spontaneously in this language. Others were hesitant to articulate "power" explanations, partly perhaps because of the elitist-conspiratorial connotations of such a conception. We therefore combined two approaches, utilizing three key, or test, questions. The responses to these questions, under certain circumstances, were considered to be evidence of the goal orientation of the leader, particularly whether or not he was "power-oriented." These three questions were:

1. "Would you have favored a stronger plank on Civil Rights (for your party's platform) even if it meant the loss of some votes?"

   We were interested here in those who were consistently "liberal" on other issue questions and who replied "no" to this question—evidence in our opinion that they were muting their liberal enthusiasm because of a desire to maximize power objectives.

2. "What type of candidate would you like to see your party nominate for president next time? Why do you feel he would be a good candidate?"

   By scrutinizing their responses we were able to get some insight as to how important success-maximization was to the respondent—whether he wanted a "winner" or whether winning was secondary or irrelevant.

3. "Was there ever a time when you thought that your party's supporters would have been justified in splitting their ballots? Under what sorts of conditions would this be?"

   Although we were predisposed to consider all "splitters" as not committed to the power goal of the party, "conditions" could be pertinent—the person

> who felt that splitting was always good ("helps keep our parties in balance") being quite different from the person who was in support of occasional splitting "because the other party had a better candidate." Generally, however, it was difficult to defend splitting in this power context.

In addition to these three questions, we screened the entire interview for fugitive evidence which might be cumulative, contradictory, or substitutive. The individual was usually classified, then, on the basis of his total response. The three questions tap different facets of the respondent's perceptions of the group's goals. No one of these questions is sufficient in its own right—the first, perhaps, being closest alone as a valid measure, but combined they produce an effective screening technique. Thus, 11 per cent of the precinct leaders were consistent liberals who balked at losing votes for civil rights(question 1); 6 per cent frankly indicated they wanted a presidential candidate who was a winner, 30 per cent wanted a candidate who supported a particular ideological position (with winning clearly subordinate), while over 50 per cent gave responses which were not as clear-cut as these (question 2). Finally, 49 per cent of the Democrat and 26 per cent of the Republican precinct leaders opposed splitting ballots under any circumstances (question 3). With these questions as a start, plus scrutiny of responses to other questions—particularly those concerning motivation, role perception, aspiration, and morale—the leaders were classified on the dimension of goal orientation. We discovered those who were clearly power salient, those who articulated other goals as primary, as well as those who seemed incapable of articulating any party goal or were in real conflict about the goals of a political party.

Political leaders have quite distinct frames of reference in terms of which they will reveal their understanding of the party's goal. They do not have uppermost in their minds and at the tips of their tongues a neat explanation of party theory.

Illustrative of the type of material which gives clues, however, is this quotation from a Republican district chairman whom we considered to be highly power-oriented:

> "One minority group in Wayne are the Mexicans. They are underprivileged, live in slums, many have become naturalized citizens. I took them down and got them registered. Some of them have been Democrats for years and would have nothing to do with Republicans. But I speak Spanish and through a Negro friend of mine I have been able to talk to their leader. At first he was quite hostile but when I told him about our interest in minorities he was willing to listen. Now for the first time in Wayne's history we have had Mexicans voting Republican. But then look at how our party treats them. I took this Mexican leader to a dinner. They refused to talk to him or accept him. This is why we will never get ahead. As some of my Negro friends tell me, 'these Republicans will never rub skins with us.' Now this kind of attitude has to be changed by the party."

A Democratic chairman revealed power-consciousness in his discussion of the candidate, civil rights, and the South:

> "The Dems in 1960 need a candidate with color who will present a cornier approach than Stevenson. Because the urban Democrat is becoming the suburban Republican the presidential candidate must have snob appeal. He must please the conformist attitude which is sweeping the United States, but he must also be a liberal to please the articulate section in American politics. The Democratic party is sincere on civil rights, but the party has the problem of the southern states. The Democratic party still needs the southern vote, and much as I would like to be able to do so I am not prepared to alienate them. I am an integrationist (I live in an integrated district), but I believe the party has gone as far as it can on civil rights."

Occasionally a leader will be very candidly power-oriented, as was this Republican executive board member:

> "The reward I got this year was seeing Ike elected. I'm in here because I want to see good people in office and I'm afraid of the CIO and the Democrats. I'm scared to death they'll get too much power. Walter Reuther was educated in Russia."

And another executive board member, a Negro Democrat, could just as frankly reveal a temporary loss of interest in gaining power:

> "I would not pass out any literature for Stevenson. That middle-of-the-road stand he took—I'll never forgive him for it. That man seemed not to know where he was going. We need a liberal thinking person. Don't worry about the South. I am interested in people, particularly my people."

From such quotations it is apparent that leaders varied in the saliency as well as the substantive nature of their goal perceptions. One man was interested in power for personal reasons: "The trouble with the Republican party today is that they don't get anybody any jobs." Another was working for the advancement of the aims of a particular interest group, such as the Negro Democratic leader. Another was genuinely issue-oriented and saw a connection between issues and achieving power:

> "I am a liberal but it is hard to be a liberal in the Republican party, because they think liberals are dangerous. We cannot have people going against civil rights. We should have developed some good issues. Instead we just attacked union leaders and lost the vote."

Still another emphasized the importance of winning to the viability of the party organization: "The major problem is to keep the enthusiasm of the people up, while elections are lost year after year." And some were thoroughly "communal action" minded, to use Max Weber's phrase. We were interested in all these varying predispositional bases for goal perception, but our primary aim was to separate those who, whatever the substantive purpose or motive, saw the party as a means for achieving social control or influence. We were concerned with those who sought to capture the top power offices in the society, which would in turn provide opportunity for decisions relevant to the ambitions, demands, and interests of the leaders and followers in the party structure. Does the party leader actually see, to use Charles Merriam's phrase, that the "party is the near government"?[4]

[4] *Op. cit.*, p. 58.

HIERARCHICAL DIFFERENCES IN GOAL PERSPECTIVES

The top executive elite was obviously the most power-oriented in both parties. This was particularly true for Democratic chairmen who had been winners in Detroit and who knew the rewards which accompany victory. The percentage of "power salients" among the Republicans at all levels was considerably smaller than among the Democrats; they were not as overt, articulate, and uncompromising on the question of winning power as the Democrats. Half of the Republican chairmen, five-sixths of their secondary cadre, and 70 per cent of their precinct leaders had subdued their power-consciousness or had rationalized their (minority) party's objectives in other goal terms. (Almost one-half of the Republican precinct leaders were "idealists" about party goals or "unoriented" in goal terms.) But this does not imply that the Democratic party machine was a unified power-winning aggregation. Democratic executive board members were particularly inclined to substitute goals other than power as primary.

The data suggest a diminution in "power-winning" perspectives as one descends the hierarchy, with the net result that large percentages at the lower echelons, especially for the Republicans, had not been indoctrinated with, or had not accepted, office-winning power as the proper and legitimate primary party goal. Nevertheless, in both parties, despite sizeable bodies of lower-echelon dissenters, the bare majority of leaders were aware of power as the goal of a political party and its implications for the activities and processes of their political group. They wanted candidates who could achieve this power objective, they knew that issue stands are related to it, and they perceived clearly that the public's voting behavior is also closely linked to the power objective. Yet, the dissenters, confused, and unoriented on goals, indicated this to be no single-minded, goal-oriented machine.

THE PUBLIC'S VIEWS OF PARTY GOALS

In arriving at criteria by which the public was to be classified in terms of the above power-saliency categories, somewhat

TABLE 9.1

PARTY GOAL PERSPECTIVES—THREE ECHELONS OF THE HIERARCHY

Categories	*Democrats*			*Republicans*		
	Chairmen	*Executive board*	*Precinct*	*Chairmen*	*Executive board*	*Precinct*
Power salients—primary party goal is to win power	67%	33%	61%	50%	17%	29%
Power latents—weak but some evidence of a power-winning perspective	33	22	18	50	43	25
Idealists—party goal other than power (ideology, group representation, etc.)	0	45	12	0	40	35
Unoriented (no evidence of any goal awareness)	0	0	9	0	0	11

different questions were employed. Even though a sizeable percentage of the public identified with one or the other of the parties, the questions used had to assume that all sectors of the public would perceive party goals from the standpoint of non-involved spectators. Consequently, we asked the cross-section sample three questions which provided both direct and indirect evidence of party goal perceptions: (1) whether, if they were interested in political action opportunities, they would prefer to work through political parties or through other political groups, and why (here we coded particularly their "power" references about parties); (2) whether they felt it made any difference which party won the election (designed to screen out those who felt there would be no consequences from a change in party control); and (3) whether they felt that party leaders were important in influencing the voting decisions of the public. These questions again tapped three different facets of party perceptions—the voting activation power of the party, the post-electoral results of party power, and a general evaluation of the party as an action group.

Considerable differences were found in the public's responses. Thus, only 47 per cent felt that it made any significant difference which party won the election. Again, only 24 per cent indicated an inclination to work through parties if they became more active, while 50 per cent preferred to work through other groups. Yet, only 13 per cent of the former group and 16 per cent of the latter explained these preferences in terms of clear perceptions of the parties as power-winning aggregations—29 per cent, thus, preferring to work through parties because they were power goal-oriented, or recoiling from parties because of such an orientation. Finally, 43 per cent of the public felt that party leaders were influential in vote mobilization (18 per cent ranked party leaders as more important than any other leadership group), while 41 per cent were not impressed with this role of party leaders. In constructing our index we included among the "power salients" those who were clearly aware of the power goals of parties on all three dimensions, the "idealists," who preferred to work through parties but for other than power reasons, and the unoriented, who felt that it made no difference which party won and expressed the opinion that party leaders were unimportant in influencing voting decisions. The "power latents" were a small residue who gave some indication that the party contest might be important, or that party leaders might have some significance in influencing the vote.

Two conclusions are obvious when the public's views of party goals are compared with those of party leaders (Table 9.2). (1) The precinct leaders of the two parties differed considerably from their respective publics in goal perceptions, with the Republican leaders revealing a relatively low level of power orientation; (2) precinct leaders of both parties were more likely, however, to have some party goal-orientation than were the loyal partisans, irregulars, and independents in the general public. On the one hand, this implies that some goal-indoctrination took place in the hierarchy for precinct leaders, but not necessarily

TABLE 9.2

PARTY GOAL ORIENTATIONS OF PRECINCT LEADERS AND THE PUBLIC

	Democrats			*Republicans*			*Inde-pend-ents*	*Entire cross-section*
	Pre-cinct	*Loyal sup-porters*	*Other*	*Pre-cinct*	*Loyal sup-porters*	*Other*		
Power salients	61%	31%	29%	29%	35%	27%	22%	29%
Power latents	18	7	8	25	17	0	0	5
Idealists	12	23	9	35	4	10	10	11
Skeptics and negativists	9	39	54	11	44	63	68	55

in terms of winning power for the party. On the other hand, a great recruitment potential existed for the party in the public, for almost one-third of the public did clearly see the party in power terms.

One of the most consistent findings was that the closer an individual identified with a party, the more likely he was to see the party in power goal terms. Only 22 per cent of the independents, but 38 per cent and 52 per cent of the loyal supporters, did have such perceptions. Conversely, those most loosely connected to a party seemed to be more skeptical of the existence of any kind of party goal—68 per cent of the independents, in contrast to 39 and 44 per cent of the loyal supporters. Those in the general public who did not see parties in power terms were not likely, however, to see parties as working for other goals or ideals—only the Democratic loyal supporters revealed any sizeable percentage of such "idealists" (23 per cent). It appeared, then, that close affiliation with a party and particularly involvement in party work had the effect of developing power perceptions of party goals. Involvement in Democratic party leadership positions in Detroit was especially significant in this respect. The majority of party leaders were either overtly or latently aware of the power-winning goals of the party, while the great mass of irregulars and independents, from 54 to 68 per cent in our study, had no real perceptions of parties in a clear and meaningful sense, or were frankly negative.

ORGANIZATIONAL VARIATIONS IN LEADERSHIP GOAL PERCEPTIONS

In searching for factors responsible for the development of power perspectives, it may be helpful to note again the differences among the six congressional district organizations, which are the basic units of party organization in the Detroit area. As Table 9.3 shows, precinct leaders did differ from one organization to the next in their goal perspectives. Democrats exceeded Republicans in power saliency in all districts except the 14th; Republicans exceeded Democrats in idealism in all districts; and the variation by district is most interesting. There was a range of almost 50 points in power saliency for the Democrats between districts 14 and 17, and between districts 16 and 14 approximately the same range obtained for the Republicans. One-fifth of the Democratic precinct leaders in three districts (13, 14, 15) seemed poorly oriented on any party goals, while the Republicans revealed the highest concentrations of poorly oriented leaders in districts 15, 16, and 17. The only plausible explanation for these differences is that they were the function of two forces—recruitment or induction into the organization, on the one hand, and indoctrination by and through the organization on the other. The association of precinct leaders formally and informally within an organizational context, and their selective recruitment by each other, produced a somewhat distinctive structure of party goal perspectives.

The much lower level of power saliency among Republicans, particularly in the 1st, 15th, and 16th districts, which are overwhelmingly Democratic, suggests tendencies in goal perceptions among the minority party leadership, in certain self-contained organizational units, which reflected the political terrain. The

TABLE 9.3

PARTY LEADERSHIP GOAL PERCEPTIONS IN THE SIX CONGRESSIONAL DISTRICTS
(Precinct Leaders Only)

Districts	*Democrats*					*Republicans*				
	Power salients	*Power latents*	*Idealists*	*Unoriented*	*Number of cases*	*Power salients*	*Power latents*	*Idealists*	*Unoriented*	*Number of cases*
1st	76%	6%	18%	0%	17	20%	30%	45%	5%	20
13th	68	5	6	21	19	39	33	28	0	18
14th	35	35	10	20	20	58	29	13	0	24
15th	78	0	0	22	18	18	24	34	24	17
16th	44	35	21	0	43	12	17	54	17	41
17th	86	5	9	0	21	39	26	22	13	23

incidence of 45 per cent, 34 per cent, and 54 per cent "idealists" among Republican leaders in districts 1, 15, and 16 was not the product of chance. The leadership group no doubt adapted to this terrain and developed a "realistic" calculation of organizational goals. Thus, the *esprit* of the organization's leadership corps, its informal associational life, as well as its political environment, together conduced toward the emergence of goal-perspective patterns which varied by geographical area. It is perhaps remarkable that in such overwhelming Democratic areas up to 20 per cent of the Republicans were power salients, and from 30 to 50 per cent of the Republicans had some power goal perspectives for their party, however subdued.

A more precise application of this interpretation is possible by examining the goal perceptions of precinct leaders by type of precinct (Table 9.4). For the Republicans, two findings fit this theory, and two findings, to some extent, may conflict with it. For all types of precincts the Republicans revealed a higher percentage of idealists than the Democrats, even the percentage of idealists among Republicans in sure Democratic precincts was relatively high (33 per cent). There were few Republicans in doubtful precincts (3 per cent) who seemed to have no goal-orientation, true also among Democrats in doubtful precincts (none in the fourth category). But the two findings possibly at odds with the theory are the relatively high percentage of power salients among Republicans in sure Democratic precincts, and the unexpectedly high percentage of Republican idealists in doubtful precincts. In terms of a theory of party competition, the Republicans did not have power-oriented leaders in doubtful precincts, where they most needed them. Here 77 to 94 per cent of the Democrats were power-oriented, while only 28 to 46 per cent of the Republicans showed this orientation. The consistent differences in power perspectives between parties on the precinct level suggest that the Republican leadership may have been more influenced in its calculations of realistic party goals by its chances of success in the Detroit area generally, which regularly votes Democratic, than by the possibilities of increasing the Republi-

TABLE 9.4

GOAL PERSPECTIVES BY POLITICAL STATUS OF THE PRECINCT
(Precinct Leaders Only)

Precinct type	Democrats					Republicans				
	Power salients	*Power latents*	*Idealists*	*Unoriented*	*Number of cases*	*Power salients*	*Power latents*	*Idealists*	*Unoriented*	*Number of cases*
Sure Democratic	56%	18%	16%	10%	79	32%	22%	33%	13%	69
Sure Republican	59	21	6	14	29	29	43	14	14	35
Doubtful	77	17	6	0	30	28	18	51	3	39

can vote in marginal precincts. The few votes to be gained by a fight in a small precinct were overbalanced by the high probability of Republican defeat in the district and the county, thus, the relatively low level of group objectives in power terms, and the justification of party activity in idealistic goal terms.

SOCIAL STRUCTURE AND GOAL PERSPECTIVES

Since there was wide diversity in goal perspectives among party leaders, it is worth while to question the relevance of personal characteristics for identifying the power salient. The ordinary demographic variables are of some, though limited use (Table 9.5). Women in both parties perceived it in a power-winning context more clearly than men, and Catholics seemed somewhat more power-conscious than Protestants. It is interesting that an inverse relation existed between education, and clarity and saliency of power perceptions—the college-educated leaders were least perceptive of the party's goals in this sense.

A return to our "subcoalitional" and "open recruitment" models of the party structure will be meaningful in a suggestive sociological basis for differential party goal perceptions. The primary subgroups in both parties presented important differences (Table 9.6). The Polish Democrats were overtly power-oriented (93 per cent), contrasted to the relatively subdued or uncertain goal orientations of the Negroes and Irish (only 53 and 44 per cent, respectively, were power-salient). This is, in a sense, parallel to the finding in Chapter 4 that the Negroes and Irish had relatively low subcoalitional party loyalty.

An augmented diversity in goal orientations appeared among Republican subcoalitions. One in three white labor union members could not clearly and consistently perceive the party goal. The percentages of "idealists" among the other subgroups were relatively large, reflecting very little consciousness of the party's goal as "communal power." The general impression is that certain Republican subgroups consisted of leaders who were more subcoalition power-oriented than party power-oriented—notably

TABLE 9.5

GOAL PERSPECTIVES BY PERSONAL CHARACTERISTICS OF PRECINCT LEADERS

	Democrats					*Republicans*				
	Power salients	*Power latents*	*Ideal-ists*	*Unori-ented*	*Number of cases*	*Power salients*	*Power latents*	*Ideal-ists*	*Unori-ented*	*Number of cases*
Sex										
Male	56%	20%	13%	11%	117	26%	24%	38%	12%	115
Female	86	5	10	0	21	43	29	21	7	28
Age										
Under 40	69	17	14	0	47	42	24	22	11	45
40–49	45	9	9	37	33	9	25	60	7	44
50–59	62	35	3	0	39	16	24	52	8	25
60 and over	68	0	32	0	19	52	28	3	17	29
Education										
Elementary	60	10	10	20	20	69	0	0	31	16
High school	65	15	10	10	80	12	29	44	15	52
College	53	30	18	0	38	33	28	36	3	75
Religion										
Catholic	63	17	14	6	65	38	6	38	18	34
Protestant	60	21	13	6	62	23	30	38	9	97

TABLE 9.6

GOAL PERCEPTIONS FOR SUBCOALITIONS AND "DEVIANTS" IN THE PARTY STRUCTURE
(Precinct Leaders)

Democratic subcoalitions	*Democrats*				*Republican subcoalitions*	*Republicans*			
	Power salients	*Power latents*	*Idealists*	*Unoriented*		*Power salients*	*Power latents*	*Idealists*	*Unoriented*
Negroes	53%	19%	16%	12%	Business-managerial whites	13%	41%	39%	7%
Poles	93	0	7	0	Other white-collar (Northwestern European)	47	18	24	11
Irish	44	28	28	0	Labor whites	35	24	12	29
Business and professional whites	79	21	0	0	Negroes	30	26	44	0
All labor	64	16	8	12	All Germans	39	43	9	9
Democratic "deviants"					All English, Scottish, Welsh	25	36	14	25
Germans	100	0	0	0	Irish and Poles	44	0	50	6
English	54	28	0	18	Other southern, central, and eastern Europeans	0	11	68	21
Business-managerial	64	7	0	29	Semi- and unskilled	43	0	38	19
Clerical and sales	27	27	27	18					

the business-managerial whites (13 per cent power salients) and the Negroes (30 per cent power salients). This, too, is a finding not in contradiction to the Republican party loyalty analysis of Chapter 4. For large numbers of Negro leaders, in both parties, the party was very secondary in terms of achieving top power positions in the political system. The same seemed to be true for other Republican subgroups, whose low level of power-consciousness was striking. This was not true for labor union members in the Democratic party, however, nor for the Poles who were ascending the party mobility ladder in increasing numbers, nor for the business and professional whites. These groups saw the Democratic party as a power instrument, a party which, by winning governmental office, could and would use its decisional power to further group aims. This was no doubt due to the fact that the Democratic party was the majority party in the area, but it is also related to the indoctrination of group leaders with utilitarian power perceptions. The Irish, and all Republican groups, conversely, seemed almost skeptical, or at least reserved, about the power utility of their parties.

The exceeding relevance of the majority status of the Democratic party can be shown by analysis of the "deviants." The Republican Polish leaders were idealists, not power salients or even latently aware of the party's power goal (only one of 10 was power-oriented). Again, only 43 per cent of the Republican semi- and unskilled leaders were power-conscious, in contrast to 94 per cent of Democratic leaders in these occupations. On the other hand, German and English Democrats were more conscious of the power-winning character of the party than were their Republican counterparts. Two-thirds of those in business and managerial occupations were power salient in the Democratic party, but only 13 per cent in the Republican party. These "deviants," rather than introducing a pattern of alien goal perspectives, seemed to assimilate the goal perspectives of other leaders in the party. They conformed more with party goal perspectives than with nationality or occupational class perceptions of the party.

CAREER STATUS AND ORGANIZATIONAL STATUS AS CONDITIONERS OF GOAL PERSPECTIVES

A recurring determinant for leadership indoctrination into the power aspirations of the party is the organizational climate. Why should Democratic unskilled workers be more power-conscious about party goals? Why should Democratic leaders in doubtful or sure Republican precincts be more power-conscious than Republican leaders? This was not a function of labor union membership alone, for, although unionism was greater in the Democratic party, Republican precinct leaders who were also union members revealed a marked confusion about party goals and less saliency about power-orientation than Democratic labor union party leaders. The suggestion is strong that the Democratic party organization subtly inoculated its leadership with clear power assumptions. Yet, not all in the Democratic party were inoculated, and this raises the question of the relevance for goal perspectives of a leader's position in the hierarchy.

In the Democratic party, the career status of a leader was indubitably connected to the content and saliency of his view of the party's goal. The top mobiles among Democratic precinct leaders were clearly power salients—91 per cent contrasted to only 24 per cent of the noncareerists. The aspiring, mobile, and continuously active Democratic leader did become aware that power is the party goal. This was not so for the Republicans, for only 13 per cent of Republican top mobiles were power salients, compared to 44 per cent of Republican noncareerists. Thus, the kind of person who moved upward in a party organization was not necessarily the kind of person who was exposed, or susceptible, to the doctrine that the party's goal is that of winning power. Even in the Democratic party 65 per cent of the nonmobile regulars were power salients. This suggests that mobility was not indispensable to power perspectives, even in the Democratic party.

It must be recognized, however, that the power salients were found, actually, throughout the structure of both parties regardless of career status. This diffusion is documented by Table 9.7.

TABLE 9.7
THE DISTRIBUTION OF GOAL PERSPECTIVES BY CAREER STATUS
(Precinct Leaders)

	Democrats				*Republicans*			
	Power salients	*Power latents*	*Idealists*	*Unoriented*	*Power salients*	*Power latents*	*Idealists*	*Unoriented*
Top mobiles	25%	4%	6%	0%	7%	19%	28%	0%
Informal influentials	32	8	24	33	17	19	10	0
Nonmobile regulars	15	13	24	0	36	25	28	40
Potential careerists	19	33	35	0	24	25	32	33
Noncareerists	8	42	11	67	16	12	2	27
Number of cases	84	24	17	12	42	36	50	15

Power salients appeared among the intermittent and sporadically active noncareerists as well as in other career categories: 8 per cent of the Democratic power salients, and 42 per cent of the power latents were found among noncareerists. Thus, although it was true that one was more likely to be conscious of the power goal of the Democratic party if he was a top organizational mobile, there was by no means a perfect concentration of power-consciousness or idealism by career classes.

If career status is only a partial answer, other internal organizational factors should be considered (Table 9.8). For example, it appeared that precinct leaders who had a very low awareness of the "state" of the organization were likely to have no goal perspectives at all for the party. In the Democratic party, particularly, few of the unaware (6 per cent) were power salients.[5] On the other hand, those who were very aware of the nature of the organization had absorbed a power goal-perspective at the same time that they learned the details of organizational operations. Therefore, power salients were not found among the organizationally ignorant in the Democratic party, though this was not true in the Republican party.

A final question to be answered is whether communication between precinct leaders and top district leaders is a critical factor in explaining goal perspectives. Does frequent contact at the top elite level lead to power-consciousness about party goals? Two-thirds of those who saw Democratic district leaders regularly were, indeed, power salient, but contact with district leaders was no guarantee that the power doctrine of the party would be communicated and absorbed (Table 9.8). This coincides with the finding in Table 9.1 that not all district chairmen and executive board members were *themselves* power salient. In the Democratic party, large proportions of precinct leaders who rarely or never came into contact with the top elite nucleus were very conscious of power as the party's goal. Therefore, although elite communicative contacts had some utility, they were by no means conclusive, and depended, to some extent, on which district

[5] See Chapter 5 for the "index of organizational awareness" used here.

TABLE 9.8

GOAL PERCEPTIONS BY DEGREE OF ORGANIZATIONAL AWARENESS AND COMMUNICATIVE FREQUENCY WITH THE TOP DISTRICT ELITE
(Precinct Leaders)

	Democrats					*Republicans*				
	Power salients	*Power latents*	*Idealists*	*No goal perspective*	*Number of cases*	*Power salients*	*Power latents*	*Idealists*	*No goal perspective*	*Number of cases*
Organizational awareness										
High	72%	13%	9%	6%	68	31%	24%	45%	0%	51
Doubtful	65	18	17	0	54	26	28	33	13	57
Ignorant	6	31	13	50	16	31	23	23	23	35
Communication with district leadership										
Often, frequently	66	16	14	4	101	37	28	34	1	86
Rarely, never	46	24	8	22	37	18	21	37	24	57

leaders one contacted. But this explanation is not completely satisfactory, since a special analysis was made of districts with power-salient chairmen, in contrast to districts whose chairmen were power latents. The finding was that a power-conscious chairman could have a relatively low proportion of power-conscious precinct leaders, as well as the reverse. The chairman did not seem, therefore, to be a principal indoctrinator of goal perspectives, due to his lack of personal control ("stratarchy"), as well as his brevity of tenure.

CONCLUSIONS

In attempting to determine the incidence of party goal-perspectives among leaders, we found a large minority at the two lower echelons of the structure who were not clearly conscious of the party as a "power group." From 20 to 45 per cent were "idealists" or unable to articulate a goal for the party. Theoretical definitions do not square perfectly with the empirical facts. If the party was primarily concerned with the drive for top power positions in the community, large numbers of party leaders were not aware of this. Party leaders were, however, more conscious of the power goal of a party than were members of the general public, two-thirds of whom did not reveal this perspective with clarity. There was, however, a considerable difference between the two parties in the Detroit area. It was consistently evident that the Republicans as the minority party rationalized their existence in other than power terms. Power as a goal was much more latent for Republican leaders, and Republican precinct leaders were willing to settle for "idealistic" conceptions of the task of the party.

In probing for factors to explain the differential goal perspectives in both parties, we found considerable evidence that the organizational climate of the party in a particular area, as well as the hierarchical status and relationships of the leader, may be relevant. For Democrats one found 77 per cent of the precinct leaders in doubtful precincts to be power salient, suggesting that the conditions of competition may be importantly related to power perspectives for the majority party in the metropolitan area, though not for the minority party. We found, further, that subcoalitions within the party structure varied in goal perspectives, some apparently seeing the party in power terms, others less conscious of power as a goal and perhaps less convinced of the party role as one of power. The top mobiles in the Democratic party tended to be power-conscious, but one found power salients, unexpectedly, among other career classes also. Further, organizational awareness and communication contacts were two variables of some value in explaining the incidence of goal perspectives.

The image of a party elite, recruiting and indoctrinating activists into a power-orientation toward party tasks, does not fit the empirical data very well. Too many nonmobile careerists with intermittent service records, and without communicative contact with the top elite were, indeed, power-conscious. In addition, a special analysis of Democratic precinct leaders revealed that only 51 per cent of those initially recruited for party work by politicians or through political organizations were power salients. This is not to deny that being in the Democratic party over time might have brought many activists to comprehend and accept the goal of the party as power, but the way in which this process of indoctrination occurred is not clear. It was, apparently, a process which was successful with some leaders while never successful with others, no matter how mobile, continuously active, or frequently in contact with the top elite they might be.

This suggests that a consciousness of power as the goal of the party is intimately related to the individual's own psychological makeup, his own ambitions, interests, and drives in political organizational life. Perceiving a party as power-winning may be part of a general motivational syndrome for the individual. To a certain extent, we found preliminary corroboration of this upon examination of Democratic precinct leaders' current motivations for politics and their own explanations of why they became active. There were two findings of interest:

1. While only 54 per cent of those who said they were

inducted into politics by others—politicians, group leaders, relatives, or friends—revealed a power orientation toward party goals, 74 per cent of those who claimed to have made the decision themselves were power-oriented.

2. Seventy-eight per cent of those precinct leaders who were admittedly in politics for personal satisfactions—to build a career, get a job, secure recognition, improve their business, etc.—were power-oriented. In addition, 70 per cent of those who were in politics for personal social rewards and gratifications were power-oriented. But only 44 per cent of those who had ideological motivations, and only 21 per cent of those who found no satisfactions they would miss if they had to leave political work, were power-oriented.

It seems, therefore, that individual motivation is clearly related to goal perceptions. While the organizational, competitive, and hierarchical milieu and status no doubt condition a party leader over time to an awareness of the party as a power group, his own internal drive and motivational predisposition have something to do with his susceptibility to organizational and environmental influences. As the political party adapts and rationalizes its existence in terms of the political terrain in which it must compete, the party leader also adapts his expectations concerning the party's goals to the power perspectives of others in the hierarchy, but only so far as his motivational predispositions coincide. Germans can enter the Democratic structure and become overtly power-conscious, while Republican German leaders will remain skeptics about the party goal of power. Polish leaders can enter the Republican party and be idealists, while 93 per cent of their Democratic counterparts are power enthusiasts. But there is always the nonconformist Pole or German with alien goal perspectives. The "open" party structure, encouraging autonomy and diversity in goal perspectives, is a structure in which the process of socialization and indoctrination is unsystematic, spasmodic, tenuous, and incomplete.

CHAPTER 10

LEADERSHIP ROLE PERCEPTIONS

It is one thing for a party leader to have a clear conception of the primary goal of the group; it is quite another, although related, matter for him to have a clear perception of his personal task or role as the holder of a position in the hierarchy. His own interpretation of his job is involved, as well as a recognition of the expectations others have about his job. Further, for an organization to be ideally effective, there should be clarity in the comprehension and evaluation of tasks associated with the positions held by others at all levels of the party structure. Although no one perspective can be considered more vital to group success than another, one would certainly hypothesize that an organization such as a political party loses effectiveness if roles are misperceived or improperly evaluated. A party with precinct activists, for example, who differ in their own role perception from that assumed by the top elite, may find itself with no effective cadre of workers implementing command strategy in the field, or with a set of precinct leaders operating independently and accountable to no central command.

We approached the study of roles empirically by asking leaders at each level to define and evaluate their own tasks as well as those of persons holding other positions in the party structure. We could philosophize at great length on party leaders' role perceptions, drawing upon a rich body of social-psychological and political literature. We were, of course, interested in the degree of bureaucratization within the party, the number of leaders who believed they possessed specialized skills (organizational, financial, communicative, etc.), how much feeling existed for personal responsibility in party decision-making, how much professionalism and amateurism was found, and many other role-behavioral problems. At the outset, however, prior to such analyses, we wished to look at the statements made by party leaders in attempting to explain their roles. In probing, we usually asked some variant of this basic question put to precinct leaders: "Aside from your routine duties, what do you consider to be your most important job or task?"

Although interechelon role perceptions will be examined more thoroughly later, it is important here to note the views which top party leaders held of the roles of those in the district organizations. The two state chairmen had very definite ideas about the conditions of their party in the Detroit area, the duties of those at the various levels of the party in Wayne County, as well as their inadequacies. Both men were critical of role fulfillment by district chairmen, for example. One state chairman felt that the major tasks of the *district chairmen* were to perfect an effective organization in their district, to improve internal communication, and to increase popular participation in party politics. But, he said, because of a lack of time and organizing ability, "they do not perform their duties adequately; they do not delegate enough; they are reluctant to give up powers; they are doing about 10 per cent of the work they could do." He concluded that the "district chairman is the bottleneck of too many operations." His fellow chairman was also critical of his district chairmen. He felt that their duty was organizational leadership, and the attraction or recruitment of people into the party through such leadership. But he said, "The type of people who are district chairmen are not the type who can lead. They came into the organization because they wanted something from it. The people who should be interested most are not."

The state chairmen's expectations concerning the roles of the *precinct leaders* differed somewhat but not essentially. There was no doubt that getting out the vote during the campaign was of central importance. One said very frankly that "their job is to deliver votes," but both also emphasized other aspects of the precinct leader's job. One chairman expressed it in the phrase "service organization." He said, "We need to be more of a service organization—disseminating propaganda and enrolling people to work" in the party. The opposing chairman took essentially the same broad view of the precinct leader's place in the party—to increase participation, to be consulted from time to time in the development of party programs, to discuss party policy with members in the precinct, to perfect organization records and files in preparation for the campaign. Both men particularly emphasized the need for precinct leaders who were interested in public issues and who provided an ideological foundation for the party. Both men also felt that although these were their role expectations, much had to be done in their respective organizations to measure up to these standards. The Democratic chairman perhaps felt somewhat more optimistic than his Republican counterpart about the progress already made in these directions and the possibilities for future improvement.

What did the district chairmen think of their own role? A careful listing of their own statements revealed a great diversity in interpretation—17 different kinds of substantive statements about the nature of their task. These included such widely varying duties as (percentages of all chairmen mentioning this role are in parenthesis): patronage distribution (75 per cent), financial solicitation (33 per cent), informing lower-level workers about party policy (82 per cent), concern for the recruiting of workers (67 per cent), screening candidates for public office (67 per cent), acting as "watchdogs" over the actions of elected representatives (44 per cent), perfecting the organization and instituting more discipline (92 per cent), providing a link between lower echelons and the county or state organization (64 per cent), educational leadership in the community (18 per cent), stimulating social activities in the party (55 per cent), providing economic help to the needy (18 per cent), promoting harmony among the party factions (92 per cent), coordinating campaigns and organizational units (100 per cent), stimulating interest in politics in the community (36 per cent), representing the interests of specific groups such as Negroes, businessmen, unions (67 per cent), and, finally, of course, "getting out the vote" (92 per cent).

These distributions in themselves are interesting. The small percentages of chairmen who were concerned with economic assistance, with stimulating political interest, and, relatively, with the watchdog function, are suggestive certainly of what the party leadership at the local level thought was *not* important. On the other hand, the fact that 12 of these role interpretations were mentioned by over 50 per cent indicates the great breadth of their tasks as these chairmen perceived them.

The range of such role statements in fact makes systematic role classification difficult. But perhaps some order can be realized from the diversity by looking at the data in terms of *three* basic dimensions—their roles in achieving the goal of winning party power, as internal organizational leaders, and as leaders of a party group interacting with and adapting to its environment. The basic question, then, is twofold: what did these chairmen define as their major task *and* their *primary "role type"*? Did they stress a "power-productive" orientation, an organizational "managerial" or "integrative" orientation, or environmental "adaptation"? A careful re-examination of the emphasis used in describing their roles indicates that most chairmen did indeed see themselves in all three leadership contexts and did tend to spell out the specific task that most preoccupied them in these contexts. All but one of the 12 chairmen had a clear view of a "power-productive" role—they expressed a concern for the recruitment of candidates, perfecting precinct campaign activities and campaign organization, training party workers in vote mobilization tactics, etc. Above all, 11 chairmen were rather explicitly aware of the importance of increasing or maintaining voting strength. For the other two role contexts, two-thirds of the chairmen emphasized their task of harmonizing factions (in the managerial context), and the same proportion saw themselves as ideological mentors (in the community adaptation and leadership context).

The problems of internal factionalism within districts were great for both parties, thus two-thirds of the chairmen saw their primary "managerial" role as one of mediating these conflicting forces. One Republican chairman, for example, stated: "The District Chairman (here) has to be a Sherlock Holmes. We have many splits in our party and there is a constant battle of wits as to who is for whom. Some factions try to trap you into making derogatory statements about Negroes, for example; then they use this against you. It was factionalism and hatred that killed Cobo in Detroit. We often fight with one another rather than discuss party issues. We have simply got to do away with factions. The party must be united to win." The number and type of factions referred to differed considerably: "old guard" and young "progressives," conservatives and liberals, racial and nationality groups, clubs versus the regular organization. Two of the chairmen went so far as to mention, respectively, eight and 11 separate "factions" within their districts with which they had to contend. It was clear that the remaining third of the chairmen who de-emphasized factionalism saw the job of perfecting the district hierarchy into an integrative unit as most important. "Pulling together" during campaigns, continually building the organization by filling precinct positions, maintaining contact with the lower echelons, and seeing that all levels worked together as a team in the promotion of party activities were cited as some of their duties. In this sense they shared the view of their role held by the state chairmen.

Less explicit was their articulation of "adaptive" roles in the community. The Republican chairmen, particularly, were not too conscious of such a role and tended to de-emphasize it. Two Republican chairmen were in fact so vague, talking in generalities about a need for better "public relations," that it is doubtful whether they could be considered aware of such a role expectation. One Democrat was quite candidly a representative of, and linked with, a particular social group and claimed he maintained a close relationship with this group. One Democrat was of the "old-style" variety, predominantly conscious of social welfare.

The remainder of the chairmen (eight of the 12) had some feeling of "ideological mentorship," i.e., leaders who felt that issues were very important, that the community had to be educated on these issues (not that the public's views were to be "followed"), and that party leaders had a definite responsibility for "leading" community opinion and stimulating community action.

The district chairmen discussed the roles of *executive board members* at considerable length, but with varying emphasis. One chairman took the position that "the District Board runs the district, by calling the plays on nominations and patronage." Another claimed that a steering committee of the executive board "did the back-room work," making basic policy and strategy decisions. Other chairmen were less impressed, one claiming that the board rarely met because of problems of factional conflict. Seven of the 12 chairmen seemed to consider the executive board an important cog in the party structure, while five were not very enthusiastic. These differences in role evaluation may of course have stemmed from structural differences in the district organization. In some districts there was no party position between the statutory board of 15 and the precincts, while others had from one to three intervening echelons: area (or ward or zone) chairmen, division chairmen, section chairmen. The executive board was elaborately legitimized in some districts, with a great proliferation of subcommittees holding special responsibilities, while in other districts there was none of this apparatus and minimal consciousness of the executive board's organizational possibilities or its prestige.

The types of roles played by the executive board were almost exclusively organizational in character. The board, when it was effective, made some policy, screened candidates for office, maintained contact with precinct leaders or leaders at the "area" or "section" level, decided on patronage, discussed issues, determined district campaign strategy. In those districts where members of the executive board also held intermediate echelon positions, as area or section chairmen, they were perceived as go-betweens linking the precinct level and the district level, communicating policy, recruiting precinct-level leaders, and, in a few cases, training precinct leaders for campaign work. The picture that emerges, therefore, is not uniform. But where executive boards were important units in the structure they had a twofold role—decision-making on a variety of organizational policy problems, and a representative as well as oversight link between precinct leaders and the top executive elite. Two qualifications of this pattern should be noted, however. It seemed to be quite possible for district chairmen to de-emphasize the executive board's role and some inclination to do so, since the members may not have been choices for the board, elected as they are officially by the district convention. Second, most district chairmen, but not all, emphasized their personal meetings and contacts with precinct leaders. District chairmen placed great importance on the support of precinct leaders (for precinct delegates elected the district chairmen at the convention), and precinct leaders were also responsible for mobilizing votes.

Executive board members, then, were perceived as an intermediary cadre with primarily organizational roles and tasks. Their "power-productive" role was secondary and only indirect. And their role as leaders in the community, in the sense of adapting to the public with which the party must work, was never really mentioned at all by district chairmen.

How did executive board members visualize their own roles? First, not all of them considered the position significant. Three-fourths, in both parties, saw the job as important, though some of these had real reservations. One-fifth viewed their position as relatively meaningless in the party structure, with the remainder either unwilling to commit themselves, or unsure. This distribution coincided closely with the views of the district chairmen. In terms of role content, the executive board members referred to a great variety of expectations; again, one-fourth saw their job as "coordinating precinct work," another 15 per cent referred to specialized organizational skills they were presumed to have in building up the precinct structure and in conducting registration drives. Another 15 per cent mentioned their communicative link between the district and precinct levels, seeing their job as one of informing precinct leaders of the "party line" and transmitting precinct opinion to the district level. Another 35 to 43 per cent mentioned some specific representative role—factional delegate to the board, nationality group ambassador, union representative, youth auxiliary delegate, or hand-picked elite appointee to the board. This is a particularly interesting finding in view of the subcoalitional image of the party developed earlier. In addition, a few mentioned other role perceptions, such as the need for legal skills on the board, for example. About 12 per cent said forthrightly that they had no role or task. (The total added up to more than 100 per cent because some board members mentioned more than one role expectation.) The distribution of role statements can be summarized in the following way, by party:

(Percentage of board members of a party mentioning a specific type of role)

	General organizational work	Specialized skills	Representative roles	No task	Other
Democrats	65%	0%	35%	18%	6%
Republicans	70%	17%	43%	9%	0%

Considerable congruence existed, therefore, in the views of the district chairmen and board members as to the roles of the executive board. More specification of role appeared when one talked to the board member, but generally there was agreement that he had an organizational set of tasks which varied, however, from one area to the next. He mediated between precinct and district chairmen, was an organizational overseer, and a communicative as well as representative link. He did not perceive himself as expected to get the vote out directly, nor was he conscious of an adaptive leadership role in the community, at least these were not the most salient expectations. In sum, the executive board member belonged to an intermediate cadre of upward-aspiring activists whose specific tasks were not unanimously defined but whose general position in the party was uniformly perceived as that of both secondary-level "manager" and representative.

One would expect the precinct leader, in his role perception, to exemplify the "power-productive" character of the party structure. We have seen that the district chairman operated in all three role contexts—winning power, running the organization, and interacting with the community, especially as an ideological leader. The executive board, however, saw itself primarily as an organizational-integrating force. Since "the votes are in the precincts," we might assume that the vote-mobilization task would be impressed on the minds of the precinct leaders. As Avery Leiserson has put it: "the central function of the precinct organization is to carry the precinct for the party"; and, "the display of reliability and efficiency (by the precinct leader), rather than of original ideas and personal prominence before the electorate, is statistically the approved way to start up the ladder within the organization."[1]

Yet, an examination of empirical facts indicates precinct leaders' roles cannot be defined so simply. When asked what they considered their major task, a majority did not respond immediately that it was delivering votes. The actual distribution for the two parties, using our previous categories, is given in Table 10.1. From this distribution one can see that precinct leaders had by no means accepted the doctrine that their *primary* task was vote production. They actually saw themselves in an important "adaptive leadership" role in the community, much like the district chairmen—a role perception executive board members generally did not share. Thus at the apex and at the base of the hierarchy the parties contained leadership conscious of its interactive potential with the public. Less than one-fifth saw this interaction as exclusively part of the old New Deal era

[1] *Op. cit.*, pp. 188, 192.

TABLE 10.1
Distribution of Role Perceptions for Precinct Leaders

Roles	*Democrats*	*Republicans*	*Total*
Vote mobilizer	45%	45%	45%
Ideological mentor	24	23	24
Social-economic welfare promoter	22	14	18
Have no role at all	9	12	10
Not ascertained	0	6	3

stereotype of getting jobs for people, attending funerals, fixing traffic tickets, and providing for the needy. Though some still insisted on the priority of the service role, one-fourth thought of themselves in the "ideological mentor" role. That is, they felt their job was to define and explain public issue alternatives to the voters, to educate and inform the public about government generally, to instigate neighborhood action, and to fight for particular social legislation. This does not mean that they had no sense of responsibility for vote mobilization—after all, they were aware, theoretically, of the pressure from above to keep voter records up to date, engage in campaign activities, and conduct house-to-house canvasses. But at least 40 per cent of the precinct leaders either considered such voting efforts secondary, or they took a broad-gauged view of how the party was to maximize its voting appeals. This view of their own role was held also by the two state chairmen, Mr. Staebler and Mr. Feikens, though not as clearly articulated by either. From our interviews with district chairmen it was obvious that only two or three of them had this conception of the precinct leader's task. With few exceptions, district chairmen said that precinct leaders were important in the organization, and as influential, or more so, as executive board members. Their frame of reference, however, was different. District chairmen referred to the collective voting power of precinct leaders (in the party convention), to the importance of precinct organizations in rounding up the vote, and only rarely, and then ambiguously, to the fact that precinct leaders were "closest to the people" and "in touch with public opinion." Only two district chairmen indicated that personal attention was given to training precinct leaders for the assumption of a community leadership or social welfare promotion role.

An interesting question arises about the efficient structuring of a party organization when only 45 per cent of those at the grass roots say their primary job is vote mobilization. On the surface this might seem dysfunctional to the success-maximization goal of the party. Yet, this must remain an open question until further analyses are made. It may very well be that the ideological mentor and social-welfare promoter is just as efficient in winning or holding the precinct for the party as the overt vote mobilizer. A further question which must also be held in abeyance pending further analysis and interpretation is whether a party system with this type of role structure from top to bottom is not in essence a better balanced set of groups functioning more meaningfully in the society and the polity than a party system in which the political groups are exclusively role-conscious in a power-winning sense. Certainly, despite allegations about party politics in the United States to the contrary, it is significant that at the lowest echelons a sizeable percentage of activists had resisted the doctrine of the decline of ideology and saw as most salient their job as ideological surrogates for the community.

A revealing by-product of investigation was the set of views of party leaders concerning the importance of their leadership in influencing the political behavior of the public. We asked respondents to rank the opinions of "leaders of a political party" (as well as the opinions of "close friends," "family members," "religious leaders," "union leaders," "employers and business leaders," "nationality or racial group leaders") as "very important," "somewhat important," or "not very important" in "helping people decide how to vote." The relative self-esteem of party leaders can be seen in Table 10.2.

Party leaders tended to have a higher esteem of their own opinion influence than did the public. This perception correlated

TABLE 10.2

RANKING OF IMPORTANCE OF LEADERS' OPINIONS BY PARTY (PRECINCT) LEADERS AND THE PUBLIC

	Precinct leaders	*Public cross-section**
Party leaders' opinions:		
Very important	45%	19%
Somewhat important	34	32
Not very important	20	49
Which opinions most important?		
Party leaders	24	21
Union leaders	26	7
Family members	17	25
Nationality or racial leaders	12	2
Close friends	10	9
Religious leaders	6	14
Employers and business leaders	2	7

* Percentage of those whose opinion could be ascertained.

well with the insistence of a large number of precinct leaders on their role of community leadership and interaction.

The image of the public differed substantially from that of the party leadership. At least 25 per cent of the public was unsure of the opinion influence role of various sectors of community leadership. But those who did commit themselves felt that union and nationality, or racial, leaders were less important than did precinct leaders, and placed somewhat more importance on the role of religious and business leaders. This differential image of political reality raises interesting questions about the perspectives of party leadership in activating the vote. This matter of the "realism" of party leadership will be examined with more care and detail in an ensuing section. Here it is important to note two tendencies. One is that the majority of grass-roots party leadership sensed the importance of its own influence role. The other observation is that, despite this tendency, one-fifth of the local leadership felt they were not influential at all, corresponding to the finding that 13 per cent of precinct leaders were unable to explicate their primary role in the party structure. The implications of these tendencies will be analyzed in Part IV in our discussion of the "functional" competence or relevance of the party machine in the social and political system.

Role expectations or assumptions apparently varied greatly among party leaders, particularly precinct leaders. A central question to be posed, therefore, is why this variation, and under what political and social conditions does one or another type of role-perception motif develop? What types of precinct leaders in what organizational and/or social context are inclined to see themselves as "ideological mentors," "welfare promoters," and "vote mobilizers"?

Congressional district organizations differed greatly in the emphasis used by precinct leaders in defining their roles. Among Democrats, for example, three-fifths of those in the 15th District but only one-third in the 1st District defined their role primarily as vote mobilizing. On the other hand, over 50 per cent in the 1st District considered themselves ideological mentors, while less than 10 per cent in the 16th District assumed this role. Similarly, among Republicans, the highest percentage of vote mobilizers (75 per cent of precinct leaders) were found in the relatively competitive 14th District, while only one-fourth were in the 16th District. The ideological mentor role did not vary as greatly among Republicans, though the 16th was high (34 per cent) and the 13th was low (11 per cent). Thus, in both parties, in districts where the smallest percentage of precinct leaders declared their job was vote mobilization, the highest percentage claimed to be ideological leaders. There was also a tendency in both parties for precinct leaders in those districts which were least sure Democratic to be vote mobilizers.[2]

Significant, too, for both parties, were those districts in

[2] The one important exception was the Democratic 17th, which was somewhat marginal but had a fairly even distribution of precinct leaders in all three role categories. This may have been due to the personal battle between the congresswoman in this district and the district chairman, with the former developing her own campaign organization, she maintained. It also must be remembered that such a balancing of roles may not in any sense be assumed as dysfunctional to party success in a district.

which the chairman was apparently most conscious about precinct delegates, asserted they were very important, claimed he saw them regularly, *and* had articulated a district organizational apparatus through which precinct leaders, he said, were consulted on party policy, trained for party work, and informed on party affairs. In these districts, two Democratic and two Republican, practically no precinct leaders replied "nothing" when asked to define their primary tasks or duties. There is a strong suggestion here, then, that these variations in role perception were linked to the competitive status of the district and the organizational plan for precinct leader communication and indoctrination.

An examination of precinct leaders' roles by the competitive status of the precinct itself (Table 10.3) adds to this analysis, and to some extent questions it, by indicating more precisely that both parties had the highest concentrations of vote mobilizing in sure Republican precincts. Although marginal precincts had a high proportion of Democratic vote mobilizers, they were not the highest.

The "get out the vote" doctrine had been communicated to the precinct leaders for the same types of districts, but with different strategy goals in mind—the Republicans seeking to hold their bastions of precinct voting power, the Democrats seeking to attack where they were weakest. Of course, role perception is not the same as "role activation," and it remains to be seen by later analysis to what extent precinct leaders' activities coincide with role evaluations. Nevertheless, it was not the doubtful precincts which revealed the heaviest concentration of overt vote mobilizers, but the definitely Republican precincts, indicating that the Democrats were competing with a vote-conscious set of precinct leaders in their weakest areas of strength. These data suggest also that the sure Republican precincts were the locale in which there may have been the most straightforward "struggle for votes," while in other precincts other types of leadership activity may have been more important. Finally, the Republican leaders were least conscious of their role in the sure

TABLE 10.3

PRECINCT LEADERS' ROLE PERCEPTIONS BY PRECINCT COMPETITIVE STATUS
(Proportions of Leaders in Each Precinct Type)

Precinct type	*Democrats*				*Republicans*			
	Vote mobilizers	*Ideological mentors*	*Welfare promoters*	*No role*	*Vote mobilizers*	*Ideological mentors*	*Welfare promoters*	*No role*
Sure Democratic	37%	30%	28%	5%	41%	22%	10%	19%
Sure Republican	66	10	7	14	60	11	9	9
Doubtful	47	20	20	13	36	36	26	3

Democratic precincts: almost one-fifth had no role perception at all.

When we join our data on the party career status of precinct leaders with role perceptions we find two career classes (those who had been party regulars and those who had achieved some upper mobility status) were least conscious of a vote-mobilization role (Table 10.4). It appeared that those precinct leaders who had served a long time in the organization without moving upward continued to work at the precinct level but perceiving themselves primarily as more broad-gauged community leaders. Vote mobilization became secondary to a great majority, about 70 per cent, of them. Similarly, from two-thirds to three-fourths of the top careerist elite among the precinct leaders, who had achieved higher positions while continuing as precinct leaders, also had a broad-gauged role perception. Vote mobilization was secondary to them, also. On the other hand, noncareerists were still relatively vote-mobilization-conscious, and thus of real value to the party machine despite their sporadic activity. But they included the largest percentage—about 30 per cent—of those who perceived themselves as having no role at all. It was the "informed influential" and "potential careerist" groups who were the vote mobilizers—those who were hoping for some eventual formal position in the hierarchy, who saw getting out the vote as the role most likely to result in political advancement. Above all, these data reveal again the great variety of personal role interpretations which prevail in a party, and suggest that the leader's own image of his present and future relationship to the hierarchy conditions his definition of his primary role. Perhaps vote mobilization is still the accepted avenue for recognition for the aspiring newcomer. But long-time precinct leaders who had begun to ascend in the hierarchy were more likely to define their job in less narrow terms. Perhaps this was because they visualized the party's place in the community in broader terms than winning elections, or they had a clearer view of how parties win elections.

In pursuing this last possibility, we correlated our data on

TABLE 10.4

CAREER STATUS AND ROLE PERCEPTIONS OF PRECINCT LEADERS
(Proportions of Leaders in Each Career Status)

Career status	*Democrats*				*Republicans*			
	Vote mobilizers	*Ideological mentors*	*Welfare promoters*	*No role*	*Vote mobilizers*	*Ideological mentors*	*Welfare promoters*	*No role*
Top organization mobiles	22%	17%	61%	0%	38%	54%	4%	0%
Informal influentials	60	8	22	11	68	0	21	5
Non-mobile regulars	29	43	29	0	32	14	32	7
Potential careerists	57	38	6	0	43	28	8	20
Noncareerists	44	20	0	32	63	0	6	31

party goal perspectives with role perceptions, with striking results (Table 10.5). It is clear that a close correspondence obtained between the two sets of perspectives. Those who did not articulate party goals in terms of winning power did not define their own role in vote-mobilization terms. And those with no party goal perspective tended to be unable to explain the expectations concerning their own role. Almost 10 per cent of precinct leaders fitted into both categories and demonstrated complete unawareness of party or their own job requirements—a significant finding in itself. On the other hand, those who were very conscious of the party goal of winning power did not necessarily see their own role as primarily vote mobilization. Fully 50 per cent saw themselves as ideological mentor or social and economic welfare promoter. This finding seriously questions the assumption that the power-oriented party leader is single-minded in his devotion to vote maximization.

There seemed, in fact, to be two distinct types of grassroots party leaders from the standpoint of role perspectives, perhaps also two types of doctrine on the meaning of a party leadership role. While there was considerable evidence that the party did communicate the concept of vote mobilization, especially in the recent joiners and upward aspiring, and in certain competitive areas and specialized organizational contexts, yet this doctrine was by no means uniform. It appeared that for many party regulars and those with some achieved status, though they were aware that the *party* goal was power, they might or might not take the view that their own role was an expanded one involving much more than merely producing votes.

There was undoubtedly also a tendency for leaders from certain social strata and backgrounds to assume particular role interpretations (Table 10.6). But for three variables (race, sex, and religion) these differences seemed to be party-conditioned. Negro Democrats were not as frequently vote mobilizers as are white Democrats, though the same distinction was not as true among Republicans. It is interesting that practically one-half of the Negro Democrats saw themselves in an ideological role, while

TABLE 10.5

PARTY GOAL PERSPECTIVES AND ROLE PERCEPTIONS OF PRECINCT LEADERS
(Proportions of Leaders in Each Goal Category)

Party goal perspectives	*Democrats*				*Republicans*			
	Vote mobilizers	*Ideological mentors*	*Welfare promoters*	*No role*	*Vote mobilizers*	*Ideological mentors*	*Welfare promoters*	*No role*
Power salients	44%	24%	27%	5%	64%	12%	7%	5%
Idealists	0	53	41	0	0	54	34	8
Unoriented	0	33	0	67	0	6	0	94

TABLE 10.6

PERSONAL CHARACTERISTICS AND ROLE PERCEPTIONS OF PRECINCT LEADERS
(Proportions of Leaders in Each Demographic Category)

	Democrats				*Republicans*			
	Vote mobilizers	*Ideological mentors*	*Welfare promoters*	*No role*	*Vote mobilizers*	*Ideological mentors*	*Welfare promoters*	*No role*
Race								
White	51%	17%	20%	11%	45%	25%	11%	11%
Negro	25	47	28	0	40	14	30	17
Sex								
Male	49	19	20	10	39	26	17	10
Female	19	52	29	0	64	11	4	18
Education								
Elementary	45	5	30	20	44	0	0	25
High school	46	22	22	10	32	30	25	11
College	43	38	16	0	53	23	9	9
Religion								
Catholic	52	17	17	12	24	35	12	18
Protestant	40	29	31	0	46	21	16	11
Nationality								
Northwestern European	56	5	29	9	47	20	7	16
Central, southern and eastern European	43	30	12	16	35	25	20	12
Family income								
Under $6,000	45	32	23	0	40	12	10	26
$6–10,000	53	9	31	7	47	28	25	0
Over $10,000	30	39	3	24	40	32	12	8
Union membership								
Belongs	43	22	19	16	43	12	12	24
Officer	48	22	30	0	*	*	*	*
Not a member	47	29	21	0	44	25	15	7

little more than one-tenth of the Republican Negroes did. Sex functioned in contradictory ways also in the two party hierarchies, Democratic women leaders infrequently defining their role as vote mobilizing (19 per cent) compared to 64 per cent of Republican women. The Democratic women tended to be ideological leaders in role perceptions. Catholics again defined their roles differently in both parties—a majority were vote mobilizers in the Democratic party but many fewer in the Republican party.

For three factors (education, nationality, and family economic status) the differences seemed to be basic and uniform for both parties. Thus, it is significant that one found those leaders with only an elementary-school background most likely unable to articulate any personal role. Similarly, leaders with a northwestern European background were more inclined to think of themselves as vote mobilizers in both parties than those from a central, southern, or eastern European heritage. Middle-income leaders were somewhat more inclined to be vote mobilizers, although a party difference was also noticeable here—the wealthy Democrats were those who saw no personal role, while the poor Republicans had the same role perception. It may be that these were the deviants in role perception in both parties, their role interpretations reflecting an awareness that they did not fit into the party's socio-economic profile.

Union members were an unusual group within both parties—representing almost 70 per cent of the Democratic precinct leaders and 30 per cent of the Republicans. Union officers had clear role perceptions, but it is strange that relatively high percentages of nonofficer union members in both parties had difficulty (or skepticism) in defining their roles as leaders of a political party. This may have been due to ambivalence about party work, or the fact that they had been recruited for party work, or agreed to undertake party work with considerable reluctance or without adequate understanding of party tasks. They may also, of course, have had grave doubts about the efficacy of party precinct activity.

Returning to our "subcoalitional" and "deviant" analysis of

the party structures, we found no exclusive preoccupation by subgroup representatives with winning votes. There was a good deal of overt commitment so far as own role is concerned with promotion of individual welfare as well as with ideological objectives (Table 10.7). Negroes, Poles, and Irish in the Democratic structure articulated roles highly suggestive of subgroup consciousness. Only the business and professional Democrats were not group-welfare-conscious. There was much less awareness of own role as well as much less concern for promoting social and economic welfare in the Republican subcoalitional structures.

The white labor element in the Republican party was a peculiar group. They were split—43 per cent seeing no role for themselves, 46 per cent saying they were vote mobilizers. The English as a Republican subgroup were almost as divided. On the Democratic side the business and professionals were also split, but they were conscious of a role for themselves—50 per cent vote mobilizers, 43 per cent ideologues. The Irish Democrats divided a different way—50 per cent vote mobilizers, 44 per cent interested in social and economic welfare promotion.

The "deviants" in both parties, except for the German Democrats (who seemed to be ideologues) were as vote-mobilization-conscious as other subgroups. The English Democrats were particularly vote-conscious. Recruitment of deviants, thus, did not seem to mean that activists from these deviant groups would be less susceptible to indoctrination by the party in the success-maximization principle.

Democratic liberals were much less vote-conscious in role interpretations than were Republican conservatives. We arrived at this conclusion after an analysis of the role perceptions of the consistent liberals and conservatives in each party, contrasted to those who were inconsistent or took middle-of-the-road positions on current issues (Table 10.8). The two issues used here were foreign aid and medical assistance through governmental action. The data revealed that one-third of the Democratic liberals viewed themselves as vote mobilizers, in contrast to 63 per

TABLE 10.7

ROLE PERCEPTIONS OF SUBCOALITIONAL AND DEVIANT GROUPS
(Precinct Leaders)
(Proportions of Leaders in Each Subcoalition)

Democratic subgroups	*Vote mobilizers*	*Ideological mentors*	*Welfare promoters*	*No role*
Negroes	25%	47%	28%	0%
Poles	38	6	32	25
Irish	50	0	44	6
Other labor				
Officers	27	33	40	0
Nonofficers	65	15	0	20
Business and professional whites	50	43	7	0
All union members	43	22	19	16
All Germans	0	91	9	0
All English, Welsh, and Scottish	64	0	18	18

Republican subgroups	*Vote mobilizers*	*Ideological mentors*	*Welfare promoters*	*No role*
Business-managerial whites	50%	30%	11%	9%
Other white collar (whites, northwestern European)	35	18	18	29
Labor whites	46	11	0	43
Negroes	40	14	30	17
All Germans	65	4	4	27
All English, Welsh and Scottish	43	7	11	39
Irish and Poles	39	33	28	0

TABLE 10.8

IDEOLOGY AND ROLE PERCEPTIONS OF PRECINCT LEADERS
(Proportions of Leaders in Each Ideology Category)

	Democrats				*Republicans*			
	Vote mobilizers	*Ideological mentors*	*Welfare promoters*	*No role*	*Vote mobilizers*	*Ideological mentors*	*Welfare promoters*	*No role*
Consistent liberals	37%	16%	35%	12%	*	*	*	*
Consistent conservatives	*	*	*	*	63%	22%	13%	0%
Inconsistent or middle of the road	50	43	7	0	29	29	20	16
Don't know, and not ascertainable	63	19	15	0	58	18	3	6

* Too few cases for analysis.

cent of the consistent Republican conservatives. In role definition, therefore, the conservatives seemed more alert to their vote-production task as party leaders. Perhaps more surprising is the fact that such a small percentage—no more than one-fifth or one-sixth of the consistent "ideologues"—actually assumed an *ideological* leadership role. This attests again to the low level of ideological saliency for many leaders. The Democrats were more inclined to be welfare promoters, the Republicans to be interested in votes. With 12 per cent of the Democratic liberals inarticulate on role, the consistent liberals seemed somewhat more confused than did the consistent conservatives. It was the ideological "fence-straddler" who was more vote-conscious and aware of his role in the Democratic party, while the Republican "fence-straddler" seemed less aware of his role and less inclined to be alert to his job of rounding up the votes in the precinct.

The power apex of each party was in charge of personnel with fairly clear role perceptions. They were aware of their jobs in a "power-productive," "community leadership," and managerial-organizational sense. Perhaps the Democrats in the Detroit area were more alert to their community adaptation responsibilities than were the Republicans. The internal management problems which beset a district chairman, however, were such in both parties that the top elite needed to concentrate the great proportion of its time on coordination, communication, and harmonizing the elements of dissension and factionalism in a local party structure. The secondary cadre of board members were strictly communicative links and representative agents of the precincts, performing organizational tasks of oversight and liaison.

It was at the base of the structure that one found a wide and unexpected role proliferation. The precincts in both parties were led by men and women with great variation in role interpretation. A majority did not see their *primary* task as vote maximization. Many felt they were ideological leaders or educators in the community, or charged first of all with the task of attending to social and economic demands of the party's constituent clientele groups. This may have been the result of the subcoalitional character of party structures. Over 10 per cent saw themselves as having no role at all. This means that the command posts in the field were populated with leaders who saw their tasks differently, however well they might perform as leaders. Why they differed in role definition is not absolutely clear, but the data suggest that the type of district party elite to which they were subordinate, and by which they were indoctrinated, may be of some relevance. Further, that the type of precinct, competitively, in which they found themselves may also be relevant. Then, too, the length of tenure in party work and the extent of their upward mobility in the hierarchy seems important—interestingly enough those who were newcomers were more likely to call themselves "vote mobilizers," while the others might define their role less narrowly. Finally, the leader's social and personal background and subgroup connections may also be related. The proliferation of role perceptions, explicable by these variables—organizational status, political milieu, personal characteristics—and so closely linked to one's view of the party's goal as well as to one's own career aspirations suggests that it is indeed a diffuse organizational and personal context by which roles are assumed.

Three observations seem overriding in this analysis. A minority of precinct leaders parroted the classical doctrine of students of party politics that precinct leaders had as their major task "getting out the vote." Second, parties did not communicate one particular role conception to rank-and-file leaders. The party line, if there was one, was confused and poorly communicated. There was much individualization and autonomy, apparently, in the taking on and defining of party leadership roles. Finally, a rather interesting balance of role interpretations emerges from our analysis—45 per cent vote mobilizers, 24 per cent ideological leaders, 18 per cent socio-economic welfare promoters. This raises significant questions. Is this balance conducive to effective party teamwork and immediate goal implementation? Does it mean that parties are effective functional groups at the grass roots in the community and the neighborhood? In Part IV we shall return to these basic queries in an analysis and discussion of the "functional competence" of parties in the society and the political system.

CHAPTER 11

MOTIVATIONAL DIVERSITY IN THE PARTY HIERARCHY

Crucial for the party's survival is the satisfaction of the personal needs of activists in the party structure. Motives of leaders, probably more than any other perspective, determine the character of the individual's relationship to the party, as well as the drive potential of the group collectively. Nothing is so disintegrative as leadership motives which diverge and detract from the implementation of party group goals. Ideological positions of leaders may, indeed, conflict; yet one senses that divergent issue positions are not critically dysfunctional to leadership activity. Interpretations of party goals may be contradictory or unclear; yet the activist continues to work energetically. Role perceptions may vary; yet he maintains his position, oblivious to the task definitions assumed by others. Although these perspectives are relevant to the party's organizational style as well as to the unity with which leadership cadres carry on their operations, they do not necessarily define the "meaning" of party work for the individual leader. His drive to fulfill a salient personal need, however, is a variable of greater theoretical validity for understanding his relationship with the party. In this chapter we examine the kinds of needs expressed by party leaders and the extent to which leaders perceived these needs to be fulfilled. Such analysis will, it is hoped, contribute to our knowledge of the party as a viable social-psychological action system.

The data on political motivation in the party hierarchy are concerned with four major aims. First is a description of patterns of leadership motivation at one point in time for the three basic echelons in each party—precinct, executive board, and chairmen. We will relate our data to different concepts of motivation, distinguishing between the personally instrumental and exploitative and the "impersonal," socially normative, or group-value-directive. A second aim is to trace certain developmental patterns in motivation. In Chapter 6 we discussed at length the career entrance motivations of leaders in terms of the personal drives most prominent when they began party work. We seek here to analyze the extent to which these entrance motivations were continued or modified during the period prior to our interviews in 1956. Further, we are interested in the phenomenon of political socialization as it relates to motivational development, particularly party differences, organizational milieu differences, and the effect of changed party leadership status on the alteration of motivational perspectives. Third, we wish to correlate again a variety of personal and social characteristics with motivational interests, to determine the relative contribution of certain social categories and subcoalitions to the emergence of the key motivational types. Finally, we intend to examine the political party collectively as a structure of motives. The basic question here is: Does "motivational pluralism" exist, and if so does it reflect such irreconcilable demands for gratification by leaders that the party as a group cannot successfully implement these personal drives? Or does such "motivational pluralism" merely reflect a predictable and natural differentiation in human needs with which the party can cope as a balanced social group without impairing the efficient pursuit of its political goals?

VOLUNTARISM VERSUS PERSONAL REWARDS

Party leaders at the lower echelons gave a great variety of answers when asked about their major satisfactions. The two state chairmen themselves, however, explained in very similar ways the motives of their activists, and in general perceived many activists as group-conscious "volunteers." One chairman said some were active out of a desire to "help shape events," others wished to associate with top politicians, and still others merely enjoyed working and associating with like-minded people. The other chairman also said that being a "part of something" and participating in the excitement of a campaign was important, emphasizing especially that for many the opportunity for meeting and working with friends was most significant. Both men felt the Democratic workers had a greater personal stake in politics than the Republicans. As one chairman commented: "Many Republicans are not hungry enough for the experience of participation in politics—they have a pretty good economic base and social life and thus have no need for the social aspect of political life. The Democrats seem to work for a political goal, and the Democratic party has worked on the psychic have-nots." Both men desired more "voluntarism" in political activity and de-emphasized the importance of patronage. One chairman claimed "there is very little patronage to dispense, and it would make very little difference if it were increased or decreased. It should be abolished as a reward for party service." For the other chairman patronage "has now only a symbolic effect; the people we appoint symbolize the party and the choice always brings out a show of force; I am not in favor of much patronage, it is a device for crystallizing groups in parties. It would not make much difference to the party if it were abolished. A little is helpful." These views were generally echoed by the county chairwomen, although one of them said, "Many people feel they should belong to a party to gain patronage. We might win more votes if there was more patronage."

This "voluntaristic" conception of party worker motivation was not unanimously shared by the men responsible for the district party machines. All of them admitted that there was patronage to be dispensed, and usually explained at some length the procedures for consultation on patronage. Almost all, however, agreed that patronage had decreased. Of interest was the fact that only one chairman spoke critically of the idea of patronage (calling it the "curse of American politics"), while seven chairmen were frankly critical of civil service and desired more patronage as a means of building up their own organizations. There was a clear-cut indication in both parties that the congressional district elite felt more people could be attracted to party work, and turnover in the precincts diminished, if party work was less altruistic and volunteer. The district chairmen were willing to admit that many people entered party work "to improve their own lot," socially or economically, and that it was difficult to satisfy these workers without more political largess to distribute. It is interesting to note in this connection that 33 per cent of the district chairmen of both parties held governmental positions in the Detroit area, 20 per cent of the executive board members did, and only 10 per cent of the precinct leaders.

A basic conflict seems to exist, then, between the "voluntaristic" ideal type of party worker conceived by the state chairmen, and the real "personal-reward motivated" person at the grass roots with whom the district chairmen perceived they had to contend. Implicit in this difference of opinion are two types of questions about party worker motivations: Are party workers involved because they see this work as "personally instrumental," as satisfying some personal interest, or are they involved impersonally for the purpose of "group realization," in order to "do a job" as a citizen or as a loyal group supporter? And if they see their work as "personally instrumental," what type of satisfactions are most prominent in their minds? The data on the various echelons of the party hierarchy will help describe the contemporary motivational patterns in the two parties in terms of these conceptual categories.

A political party machine has two tasks: keeping its hard-core activists personally satisfied, and at the same time marshalling its best efforts in mobilizing votes for support of its elective leadership. A political party which can dispense patronage, in jobs or in other forms to 100 per cent of its activists can be a highly effective political team, as other studies have shown.[1]

[1] See, for example, Gosnell, *op. cit.*, Kurtzman, *op. cit.*, or Rossi *et al.*, *op. cit.*

Today, however, in most communities such a completely patronage-based machine is rare. In Detroit, patronage as a reward for party service was possible for only a small minority of activists. This created for the party the dilemma of satisfying those who seek personal rewards, while moving the party ahead toward its political objectives, and this was no mean task. In Detroit almost 50 per cent of the precinct activists in 1956 had begun work only recently; almost one-fourth had no experience prior to 1956. This high turnover underscores the problems of motivational fulfillment. Are the motivational expectations of American party workers such that their personal relationship to the party will in all probability be tenuous and short-lived? Do they enter the party with drives which are eventually unfulfilled and thus induce frustration?

The study of "motivation" is admittedly a difficult undertaking, and we should be clear about the conceptual context in which it was pursued in our study. It is difficult *for the researcher* because of the many meanings and connotations attached to the term. It is difficult *for the political leader* who is asked direct or indirect questions about motivation, either because he is unwilling to explain his motives frankly, or because he is confused about his actual primary and secondary personal interests in political party work. Which terms are most meaningful or "real" to the party worker—"aspiration," "drive," "motivation," "interest," "satisfaction," or "reward"? And what indirect evidence, admitting that all party leaders cannot be forthright and frank, is acceptable and demonstrative? Our investigation proceeds on the assumption that "motivation" is a "three-layer phenomenon." We believe, first, that every individual has deeply imbedded "needs" which he feels, with greatly varying intensity, must be fulfilled—prestige, power over others, feelings of contributing to some social goal, economic status, social interaction, etc. These "needs" lead to "drives" or determinations to satisfy these "needs," though again, with varying urgency. The consequence of the activation of these "drives" over time is a resultant feeling of some degree of fulfillment (or nonfulfillment) of needs, or "satisfaction" (dissatisfaction). In interviewing party leaders about their "motivations" we can certainly secure some evidence of whether they sense a "satisfaction," and of whether the particular substantive type of satisfaction which they claim has or has not been fulfilled. We can also attempt to deduce from this and other interview responses what the "drives" and "needs" of the party leader were, or are. But we should not delude ourselves into thinking that we have secured complete insight into the motivational orientation of the leader. The fact that he tells us he has secured a certain satisfaction from the social contacts, or economic gain, concomitant with his career in the party is not necessarily the whole motivational picture. He may hide from us the fact that there were other "needs," such as a craving for personal political recognition, evoking "drives" which were never implemented. Thus, in presenting our data on "motivation," we wish it to be understood that these data may only be describing the peak of the "motivational iceberg." We will discuss "satisfactions" or "rewards" (the things people say they would miss if they were forced to leave party politics), and these may be probes in depth of basic personality needs and drives, but we cannot be sure.

HIERARCHICAL DIFFERENCES IN WORK SATISFACTIONS

What type of responses did we get from party leaders about "satisfactions" derived from party work, or what they would "miss" if forced to drop out of political activity tomorrow? As Table 11.1 reveals, the "satisfactions" differed for both parties, and by leadership status.

If these data are accepted under the conditions used in securing them, and despite obvious limitations, they do show some interesting contrasts.

Precinct leaders in both parties frankly revealed the personally instrumental nature of their involvement much more readily than did leaders at the upper echelons. This was particularly distinctive in the Democratic party where 76 per cent

TABLE 11.1

CURRENT SATISFACTIONS FROM PARTY WORK

	Chairmen and executive boards		*Precinct leaders*	
	Democratic	*Republican*	*Democratic*	*Republican*
Personally instrumental satisfactions				
Social contacts	21%	34%	63%	47%
Political fun (and inside information)	4	10	12	8
Business, economic, and political gain	25	24	1	1
Group and society-related satisfactions				
Moral and philosophical satisfactions	21	17	4	3
Ideological or issue satisfactions	29	10	3	17
No satisfactions received (nothing would be missed)	0	3	15	22
Number of cases	24	29	138	143

of the precinct leaders, contrasted to 50 per cent of the upper elite, gave such responses. Precinct leaders were also willing to admit their low level of motivational fulfillment—15 to 22 per cent—admitted there was nothing to be missed by leaving party work. But the upper organizational leaders were more willing to reveal a personal political or economic drive satisfied through political work—one-fourth citing this as a major satisfaction, while only 1 per cent of the precinct leaders did. Contrary to expectations, the majority of party leaders did not lapse into philosophical rationalizations in explaining their satisfactions in party work. Not all of them appeared to be hiding their motivations and gratifications. The picture that emerges is one of considerable disillusionment motivationally among precinct leaders, coupled with high personal need fulfillment (especially a desire for social contacts and association with friends), and very few ideological-philosophical gratifications. Above all, politics seemed to be socially gratifying for a large percentage of precinct activists, while social interaction was either a less dominant need for the upper organizational elite or it may have been a need, but fulfilled adequately for only a small minority.

The question can well be raised: How much evasion existed at all levels—how much unwillingness to admit they were in politics for the fulfillment of personal, economic, or political objectives? A variety of evidence suggests that the percentages in the table are too low. Thus, though only 1 per cent of the precinct leaders openly admitted such needs existed, about 17 per cent had already demonstrated some upward mobility in the hierarchy, and from 10 to 12 per cent held some type of governmental position, or their husbands did (16 per cent of the Democratic precinct leaders, 9 per cent of the Republicans). Further, 57 per cent of the precinct leaders said they might aspire to a higher party position if it was offered them.[2]

Similar data are suggestive for higher echelon leaders. Although only one-fourth of these admitted deriving satisfactions related to personal economic and political power drives, over 70 per cent might conceivably have had such drives, based on the data concerning their past, attempted, or present governmental employment (42 per cent of the Democrats, 46 per cent of the Republicans), on their aspirations for governmental careers (67 per cent of the Democrats, 46 per cent of the Republicans), plus other indications that they saw politics as a means to implement their own personal ambitions. It is extremely difficult of course clearly and confidently to deduce "motivation" from upward organizational mobility or interest in, and tenure of, a governmental patronage position. But if one uses such indirect evidence, the probable proportions of those interested in a per-

[2] Using "aspiration" as a clue to "motivation" seems highly questionable. A person may be willing, even eager, to move to more responsible positions in the hierarchy, and yet his personal linkage to the party and the satisfactions he derives or expects from party work may be other than personal political gain.

sonal economic and political power satisfaction is as shown in Table 11.2.

TABLE 11.2

PROPORTIONS OF LEADERS INTERESTED IN PERSONAL ECONOMIC AND POLITICAL POWER SATISFACTION

	Democratic	*Republican*
Chairmen	83%	83%
Executive board	78	70
Precinct leaders		
On the basis of governmental position held	16	9
On the basis of party organization mobility	17	17

Much more decisive data are necessary before determining to what extent personal entrepreneurial ambitions were primary. It is possible to consider the responses to direct questions about satisfactions as honest. Thus, while 17 per cent of precinct leaders *may have been* personal entrepreneurs about politics, most of them realized currently that this was not their primary satisfaction nor the reason they stayed in politics. Only 1 per cent may in fact have considered this the primary satisfaction, while the others stayed in politics for the reasons they gave us, with 15–22 per cent seeing no need fulfillment whatsoever in politics. By the same token, the vast majority of upper echelon leaders may have been personal entrepreneurs about politics at one time, but in fact may have reassessed the reasons for their involvement and their satisfactions. Only 25 per cent continued in politics because of the satisfactions of personal ambition, and the remainder genuinely experienced the fulfillment of other needs, particularly sensing more philosophical and ideological satisfactions from party work than did the precinct leaders. More "depth" data on motivational drives are needed to ascertain exactly which interpretation is correct.

NONCONGRUENCES IN MOTIVATIONAL PERCEPTIONS

Since the party is presumably an organizational team of workers, leaders' perceptions of the motivations of others, particularly in comparison with their own alleged motivations, are important, psychologically as well as politically. The two significant phenomena are, of course, "projection"—ascribing one's own motivations to others—and "incorporation"—assimilating the perceived satisfactions of others.

TABLE 11.3

MOTIVATIONAL PERCEPTIONS OF "OTHERS" AND "SELF"
(Precinct Leaders)

	Self perceptions							
	Democrats				*Republicans*			
Perceptions of "others'" motivations	*A*	*B*	*C*	*Number of cases*	*A*	*B*	*C*	*Number of cases*
Social contacts	87%	0%	13%	15	67%	0%	0%	18
Ideological satisfaction	68	6	9	53	43	22	6	81
Fun, excitement	40	0	0	23	56	25	0	16
	D	*E*	*F*	*Number of cases*	*D*	*E*	*F*	*Number of cases*
Personally instrumental	71	9	19	68	79	11	9	47
Impersonal task-oriented	82	5	11	62	51	29	20	84
Nothing—no rewards	*	*	*	6	18*	0*	82*	11

* Too few cases for reliable analysis.

Our data suggest minimal projection and incorporation (Table 11.3). The best examples of incorporation were, first, a small minority (11 to 13 per cent) of Republicans and Democrats who thought other precinct leaders were in politics for social contacts, and from 67 to 87 per cent of these groups who said that they were also in politics because of that satisfaction. Second, a very small minority of Republicans (8 per cent) said their fellow workers got no rewards out of political work, and 82 per cent of these admitted the same disillusionment. Such coincidence was the exception, however, rather than the rule.

In fact, if we invert Table 11.3 and ask what percentage of those who responded about "self" in a particular way ascribed the same motivation to others (the phenomenon of "projection"), we find a very limited amount of mutuality in motivational perceptions. Thus, although 63 per cent of the Democrats claimed their main satisfaction was social contacts, only 15 per cent of the group saw this as a satisfaction for other leaders. The same was true for Republicans—48 per cent saw social contact as the major satisfaction for self, but only 18 per cent of these perceived it as a primary motivation for others. Further, only 5 per cent of Democrats and 29 per cent of Republicans who said they derived no satisfactions from political work felt this was true for other party leaders.

Particularly significant, and indicative of the frankness with which these politicians responded, was the tendency to ascribe altruistic motivations to others but deny them for themselves. Of the Democratic precinct leaders, 36 per cent said that other leaders were receiving ideological satisfactions—working for things they believed in—but only 6 per cent claimed this satisfaction personally. The percentages for the Republicans were 57 per cent ascription of this satisfaction to others, but only 22 per cent of the group declaring this to be their own satisfaction. Conversely, 76 per cent of the Democrats and not quite 60 per cent of the Republicans claimed "personally instrumental" satisfactions for themselves, but only 46 and 45 per cent of these leaders, respectively, ascribed such motivations to others.

In sum, our analysis of specific motivational perceptions for others and self reveals that 84 per cent of the Democrats and 72 per cent of the Republicans did not share motivational perceptions. There seemed to be great confusion about why the "other fellow" was involved in party work, as well as a tendency to think that he was more ideologically committed and satisfied than was one's self, and than was realistically the case. Whether this condition resulted from misperceptions of reality, or from difficulty in generalizing about the satisfactions of others, the finding points to the incohesiveness of the party group as an action system. The existence of "motivational pluralism" in the organization has been demonstrated. We now find, in addition, the existence of marked confusion about why one's fellow workers were involved in political life. The resulting impression is that the local party organization was not a tightly knit associational team, but consisted, rather, of a set of individuals pursuing particular needs and deriving satisfactions, irrespective of the motivation of other workers. The party was a tangled web of personal motivational relationships between activists and the group, with a minimal amount of awareness by each activist of the motivations that drove his political confreres on with party work.[3] These findings are highly supportive, of course, of the "stratarchical" model of the party structure.

CAREER FACTORS AS EXPLANATIONS OF MOTIVATIONAL DIFFERENCES

As noted before, a high percentage of precinct leaders seemed to derive personal, social gratification from politics, with one-tenth seeing ideological-philosophical satisfactions as primary, and almost 20 per cent sensing no motivational fulfillment. Differentiations in terms of career tenure appeared, however, for the precinct leaders of both parties (Table 11.4).

One set of differences emerged when precinct leaders were grouped by the era in which they began party work. The recent joiners, since 1952 in the Republican party and since 1955 in

[3] When asked whether the party workers of the opposition differed "at all in the rewards and satisfactions which they get out of political activity," 53 per cent of all precinct leaders said there were no differences (65 per cent of the Democrats, 41 per cent of the Republicans), with about 10 per cent in both parties uncertain.

TABLE 11.4

ERA OF CAREER ORIGIN AND CURRENT SATISFACTIONS
(Precinct Leaders)

Career era (first campaign)	*Social contacts*	*Other personally instrumental satisfactions*	*Imper-sonal satis-factions*	*No satis-factions*	*Num-ber of cases*
			Democrats		
1956	53%	6%	0%	38%	32
1952–55	59	17	10	10	29
1940–51	73	10	3	13	30
1932–39	70	22	0	4	27
Before 1932	60	10	25	5	20
			Republicans		
1956	53%	19%	16%	9%	32
1952–55	42	0	17	42	36
1940–51	54	21	8	18	39
1932–39	40	0	47	13	15
Before 1932	48	0	38	14	21

the Democratic, seemed to be the most frustrated and at a loss to discuss their satisfactions with party work. Further, it is clear that long-time members were much more likely to be impersonally motivated and satisfied ideologically with party work. Over 40 per cent of the Republicans who began in party work before 1940 did not have a personal entrepreneurial motivational perspective, as was the case for one-fourth of the Democrats who began before 1932. Either of two explanations may hold: the old-timers may have been transformed into task-oriented ideologues over the years and thus lost a personal entrepreneurial approach to politics, or contemporary party leadership elites have been unable to recruit, educate, or transform the activist cadre, in keeping with their "voluntaristic" and "idealistic" model of the party organization.

A further analysis of precinct leaders by career status, using the categories suggested in an earlier chapter, indicates the relevance of this status to personal motivational relationships to the party (Table 11.5). Two characterizations are determined from these data. One concerns the top organizational mobiles (precinct leaders who have been conspicuously active, moved upward in the hierarchy, and aspire to higher positions). This group placed the highest premium on social contacts as a personally instrumental type of satisfaction most important for them. They were also the least disillusioned about party work (only 4 per cent in both parties said they would miss nothing if they had to leave party work). On the other hand, the noncareerists stood in sharp contrast. They were the most disillusioned (36–44 per cent), and they had a relatively low proportion deriving social gratifications

TABLE 11.5

MOTIVATIONS OF PRECINCT LEADERS BY CAREER STATUS

	Instrumentalists		*Ideologues and Philosophers*	*Disillusioned*	*Number of cases*
	Socializers	*Others*			
			Democrats		
Top organizational mobiles	83%	4%	9%	4%	23
Informal influentials	76	8	0	16	37
Nonmobile regulars	52	29	10	5	21
Potential careerists	59	25	3	13	32
Noncareerists	40	0	16	36	25
			Republicans		
Top organizational mobiles	67%	0%	29%	4%	24
Informal influentials	63	32	5	0	19
Nonmobile regulars	39	2	20	39	44
Potential careerists	35	18	30	15	40
Noncareerists	56	0	0	44	16

from politics. Aside from these findings, the differences are not generalizable for both parties. For example, the Democratic potential careerists were a socializing group, while the Republican potential careerists had a relatively high proportion of ideologues. The Republican nonmobile regulars were rather disillusioned, while the Democratic regulars still viewed party work in terms of personal rewards. These variations in the extent and type of satisfaction derived from party activity suggest, then, that career status differences may determine one's motivational emphasis, and, further, that generally only certain types of individuals with particular drives will succeed to top party career positions.

MOTIVATIONAL REORIENTATION

The foregoing leads into a discussion of developmental patterns in party worker motivations. We are, on the one hand, interested in the contemporary structure of political motivations in party organizations. We are also concerned with the modification and transformation of motivational perspectives in the party worker from the time he joined the party to the present. Is the party worker "socialized" over time, and do his personal needs, drives, and satisfactions change? Or does he come into the party with certain needs and motives which remain constant throughout his career and whose fulfillment condition his tenure in the organization? Since we asked party leaders why they first became active, as well as about their current satisfactions from party activity, a developmental analysis, though only suggestive, is possible.

Upper echelon party leaders were quite frank in admitting that they began their careers with a desire to fulfill personalized drives, and maintained this drive perspective, or changed to another personalized motivational orientation. The reverse tended to be true for the precinct leader (Table 11.6). The elite leader wanted something personal out of politics when he became involved initially, or he was soon socialized to this expectation. The precinct leader ordinarily did not assert that he thought in

TABLE 11.6

CHANGES IN GENERAL MOTIVATIONAL ORIENTATIONS DURING PARTY CAREER

	Upper echelons		*Precinct leaders*	
	Demo-crats	*Repub-licans*	*Demo-crats*	*Repub-licans*
Began with personalized motivation	67%	45%	26%	15%
Remained unchanged	75	92	97	57
Changed to or toward impersonal orientation	25	8	0	24
Became disillusioned	0	0	3	19
Began with impersonalized motivation	33%	55%	74%	85%
Remained unchanged	37	50	12	22
Changed to personalized motivation	63	50	68	57
Became disillusioned	0	0	20	21
Total percentage changing motivational direction	38%	31%	66%	73%
Number of cases	24	29	136	137

terms of personal gain when he began party work. However, the grass-roots activist soon took on personalized motivational perspectives, if he did not start out with them. This observation is borne out by our data: 60 per cent of the top elite began with personalized motivations and 79 per cent held such motivations currently, while only 21 per cent of the precinct leaders began with personal political drives and 68 per cent were thus motivated currently. In Detroit this was somewhat less true for the Republican precinct leaders—60 per cent were currently preoccupied with personal satisfactions as against 76 per cent of the Democrats. There was less tendency for the Republican precinct leader to discard his ideological-philosophical and task motivations.

It is also significant that the upper echelon leader did not vacillate, motivationally, during his career as much as the precinct leader. Only one-third of upper echelon leaders said that the satisfactions currently derived from politics differed from their original drives, while two-thirds of the precinct leaders said they had changed. This seemed to be related to hierarchical status or to other characteristics, and not to lengthy tenure in party service, since precinct leaders who began party work before 1940, but who had not become members of the elite corps, changed motivational orientation almost as much as did other precinct leaders (see Table 11.7).

The differences in motivational development by time period of entrance into party work are interesting. The old-timers (began party work before 1940) actually were more "personal-drive-conscious" when they began their work than those who began after 1940 (especially the "newcomers" group of 1952–56). But they tended to change more away from this personalized perception of relation to the party, or changed less to personalized motivations from impersonal motivations (the Republicans accounted for almost all of the difference here). Thus only 46 per cent of the old-timers were currently (in 1956) motivated by overt self-interest, while 62 per cent of the newcomer group and 83 per cent of the group joining the party cadre in the 1940–51 period were so motivated. Recent precinct leaders were much more likely to begin with idealistic motivations (from 73 to 94 per cent since 1940), but they took on personal motivations and left idealism behind much more than those with 15 to 30 years of party service.

Especially noticeable is the large number of idealistic recent joiners who became disillusioned. The "realists," except for Republicans who joined from 1940 to 1951, gave no inkling of disillusionment comparable to the feeling of dissatisfaction among those with impersonalized motivational directions.

We have noted before that at least 55 per cent of precinct leaders currently reported their primary satisfaction was social contacts and friendships. In one sense this is strange, because only 5 per cent reported this as the initial reason they began to work. What were the initial drives and what happened to them in the

TABLE 11.7

Motivational Constancy and Change By Era of Entrance Into Party Career
(Precinct Leaders Only)

	Era of career origin					
	1952–56		*1940–51*		*Before 1940*	
	Democrats	*Republicans*	*Democrats*	*Republicans*	*Democrats*	*Republicans*
Began with personalized motive*	14%	6%	27%	18%	40%	32%
Remained unchanged	100	100	100	43	94	50
Changed to impersonalized motivation	0	0	0	0	0	50
Became disillusioned	0	0	0	57	6	0
Began with impersonal motive	86%	94%	73%	82%	60%	68%
Remained unchanged	9	17	5	10	20	47
Changed to personalized motivation	61	56	77	81	75	29
Became disillusioned	30	27	18	9	5	24
Percentage changing						
From one specific motive to another†	96	77	53	91	74	65
From one category of motivation (personal, impersonal) to another‡	78	78	70	85	51	52
Number of cases	59	67	30	39	45	31

* The *N*'s in the subcells of this group were very small and the results are therefore suggestive only.
† The *N* used here is smaller than the total *N* indicated, because not all responses could be placed in precisely comparable categories.
‡ Includes changes to disillusionment ("nothing would be missed," etc.).

course of their careers (Tables 11.8 and 11.9)? Those who began with a desire to influence governmental policies (21 per cent of the sample) seem to have turned to personalized satisfactions. No Democrats, and only one-fourth of the Republicans remained ideologues. Those who began work because of a desire to help a candidate friend (12 per cent) were the most disillusioned group in the sample—over 50 per cent in both parties reported no current satisfactions. The philosophers, both those who said they began because "politics is part of my way of life" (11 per cent) or because they had to "fulfill a sense of community obligation" (20 per cent), were highly socialized in the direction of social contact and other personal satisfactions, with the Republicans tending to become quite disillusioned, and only a small percentage of these two categories combined remaining philosophical about politics (16 per cent Democrats, 12 per cent Republicans). One of the highly disillusioned groups was the "party loyalists," who began because of their belief in the party. From one-fifth to one-third of these were currently dissatisfied, and most had also become socialized in the direction of personalized expectations about politics. On the other hand, the Democrats who reported frankly that party work was for them meaningful from the outset in terms of a personal need or drive, overwhelmingly remained committed to this perception. This was not as true for the Republicans, as noted earlier, many of whom became dissatisfied (24 per cent) and some of whom shifted to an ideological motivational direction (24 per cent).

These patterns of motivational stability and change are indeed significant. They suggest that while grass-roots workers and leaders may have been recruited under the guise of the "voluntaristic-idealistic-impersonal-task-oriented" concept of party work outlined earlier by the two state chairmen, these precinct leaders in large numbers changed motivational direction during their careers. Many became disillusioned; the majority soon articulated personal demands, needs, and satisfactions to be derived from party activity. In reality this means that the majority of precinct leaders changed their motivational relationship

(Precinct Leaders)

Original perceived motive	Current satisfactions					
	Ideological achievement	*Other impersonal philosophical satisfactions*	*Social contacts*	*Other personalized satisfactions*	*No satisfactions*	*Number of cases*
Policy influence						
Democrats	0%	0%	58%	23%	19%	26
Republicans	26	12	44	14	3	34
Candidate friendship						
Democrats	0	0	38	0	56	16
Republicans	11	0	37	0	53	19
Philosophical orientation ("politics is part of my way of life")						
Democrats	9	23	59	9	0	22
Republicans	10	0	30	40	20	10*
Sense of community duty						
Democrats	0	0	77	14	5	22
Republicans	15	0	58	3	24	33
Party loyalty						
Democrats	13	0	33	13	33	15
Republicans	10	5	48	19	19	21
Personal drives: social contacts, fun, political position, business contacts, desire to be close to important people, recognition in community						
Democrats	0	0	81	15	3	35
Republicans	24	0	48	5	24	21

* Too few cases for reliable analysis.

Note: When the total percentages do not add up to 100%, the balance represents those who were unclear or unascertainable on current motivations.

TABLE 11.9

CURRENT MOTIVATION OF ALL THOSE CHANGING MOTIVATIONAL DIRECTION, BY ERA OF CAREER ORIGIN

Current satisfaction	*Era of career origin*						*Total*	
	1952–56		*1940–51*		*Before 1940*			
	D	*R*	*D*	*R*	*D*	*R*	*D*	*R*
Ideological	5%	3%	0%	5%	3%	44%	3	12
Other impersonal	0	8	0	0	0	0	0	4
Social contacts	56	49	73	57	80	36	66	49
Other personalized	12	10	9	19	11	0	11	11
No satisfaction	27	30	18	19	6	20	18	24
Number of cases	57	61	22	37	36	25	115	123

to the party. This is perhaps not unexpected, but the changers did not move in the direction of ideological rationalizations of party activities (except perhaps the old-timer Republicans who joined before 1940). Nor did they even become philosophical generalists about their tasks. They either became disillusioned, or they conceptualized their relationship in terms of social friendship satisfactions (66 per cent of the Democrats, 49 per cent of the Republicans), a desire to be "in the know" and gain prestige in the neighborhood (4 per cent of the Democrats, 6 per cent of the Republicans), or they saw other personalized satisfactions such as the enjoyment of the "fun and excitement" of a campaign (6 per cent of the Democrats, 4 per cent of the Republicans).

INCONSISTENCY IN PERSPECTIVIST PATTERNS

Not only was there great "mobility" in the precinct leader's motivations during his career, but his current perspectives toward party activity exhibited considerable disjunction. One might expect a certain consistency in the concentrations of activists in the perspectivist categories used in preceding chapters. The person who perceived his role as "ideological mentor," for example, and the person who was consistently liberal or conservative on public issues might be expected to give motivational responses indicating he derived the greatest satisfaction in party work from promotion of ideological causes. But this is not the case (Table 11.10). Less than one-fifth of the consistent ideologues in both parties seemed motivated and satisfied by ideological or philosophical interests. Less than one-tenth of the Democrats and only 30 per cent of the Republicans who defined their role ideologically derived their greatest satisfaction from the party ideologically. Further, only small percentages (6 per cent Democrats, 22 per cent Republicans) of those who saw the party's goal as fighting on the issues and problems of the day, related themselves personally to the party in these terms. Thus, the political orientations of party leaders were multidimensional, and their orientations toward the party were separable, not cumulative.

The one striking consistency of perspectives emerging from this analysis is that those activists who were unable to articulate the goal of the party, and those who had no clear perception of their own role, were definitely inclined to be disillusioned motivationally. Otherwise there seems to be a limited correlation between perspectives. The inconsistent ideologically were no less "socializers" than the consistent ideologues. The power salients, who saw the party's goal clearly in terms of winning elections and power, were distributed motivationally very similarly to those who had no such goal orientation for the party. Two general conclusions are suggested, then: (1) the particular content of a person's ideological position, or conception of what the party should be fighting for, or his own role in the party structure, was not necessarily related to the satisfaction he derived from party work. *Goal*, *role*, and *ideology* might be in one compartment, motivation in another. (2) The "social contacts" type of motivational response was so frequent and normal, particularly in the Democratic party, that even though a precinct leader clearly understood the party task to be winning power,

TABLE 11.10
CONGRUENCE OF PERSONAL PARTY PERSPECTIVES
(Precinct Leaders)

Categories of other perspectives	*Motivational perspectives*									
	Democrats					*Republicans*				
	Instrumentalists					*Instrumentalists*				
	Social-izers	*Others*	*Ideologues-philosophers*	*Disillu-sioned*	*Num-ber of cases*	*Social-izers*	*Others*	*Ideologues-philosophers*	*Disillu-sioned*	*Num-ber of cases*
Ideology:										
Consistently liberal	63%	14%	13%	8%	63	*	*	*	*	9*
Consistently conservative	*	*	*	*	6*	41%	16%	16%	25%	32
Middle of the road (not consistent)	67	14	2	17	42	48	9	22	22	69
Party goal orientation:										
Power salients	72	16	6	5	85	43	17	26	14	42
Power latents	50	13	13	25	24	64	8	19	8	36
Idealists	82	6	6	0	17	50	8	22	18	50
Unoriented	0	0	0	90	12	13	0	0	87	15
Personal role perceptions:										
Vote mobilizer	58	19	8	15	62	59	14	19	8	63
Ideological mentor	61	12	9	15	33	48	0	30	18	33
Welfare promoter	90	7	3	0	30	60	5	10	25	20
No role	33	0	0	58	12	6	24	6	65	17

and his own task to be mobilization of votes, yet his satisfaction was inclined to be highly personalized and instrumental. The *party* was striving for power. The majority of individual leaders were striving for social gratifications and personal status.

Analysis of current motivations by the social strata and social characteristics of precinct leaders gives us clues about the types of individuals in both parties who derived particular motivational fulfillment (Table 11.11). First, these data suggest that the disillusioned minority originated in politically deviant social sectors. One-half of the wealthy Democrats would miss nothing if they had to step out of party work; there was a similar slight tendency for those among the lower-income Republican leaders to be disillusioned. Republican Catholics had a high percentage of disillusioned (47 per cent) and up to 50 per cent of the leaders in both parties whose family origin was in eastern and southern Europe were motivationally unhappy. Second, the ideologically motivated leaders came from different social sectors for both parties. For the Democrats the highest percentages were found among those in the lower income brackets and the college-educated, but they were only one-fifth in each such demographic category. The Republicans with ideological motivation were distributed in a less discernible pattern of regularities. Besides the college-educated, who were one-third ideological, the women leaders were also relatively high in this respect. But all Republican social groups with few exceptions, the most notable being the lowest income group, tended to exhibit more ideological motivation than did the Democrats.

A third question is, Which social strata produce the "socializers"? The most significant concentrations in both parties were found among the Negroes and the Protestants. The Catholics were particularly low in this satisfaction in the Republican party, where, as noted previously, almost half were disillusioned about satisfactions received from party work. It is interesting to note also that there was a great percentage difference in social gratifications among the upper and low income groups in the Democratic party, and to a lesser extent in the Republican party, with

TABLE 11.11
CURRENT MOTIVATIONS BY SOCIAL STRATA
(Precinct Leaders)

	Democrats					Republicans				
	Instrumentalists					Instrumentalists				
	Social-izers	*Others*	*Ideologues-philosophers*	*Disillu-sioned*	*Num-ber of cases*	*Social-izers*	*Others*	*Ideologues-philosophers*	*Disillu-sioned*	*Num-ber of cases*
Income (family)										
Under $4,000	80%	0%	20%	0%	10	33%	43%	0%	24%	21
$4–6,000	70	27	0	3	37	41	0	28	31	29
$6–10,000	72	2	10	14	58	72	8	8	11	36
Over $10,000	29	8	4	50	24	44	4	28	24	50
Race										
Negro	81	3	3	13	32	74	22	4	0	23
White	58	16	8	16	106	43	8	22	26	120
Sex										
Female	67	33	0	0	21	36	25	32	4	28
Male	62	9	8	18	117	50	6	17	26	115
Age										
Under 30	*	*	*	*	7	40	16	24	20	25
30–59	59	16	6	18	112	56	2	17	24	89
60 and over	84	0	11	0	19	34	22	27	17	29

TABLE 11.11 (continued)
CURRENT MOTIVATIONS BY SOCIAL STRATA
(Precinct Leaders)

	Democrats					*Republicans*				
	Instrumentalists					*Instrumentalists*				
	Social-izers	*Others*	*Ideologues-philosophers*	*Disillu-sioned*	*Num-ber of cases*	*Social-izers*	*Others*	*Ideologues-philosophers*	*Disillu-sioned*	*Num-ber of cases*
Education										
Elementary	60	15	5	15	20	25	25	25	25	16
High school	65	14	0	20	81	60	2	2	36	53
College	59	21	22	5	37	43	12	32	11	74
Religion										
Catholic	60	14	6	15	65	29	16	15	47	34
Protestant	77	6	6	10	62	56	12	19	13	97
Nationality										
Northwestern European	56	11	13	18	45	27	9	29	33	45
Central European	63	23	2	10	41	59	3	15	24	34
Eastern and southern European	40	10	0	50	10*	28	0	28	44	18

* Too few cases for analysis.

the findings somewhat reversed for the two parties. That is, low-income Democrats were "social-contact conscious" while low-income Republicans were not; but in both parties fewer of the wealthy were in politics for social rewards. Women differed also by party in this respect—Democratic women were much more likely to be socializers than their Republican counterparts. The same was true for the older leaders, those with an elementary education, and those with a northwestern European family origin. Thus, while race and religion may have been common social-group factors for both parties, there is evidence that other social factors were not generalizable, and that the differences in motivational perspectives for population subgroups stemmed from internal party conditions and environmental factors.

MOTIVATIONAL VARIATIONS WITHIN DISTRICT ORGANIZATIONS AND PRECINCT TYPES

The pluralistic motivational structure of the party elites has been apparent in the analysis presented thus far. The question remains as to whether there is more homogeneity within the party if we look at the "party," not as a mammoth county hierarchy, but as a series of fairly autonomous districts and precincts. The distribution of motivations and satisfactions by the six congressional districts is presented in Table 11.12, and it can be seen that precinct leaders may vary considerably by district.

The 1st District of Congressman Machrowitz, made up primarily of Negroes and Poles, included a high proportion (82 to 95 per cent) of "socializers" in both parties. The 17th District of Congressman Martha Griffiths, a more marginal area, had a relatively low proportion of "socializers" (38 to 39 per cent) in both parties, more activists (particularly among the Democrats) who were interested in other kinds of personal aims, Republican ideologists, and a larger percentage of disillusioned precinct leaders (particularly among the Republicans). Other districts were outstanding in other respects, although the reason for this is not so readily apparent. Why should 50 per cent of the Republicans

TABLE 11.12

MOTIVATIONS WITHIN THE DISTRICT HIERARCHIES
(Precinct Leaders Only)

Districts	*Democrats*					*Republicans*				
	Instrumentalists		*Ideologues-philosophers*	*Disillu-sioned*	*Number of cases*	*Instrumentalists*		*Ideologues-philosophers*	*Disillu-sioned*	*Number of cases*
	Socializers	*Others*				*Socializers*	*Others*			
1st	82%	0%	6%	6%	17	95%	0%	0%	5%	20
13th	68	0	0	21	19	28	22	50	0	18
14th	35	30	10	25	20	46	25	21	8	24
15th	67	6	6	22	18	35	6	0	59	17
16th	77	2	9	9	43	44	0	24	29	41
17th	38	43	5	14	21	39	13	22	26	23

in the heavily Negro 13th District have been ideologically motivated, with practically a total absence of Democratic ideologists in the same district? Why should there have been such a high proportion of disillusioned Republicans in the 15th District? These and other differences hint again at such possible controlling factors as the conditions of party competition, top elite recruitment of precinct leaders, and organizational morale as basic to understanding the motivational structure of the party, a structure which is geographically and organizationally non-monolithic.

If our precincts are divided on the basis of competitive status, we derive some help in explaining differences in motivation (Table 11.13), but these differences occurred by party. It is true that sure Republican and Democratic precincts had the highest percentages of "socializers," but the differences (particularly among Republicans) were not significant. Also, the marginal precincts seemed to have the highest proportions of ideologically motivated, but again the Republican differences were small. Marginal areas may have had few or no disillusioned workers (Democrats) or a relatively high percentage (31 per cent among the Republicans). The differences, thus, seemed to be within party by type of precinct, rather than generalizable for both parties. The Republican picture was quite disorderly; the Democrats revealed more uniformities. Their sure districts were heavily composed of "socializers," the opponents' sure districts included Democrats relatively disillusioned, and the marginal districts found Democrats more ideologically motivated and apparently fairly well satisfied about their personal motivational relationship to the party.

Some patterns are also observable if we divide the precinct by turnout level. Those areas where the voters were apathetic tended to be neighborhoods where the precinct leaders enjoyed social gratification from party work, where the Republicans were ideologues but the Democrats were not, and where there tended to be fewer disillusioned party leaders. On the other hand, in high-turnout areas, Democrats and Republicans expressed the

TABLE 11.13

Motivational Patterns by Precinct Types

	Democrats					*Republicans*				
	Instrumentalists					*Instrumentalists*				
	Social-izers	*Others*	*Ideologues-philosophers*	*Disillu-sioned*	*Num-ber of cases*	*Social-izers*	*Others*	*Ideologues-philosophers*	*Disillu-sioned*	*Num-ber of cases*
Competitive status of precincts										
Sure Democratic	80%	3%	1%	15%	79	51%	13%	20%	16%	69
Sure Republican	34	25	7	31	29	46	11	17	23	35
Marginal	47	33	20	0	30	44	2	23	31	39
Turnout level of precincts										
High	47	21	11	18	74	46	9	15	29	79
Medium and low	81	4	2	13	64	50	11	27	13	64

greatest dissatisfaction with party work, perhaps because so many of them were seeking social contacts and the character of the party operation was less conducive to promotion of this type of satisfaction. A somewhat paradoxical situation obtained, therefore: where voter interest and participation were high, partly due no doubt to the hard work of the party machine, in such neighborhoods party activists' satisfactions with party work were low!

CONCLUSIONS

In this chapter we have documented certain prominent aspects of the motivational structure of the party. It seems clear that the party structure comprehends leaders with a great variety of drives which may or may not be satisfied. The party is a motivationally complex and pluralistic structure. We have seen how these satisfactions differed for the top elite and the grass-roots actives. Among the latter motivation might differ by type of district or neighborhood in which one worked, by tenure and career status in the organization, as well as by the type of social strata in which one has been reared.

Aside from this diversity in motivational patterns hierarchically, areally, and organizationally, great perceptual confusion was displayed among party leaders as to why their colleagues were involved in party work. Fully three-fourths of precinct leaders ascribed motivations to others different from their own, and not borne out by reality.

A further analysis which complicates the picture is the considerable movement and change in motivation from the time of career origin to the present. The great majority (over two-thirds) of precinct leaders changed motivational direction after beginning party work, whether they began before 1940 or after.

Finally, the disjunction and noncongruence of motivations in relation to other personal political perspectives adds to the puzzle. There seemed to be considerable inconsistency between role perception and goal conceptualization for the party when placed alongside motivation. But it is important to realize that what the individual personally felt he got out of politics may be one thing, while what he realized was his role, and what the party's goal was, might be quite other matters. Personal goals and group goals, as perceived by the party leader, did not often coincide.

That no more than 10 per cent of the precinct leaders of the parties (actually only 3 per cent of the Democrats) were ideologically motivated in their work may be a disturbing fact, but it is a fact which should be clearly recognized. A party is a social group, and the personal motivational relationship in the party is basically the same, apparently, as in other social groups. Social friendships, rewards, and other personally instrumental satisfactions were most salient in the minds of the precinct activist, as well as in the minds of the top organizational mobiles and those who had arrived in the top elite positions. They may have started out as idealists (especially those who were at the lower echelons and nonmobile), but they were soon acclimated and socialized to expect personal satisfactions and to stay in party work because of them. Though party work was "voluntaristic," since there were few real patronage jobs to dispense, it was not "ideological" as those with reformist visions might have hoped. The political party unites an agglomeration of people with a rich variety of motivations, drives, and needs. As such it is a very incohesive team of leaders and workers. But it is clear that the vast majority of these people sought some personalized satisfaction—whether good fellowship, excitement, social recognition, prestige, money, or friendship. In a broader sense, this is the "patronage" they expected, and this "patronage" produced not only personal contentment but probably also induced them to continue work, be maximally productive in their roles, and inspired the fight for higher status in the party machine.

CHAPTER 12

ENVIRONMENTAL AND VALUE PERSPECTIVES OF PARTY LEADERS

The ideas and understandings of a party leader about the social and political world in which he and his party must work provide clues to the nature of the party's "adaptive" posture and potential. The political party leader has to contend with an "environment" which includes many "objects"—the "other party," current political issues, the social structure and organized groups in the community most relevant for politics, the governmental apparatus he seeks to control, the mass media available to him. In addition, part of the leader's environment is "atmosphere," more abstract understandings about the game of politics, and how it is to be played. Thus, there are certain moral norms and operational proprieties to be observed and of which he must be conscious. These concern particularly the proprieties of alternative competitive strategies and activities open to him. For example, house-to-house and doorbell campaigning is frowned on in certain countries (and in certain areas in the United States) because, among other reasons, the practice allegedly invades the privacy of the home. But, in addition, abstract understandings about the character of the political order are also involved. In a "democratic" society expectations develop which require a party leader to conform to a particular set of values concerning human relations, group process, and governmental behavior patterns. These value expectations may vary specifically from one democratic culture to the next. Politicians in one country may be much more self-conscious about mobilizing consent, or about committing themselves if elected to implementing the popular "mandate," than in another country. Thus, a great range of environmental conditions and political norms, with variable content, may exist in political systems. The party is seeking to maximize its support and status in this environment. The party leader is aware of the milieu and brings to his work, or subsequently develops, a basic set of perspectives about his personal relationship to the milieu in his capacity as a political agent.

The analysis of environmental perspectives has greater significance than mere description, although this aim has never been carefully fulfilled. Nor is its utility to be defended exclusively on the grounds that the knowledge of such perspectives leads to a clearer understanding of the integrative relationships between political party and "the system," though this is an important purpose here. The structural character of the party, its functional performance in the pursuit of power, and its place in the society are partly deducible from the distribution of such perspectives in its elite cadres. But it is also important to bear in mind that a political party elite disposes of large amounts of important values in a society by frequent interaction with its own "clientele groups" as well as with the public generally. It can thus reinforce or disturb accepted value references about politics. The public's image of the party elite as well as of the political system is derived in large part from its interpretations of the elite's value perspectives. In the larger view, therefore, the assumption is made that elite perspective analysis has great value-relevance for knowledge about cultural variations in democratic belief and norm.

Two major types of perspectives can be identified, the one perceptual, the other evaluative. The first of these embraces the understandings of a democratic party leader about the "outside world," percepts which he will incorporate into his decisions and plans for fulfilling his organizational responsibilities. He should make "realistic" or "rational" decisions, reflecting an awareness of the milieu and suggesting the best way to exploit, manipulate, or manage it tactically for the party's objective of power. As Harold Lasswell has put it, the leader does not project his personal "fantasies" onto the outside world. He is realistic about his environment, as he is realistic about himself, and his realism is not necessarily cynical. For example, he acknowledges and adapts to "ideological" demands just as he reacts to a recognition that some demands are "self-interested." As a realist he is, therefore, informed and observant about his world, coping with the sociological and psychological facts of political life despite personal preferences, carefully applying his intelligence to problems of political strategy, and tough-minded in the analysis of failure or success. An exploratory attempt will be made to tap the first dimension, of "realism" at one end and "fantasm" at the other end, by a look at some of the data on party leaders in Detroit.

The second dimension is evaluative. The democratic party leader does not merely perceive accurately, he believes in the democratic rules of the game. He knows and accepts the proprieties and acts accordingly, and he does this not merely because he fears defeat or loss of votes. He prefers defeat to responsibility for violation of the code of democratic practice. For example, he would avoid circulation of fraudulent petitions, not because it is impractical but because the system proscribes it. But his value perspectives are not merely negative avoidances of error in the interpretation of the code. They are also positive. He believes in the freedom of competition, positively; he accepts to some degree the idea of popular consultation and consent for decision-making, whether in his own organization or in official government. He believes in the basic integrity of democratic institutions and processes, despite their imperfections, and does not condemn all politics as "dirty" and "corrupt." The party elite thus share and reinforce democratic perspectives, defending the system, not just tolerating it. The extent to which the party leadership cadres do indeed reveal such democratic beliefs, or, conversely, the extent to which they reveal an anti-democratic value position, will be explored with the data available in our study. In so doing, we are wrestling with an attitudinal syndrome which may be akin to the "authoritarian" scale developed by others; yet it has a basically different character. We are not so much concerned here with our leaders' attitudes toward authority as we are with their incorporation of certain values concerning the *process* of party politics—internal party process—and the tactics parties utilize in the pursuit of their legitimate goals.

Various kinds of data about party leaders might be consulted in determining the realism with which leaders perceive their external environment and the extent to which they have internalized democratic values. The data on social backgrounds and political careers, as well as patterns of political behavior, might permit inferences to these two dimensions, but they would be an unstable basis on which to generalize. One could question the leader directly about reactions to his environment and values which seem most important to him personally. Ambiguities in meaning, however, might preclude the acceptability of such evidence. A third approach, attempted here, was to deduce the level of realism and the depth of value commitment from the responses to questions ostensibly directed toward other interview objectives. Thus, we asked the leader, "What do you particularly like about your own party? and, "What, if anything, would you say you *dislike* about your own party?" Ostensibly aimed at a specification of party image, this question can elicit suggestive responses concerning the leader's evaluations of democratic competitive party process. By coding and weighting these "unsolicited hints," we developed indices of "realism-fantasm" and "democratic–pseudo-democratic" value position. Probing such environmental perspectives is one of the most difficult problems in political analysis. Only a beginning has been made here, and our findings are no more than suggestive. A subsequent design, more self-consciously and at greater length devoted to these objectives, will no doubt be of value.

THE POLITICAL REALISM OF PARTY LEADERS

The "picture" in the mind of the party leader about the outside world is a mosaic of perceptions. Among the many components of this picture which interested us was his view of the political competition environment of the Detroit area in which he worked. As noted in Chapter 1, although Wayne County was consistently Democratic in presidential elections, it was not a one-party enclave. The Democratic percentage in 1956 was 57.9. Further, only one congressional district, the 1st, was one-party, voting over 80 per cent Democratic since 1948. Two of the districts were rather marginal in recent congressional elections, and quite a number of marginal precincts hovered between Republican and Democratic majorities. There were as well moderately and overwhelmingly Republican precincts.

It is interesting, therefore, to note the responses to questions concerning the competitiveness of party politics. Two series of questions were used, one which asked whether there were important differences between the parties (and what these differences were), and the other concerning the number and nature of the campaign issues in the 1956 election. The range of the percentages of precinct leaders who were unaware of a "competitive political milieu" on the basis of these questions, or who were only minimally conscious of party conflict, is observable from the distributions in Table 12.1.

It would not be surprising to find members of the apathetic public who fail to perceive party conflict differences in Detroit,

TABLE 12.1

RANGE OF PERCENTAGES OF PRECINCT LEADERS UNAWARE OF A COMPETITIVE POLITICAL MILIEU

	Democrats	*Republicans*
Political parties are the same—no differences	22%	48%
Political parties differ—but only in organization and campaign techniques	10	10
No issues existed in the last campaign	7%	7%
Candidate personality was the only issue in the last campaign	3	7

but it is more significant to discover upwards of 10 per cent of precinct leaders asserting that there were no campaign issue controversies. One assumes that involvement in the party operation in Detroit, an area of considerable publicity of Democratic and Republican differences in presidential (as well as gubernatorial) elections, would certainly educate party leaders to an expectation, perception, and assertion of conflict. But, it may be argued, the precinct leader might be reacting only to the conditions of interparty warfare in his own particular constituency, and those leaders who are unaware of conflict come from sure Democratic or Republican precincts where the opposition is overwhelmed and does not contend for power. The facts, however, do not bear this out. For example, only 11 per cent of those who perceived no campaign issues were active in precincts either overwhelmingly Republican or Democratic; and almost 50 per cent came from fairly "marginal" precincts (based on the vote in the previous three presidential elections). Further, 42 per cent of the precinct leaders who saw no differences between the parties came from precincts which were "critical marginal" areas. This suggests that a small minority of precinct leaders were not "realists," in the sense that they were living in a competitive environment but perceived no real conflict between the party groups. Despite the "Tweedledum-Tweedledee Theory" of American politics (that there are no real issue and ideological differences between the two parties), it is indeed peculiar to find such a large number of party leaders advancing this perception in precincts of intensive party combat. Aside from their socialization to accept such a theory, one would expect them to have incorporated the concept of party competition as a result of task performance in the precinct, to say nothing about their indoctrination through the national and state party hierarchies. Many of these leaders lived in areas of considerable party conflict over the vote, yet they took the position that there was no difference between the parties and no campaign issues.

There are, no doubt, many good explanations. Some leaders who did not perceive party conflict may not have lived long in the Detroit area, may have become active only recently in the party, or may have been merely perfunctory in the position of precinct leader. Whatever the reasons, to be explored later, one must admit presumptive evidence here of political nonreality. Given the premise that parties did compete in Detroit as well as nationally, that there were issues (even if only based on the personality and qualifications of the candidates), and that their own precincts exhibited evidences of party conflict, assertions of the lack of party competition raise questions about the extent to which these leaders were in close contact with their political world, and the accuracy of their perceptions of it.

Another quite different test of reality contacts and perceptions can be employed by asking precinct leaders specifically about the division of the party vote in their precincts. We did this by asking for the presidential vote in 1956, how the people in the precinct "as a whole usually vote," and whether their party's vote increased or decreased in the precinct in the past presidential election. Admittedly this may be construed as a test of specific knowledge and recall, but it also gives clues as to the closeness of the leader's contact with his own political bailiwick and the accuracy of his perceptual image. A leader who told us that Eisenhower received 70 per cent of the vote in his precinct when actually Eisenhower received 40 per cent is an individual who obviously was not in close touch with the facts of political life in his precinct, and, in addition, might be the type of person who is unconcerned about political reality. The distributions in Table 12.2 indicate the wide range in accuracy of perceptions. A bare majority of precinct leaders had precisely correct estimates of voting patterns in their precincts, and from one-fifth to two-fifths were inaccurate, depending on the rigor of the test. Perhaps the expectation that a precinct leader should know the exact percentage, within 5 percentage points, is too restrictive. But certainly the 14 per cent of Democrats and the 23 per cent of Republicans who were 20 percentage points off in their statement of the presidential vote raise serious doubts about their contact with political reality!

TABLE 12.2

ACCURACY OF PERCEPTIONS ABOUT VOTING PATTERNS IN OWN PRECINCT

	Democrats	*Republicans*
Perception of how precinct usually votes		
Correct	52%	54%
Somewhat inaccurate	27	22
Very inaccurate	21	24
Perception of 1956 vote		
Correct within 1 per cent	7	8
1–5 per cent off	16	19
5–10 per cent off	23	19
10–20 per cent off	19	17
Over 20 percentage points off	14	23
Don't know and not ascertained	21	14
Perception of gain or loss in vote in last two elections		
Correct		
Gained	30	31
Lost	19	5
About the same	3	5
Incorrect		
Claimed party gained	14	34
Claimed party lost	11	3
Claimed vote about the same	11	5
Don't know and not ascertained	12	17

Finally, we were interested in reality perspectives in a more general sense—the level of sophistication of the leader concerning the conduct of politics, tendencies in voting behavior, and factors that shape voting decisions. A variety of questions had the objective of determining the level of generalized reality about the political and voting process, although in answering these questions the leader was asked to keep his specific electoral or geographical context in mind. Paraphrased, these questions were: Do organizations affect the way people vote? Do people (in your precinct) ever have conflicts or problems in voting because they belong to groups with different views on political matters? Is politics a "dirty game," and in what way? Have you ever been really disgusted with the campaign activities of anyone in your own party, or in the opposition party? What types of activities were these?

The social scientist studying politics receives a considerable jolt from some of the responses of precinct leaders to these questions. What interpretation is to be placed on the fact that over one-third (49 per cent Democrats, 25 per cent Republicans) felt that organizations had no influence on the way people voted in their precinct? Is this fantasy or rationalization, in view of the politically active role of labor and business groups in Detroit politics, to say nothing of other group influences? Were these leaders simply not in close enough contact with their constituencies to understand the kind of forces operating on the American voter? Or were these voters in fact insulated from group influence? Another finding, perhaps more disturbing, is that precinct leaders thought that multiple group membership in politically divergent groups created no "cross-pressures" or "conflicts" for their constituents in decisions about voting—81 per cent of the Democratic leaders felt this way and 77 per cent of the Republicans. Does this vitiate the "cross-pressure" hypothesis for four-fifths of Detroit area precincts? Or does it mean that the vast majority of precinct leaders were quite unsophisticated about the determinants and characteristics of the voting decision?

On the other hand, precinct leaders seemed to be quite "realistic" about whether politics is "dirty." The other party is, of course, less moral than one's own—from 45 to 50 per cent said they had never been disgusted with the campaign activities of their own party, while only 23 to 30 per cent said they had never been disgusted with the opposition. Yet, less than one-fifth responded generally that politics is not "dirty," and if we code their responses on all questions concerning this subject, less than 10 per cent of responses consistently indicated unawareness of any irregularities or questionable campaign practices—8 per cent of all Democratic precinct leaders and 3 per cent of the Republicans.

After elimination of questions not sufficiently discriminating on the reality dimension (such as the group cross-pressures query), and screening the responses on all other questions, assigning proper weights to the nature of the response, we reached the following distribution of precinct leaders:

	Democrats	*Republicans*
Consistent realists	43%	48%
Some evidence of nonrealism	39%	30%
High degree of nonrealism	18%	22%
Number of cases	138	143

This is probably a higher level of realism than one might secure from the general public, but it is significant to locate such a sizeable minority of nonrealists among party activists. The finding, no doubt, reflects the haphazard recruitment procedures of the two parties as well as the inadequacy of the party's training and socializing of activists for party tasks. Whether this level of nonreality was damaging for the party in the performance of precinct tasks is, of course, another critical question.

It is interesting to compare the top leadership nucleus (district chairmen and executive board members) with precinct leaders on the reality dimension. A good majority of the top echelon leaders were consistent realists. They were knowledgeable, aware of the competitive character and implications of party conflict, not naive about the nature of party tactics, and rather sophisticated in their theories of the causes and forces explaining voting behavior. But all of them by no means were realists, and the evidence was at times both peculiar and dramatic. For example, two Republican district chairmen steadfastly claimed that their party had been making gains in the congressional and presidential vote in their districts, despite objective election statistics to the contrary, and both of these men were extremely unclear as to differences in the aims and purposes of each party. Further, although most of those in the top nucleus had detailed (and frank) explanations of how the organization operated, formally and behind the scenes, as well as of the intricacies of patronage distribution, factional warfare, and other details about party life, some were obviously less perceptively realistic. One board member was unaware of the existence of the county chairman, several others denied the existence of precincts, and one member was at a loss to explain why he had ever been picked for the board. Finally, there were leaders with very little feeling about the determinants of the voting decision and unable to offer any explanation of why Cobo lost in the gubernatorial race. Thus, for a minority of these leaders there was evidence of lack of knowledge about party politics and lack of perceptive insight into the mainsprings of political organizational and electoral activity. The Democratic district chairmen were a hard-headed, realistic group, and all six of them were classified as "consistent realists." Four of the six Republicans were considered in this category, the other two placed in the intermediate category of "realism with serious qualifications." The final distribution of board members is given in Table 12.3. Thus, on the basis of these data,

TABLE 12.3

Distribution of Executive Board Members on the Dimension of Realism

	Democrats	*Republicans*
Consistent realists (few if any reservations)	75%	59%
Realists (some serious reservations)	25	23
Nonrealists (great reservations concerning their realism)	0	18

there was a significantly higher proportion of nonrealism at the precinct level than at the two upper echelons, and more nonrealism among Republicans than Democrats at all levels.

THE "DEMOCRATIC VALUE" PERSPECTIVES OF PARTY LEADERS

Value orientations are more difficult to identify than any other perspective, yet knowledge of them is essential in order to gain a proper understanding of where the party leader stands vis-à-vis his environment. A wide range of specific value positions are involved. When we generalize about the distinctiveness of a "democratic" society or culture, we often consider two differentiae critical—the willingness of political leadership to tolerate, and not suppress, the opposition; and the readiness of political leadership to accept the consequences of electoral defeat and to withdraw from political office peacefully subsequent to defeat. These loom as basic value perspectives in contrasting democratic with anti-democratic or developing democratic societies. Yet, the analysis of democratic leaders exclusively and overtly preoccupied with these two value positions concerning the rules of the political game would not be very profound or useful in the United States. Societies, and the political leadership cadres in them, vary greatly in the extent to which they have crystallized and internalized the rules of the political game. And the above criteria are by no means sufficient for detecting the subtler differences in value position found among leadership groups within a "Western type" democratic society. All of the Detroit area party leaders would have acquiesced openly in the above value standards of democratic political life, but they all may not have been as firmly committed to democratic norms less obviously or visibly part of the political code. It is the nuance and subtle shading of meaning in the party leaders' interpretation of "democratic polities" which interests us and which we sought to investigate by inference from responses to interview questions.

The detection of "anti-democratic" value perspectives is indeed difficult, particularly when one seeks evidence exclusively concerned with attitudes toward the political process, not attitudes toward social relationships generally. Bearing the political context in mind, we first operationalized a value component perhaps best named the "value perspective toward critical clientele groups." The explanation of this label is as follows. We can assume that in a system such as ours with two major parties loosely structured and characterized by fluid interchanges of potential voters from one to the other—a party system in which neither party is fixedly class- or group-bound—the party must maintain its image of a "mass" party, appealing to and accepting support from all significant citizen and opinion sectors in the society. In such an environment one would not expect the party leader, on the basis both of pragmatism and his democratic value-orientation, to take an exclusivist and prejudicial view of those significant voting blocs to which his party must appeal. For example, in Detroit one would expect the party leader to be fairly well adjusted to the idea of the party appealing to Negroes, labor union members, nationality groups, etc. Any indication that the party should be "highbrow" or exclusive in its interactions with such groups might well be construed as a type of "anti-democratic nonrealism."[1] Two possible exceptions to this must be incorporated into any analysis. The first is the person who might be excepted because his anti-minority groups or anti-civil rights attitude is part of a conservative ideological syndrome—his attitudes on all issues and in terms of all public objects and questions are conservative. He is against minority groups and civil rights legislation just as he is against health insurance legislation or foreign aid. (The proportion of ideological conservative leaders was presented earlier.) But his political issues position should be separated from his democratic value position, and, thus, responses which indicate that the latter is probably subordinate to the former must be carefully screened out in the categorization attempted here, though admittedly the distinction is often ambiguous and possibly difficult to defend. A second exception is the person who has a national image of the party and who, though liberal, sincerely believes, since he is conscious of the party's primary task of winning power, that the party should not go too far in its pro-minority group and pro-civil rights advocacy for fear of losing votes in certain sections (such as the South), which in his opinion are required for party success. Where party leaders are clearly identified in these terms, their superficially

[1] This differs practically, of course, from one section of the country to another, depending on the interpretation of those voting groups critical for party success (e.g., the South)!

appearing anti-democratic responses must also be screened out and excluded in the classification of their value position. With these two exceptions, we utilized the attitudes of party leaders toward "minority-group" sectors of the population as one indicator of their democratic value position. We found that 9 per cent of our precinct leaders were classifiable as anti-democratic under this component.

A second component is named the "value perspective toward intragroup decisional style." The democratic party leader is presumably interested in organizational efficiency and is realist enough to expect a certain amount of managerialism in the conduct of the party machine by the upper leadership nucleus. On the other hand, he is also wise enough and "democratic" enough to realize that a certain amount of involvement of the lower-echelon hard-core activists in the decisional activities of the organization is desirable and expected. Consultation of precinct leaders may not indeed influence decisions, but consultation at a minimal level is a value important in a democratic society's group life. One would particularly expect precinct leaders to value a minimal amount of consultation by the upper echelons of the party. Since we were particularly concerned with the study of organizational relationships in the party, we probed the views of party leaders on all levels about their relationship to the party decision-making process. It was thus possible to isolate those precinct leaders who felt that precinct leaders had absolutely no say in party decisions *and* who considered this the appropriate way to run a party group. The presence of this value position was used in the construction of the index of "anti-democratic nonrealism." We found 16 per cent of precinct leaders holding anti-democratic values under this rubric, half of whom took an extreme "authoritarian" position.

Finally, we utilized the component of "overcompulsiveness concerning the immorality of political-party tactics" in constructing our democratic values index. The democratic party leader should be acquainted enough with party life to realize that some "dirty politics" occurs. On the other hand, he should not be so preoccupied with dirty politics, both within his own party and the opposition, that he loses confidence in the morality of parties and the party action process. Such overcompulsiveness may reflect a general hostility, suggestive of the "authoritarian syndrome," with the immoral "goings on" of society, or they may be related exclusively to political happenings, events, and activities. Whatever the case, one should not expect such extremist value interpretations from those in positions of party activism in a democratic system. Their presence not only raises questions concerning the kinds of values "disposed" by party leaders, they also suggest that such interpretations may be only part of a more inclusive orientation toward the entire system. Under this third rubric we found 8 per cent of precinct leaders inclined to be overcompulsive.

Using these three components and the data available from our leadership interviews, we found the distributions for precinct leaders given in Table 12.4. Although this is admittedly only an exploratory attempt at the identification of the value perspectives of party leaders toward the party process, it is valuable as an indication of party differences and the extent of commitment to democratic perspectives in the party hierarchy. We

TABLE 12.4

Distribution of Precinct Leaders on Democratic-Authoritarian Criteria

	Democrats	*Republicans*
Strong evidence of "authoritarianism"	1%	5%
"Authoritarian" tendencies	8	5
Moderately "authoritarian"	4	24
Overcompulsive about morality only	10	3
Suggestive evidence of "authoritarianism," not convincing	1	8
Total	24	45
Consistent on democratic values	76	55

found 5 per cent of the Republican leaders and 1 per cent of the Democratic leaders to be explicitly and extremely anti-democratic. On the other hand, an additional 12 to 29 per cent revealed authoritarian tendencies of a definite or moderate type which, though not confirmed completely by their other responses, suggested the possibility of anti-democratic proclivities. While the majority were consistent "democrats," at least a small minority of precinct leaders were possibly not completely committed to democratic practices and relationships in political life.

One might expect top-echelon leaders in both parties to exhibit anti-democratic value perspectives more frequently than precinct leaders, due particularly to the fact that they would be more preoccupied with problems of "power," both concerning their own hierarchical status and the goals of the party. On the other hand, the opposite possibility might be suggested, that the top elite would be better aware of the "value" terrain within which the party functions and more adaptable to and realistic about it. Whatever the expectation, we found no great differences in the degree of "authoritarianism" of party leaders at the grass-roots and top decisional levels. If anything, there was less authoritarianism at the top, particularly among the Republican executive elite. Only two top-echelon leaders, both Republicans, could be considered overt and consistently anti-democratic. But, though not extremely anti-democratic, we did find from one-fifth to one-fourth of executive board members in both parties who were not consistently "democratic" in their perspectives, either. The Republican chairmen were a special case—one overtly authoritarian, two others moderately so—while only one Democratic chairman could be categorized as moderately anti-democratic. The distribution was as follows for executive board members:

	Democrats	*Republicans*
Anti-democratic (overt, consistent)	0%	5%
Moderately anti-democratic	19%	23%
Some evidence, but slight	6%	9%
Consistently democratic	75%	64%

Thus the Republicans were again more inclined than the Democrats to be anti-democratic. But upper-echelon Republican leaders (except for their chairmen, three of whom were not consistently democratic) were more democratic than their precinct leaders. It is interesting to note that only one out of these 50 top-echelon leaders was overcompulsive about the "dirtiness" of politics. It is also important that 85 per cent of these leaders, despite their position at the top, were "democratic" so far as intraparty leader-led relationships were concerned. Although a larger percentage were "exclusive" in their perceptions of the party's responsibility and relationship to minority groups, the vast majority felt that those in precinct leadership positions should be consulted and involved by the top elite in party discussions and decisions. Most of those in the top leadership nucleus considered the precinct leader a significant cog in the machine, and they had a healthy respect for the people who assume precinct posts.

FACTORS ASSOCIATED WITH ENVIRONMENTAL AND VALUE PERSPECTIVES

From the previous analysis it is clear that we found more convincing evidence of "nonrealism" among party leaders than "authoritarianism." While one-fifth of both parties' precinct leaders seemed nonrealist about their political milieu, using our criteria, less than 5 per cent of the total were overt "authoritarians." This is a remarkably low score, and is still more remarkably low among top-echelon leaders, particularly in the Democratic party.

An analysis of the factors related to nonrealism among party leaders is not very rewarding. Personal-social characteristics do not suggest many significant relationships. For example, one might hypothesize that the youngest members would be least in contact with reality, and the older party activists most realistic. A glance at Table 12.5 reveals that leaders under 35 years of age did tend to be less realistic than those over 60, but the dif-

TABLE 12.5
PERSONAL FACTORS AND LEADERSHIP REALISM
(Precinct Leaders)

Factor	*Net realism score**	
	Democrats	*Republicans*
Education		
College	+33%	+ 5%
Elementary	− 5	+26
Age		
Under 35	+ 6	−14
60 and over	+ 9	+24
Nationality		
Northwestern European (including Germany)	−19	−15
Central, southern, and eastern European	+ 7	+41
Irish only	−21	†
Race		
Negroes	+ 1	− 8
Religion		
Catholics	− 1	+27
Protestants	0	+12
Occupation		
Professional	+48	−19
Managerial	+22	+31
Clerical, sales	+ 8	+37
Skilled labor	+ 2	− 4
Unskilled and semiskilled	−37	+19

* The "realism score" is derived from a five-point scale, the computation representing the difference between the combined percentages of the upper two and lower two points on the scale. A plus sign (+) indicates a tendency toward "realism," a minus sign (—) a tendency away from "realism," and a zero (0) an even balance on the realism index for the particular category of persons.
† Too few cases for analysis.

ference varied greatly by party, and the difference on the Democratic side was exceedingly small. Again, one might expect college education to produce a realistic party leadership, but among Republicans those with only an elementary education were most realistic. Catholics and Protestants did not differ sharply on the Democratic side, although Catholics were more realistic among Republican leaders than Protestants. And there seemed to be no consistency among occupational groupings; there is less realism among Democrats as one descends the occupational ladder (the unskilled and semiskilled being most nonrealistic), but this was not so among Republicans.

The one observation which may be supported by evidence is that those demographic categories most "deviant" from the group (deviant in the sense of constituting a small minority and being "unexpected" activists in a particular party) seemed to be the most realistic. Thus, the well-educated, professional, and managerial occupational groupings seemed to be most realistic among Democrats. Those with an elementary schooling, the Catholics, and those in the unskilled and semiskilled occupational groups were most realistic among the Republicans. This suggests that upward mobility of such deviants requires and results in a higher degree of awareness of, and contact with, political reality. It is interesting in this connection to note that the newer immigrant groups infiltrating both parties—those from central, eastern, and southern Europe—were more realistic (particularly in the Republican party), than the old, established nationality groups of northwestern European origins. The "decline of the Irish" in the Democratic party in Detroit cannot be more eloquently documented than by their relatively high nonrealism score.

Since realism about politics should presumably be related to the extent and character of social interaction, we devised a series of tests of this hypothesis (See Table 12.6). From these findings we noted that although membership in a large number of voluntary groups did not necessarily produce a high realism score (though it seemed somewhat related), union activity was significant. Union officers in the ranks of Democratic precinct activists were the most realistic about politics, and, particularly among Republicans, even union affiliation made a great deal of

TABLE 12.6

BASIC FACTORS RELATED TO LEADERSHIP REALISM
(Precinct Leaders)

Factor	*Net realism score**	
	Democrats	*Republicans*
Union affiliation		
Member	− 7%	+33%
Officer	+49	†
Nonunion	−23	0
Number of groups belonged to		
2 or less	0	+12
6 or more	+17	+17
Frequency of district party contacts		
Often	+31	+22
Frequently	−16	+ 2
Rarely	−37	+12
Never	†	+ 3
Political activity of factor		
Active	0	+12
Not active	− 5	+ 4

* The realism score is derived from a five-point scale, the computation representing the difference between the combined percentages of the upper two and lower two points on the scale. A plus sign (+) indicates a tendency toward "realism," a minus sign (—) a tendency away from "realism," and a zero (0) an even balance on the realism index for the particular category of persons.

† Too few cases for analysis.

difference. Another type of test of social interaction used was the frequency with which the leader had party contacts in the district, and this again revealed a fairly consistent relationship. Among Democrats, about 60 per cent of those with high frequency of contact with other leaders were realists. The percentage for the Republicans was 48 per cent with only 10 per cent nonrealists. Other tests, such as the political activity of the father, did not reveal as great a difference, although it was in the right direction. The causal direction implied by these relationships may be questioned (particularly whether realists are affected by group association and leadership contacts or, conversely, whether they seek out such contacts). A pattern of interrelated behaviors seems apparent here. Realists may be somewhat socialized to political realism in the family, become more perceptive in their group associations, and, by conscious effort or otherwise, become further aware of political reality through party work and by "rubbing elbows" with fellow activists, depending upon their career orientations and status. Although we found no clear relationship between such orientations as the leader's role perception and his realism, there did seem to be a definite connection between his career pattern and his reality contacts (see Table 12.7). Among Democrats the two top groups of mobiles had the highest realism scores, while those without status were least perceptive of reality. It is interesting that the "top organization mobiles" among Republicans were inclined to exhibit a negative net realism score. Their nonmobile regulars were more realistic, however, and their "informal influentials" were particularly high on realism. In fact, in the analysis of career status, as elsewhere, Republican precinct leaders exhibited no significantly lower level of realism generally than did the Democrats (and in a few instances, considerably higher). The Republican top mobile elite, however, was less realistic.

THE AUTHORITARIAN PROFILE OF PARTY LEADERSHIP

With so few extreme authoritarians in the leadership sample (13 Democratic cases, 14 Republican cases), only a suggestive profile can be attempted. We found, for both parties, no Negroes in the authoritarian group. A majority (63 per cent) had a northwestern European nationality background. They tended to be middle-aged and over 60 in the Republican party, middle-aged and young in the Democratic party. They were found among Catholic leaders in the Democratic party (70 per cent) and among Protestants in the Republican party (also 70 per cent). They were the middle-income and wealthy Democrats, the

TABLE 12.7
POLITICAL MOTIVATION, CAREER STATUS, AND LEADERSHIP REALISM
(Precinct Leaders)

	Net realism score	
	Democrats	*Republicans*
Career type		
Top mobiles	+ 9%	− 8%
Informal influentials	+47	+58
Nonmobile regulars	−16	+18
Potential careerists	−34	−10
Noncareerists	−28	+ 7
Political motivation		
Socializers	− 6	+ 6
Other personal motivation	− 6	+35
Ideologues	*	−18
Nothing	− 9	+26
Goal orientation		
Power salients	− 4	+ 4
Power latents	−17	−11
Idealists	+30	+20
Unoriented	*	+40
Role perceptions		
Vote mobilizer	+10	+ 5
Ideological mentor	+10	− 6
Social welfare promoter	−13	+75
No role	−67*	+25

* Too few cases for analysis.

middle-income and poor Republicans. The only occupational finding of any consistency is that none of them came from the unskilled or semiskilled working groups. Union members contributed only one-third in both parties, and leaders with a non-union background comprised two-thirds. None of the union officers who were Democratic precinct leaders revealed any real authoritarian inclinations in our data. Finally, of special significance is the fact that none of these 27 authoritarians was found among the top organization mobiles in their parties. Twenty of the 27 were potential careerists or noncareerists. It seems, then, that perhaps with the exception of the finding on religion (reversed for the two parties), authoritarians where found in the precinct leadership cadre, were not found in the critical leadership sectors or centers of the party structure. The peripherals, the aspiring careerists, and the noncareerists produced that small number of authoritarians which did exist. The Negroes, Poles, and other central, southern, and eastern European nationality groups, the union leaders, the professional-managerial occupations (so crucial to the Republicans), the skilled and, particularly, the unskilled (so crucial to the Democrats) were not the contributors of an abnormally large group of party leaders who were predominantly authoritarian.

In a final summary analysis we have combined "realism" and "democratic-value" perspectives and inspected the two extreme groups—those leaders who were "realist-democrats" and those who were "nonrealist-authoritarians." It is this latter group of "fantasts," rather completely out of touch with political reality and theoretically the most dysfunctional to party life, which particularly attracts our attention. One wonders how it is possible for such individuals to be accepted at all into party leadership positions. In order to characterize them, it is necessary to contrast and compare their profile with that of the consistently democratic realists (Table 12.8).

Many of the same characteristics of the authoritarians were duplicated for the nonrealist-authoritarians. Comparison with both the percentages found among realist-democrats and in the total sample emphasized the following composition of these visionaries: few Negroes, northwestern European nationality (although one-fourth of the Democrats in the fantast group were Poles), the Irish with a disproportionate contribution to both parties, and large numbers from the managerial and professional occupational groups. In addition, it is interesting to see the very small number of women (5 per cent) among Democratic fantasts and the very high percentage of women (53 per cent) among the Republicans.

TABLE 12.8

PROFILES OF TWO CONTRASTED GROUPS OF LEADERS: "REALIST-DEMOCRATS" AND "NONREALIST-AUTHORITARIANS"

Characteristic	*Realist-democrats*		*Non-realist-authoritarians*		*Percentage of sample*	
	D	*R*	*D*	*R*	*D*	*R*
Sex						
Percentage women	20%	21%	5%	53%	15%	20%
Age						
Under 35	28	33	15	47	23	24
60 and over	13	24	5	5	14	20
Education						
Elementary	17	3	5	0	14	11
College	33	62	19	63	26	51
Religion						
Catholic	54	47	52	26	47	24
Protestant	44	53	29	47	45	68
Income						
Under $4,000	4	9	5	5	7	15
$4–6,000	26	14	5	42	27	20
Over $10,000	24	53	24	42	17	35
Occupation						
Professional	24	6	10	43	16	19
Managerial	13	53	35	21	10	36
Clerical, sales	13	25	20	7	17	14
Skilled	35	3	30	0	35	16
Semi- and unskilled	15	13	5	28	22	15
Nationality						
Irish	8	8	19	26	13	6
German	13	4	5	26	8	16
Poles	13	16	24	0	12	7
Other northwestern European	15	32	33	21	20	25

TABLE 12.8 (continued)

PROFILES OF TWO CONTRASTED GROUPS OF LEADERS: "REALIST-DEMOCRATS" AND "NONREALIST-AUTHORITARIANS"

Characteristic	*Realist-demo-crats*		*Non-realist-authori-tarians*		*Per-cent-age of sample*	
	D	*R*	*D*	*R*	*D*	*R*
Nationality						
Other central, southern, and eastern European	23	20	10	26	18	13
Race						
Negroes	28	20	10	0	23	16
Number of groups belonged to						
0–2	17	32	47	26	16	24
3–5	20	38	44	58	34	47
6 or more	63	30	9	16	50	29
Union affiliation						
Member	54	21	48	21	56	29
Officer	33	0	0	0	17	1
Nonunion	13	79	52	79	27	70
Career status						
Top mobiles	26	3	5	0	17	17
Top influentials	35	9	29	5	27	13
Nonmobile regulars	7	53	10	42	15	31
Potential careerists	13	24	10	26	23	28
Noncareerists	20	12	48	26	11	18
Number of cases	46	34	21	19	138	143

Note: We have included in this analysis of the nonrealist-authoritarians those authoritarians who were most extreme as well as a small number of moderate authoritarians who revealed definite authoritarian tendencies (8 Democrats and 5 Republicans).

"Fantasm" seemed to be a middle- and upper-income class phenomenon, particularly in the Democratic party. The relationship of religion was questionable, with a fairly even split, relative to the proportions of Catholics in the population, though Protestants represented a smaller proportion in the fantasm column than might be expected. Thus, Republican fantasts tended to be of older immigrant origin, a young and middle-aged group of people, more female than expected, with considerable education and fairly well off, whose head of household's occupation was white collar (plus one-fourth from the semi- and unskilled occupational categories). The Democratic fantasts were male, middle-aged, with a high-school education, more Catholic, fairly well off, white collar (except for 30 per cent skilled blue collar), primarily northwestern European (though one-fourth were Poles). Union officership, and to some extent union membership, seemed to conduce to realistic-democratic perspectives. Again, finally, it is significant that although some fantasm was found in the higher reaches of the party hierarchy, it was minimal (5 per cent of Democratic fantasts were found in the top mobile career clan, and no Republicans). We find most of this phenomenon, then, in its extreme form, among the nonmobile party regulars, aspiring careerists, and the "fly-by-nighters."

CONCLUSIONS

In this chapter we have explored two new perspectives, political realism and value positions, in relation to the environment in which the party leader functions. After operationalizing these perspectives for our purposes, we examined the data to determine their incidence at various levels of the party hierarchy. More consistent, valid, and reliable evidence of nonrealism was detected than of anti-democratic perspectives. Both were found, however, and since both theoretically are relevant to the nature of the party as a functional unit in the system, as well as to the distribution of perspectives and values within the society generally, we analyzed the correlates of these perspectivist patterns.

The most suggestive discoveries are three in number. First, that the so-called deviant minorities in a party coalition, those groups seeking to establish a place for themselves and move inward and upward in the party machine, tended to exhibit the most realism and least authoritarianism. Second, there is considerable evidence that group life is beneficent and salutary—those who had a high level of social interaction experience, in formal groups and in political contacts, with other leaders and in the precinct were less likely to be nonrealist and authoritarian. And, finally, career status—length of tenure, continuity of experience in party work, and upward career mobility—seems associated with realistic democratic perspectives. We found less fantasm in the top executive elite, particularly in the Democratic party, and among the top mobiles of the precinct leaders than among the *nouveau politiques*. This suggests that these anti-pragmatic environmental and value perspectives, though producing problems in particular sectors and in specific intraparty relationships, are not as dysfunctional for the party organization at its management levels as might have been supposed. The extent to which they are dysfunctional in the precincts, at the grass-roots level where the vote-mobilization process is vital, remains to be explored. It is hoped that this attempt to identify, isolate, and empirically investigate these two perspectives will not only be suggestive of further methodological approaches, but also shed light on a crucial problem of the party group process in a democratic society.

PART III

THE PARTY AS AN ORGANIZATIONAL SYSTEM

INTRODUCTION

We have been concerned, thus far, with the content of individual perspectives at different levels of the organization, but a party as a durable social group is more than an aggregate of perspectives. The party is an identifiable set of relationships and interactions of actors in positions of a structure. It is to various aspects of these structural networks that we now turn, deriving from the theoretical foci outlined earlier the specific operational constructs considered most useful in an analysis of the dynamics of party structure.

Many conceptual emphases can be utilized in the explication of internal party structure, as the literature on organizational theory and behavior reveals. An eclecticism of insight should instruct the researcher who ventures into the uncharted area of internal party dynamics, for party organizational reality is too complex to be dealt with satisfactorily by testing one body of theory. A single-minded commitment to a "theory of oligarchy," for example, traditionally the major full-bodied theory of party structure, will not suffice. Other theoretical explorations are needed and may well lead to new knowledge.

As a structural aggregate of roles and relationships the party can be viewed from three primary theoretical vantage points. First, as a group competing for power, the party is a *task group* and certain key activities are requisite, particularly in leadership selection and support mobilization, if the group is to maintain itself. Although the particular types of tasks engaged in vary greatly, depending on the political culture and social context, efficiency in performance relevant to group goals is a critical dimension applicable to organizational relationships and actions. Indeed, the "efficiency structure" of the party may have genuine conceptual priority. As Avery Leiserson has put it, "In all parties the institutional context is that of efficiency, whether in controlling votes or for other purposes. . . ."[1] Structural efficiency is not, however, to be viewed narrowly. It is heavily involved in the operational and tactical styles of party leaders at the different echelons, the performance of those internal activities peculiarly relevant to success in a particular social milieu, as well as in the structure's adaptive relationships with its environment. One cannot conceptualize the party in a social vacuum. "The power process is not a distinct and separable part of the social process, but only the political aspect of an interactive whole."[2] The party structure, if efficient, responds to, as well as influences, social conditions. Strategy and character of adaptive contacts vary greatly. They may be manifested in the multiple-group memberships of party activists, the formal or informal processes by which social interests are given a "hearing," the acceptance of "deviant outsiders" into the structure, and in the subtle techniques by which party and other group activists mutually "infiltrate" each others' organizations. These "intelligence" and "support" mobilization interactions are crucial to efficiency; and efficiency is crucial to structural viability.

Second, the party structure can be conceived as a *communication subsystem.* Whether viewed as a social or political group, the party cannot be understood unless the patterns of interaction between actors, between echelons, and between subcoalitions are identified and evaluated, for the party is more than a set of discrete roles, sectors, or levels. Its basic functional character emerges in one respect from the interrelations of these parts, in the formulation of group objectives as well as in their execution. Because of the critical interdependence of goal strategy and tactical implementation in a party, one might, indeed, theorize

[1] *Op. cit.*, p. 192.
[2] Lasswell and Kaplan, *Power and Society*, p. xvii.

that the nature of "information flow" in a party structure may be more important than in other large-scale organizations. Thus, Rossi and Cutright observed in their discussion of party organization in "Stackton": "Party workers through frequent contact among themselves and with party officials and office-holders diffuse a consensus over goals and methods and sustain in each other a sense of the importance of their activities."[3] On the other hand, one may hypothesize, on the basis of other characteristics of American parties, that communication patterns are entropic. This was suggested by V. O. Key, who observed the continual "fractionalization" of the internal party structure.[4]

In the analysis of communicative relationships, it is necessary to study the *direction* of the contacts maintained, that is, which parts of the structure are communicating with other parts. This includes analysis of the extensiveness of contacts as well as the degree of reciprocity in the relationships; the *content* of communication (aspects of organizational life about which conversations and involvement occur); and the *process context* in which these contacts take place (the organizational and time contexts in which interactions occur).

The nature of communication in the party group is intimately bound up with key functional problems. A party needs stability of relationship in all sectors of the structure, enduring patterns which will help the group maintain itself as a working collectivity despite the presence of divisive, pluralistic forces and subunits within. As a conflict structure, the party is always subjected to internal threats. In the face of these threats there is need for constant modification of the leadership substructures, as well as the social interest subcoalitions. The party must develop an integrationist modus vivendi. It may "aggregate" or dissipate conflict, or merely contain it. But if the party is to be a viable structure it must, for power-maximization purposes, demonstrate sources of structural strength which supravene separatist conflict. The communication process of the internal party

[3] In Morris Janowitz, ed., *Community Political Systems*, p. 95.
[4] *Op. cit.*, p. 377.

organization is important to such internal structural adaptation.

Further, the patterns of communication are intimately related to the state of "power consensus" and the level of morale within the structure. The party structure has a mission of indoctrination, seeking to shape attitudes and perceptions of group goals and tactics. This is, of course, not merely a matter of explicit and visible interpersonal contacts. It is also to be perceived as a long-range process of socialization taking place over extended periods of time, and resulting from a variety of subtle, scarcely visible associations and influences. The flow of information in the structure will determine whether group goals are comprehended, or whether they are gradually displaced by private motives, or by social, nonpower, aspirations. Related to this, but analytically separable, is the problem of the morale of activists. The content of individual satisfactions held by the party activist with his role, tasks, and relationships in the structure, dependent on his own criteria for satisfaction, condition considerably the strength of his identification. The internal mechanisms by which the party attends to morale needs are critical to structural viability. They can be investigated partially, at least, through the analysis of communication relationships.

Third, and finally, the party structure must be viewed as a decisional group. A great many decisions are made concerning the operation of the party apparatus, tactics to be employed at a given time in the pursuit of power goals, and opportunities for the individual activist in that structure. Specifically, decisions are made on strategy, finance, candidate selection, allocation of skills and other resources, ideological positions, hierarchical relationships and organs, and a host of other matters. How much interest the ordinary activist has in these matters, the degree of his participation in decision-making, and the extensiveness of organizational consultation and consent for these decisions, are important analytical questions. They are also normatively exciting. Political scientists have traditionally called for more "intra-party democracy." Just how important is such democracy in the party structure to viability is at the present a great mystery.

It may be that, realistically, our expectations should not be too high. Seymour Lipset has pointed out, "Even in trade unions and professional associations which vitally affect the individual's occupational role, such membership apathy is the usual state of affairs."[5] Yet, if the "rationality model" of Anthony Downs is valid, the consent structure of the party is vitally related to its power-winning probabilities.[6] This position contrasts strikingly with that of Avery Leiserson:

> Although all parties profess the importance of membership participation, criticism, and consultation, they differ only in degree with respect to which party members at the base are permitted to engage in any pretense of deliberation or policy discussion beyond the limits of how best to execute the tasks assigned to them in the organizational effort.[7]

Despite our value preferences, it is necessary to unravel as best we can, both descriptively and analytically, the consent pattern in the party structure and its relevance to internal viability. Relevance, in this instance, depends on the nature of activist demands, which will in turn vary considerably from one society and culture to the next. Yet, it is hard to conceive of organizational consent patterns as totally irrelevant, even if one is concerned only with the dimensions of efficiency, morale, and group goal achievement. Furthermore, decisional participation and consent may be, theoretically, relatively inconsequential for internal viability, but may have great bearing on the party's performance in the total political system. In leadership recruitment, for example, consent may be a criterion critical to the system, determining in part the quality of performance and characteristics of those who achieve top power positions in the society, even though the apathy of the activists may not pose a threat to internal structural viability. The analysis of the party structure as a decisional group, therefore, is not only a natural interest with normative implications, but necessary for understanding

[5] *Op. cit.*, p. 373.
[6] See *An Economic Theory of Democracy*, p. 28.
[7] *Op. cit.*, p. 191.

the total character of the party as a structural entity and its performance in the larger system.

The party structure is, then, a task group, a communication network, and a decisional subsystem. We do not mean to imply, however, that analytically these conceptions are completely distinct, nor that each of them alone explains the basic properties of the party structure. Clearly, the efficiency level at which the party operates as a task group is interrelated with the communicative pattern of the structure and probably also with the mode of decision-making activity. In addition, certain properties of the total organization, the extent of integration of the party structure, the conflictual nature of the structure, the level of activist morale, the degree of organizational deliberation or manipulation, can only be explained through a combined analysis of the party as a task group, communication network, and decisional subsystem. At least it would seem to be a valid assumption that morale, for example, is functionally related to the individual activist's place in, and perception of, the efficiency structure, the flow of communication, and the process of decision-making.

If one utilizes these three basic conceptions of structural relationships, it is possible to identify various types or models of party structures. Thus, the old "boss-ridden machine" structure conforms to expectations of high efficiency in task performance, a communication pattern emphasizing low reciprocity, instrumentalist content, and bureaucratic conformity, with limited involvement of lower-level activists in decision-making. At the other theoretical extreme is the "ideological party association" of doctrinaire idealists, in which decisional participation is high and communication not restrictive, but whose task performance is at the lower end of the continuum. A further variant is the "status-oriented" structure, perhaps of a minority party in an overwhelmingly one-party area, in which the structure may be deficient in all three respects, although a minimal level of communication takes place if the party, under such circumstances, is to be characterized in any sense as a meaningful structural entity. Finally, the juxtaposition of these concepts may lead us to the Downs model, which hypothesizes high expectations for the party structure in all three contexts. To Downs the party is a "team," "a coalition whose members agree on all goals," who "formulate policies in order to win elections." As Downs has said, "the informal structure, i.e. that structure centering around the private motives of those who run each party," is highly significant in analyzing the party.[8] Implicit in his model is the expectation of effective communicative relationships, high efficiency, and high decisional involvement. This "team concept" of the party, with its heavy emphasis on complete knowledge of the objectives of the party group, its implicit assumption of complete assent for party decisions, and its insistence that the activists are highly motivated to task productivity, is a model worth testing, but which probably does not square with empirical fact. Yet, the social climate and political culture of a society no doubt determine the reality limits of the model.

In modern, moderately pluralized, industrial (or postindustrial) societies, such as the United States, we would expect only partial approximations of the Downs model. In metropolitan and urban environments where there is considerable, though varying, two-party competition, and where the two major parties are power-oriented, one would expect no neat implementation of the "ideal" type of structural requisites. Rather, it seems that the four basic images of the party utilized in this study previously (open clientelism, subcoalitional character of party subgroups, stratarchical nature of internal power patterns, and pluralistic type of careerism in modern parties) would conduce to the emergence of a type of party structure only partially reflective of ideal expectations. First, one would expect a degree of "organizational slack" in task performance due to the absence of central control, inadequate indoctrination in efficiency functions, varying needs for efficiency because of the differential competitive status of precincts, and the motivational pluralism of the activists. Second, patterns of "partial communication" probably

[8] *Op. cit.*, pp. 25–30.

exist in such party structures, due to the presence of large numbers of social deviants recruited for party work, the unequal status of the subcoalitions in the structure, the isolation of the individual activist within the organization, and the differential mobility aspirations of the careerists. Third, one must hypothesize the "autonomization of decision-making" within the structure, with at least two separable levels of decision-making—localist-oriented decision-making, which is preoccupied with those activities, tactics, and tasks related to the instrumentalist function of winning the vote in the precincts, and centralist-oriented decision-making, preoccupied with more substantive matters of organizational policy and status. It is conceivable that a third sector of decision-making must also be explored, that of the middle-level activists who sit on executive committees and deal with issues and problems related to the coordination of instrumentalist activities for certain grass-roots subunits, on the one hand, and the preliminary screening and discussion of basic conflicts relevant to organizational policy on the other. This third sector may thus function as a "buffer" for the top executive elite and a transmission belt for demands from the base of the organization, in addition to assuming certain intermediate submanagerial responsibilities.

These considerations suggest that the modern party structure is indeed a hybrid, not conforming well to ideal expectations. The precise degree of efficiency, communicative interchange, and decisional consent require careful analysis in order to determine the extent to which the structure does approximate ideal conditions, the conditions under which it deviates, and the factors which best explain the components and extent of structural viability. In the following discussion, we will first analyze the party structure separately for each of these conceptual vantage points—as task group, communication network, and decision group. We will then discuss the interrelationships of these three bodies of theory and data. Finally, we shall attempt to explain the findings by utilizing those independent variables, both inside and outside the party structure, which seem to be most promising for explication.

CHAPTER 13

THE PARTY AS A TASK GROUP

From interviews with district chairmen and board members it is clear that the great majority were dedicated to developing an efficient organization. They were not merely titular leaders, resting on their laurels after a long career in politics which, for a few, had meant a patronage position. "The district chairman must sell his ideas and keep the place efficiently organized." "The district chairman's main job is to win elections; to do this he must organize the district." "My job is to build a foundation for a Republican vote—to do this I must keep in touch with the organization, keep the workers active, maintain harmony." "There is no letdown for the district chairman even between elections. He has to supervise all political activity within the district—it can be a very positive job giving the chairman real power of initiative." These recurring opinions suggest that most top echelon leaders had achieved that position because they were conscious of the need for effective organizational leadership and spent a great deal of time in the performance of organizational tasks. The chairmen reported that they devoted all or most of their leisure time to the party during the campaign period; 70 per cent of executive board members reported over five hours a week during the campaign, and almost 50 per cent spent over 10 hours a week.

The particular tasks in which these leaders were interested, and on which they claimed to concentrate their energies, reveal their organizational leadership perspectives. Four task areas appeared to predominate in the minds of the majority: promoting factional harmony, allocating patronage, planning campaign strategy, and developing organizational policy. In addition, the Democratic leaders were preoccupied with finance. Close to 50 per cent of all leaders emphasized the recruitment of lower-level activists, as well as the task of working with and supervising precinct workers. On three other types of tasks, however, much less emphasis was placed in both parties: candidate selection, discussion of issues, and contacts with elected representatives (at the county, state, or national levels).

The heavy emphasis on patronage and factional harmony represented a concern for long-run organizational viability—the need to hold the structure together by satisfying worker demands and moderating internal disagreements. There is no doubt that much top echelon activity was preoccupied, whether successfully or not, with these concerns. This interest in structural relations was manifested also in the great amount of time devoted at monthly board meetings to the details of organizational policy—committee assignments and work reports, scheduling and planning party events, determining the nature of the organizational substructure and responsibilities, etc. Preoccupation with worker recruitment reflected long-range concerns about the "turnover" of personnel at the grass roots, as well, no doubt, as the leaders' own interests in developing support for themselves and their policies. On the other hand, the emphasis on campaign strategy (and finance, on the Democratic side) was the major explicit concern with short-run implications. Though the other tasks allegedly performed by leaders were not irrelevant to short-run goals, they were not as exclusively meaningful. It appears that the discussion and development of strategy for the next campaign was the major task for a large number of the top leadership nucleus, directed at immediate vote maximization. The selection of candidates was much less emphasized, and the same was true for the development of issues. Over half of the top leaders did mention their supervisory responsibilities for a group of precincts (virtually all were board members), but practically none of them discussed actual problems and procedures of registration, files, canvassing, and election-day activities. Their silence on these matters gave the impression that they viewed their task as strategic, supervisory, even tactical, and operational in terms of planning, but not performance.

There was not always agreement between chairmen and board members about which tasks were most important, or actually performed. Board members in both parties, for example, de-emphasized the candidate selection function (only 26 per cent mentioned it as an important activity of the board), while three-fourths of the chairmen emphasized this activity. One is also led to believe that the selection of candidates was "back-room work," as one chairman put it, proscribed by party norms (since pre-primary endorsement was vigorously opposed by the leadership in all but one district), or that the "self-starter" type of candidate actually took this decision out of the hands of the leadership. Internal schisms in the party, as well, seemed to dictate a "hands-off" policy by the organizational leadership.

Although the top leadership appeared, therefore, to be dedicated to efficiency, did spend time on these various tasks, and did identify certain tasks considered critical for building, maintaining, and motivating the organization, the key question remains: Just how efficient was the executive nucleus? "Efficiency" is difficult to define, its components are elusive, and all of the evidence cannot easily be marshalled. Certainly the level of vote production or the margin of victory is not in itself convincing, since actual votes must be construed in terms of "potential," and the relationship between top leadership task performance and lower-level vote production cannot be assumed. Further, we are interested in various aspects of organizational efficiency which are not proximate to vote production, though this may be their long-run relevance. Certain types of evidence and lines of argument can be presented, however, despite the difficulty of measuring efficiency absolutely.

One notices, first, that most chairmen themselves were not satisfied. All but two of the chairmen made criticisms of their organizations which reflected on their own efforts. They were particularly conscious of the low level of precinct leaders' participation, the lack of coordination in organizational activity, and the continued existence of factional conflict. This criticism was shared by the board members, two-thirds of whom felt there was not maximum efficiency, 54 per cent making some criticism of the way the chairman performed. One-fourth of the board members were very critical.

Second, in addition to this self-criticism, the relative absence of interest in, or control over, certain organizational responsibilities was significant. Over 60 per cent of the top leaders said they did not concern themselves with candidate selection and the development or articulation of issues; from 40 to 50 per cent did not perceive lower-echelon worker and leader recruitment as an important task. These were blind spots in organizational task perspectives.

Third, certain internal "reality checks" were possible which indicated less than maximum efficiency. For example, all chairmen discussed the recruitment of precinct personnel and a desire to maintain contact with these activists. Yet, when asked how frequently they, as chairmen, saw their precinct leaders, only two chairmen (one Republican, one Democrat) admitted that they saw them as much as once a month during the campaign, and four admitted that they rarely saw precinct leaders. The majority of chairmen admitted also that they had little or nothing to do with the training of precinct workers.

Another "reality check" concerns the matter of deliberation over party issues. It is significant that two-thirds of the board members who perceived issue development as an organizational task admitted that they had never attempted to organize discussions of issues for precinct leaders or workers. Of more importance, in this connection, is the fact that 60 per cent of board members stated, when asked, that "issues" were more important to their workers than "candidates." Yet, only 38 per cent of the board members claimed that they had at some time organized discussions of the issues. Calculated somewhat differently, this means that 65 per cent of board members did not engage in the discussion of issues, even though they were fully aware that their workers were issue-oriented.

A different type of "reality check" emerges from responses of precinct leaders. Since almost all district chairmen and the great majority of board members professed an interest in the lower reaches of the hierarchy (even though they did not all feel that precinct-leader recruitment and activation was a major task), it is well to check this interest against the reports of precinct leaders. Although the development of campaign strategy was apparently a crucial top-echelon task, 18 per cent of the precinct leaders claimed that they knew of no over-all strategy for the campaign. Again, board chairmen often mentioned that they supervised a "section" or "ward" (a number of precincts), yet over 30 per cent of the precinct leaders had no knowledge of wards, or reported no contact at the ward level (in districts where such an intermediate organizational level did in fact exist). Further, as reported previously, if the strengthening of the organization at the precinct level is the concern of top leadership, it is a task not satisfactorily followed through, as evidenced by the large number of precincts with virtually no activists engaged in campaign work. Of the 80 precincts in which interviews were taken, 34 were virtually unstaffed and inert in the Republican organization, and 23 in the Democratic organization. This evidence suggests that the level of performance left much to be desired, even for such major tasks emphasized by the top leadership as strategy development, precinct supervision, and the strengthening of the organization.

The analysis leads strongly to the conclusion that task performance was minimal, not optimal, at the top executive level. There was inefficiency in a qualitative sense, i.e., in the types of tasks de-emphasized and not, admittedly, well performed (as in issue education and discussion), as well as inefficiency in a quantitative sense, i.e., in the percentage of precinct leaders not activated or influenced by top-level task performance which, presumably, had lower-echelon relevance. Further, though variations by districts existed, one does not gather the impression, from a reading of the interview material, that the top leadership was in fact a collaborative efficiency "team" or "machine." There was much confusion and disagreement, both about task priorities and the level of performance.

Inefficiency in the party structure seemed to be a function of personal incompetence, inaction, and lack of imagination, with a good deal of "slack" in personal effort, but this was also an attribute of the system. Basic organizational conditions made efficient task performance difficult—the nonsalaried segments of district leaders, the custom of avoiding premature involvement in candidate selection, the factional conflicts over patronage and policy, the dispersion of control and pluralization of power in the organization, and the autonomy of the precincts. Indeed, top district leaders were the greatest complainers about "the system"—50 per cent would have liked more discipline in the organization, and the great majority (all but one of the chairmen) were strongly in favor of more patronage in order to maintain interest and motivate workers. It is significant that the chairmen did perceive the precincts as fairly autonomous, and that only one-third sincerely approved of this. Significant also is the fact that not one chairman insisted he had any meaningful sanctions to invoke over subordinates, and only one chairman felt he had any control over elected representatives. Under these organizational conditions, as perceived by the executive nucleus, top leaders probably could not have achieved peak efficiency even if they worked continuously and with vigor at their major tasks. The fact that the top leadership ignored certain tasks, and worked somewhat less than arduously at others, may well reflect their feelings of frustration. The probability that candidate selection, precinct leadership training and supervision, ideological clarity, and organizational perfection could be effectively sought, under the extreme stratarchical conditions of the system, was low. Though efficiency could be improved, miracles could not be accomplished. Thus the chairmen sought to maintain a "holding operation" by keeping the loose aggregation of top-level leaders in a moderate state of agreement, and working on problems at the peak of the organization, without seeking to innovate, and without disturbing the prerogatives and status of those at the precinct level of the hierarchy. The top nucleus, no doubt, settled for less than it should. It sought to maintain a factional modus vivendi, discussed strategy, allocated patronage, and acted on organizational trivia, while the conditions of organizational life at the base of the party remained relatively undisturbed.

TASK PERFORMANCE OF THE PRECINCT CADRE

Any student of the American party with experience at the grass-roots level, who has also retained a broad-gauged organizational perspective, can specify the efficiency characteristics of the "ideal" precinct leader. Such a leader, first, meets certain organizational criteria for task performance, such as having complete records of the residents in his area, an adequate number of competent workers, and means for the coordination or direction of these workers by frequent meetings or other directive techniques. Next, he fulfills expectations concerning the activity patterns of the precinct worker group during the campaign: registration and fund drives, literature distribution (if these are considered worth while), house-to-house canvassing (and/or telephone canvassing), rallies, and the climactic activities of election day itself. The use of other media, posters, sound trucks, etc., might be added to this list. Third, the efficient precinct leader is active in the planning and execution of long-run, between-election activities, as social and political meetings in the precinct, training of workers, maintaining contacts with old and new residents, giving advice and providing economic assistance to people in the district. Finally, the "ideal" precinct leader is characterized as maintaining an adaptive set of relationships between his organization and the leading social sectors, the most important social groups, and the most influential leaders in his bailiwick. Efficiency for the precinct leader can be operationalized, therefore, without evidence that some of these components are more significant than others, as requiring a sound organizational base, short-run and long-run activities with a high probability of competitive and integrative "payoffs," and environmental adaptation.

In the interviews with Detroit area precinct leaders a mass of detailed information about their precinct operations was secured which permitted determination of the level of efficiency on all the above criteria. We were surprised, first, to find so few precinct leaders who met the basic *organizational* criteria. Only 3 per cent of the Republican leaders and 13 per cent of the Democratic leaders met all three criteria (records, workers, and worker meetings) satisfactorily.[1] About one-fifth of both parties' leaders met two of the criteria; about one-third met only one criterion (usually the records requirement). This means that about one-half of the Republican leaders and slightly more than one-fourth of the Democratic leaders were poor on all three criteria.

Very similar proportions of leaders in both parties had adequate records—48 per cent for the Democrats, 44 per cent for the Republicans.

Our findings on these organizational criteria suggest the organizational "styles" used in Table 13.1. The large percentage of precinct leaders who operated alone can be seen from this analysis. In addition, one-fourth of the Republicans and 40 per cent of the Democrats ran their precincts with an "in-group" of family members and friends.[2] Those most efficiently organized for precinct work, "the enterprisers," represented only 20 per cent of Republican leaders and 44 per cent of Democratic leaders. One must be cautious in the use of these data, however. Efficiency cannot be inferred from them alone. The "loner" may have exerted herculean vote-mobilization efforts, while the "enterpriser" may have had a sound organizational base but have been inefficient in task performance.

[1] The standards set for satisfactory organizational conditions were not very vigorous: up-to-date records, at least three other workers, and at least two meetings with precinct workers during the campaign.

[2] Another interesting datum is that while 20 per cent of Republican leaders admit getting help in the form of additional workers from "outside" the precinct, 39 per cent of the Democratic leaders informed us that they received such help.

TABLE 13.1

ORGANIZATIONAL STYLES OF PRECINCT LEADERS*

	Republicans	*Democrats*
"Lone operator"	47%	20%
"Marginal"	33	36
Family or friends "machine"	22	13
Mixed "machine"	11	23
"Enterpriser"	20	44
Family or friends "machine"	2	17
Mixed "machine"	18	27

* "Lone operator"—reports no helpers' or workers' meetings.

"Marginal"—no more than 3 helpers ordinarily, and no more than 2 helpers in the campaign; one or no meeting of workers in the campaign; little evidence of systematic direction of campaign work.

"Enterpriser"—at least 4 workers ordinarily, and 3 in the campaign; at least two meetings of precinct workers in the campaign; evidence of personal, systematic direction of campaign work.

Experience with party campaign work suggests *three* critical types of activities superseding the others in importance—registration drives, personalized canvassing (either house-to-house or by telephone), and the election-day roundup of votes. Admittedly, the importance of these may vary by party and by precinct, but generally one can consider them more important than literature distribution, rallies, etc. If we consider these three tasks as critical, a minority of precinct leaders reported engagement in all three, and about half reported involvement with only one of the three, or with none. (Table 13.2).

Registration was the one critical task performed by the largest number of precincts, but apparently the follow-up job of mobilizing registered voters did not take place in many precincts. A more detailed analysis revealed only 1 per cent of precinct leaders performed seven types of tasks, another 10 per cent performed five or six tasks, while 18 per cent performed four tasks. The Democratic leaders had a better record than the Republicans—39 per cent as compared to 21 per cent performing four

TABLE 13.2

PERFORMANCE OF CAMPAIGN TASKS BY PRECINCT ORGANIZATIONS

Task patterns	*Reports by:* *Democratic precinct leaders*	*Republican precinct leaders*
All 3 critical tasks: registration, canvassing, election-day roundup	17%	25%
2 critical tasks		
Registration, plus one other	38	19
No registration, but other two	0	3
Only one critical task	31	23
No critical tasks, but did report other types of activities	4	12
None of the 8 tasks performed	10	18

or more tasks, although, as Table 13.2 indicates, a larger percentage of Republicans performed all three critical tasks.

Combining an analysis of organizational conditions and campaign activities reveals the small number of precinct leaders who met "ideal" requirements. Rather than be too rigorous, we specified as the "ideal" precinct leader the one whose organization maintained adequate records, workers, and direction of workers, on the one hand, and engaged in at least two of the three critical tasks. Only 7 per cent of Democratic precincts and 3 per cent of Republican precincts met these criteria of task performance. Another 14 per cent of Democrats and 13 per cent of Republicans met two organizational criteria and two critical campaign-task criteria. At the other extreme were those who met none of the criteria—10 per cent of Democrats, 14 per cent of Republicans. Thus, by this combination, only 21 per cent of Democrats and 16 per cent of Republicans could be construed as operating near the peak of potential performance, another third in both parties were at the "middle level" in performance, and the balance had a dubious record. The differences by parties in this analysis were not striking.[3]

Certain puzzling findings raise questions concerning precinct efficiency. There were precincts which seemed "organization minded," but did not put the organization to work—20 per cent of Democrats, 11 per cent of Republicans. On the other hand, there were active precincts without proper organizational conditions—34 per cent Democrats, 32 per cent Republicans. Specifically, many precinct organizations never used their good records on election day—32 per cent of the Democrats with such records admitted this, 20 per cent of the Republicans. At the same time, 30 per cent of the Democrats and 17 per cent of the Republicans who engaged in election-day activities admitted that their records were not good. Many precinct leaders had workers but admitted that they never met with them—37 per cent of the Democrats with worker teams admitted this, 78 per cent of the Republicans. Perhaps even more significant were the percentages of those precinct worker "teams" which did *not* engage in the following crucial activities:

	Democrats	*Republicans*
Election-day work	66%	20%
Registration	7%	20%
House-to-house canvassing	54%	68%

The potential for vote maximization with current party personnel was obviously great!

The activities of the precinct leader between elections may be highly indicative of the efficiency of his organization. We asked precinct leaders to describe the types of party organization activity engaged in between election campaigns, what the leader's role was, whether the leader gave advice or assistance to people in the precinct, and the precise nature of this contact with the public.

[3] An Index of Precinct Organization and Campaign Task Performance was developed for these 12 criteria. The maximum score was 38. Only 1 per cent of the precincts had a score of at least 24, about 17 per cent had a score of 16 to 23, and 10–14 per cent had a score of zero.

Local party organizations were less quiet between elections than might be expected. Close to 69 per cent of Republican leaders and 91 per cent of the Democrats reported some type of interelectoral activities. As Table 13.3 indicates, a larger percentage of precinct leaders provided assistance to constituents than engaged in actively promoting social events or rallies in their precincts. The precinct leader who was concerned with and contacted by the public had not completely disappeared from the metropolitan community—58 per cent of the Democratic leaders were "advisors" or "welfare promoters," and 38 per cent of the Republicans were, even though our analysis of role perceptions revealed they did not see this as their major task. Nor did they see the planning of precinct social events as their own major responsibility, since 62 per cent of the Democratic leaders and 45 per cent of the Republicans left the organizing of such functions to subordinates. In sum, on the basis of available evidence, the

TABLE 13.3

PATTERNS OF PRECINCT ACTIVITIES NOT DIRECTLY RELATED TO THE CAMPAIGN

	Democrats	*Republicans*
Meetings, rallies, and social events in the precinct between elections	81%	46%
Precinct leader took active role in organizing	19	1
Precinct leader gave advice and assistance to constituents	58	38
Domestic and personal advice	28	20
Economic assistance	18	9
Participated in the solution of neighborhood problems	24	13
Meetings, rallies, etc., were held in precinct, *or* leader gave advice, etc.	91	69
Meetings, rallies, etc. were held in precinct, *and* leader gave advice, etc.	39	11
Precinct leader participated actively in the meetings, rallies, or social events—by organizing, performing services, or attending such functions	30	9

Republicans had a larger percentage of inert metropolitan precincts than the Democrats—one-third in contrast to one-tenth—but from 40 to 60 per cent of the precinct leaders in both parties still appeared to act, even though sporadically, as "brokers" or "mentors" in individual or neighborhood problem-solving situations.

The "ideal" precinct leader in the old tradition is supposed to be active during campaigns *and* between elections. We found 19 per cent of the Democrats and 4 per cent of the Republicans who fulfill this expectation. This means that many precinct leaders performed one *or* the other of these types of activities well. Thus, 75 per cent of the Democrats who performed very poorly or not at all during campaigns revealed some activity or "broker role" between campaigns. The same was true of 52 per cent of the Republicans with a poor campaign performance record. There was indeed some overlap, but the correlation was by no means significant. The result was that only 11 per cent of the Democratic leaders performed poorly during the campaign *and* throughout the year; the same was true of 26 per cent of the Republican leaders. This gave a decided advantage numerically to the Democrats. But the question still remains, "What kinds of precincts were these, and how damaging was the inertness of the precinct leader and his organization to the party's cause?" An analysis of the most inert type of precinct will be made subsequently.

The "ideal" precinct leader also maintains adaptive relationships with the environment in which he seeks to gain support. He is, theoretically, a "joiner" of nonparty groups, he works with the leadership and membership of important organizations in his neighborhood, and he associates politically with individuals drawn from social strata other than his own. This image we found to be relatively true of approximately 67 per cent of Democratic precinct leaders, and about 40 per cent of Republican leaders (Table 13.4). Only 2 per cent of all leaders belonged to no groups, and about 40 per cent belonged to six or more. The political associates of over 80 per cent of the leaders re-

TABLE 13.4

ADAPTATION EVIDENCE FOR PRECINCT LEADERS BY TYPE OF ORGANIZATIONAL STYLE

	Lone operators		*Marginals*		*Enterprisers*		*All leaders*	
	D	*R*	*D*	*R*	*D*	*R*	*D*	*R*
Adaptation criteria:								
Group affiliations								
Belong to no groups	19%	0%	0%	0%	0%	0%	4%	0%
Belong to 1–2 groups	19	40	16	13	7	3	12	24
Belong to 3–5 groups	26	27	40	70	33	55	34	47
Belong to 6 or more groups	36	33	44	17	60	42	50	29
Worked with nonparty groups in the precinct during the campaign	19	15	19	32	46	28	30	23
Occupations of the three political associates of the precinct leader								
All the same as leader	26	16	4	13	7	14	9	15
Different, and included blue-collar workers	26	16	42	2	47	0		
Different, and included white-collar workers	39	44	29	60	13	28		
Adaptation index*								
High score								
26–32	0	0	10	0	16	0	11	0
21–25	4	6	18	26	36	21	23	15
16–20	33	15	32	21	34	52	33	24
11–15	19	21	32	40	5	21	17	27
5–10	22	30	6	13	9	6	10	20
Low score								
Below 5	22	28	2	0	0	0	5	13
Number of cases	27	67	50	47	61	29	138	143

* This Index was based on the following items besides the three criteria used in this table: relationship of helpers to leader, number of helpers, communication patterns in the party hierarchy, and whether the precinct leader worked with nonparty group leaders outside of the precinct. Maximum score possible was 32.

vealed considerable occupational breadth. True, only a minority of the leaders—30 per cent Democrats and 23 per cent Republicans—claimed that they worked fairly closely with important nonparty groups in their precincts during the campaign. Yet, many of those who maintained no such formal group political contact did demonstrate considerable adaptiveness in their personal interaction patterns.

Adaptiveness varied by the organizational style of the precinct leader. The "enterpriser" who had a team of workers and directed them carefully was also the leader most likely to work closely with nonparty groups and to maintain extensive contacts. The "lone operator," who ran his precinct virtually by himself, tended to be in less contact with the social structure. From 40 to 60 per cent of the latter had low adaptation index scores (below 10), while less than 10 per cent of the enterprisers had low scores. Yet, even the lone operators were not completely isolated from other groups and group leaders. One-third belonged to over six formal groups; close to 20 per cent worked with nonparty groups in their precincts. In fact, only one-fourth of all lone operators seemed to be isolated both hierarchically and in reference to their social environment. Thus even the leaders who seem to be most status-minded or least vote-maximizing in the party structure did reveal some evidence of political interaction with the social structure.

CONCLUSIONS

Two basic images of the party as a task group emerge from this discussion. At the top was an executive nucleus which performed certain responsibilities irregularly and ineffectively, if at all. The top nucleus seemed confused about which tasks could and should be performed, who could perform them, and who was and should be involved. Above all, there seemed to be considerable "system frustration" in the attitudes of these leaders. At the base of the hierarchy, on the other hand, were the precinct leaders who seemed free to develop their own suborganizations and operational styles. Some appeared to run the precinct without help, others are assisted by friends and family, still others had an effective and representative cadre of workers. From 5 to 20 per cent of the leaders seemed to be approximating the "ideal" requirements for performance efficiency (depending on the rigor of one's expectations). But the great majority—82 to 90 per cent—engaged in *some* types of *campaign* activities, from 69 to 91 per cent reported *some* type of *interelection* activity, and from 87 to 95 per cent reported *some* adaptive contact with the social group structure or social strata of the community. This is hardly a power-maximization image of the party. The party is not a monolithic efficiency structure. It is actually a stratarchy with great tolerance for inefficiency and autonomy in task performance.

CHAPTER 14

THE PARTY AS AN INFORMATION NETWORK

The evidence from the analysis of communicative relationships demonstrates that the party is more than an aggregation of individuals; it is an interacting organizational system. The top executive nucleus (the district chairmen) reported, though not unanimously, that they saw each other at least weekly during the campaign, but less frequently after elections. The county chairman usually participated in these elite sessions. The state chairman was often present also, though this seemed less regular and formalized in the Republican party. Executive board members met with their chairmen at least monthly. The pattern of interaction of the ward or section leaders (the intermediate cadre) with the top nucleus was more variable between districts, but some informational relationships were suggested by our interviews, even though these may sometimes have been highly personalized. The precinct leader reports indicated that 40 per cent of them contacted their district leaders "often" (throughout the year) and another 25 per cent saw them frequently during the campaign. About the same proportions communicated with their ward leaders and precinct leaders. Only 15 per cent said they never saw their district leaders, 11 per cent apparently had no contact with ward leaders, and only 2 per cent did not interact at all with other precinct leaders. If communication is an important criterion of organizational existence, these party leaders revealed that they did indeed constitute an "organization."

Communication contacts in the party structure weave a complex web theoretically, if only in terms of the number of concrete units with which the individual activist's relationships must be plotted: the chairman, individual board members, the board as a collective meeting perhaps once a month, the county chairman, the state chairman, the national committeeman or woman, elected representatives, the ward chairman, the district committees, the youth, women's, or other auxiliary subgroups, other precinct leaders, precinct workers, township or city party organization personnel, and particular political clubs. Our investigation permitted the plotting of some, but not all, of these relationships for three echelons of activists. If we concentrate on the most critical relationships, an "index of interaction" can be constructed, emphasizing the extensiveness of contacts and their frequency. We were interested in each individual leader's interaction with four important parts of the structure, including hierarchical and lateral relationships.[1] Table 14.1 reveals differences by echelon and by party. The Democrats were consistently higher, and the chairmen revealed the best scores by party. But Democratic precinct leaders attained as high a mean score as the Republican chairmen!

TABLE 14.1

INDEX OF PARTY LEADERSHIP INTERACTION WITHIN THE STRUCTURE (Maximum Score Possible = 24)

	Range in scores		*Mean score*
	Low	*High*	
Democrats			
Chairmen	12	20	18
Executive board	8	18	12
Precinct leaders	2	24	15
Republicans			
Chairmen	6	22	15
Executive board	2	22	11
Precinct leaders	0	24	11

[1] Thus the index calculated a score for district chairmen based on their contacts with board members, precinct leaders, other district leaders, and the state chairmen. For precinct leaders the contacts used were state chairman, county chairman, district leader, and other precinct leaders. The score differentiated four degrees of frequency: often, frequently, rarely, never.

Some (14) precinct leaders interacted often with all the critical levels of the structure and actually achieved maximum scores, while chairmen, primarily because of their infrequent contacts with precinct leaders, did not achieve maximum scores. The data indicate great variation in communicative involvement, yet the average chairman exploited about two-thirds of his contact opportunities, the average precinct leader and executive board member approximately one-half.

Although formal channels for interaction were provided by state and party statute—annual district conventions, monthly board meetings, weekly meetings of district leaders with the county leader (during the campaign), our interviews suggested that different communication "styles" develop. These result from special organizational conditions, individual differences in motivation, effective personal associations, perceptions, and knowledge of the organization, and the amount of time the activist can give to party affairs. One chairman said he was opposed to the state chairman, felt he was a man of poor tact, and saw no need or possibility of interaction. Another said that intense factional conflict meant that he interacted poorly with his own board members. A third said he disapproved of youth groups and so had no contact with them. A fourth said he was so busy with other work that he never saw his precinct leaders, even during a campaign. Thus, although there was conscious maintenance of certain types of structural opportunities for interaction, one senses also that there was a certain "anarchy" in communicative interaction in the party. Personal relationship patterns developed. Contacts might be haphazard and unplanned. And the individual leader was free to develop his own communication lines according to his own drive, whim, and time determinations. District chairmen *could,* and did, ignore contacts with state chairmen, when the risks were perceived as minimal and the mutual support needs nonexistent. Similarly one-third of precinct leaders reported no contact with their ward leaders who were supposed to supervise, assist, and coordinate precinct leader activities. This "non-coercive" character of the communicative structure of the party had significance for organizational consensus and task performance.

Despite this sense of individualization in the development of communication relationships, and despite a nonrigid structure, certain patterns are clearly observable. Table 14.2 presents a strong localist orientation of precinct leaders' contacts, if one looks only at frequency of interaction by specific echelon. Two main observations stand out. Interaction of precinct leaders improved from the state to the precinct level; that is, precinct leaders saw each other rather frequently (from 70 to 80 per cent do), but their contacts, *in aggregate terms*, became more and more entropic as one views precinct leaders' relationships with county and state leaders (only 28–40 per cent saw these top leaders frequently or often). Thus the precinct leaders as a group were "district-oriented," and, within the district, were particularly interactive with their own counterparts. Second, fewer Republican leaders had frequent contacts with leaders at all levels than did the Democrats; the Republicans were a strikingly localist-oriented structure.

Although it is natural to assume a "pyramiding" of communicative relationships[2] (that is, a progressively smaller proportion of the 70–80 per cent of precinct leaders who interacted frequently with each other would interact with ward, district, county, and state leaders), a progressive narrowing of interactions is not entirely supported by the data. This is connected to the differential "styles" of communication contacts which one was free to develop within the party. Precinct leaders could indeed bypass the "chain of command" or the expected norms of communicative contact within the hierarchy (Table 14.3). Precinct leaders who communicated upward might ignore certain strata and interact with leaders at particular levels. Many apparently ignored the ward leader (or were ignored by him), and of those precinct leaders who had contacts at the state level (often or frequently), sizeable percentages (30 per cent Demo-

[2] See George C. Homans, *The Human Group* (New York: Harcourt, Brace, 1950), pp. 103–6.

TABLE 14.2

FREQUENCY OF COMMUNICATION BY PRECINCT LEADERS WITH SPECIFIC ECHELONS

	Sees specific leaders:									
	Often		*Frequently*		*Rarely*		*Never*		*Combined rarely or never*	
Contact of precinct leaders with:	*D*	*R*	*D*	*R*	*D*	*R*	*D*	*R*	*D*	*R*
State leaders	23%	6%	25%	22%	37%	43%	12%	29%	49%	72%
County leaders	31	6	27	18	24	42	18	34	42	76
District leaders	51	29	22	30	20	17	7	24	27	41
Ward leaders*	52	34	20	16	20	16	8	34	28	50
Other precinct leaders	41	42	39	29	19	25	1	4	20	29

* The precinct leaders in the districts where no ward structure *actually* existed were excluded from this analysis.
Note: Each percentage is a proportion of all Democratic or Republican precinct leaders.

TABLE 14.3

PATTERNS OF COMMUNICATIVE INVOLVEMENT—PYRAMIDAL AND NONPYRAMIDAL

(Precinct Leaders)

	Democratic leaders	*Republican leaders*
Pyramidal patterns (for precinct leaders who see other precinct leaders often or frequently):		
See district leaders often or frequently	82%	63%
See district *and* county leaders often or frequently	63	22
See district, county, *and* state leaders often or frequently	43	13
Nonpyramidal patterns (for *all* precinct leaders):		
See precinct leaders and district leaders but skip ward contacts	22	22
Communicate with district, county, and state but not with other precinct leaders	9	16
Communicate upward, but not at county level	7	7
Communicate with county and state leaders, but not with district leaders	10	6
Total "nonpyramidal" or "broken" communication patterns	24%	31%

crats, and 67 per cent Republicans) did not have progressive patterns of interaction at lower echelons. In fact, 10–15 per cent of precinct leaders who had state-level contacts seemed to bypass district leaders (or were ignored by them). These various exceptions, if cumulated, reveal that in the aggregate 24 per cent of Democratic leaders and 31 per cent of Republican leaders had "broken" or nonpyramidal patterns of communication.

The major types or "styles" of communication can be clearly typologized for analytical purposes (Table 14.4). The two parties differed sharply in the percentage of "cosmopolitans" among precinct leaders (those with wide contacts throughout

TABLE 14.4

STYLES OF COMMUNICATIVE RELATIONSHIPS
(Precinct Leaders)

	Democrats		*Republicans*	
Cosmopolitans (wide contacts throughout the structure including precinct level)	58%		28%	
Elite associates (little interaction at the precinct or ward levels)	15		19	
Localists (exclusively interacting at the district, ward, and/or precinct level	18		38	
Precinct and district		9		21
Precinct only		9		17
Isolates (no significant contacts with any part of the structure)	9		15	
	100%		100%	

the structure). Almost 60 per cent of the Democrats but less than 30 per cent of the Republicans fell into this category. "Localists," at the other extreme, predominated in the Republican party, particularly those who saw other precinct leaders, and no one else, in the hierarchy. An intermediate group of "elite associates" who interacted at district, county, and state party levels included a larger percentage of Republicans. Finally, "the isolates" made up 10 per cent of the Democrats and 15 per cent of the Republicans. The relationship of these communication pattern types to perspectives and efficiency will be explored later. An interesting query, of course, is whether the primarily "cosmopolitan" communicative pattern of the Democratic structure, or the "localist" orientation of the Republican structure, is more conducive to congruence and functional competence.

The selective patterns of communication not only violate the concept of "the pyramid," they must also be understood in terms of the substructural reality of the party organism. Previously we noted the subcoalitional character of the party and identified the most prominent socio-economic "factions" within each party. As Table 14.5 reveals, communicative styles differed for these subcoalitions. Among Democratic subgroups, labor members (particularly labor union officers) and Negroes had the most extensive contacts; the Poles were heavily localist in their

TABLE 14.5

THE SUBCOALITIONS AND SELECTIVE COMMUNICATION PATTERNS (Precinct Leaders)

	Cosmopolitan and elite patterns	*Localists*	*Isolates*	*Number of cases*
Democratic subcoalitions				
Labor officers	92%	4%	4%	23
Labor members	78	22	0	77
Negroes	88	12	0	32
Irish	66	0	33	18
Poles	56	44	0	16
Business and professionals	43	21	36	14
Germans and English	73	12	15	33
English alone	86	14	0	22
Republican subcoalitions				
Business-managerial whites	35	57	8	46
Other nonlabor whites				
White-collar northwestern European	47	35	18	17
All labor	60	19	21	43
Labor whites	60	15	25	34
Blue collar only	48	20	32	25
Negroes	61	22	17	23
Germans	74	22	4	23
English (Welsh and Scottish)	29	39	32	28
All nationality "deviants"	36	48	16	42
Irish and Poles	44	44	12	18

communications; one-third of the Irish and business and professionals were isolates. But, compared to the Republican structure, the Democratic party was an open and diffuse communication network. Among the Republican subgroups, labor, the Negroes, and the Germans had most extensive contacts in the hierarchy; the business-managerial whites were very "localist"; one-third of the English and blue-collar subgroups were isolates. Variation in communication patterns of the nationality "deviants" in both parties was marked: in the Democratic party large proportions of German and English had extensive contacts, but this was much less true of the Irish, Poles, and other deviants of central, southern, and eastern European origins who were precinct leaders in the Republican party. One senses, then, that while no subgroup was isolated in either party, certain "subcoalitions" utilized communication opportunities more than others. Or, to put it another way, certain subgroups were much more "involved" with the party's organizational leadership and operations.

This partiality in communication relationships is also important in distinguishing the career types identified previously, bearing in mind again party differences in communication. (Table 14.6). It is significant that no isolates were found among the two top career categories in either party (the organizational mobiles and the informal influentials). On the other hand, from 20 to 30 per cent of the noncareerists, as well as other career groups, were isolates. The Democratic top organizational nucleus was cosmopolitan in its contacts, while the same group in the Republican party was heavily localist in its contacts. Of significance, perhaps, is the fact that the nonmobile regulars (those precinct leaders who had long and continuous service but no chance to move upward) had more extensive contacts than one might have hypothesized. Though below the norm in both parties, from 40 to 57 per cent did have cosmopolitan and elite contacts. While this may have prevented them from withdrawal from party work, it must also be recognized that large proportions of these regulars seemed to be relatively parochialized or isolated in their contacts; and still they continued to work for the party.

TABLE 14.6

THE COMMUNICATION PATTERNS OF CAREER TYPES
(Precinct Leaders)

Career types	*Cosmopolitans*		*Elite associates*		*Localists*		*Isolates*		*Number of cases*	
	D	*R*	*D*	*R*	*D*	*R*	*D*	*R*	*D*	*R*
Top organizational mobiles	91%	21%	5%	25%	5%	54%	0%	0%	23	24
Informal influentials	43	47	35	42	22	11	0	0	37	19
Potential careerists	75	38	16	3	6	35	3	24	32	40
Nonmobile regulars	52	16	5	23	14	45	29	16	21	44
Noncareerists	32	25	4	13	44	31	20	31	25	16

Does the party tend to break off communication with those who are ideologically not in accord with the majority? Or, put another way, is there a relationship between communication patterns and ideological conformity? The evidence suggests that the Republican party in Detroit may have developed partial communication relationship with the nonconformist, that is, tended to isolate the "liberal," or "moderate," whereas this was not true for conservatives and moderates among the Democrats (Table 14.7).[3] Thus, close to 80 per cent of Republican conservatives and Democratic liberals had extensive hierarchical contacts, and few (6–7 per cent) of these conformists were isolated. But while 80 per cent of the ideological nonconformists had extensive communication patterns in the Democratic party, less than 40 per cent did in the Republican party. Fully one-fifth of the liberals and moderates were isolated within the Republican structure; only 1 per cent of the conservatives and moderates were isolated within the Democratic structure. Whatever the basis for such exclusion or selectivity, whether by personal choice or by the "party," it seemed that unquestionably a subtle process of partial communication did take place among Republicans and many of the ideological deviationists were cut off.

The degree of communicative involvement also seemed to correspond with, or lead to, more conservatism in the Republican party. There was no conclusive evidence of such a relationship in the Democratic party, however, although the Democratic precinct leaders were more conservative, though not less liberal, as their communication relationships became more entropic (Table 14.8). The Republicans, on the other hand, were definitely more liberal or moderate, and decidedly less conservative, as they became more parochial and isolated. Thus, 48 per cent of the cosmopolitan and elite communicators were consistent conservatives in the Republican party, whereas only 12–13 per cent of those cut off from the top elite levels were reliable conservatives. This suggests the relevance of information networks to the development of perspectives and consensus.

[3] See Chapter 8 for a description of how these ideology groups were operationalized.

TABLE 14.7
COMMUNICATION PATTERNS BY IDEOLOGY
(Precinct Leaders)

	Cosmopolitan and elite contacts		*Localists*		*Isolates*		*Number of cases*	
	D	*R*	*D*	*R*	*D*	*R*	*D*	*R*
Liberals*	76%	–	17%	–	7%	–	63%	–
Conservatives†	–	78%	–	16%	–	6%	–	32%
Liberals and moderates	81	35	14	44	5	21	105	78
Conservatives and moderates	80	49	19	37	1	14	48	101

* Too few Republicans for separate analysis.
† Too few Democrats for separate analysis.

TABLE 14.8

THE IDEOLOGICAL "CONSEQUENCES" OF COMMUNICATION PATTERNS
(Precinct Leaders)

	Democrats			*Republicans*		
	Liberal	*Moderate*	*Number of cases*	*Conservative*	*Moderate*	*Number of cases*
Cosmopolitan and elite communication	56%	43%	86	48%	46%	52
Localist communication	55	20	20	13	82	39
Localists and isolates	60	20	25	12	78	58

Before pursuing this point, however, it is important to look at the context and content of communication contacts in the party structure. In general, it was possible to distinguish three themes in the content of discussions by party leaders and activists: (1) the exploitation of party goals, issues, and images; (2) discussions of organizational details, needs, and problems; and (3) the description of preferred strategies and tactics, particularly for vote-mobilization activities. In our interviews with precinct leaders, for example, when asked to describe the "sorts of things you discuss" with the district leaders, their responses fell rather clearly into these three categories. The 84 per cent who had some contact with district-level leaders gave responses which emphasized strategy and tactics (59 per cent), referred to party issues and goals (14 per cent), and emphasized organizational matters (20 per cent). In the interviews with the district chairmen and executive board members the same three foci of communication emerged, depending on the context and echelon of the organization in which discussions took place. District chairmen and board members tended to concentrate on organizational matters and long-range strategy, discussing problems of finance, patronage, and candidates in a developmental organizational perspective. They did not seem to place great emphasis on specific issues in their references to contacts with state and county chairmen, other district leaders, or board members (only 3 of 12 chairmen and 9 of 40 board members emphasized issues). True, they did not self-consciously differentiate the three content areas distinguished here. It was, however, fairly obvious that they were preoccupied in elite-level discussions with two major concerns: What should be their short-term and long-term strategy as an organization? And how can the organization be perfected, unified, and brought to maximal performance? A third question about specific goals and issue positions that should concern the party occupied only a minority seriously.

In the analysis of the communication content patterns of precinct leaders this relative de-emphasis on party goals and issues is replicated. As Table 14.9 reveals, discussions of vote-getting

TABLE 14.9

CONTENT OF DISCUSSIONS OF PRECINCT LEADERS WITH OTHER LEADERS*

Content of discussions	*With state leaders*		*With county leaders*		*With district leaders*		*With ward leaders*†	
	D	*R*	*D*	*R*	*D*	*R*	*D*	*R*
Party goals, issues	15%	19%	12%	18%	19%	12%	24%	26%
Organizational matters	18	18	25	17	22	16	25	14
Vote-getting strategy and/or tactics	54	55	53	61	54	65	51	59
Nonpolitical and miscellaneous	13	8	10	4	7	7	0	1
Number of responses	186	153	182	115	213	161	143	77
Percentage of all precinct leaders who had no contact	12%	29%	18%	34%	7%	24%	8%	34%

* Since two responses were used, these are percentages of all responses given by those who had some contact with the particular category of leaders used.

† Only for those leaders in districts with wards.

problems consumed from 50 to 65 per cent of the time spent in communication. At the ward level about one-fourth of the responses revealed a "goal" or "ideology" content. At other levels the proportion of responses indicative of such content dropped below 20 per cent. These data attest consistently and dramatically to the great preoccupation of party leaders with the tactical and organizational problems of "getting out the vote." At all levels of the hierarchy, discussions of party goal perspectives seemed to be minimized. The party did not appear to be a team of activists seeking consensus on broad goals or specific issues.

Before reaching this conclusion completely, however, it is necessary to examine the communicative content of each individual activist. How many local leaders were exposed *at all* to discussions of broad party goals and policies? It is one thing to note that the precinct leader's interaction with leaders at all levels was heavily vote-oriented; it is another matter to determine whether he was completely isolated from broad policy discussions. Our data reveal, as a matter of fact, that the communication networks of 57 per cent of the Republicans and 67 per cent of the Democrats included contacts with other leaders in which such broad questions as party goals, issues, and images *were* dismissed. The remainder seemed isolated, either in terms of any contacts, or in terms of contacts which were exclusively narrow and vote-oriented in focus. Combining communication "content patterns" with "style patterns" results in the distributions of Table 14.10. Although those who interacted widely and at the elite levels of the hierarchy tended to be exposed to "broadening" influences and to discussion of party goals and issues, the differences were not great. From 56 to 64 per cent of those who interacted only at the local level of the structure were also exposed to such "broadening" influences. Thus, the majority of precinct leaders were involved in communication networks which at some time forced them to reflect on broad party goals, whether they interacted with the top executive elite or not. In fact, among our career types, particularly for the Democrats, those not in the category of "top organizational mobiles" tended to have had a broader communication perspective.

TABLE 14.10

CONTENT AND STYLE PATTERNS OF COMMUNICATION
(Precinct Leaders)

Style patterns	*Broad content: exposure to discussions of party policy and issues*		*Narrow focus: exposure to strategy and tactics only*		*Number of cases*	
	D	*R*	*D*	*R*	*D*	*R*
Cosmopolitan contacts (and elite contacts only)	74%	69%	26%	31%	101	67
Localist contacts	64	56	36	44	25	54

Yet, this transmission of ideas on party goals and issues appeared to have relatively little impact, whether because of the infrequency of such contacts or for other reasons. Precinct leaders exposed to an information flow which included discussions of party goals and issues tended to be somewhat more ideologically conformist in the Republican party (that is, more conservative) while less conformist (also more conservative) in the Democratic party (see Table 14.11). They also seemed more likely to take on the role of "ideological mentor." The leader who was preoccupied with vote-getting tactics was more apt to see his role as that of a socio-economic welfare promoter. But, having noticed these relatively slight differences for both parties, one discovers very little other evidence that the content of communication is powerful as an explanatory variable. Those precinct leaders with a "narrow" content focus were more likely to be vote mobilizers and power-oriented in the Democratic party, but not in the Republican party. Republican precinct leaders with a narrow focus were not likely to be enterprisers, but this was not so for the Democrats. The data, in sum, do not support the expectation that communication content influences behavior. Rather, one gets the impression that all precinct leaders were so deeply immersed in a network which stressed vote-maximization details that whatever broader issues were discussed, at any level, made very little impact.

TABLE 14.11

THE INTERRELATIONSHIP BETWEEN THE CONTENT FOCUS OF COMMUNICATION IN THE HIERARCHY AND ACTIVISTS' PERSPECTIVES AND OPERATIONAL STYLES (Precinct Leaders)

	Democrats		*Republicans*	
"Dependent" variables	*Narrow focus*	*Broader focus*	*Narrow focus*	*Broader focus*
Ideology				
Liberals	57%	40%	–	–
Conservatives	–	–	16%	27%
Role perception				
Vote-mobilizer	50	42	36	51
Ideological mentor	20	26	15	29
Socio-economic welfare promoter	28	18	23	7
No role articulated	2	12	26	13
Goal perspective				
Power-oriented (overt)	63	61	21	35
Power-oriented (latent)	26	13	20	30
Ideology implementation	11	13	41	30
No goal perspective	0	13	18	5
Operational style				
Lone operator	20	20	69	30
Marginal	43	43	18	44
Enterpriser	37	37	13	26
Number of cases	46	92	61	82

Ironically, one particular analysis we made questions the relevance of upward elite-oriented communication for the transmission of strategy plans. It also furnishes further evidence of the localist, stratarchical character of party strategy decision-making. The question asked of precinct leaders was, "In your opinion, was there a fairly clear plan for your party in Wayne County for the types of activities to be followed during the campaign?" The responses were: 83 per cent yes, 16 per cent no, and 1 per cent don't know. If we look at the communication patterns of precinct leaders, we find that those who interacted at the elite levels of the county and the district were more likely to say there was no strategy than if they had been exclusively oriented toward the precinct level (Table 14.12)! In fact, only 8 per cent of the Democratic isolates said there was no strategy, while 16 per cent of the Democrats interacting at the elite level gave the same response. This raises the question whether (1) there was indeed a strategy plan at all, or (2) whether the party was in any sense

TABLE 14.12

THE TRANSMISSION OF PARTY STRATEGY AT ELITE AND LOCALIST LEVELS (Percentage of Precinct Leaders Asserting There Was No Strategy Plan)

Level of communication	*No strategy*	
	Democrats	*Republicans*
At county and/or district level	16%	32%
At ward level in addition	6	13
At precinct level only	0	0
Isolates—no communication	8	38

efficient as a communication structure in the transmission of the one type of content on which party leaders placed so much emphasis—the transmission of the tactical battle plan.

The communication system of a group such as a political party, which is a loose association of individuals in a fluid coalitional and structural state, is, as expected, incomplete and imperfect. While it may be imperfect as a transmission system for strategy, there is evidence that the extensiveness of hierarchical communication on the part of the local activist is highly relevant to his comprehension of the total organization. Table 14.13 shows, for both parties, those who had wide communicative contacts were very aware and informed of the nature of their district party's structure and activities. None of the Democratic isolates were very aware and only 5 per cent of the Republican

TABLE 14.13

THE IMPACT OF COMMUNICATION ON ORGANIZATIONAL AWARENESS AND LOYALTY
(Precinct Leaders)

	Democrats				*Republicans*			
	Cosmo-politan interactors	*Elite associates*	*Localists*	*Isolates*	*Cosmo-politan interactors*	*Elite associates*	*Localists*	*Isolates*
Level of organizational awareness								
Very aware	65%	71%	4%	0%	45%	48%	35%	5%
Doubtful	29	5	72	100	43	30	46	32
Ignorant	6	24	24	0	13	22	19	63
Party loyalty								
Splitting approved	43	86	48	42	48	67	89	95
Splitting condemned	57	14	52	58	52	33	11	5
Number of cases	80	21	25	12	40	27	54	22

isolates were aware. Further, relatively small percentages of precinct leaders whose contacts were localist in focus had a considerable understanding of the party structure. As Table 14.13 also shows, extensive communication did not seem to produce, or be related to, increased Democratic party loyalty (operationalized here simply on the basis of approval of splitting one's ballot), though it did appear clearly related to Republican party loyalty. A 52 per cent majority of Republican cosmopolitans believed in voting a straight party ticket, but only 11 per cent of the localists and 5 per cent of the isolates held this belief. Finally, in this same vein, our analysis of goal perception revealed the following differences for precinct leaders on the basis of communication with district level leaders:

Percentage of precinct leaders who were unable to articulate the party's goals	*Had contacts with district leaders often or frequently*	*Rarely or never saw district leaders*
Democrat	4%	22%
Republican	1	26

This type of evidence strongly indicates that the actuality and character of communication in the political party are significant for the maintenance of the party as a viable socio-political subsystem of action. The communication lines in the party were not a perfect pyramid; communication was highly voluntaristic and noncoercive. From one-fourth to two-fifths of the precinct leaders did not have contacts with their district leaders, and from 10 to 15 per cent seemed almost completely isolated. Further, the content of communication in the party seemed highly preoccupied with "vote getting" and campaign tactics. Nevertheless, a large proportion—from one-half to two-thirds—did at some time become involved in broader questions of party policy, even though this may have been perceived as having a secondary priority. There is evidence that the limited cohesion of parties, the ideological congruence that may exist (especially for the minority party), and the agreement on goals, are partly attributable to the communication network, however anarchic and entropic, in which activists find themselves. The party is certainly not the collaborative group with preponderant consensus or even awareness of goals and tactics which the ideal model would specify. Nor, however, is it an aggregation of individualized actors isolated by echelon and precinct. The party does indeed communicate, and the imperfect "information flow" which occurs as a result of the interaction of these actors between echelons, while not resolving conflict, at least contributes to the minimal stability, organizational adaptation, awareness, loyalty, and aspirations which a party needs if it is to survive.

CHAPTER 15

THE PARTY AS A DECISIONAL SYSTEM

Decisions are acts of power which have consequence for the achievement of group goals and the maximization of group "drive." A multitude of decisional acts occurs within the group, and to separate those with significance is extremely difficult. In a political party are the most important decisions those involving patronage, finance, the recruitment of workers, committee assignments, or registration tactics? Is a decision to adopt a liberal position on Medicare more important than to endorse a particular candidate, or to hold a campaign rally? To rank the diversity of decisions at various levels of the hierarchy confounds all yardsticks and criteria. Doctrinal, strategic, morale-building, candidate-selecting, financial and tactical decisions—all of these may be critical to the organization's existence. To restrict an analysis, therefore, to those decisions made by the top executive nucleus of the party structure would misrepresent the total nature of decision-making reality. For, in a political party particularly, the "little" decisions made at the base of the structure, where votes are mobilized or lost, in their cumulative impact, may be as relevant to the achievement of goals as the "grand" decisions of the upper elite.

Nor is the meaning of the power relationship to be construed narrowly. In a party group it is not sufficient to determine the simple relationship of leader X to leader Y, in a strictly interpersonal sense, and perceptions or reputations of influence, though important, cannot be considered conclusive. A third conceptualization of the influence relationship which sees decisions as power acts reflecting both the interests and demands of "others" in the organization, and having consequences for the behavior of the "others," is necessary. Thus, for example, a patronage decision by top-echelon leader X to "appoint" Jones to the board of chiropractors may be reputationally a power act, may be a power act if viewed interpersonally, in the relationship of X to Y, but it is conceivably relatively unimportant as a group power action. The contingencies in such a case are, (1) Who was concerned or involved in this patronage decision? and (2) Who was affected by it?

To determine, therefore, who has power in a group (and, conversely, who is uninvolved), as well as which decisions are acts of power in a group sense, calls for the identification of the "decisional reference group" of the decision makers. This reference group consists of two separable aggregates—the "interest clientele" (those actors in the group who, with varying degrees of proximity to the decision, are enough concerned about the decision that they must be reckoned with, considered, or "consulted" by the decision maker), and the "impact clientele" (those actors in the group whose behavior is so relevant to group performance that their compliance, support, and implementation of the decision has to be solicited and mobilized). If there is no interest clientele or impact clientele for a decision, from the point of view of the group one can seriously question whether the decision was a group power act; if one *or* the other exists, the decision may be group-oriented, but it will either be dictated or inconsequential. This operationalization emphasizes, above all, the importance of identifying the "concentric circles of varying interest" in the decision by subordinate actors in the group, as well as the "concentric circles of varying compliance" with the decision by the subordinate actors, and determining the extent to which these concentric circles intersect. In a political party structure which is nonbureaucratic, noncoercive, stratarchical, coalitional, and open, the concept of the decisional reference group, particularly the concept of the impact clientele, is highly relevant. Decisions, to be significant for the group, need impact and reciprocal implementation. One strongly suspects that at both ends of the party hierarchy there may be limited interest or involvement in, and limited impact for, the decisions reached at the opposite end of the hierarchy. Thus, within the hierarchy we may possibly see the phenomenon of the autonomization of decision-making relationships.

We shall seek to explore the utility of this theory by examining decisional relationships at the upper echelons of the party structure and subsequently those at the lower echelons. In both analyses we shall concentrate on those who allegedly make the decisions, the perceptions of their power, and their decisional reference groups. Through such empirical analysis we can begin to understand the limits of decisional power and the extensiveness of decisional involvement.

DECISION-MAKING OF THE TOP EXECUTIVE NUCLEUS

Several themes recurred consistently in the interviews with district chairmen as they discussed their organizational influence. First, they insisted that they were not dictators. "I don't know about other districts, but I deny that I control the district board or precinct people under me," said one Republican chairman. A Democratic chairman made this comment:

> "A key problem is responsibility and control in a democratic political system. We have had examples of control in American politics. We had the era of boss rule here in Wayne County, but we then moved away towards anarchy. The most difficult problem is to strike that balance where you can control and yet not be a dictator. I would say our organization needs more control, as well as coordination."

A second impression is of considerable competition, criticism, and opposition within the party structure. Chairmen almost unanimously explained in great detail the types of subgroups and opposition leaders seeking to be heard within the organization as well as seeking control of the chairman's position itself. "I had to club my way in," said one Democratic chairman, but once in, "I had to work for two years with an executive board which disagreed with me on most issues, and when decisions were made through the democratic process, I had to do all I could to carry them out." Another chairman, a Republican, explained that the only way he could keep his organization integrated was to "try to find a basis of agreement with all groups."

A third recurring theme was that all chairmen saw the need to consult widely many individuals and subcoalitional leaders. The accessibility of the chairman was continually underscored in his description of his own activities. Even though, as indicated earlier, we found only limited evidence of frequent and continuous contact with precinct leaders on the part of some chairmen, almost all emphasized the need to "keep in touch" with the local precinct delegates. As one Republican chairman put it:

> "My field work committee is the most important. Its members contact delegates in the precincts. . . . I am much more in touch with party workers than my predecessor. He was from the upper strata of society and found it difficult to converse with all levels of workers. . . . My public contacts committee keeps in touch with civic and fraternal organizations. And the steering committee, which does the back room work, *formulates decisions which it hopes will be accepted by the delegates.*" (italics supplied).

Similarly, a Democratic chairman said:

> "My predecessor had virtually no organization. He only called two meetings of delegates in two years. Delegates were never informed or consulted about the chairman's actions. I have corrected most of these conditions, and I keep in constant touch with my delegates both personally and formally."

This emphasis by chairmen on the sharing of power in the face of tenuous control and continual internal conflict should not obscure the real possibility that these chairmen had more decisional power than they would admit. And indeed if their power was limited, the exact degree of their dependence on others needs careful empirical exploration. That they did participate centrally in the making of certain types of critical decisions was not denied—decisions over patronage, strategy, and organizational activities, primarily, and for a minority, decisions over candidates, issues, and finance. These were the major areas to which chairmen and executive board members referred, and which other interviews and observations corroborated as most important. Thus they were the areas in which the power of the chairmen and their elite associates should be probed.

Ascriptions of power and influence by chairmen and board members were actually contradictory to some extent. As Table 15.1 indicates, both board members and chairmen suggested that the executive boards of the districts were important in making decisions. In fact, the chairmen were more insistent on this point than the board members. On the other hand, chairmen did not underestimate themselves, particularly in the Democratic party, and the board members also perceived the chairman as having "influence," again especially in the Democratic party. These two findings are separable, because we operationalized the problem in two different ways, asking (1) What is the role of the board in making decisions in the district, and how much power does the district board have? as well as (2) How influential is your own chairman in the county organization? As a consequence, it was very possible, theoretically, for a leader to say that the board had "power" and the chairman also had "influence." The picture which emerged was generally one of diffusion or nonconcentration of decisional power when the roles of the two were separated.

A more precise analysis of each individual leader's perceptual relationship to leaders, by district, reveals, however, considerable noncongruence or confusion over power perceptions. We asked both the chairmen and each of the board members to discuss only the board's powers in their own district (Table 15.1). Over 50 per cent of these perceptual relationships were noncongruent (in most cases this meant board members felt the board was less important than the chairman indicated). Other measures of "ascription disagreement" in Table 15.1 further substantiate that close to, or over 50 per cent, of these mutual power per-

TABLE 15.1

ASCRIPTIONS OF DECISIONAL POWER AMONG THE TOP NUCLEUS LEADERS

	Perceptions held by board members		*Perceptions held by chairman*	
	D	*R*	*D*	*R*
Perceptions of board powers, generally				
Board has most, if not all, power	25%	33%	20%	40%
Board shares power with chairman	57	48	80	60
Board has little or no power	18	19	0	0
Perceptions of chairman's influence, generally				
He has much, if not great influence	72	37	60	40
He has some influence, unsure how much	17	21	20	0
He has little or no influence	11	42	20	60
Summary of ascription	*Democrats*		*Republicans*	
Disagreements (board members and their chairman)				
Board members who disagree with their chairman on the board's powers	56%		52%	
Board members disagreeing with their chairman on the chairman's influence	39		68	
Board members disagreeing among themselves on their board's powers	57		48	
Board members disagreeing among themselves on their chairman's influence	48		50	

ceptions were divergent. Board members in the same district revealed a remarkably high degree of confusion over the location of the power.

If we examine decision-making power perceptions in particular decisional areas—notably patronage, strategy, and candidate selection (where our data are most complete)—we find further corroboration of this confusion in perceptions (Table 15.2). In the aggregate, it would appear that the Republicans were fairly well split in their power perceptions concerning, for example,

TABLE 15.2

POWER SELF-PERCEPTIONS OF BOARD MEMBERS IN SPECIFIC DECISIONAL AREAS

	Democrats	*Republicans*
Aggregate distributions		
No power on patronage	24%	41%
No power on patronage and strategy decisions	12	9
No power on patronage and candidate selection	24	23
No power on all 3 decisions	6	5
Much power on patronage	60	41
Much power on patronage and strategy decisions	24	18
Much power on patronage and candidate selection	12	0
Much power on all 3 decisions	6	0
Specific disagreements in power of the board, by district		
Board members disagreeing among themselves on patronage powers	52	72
Board members disagreeing among themselves on strategy decisional power	47	57
Board members disagreeing among themselves on candidate decision power	47	34

patronage decisions, while the majority (60 per cent) of Democratic board members seemed to feel that the board had considerable power. (Only 31 per cent of the Democrats felt the board had much power on strategy decisions, however, and 13 per cent feel the same on candidate selection; for the Republicans the figures were 38 and 14 per cent, respectively.) Again, Table 15.2 presents a high percentage of noncongruence among board members when their individual perceptions are examined by district. Close to, or over, 50 per cent did not agree on the amount of power wielded by the individual boards in patronage, strategy, and candidate decisions. There was undoubtedly great incoherence and lack of clarity in the specification of power prerogatives at the top-elite level in the party structure.

As indicated above, however, power ascriptions do not determine power reality. Less subjective data can be marshalled. We have sought to determine the "decisional reference-group" status of each board member, vis-à-vis the chairman, by combining power self-perceptions with the following types of data: his organizational awareness, the extensiveness of his communication within the hierarchy, his demand for decisional involvement (these three constitute a measure of his interest in and concern about decisional involvement); whether he was a member or representative of a major political faction or subcoalition, whether or not he was ideologically orthodox, and whether he held positive career aspirations (these three constituted a composite measure of his decisional "impact" status). This operationalization distinguishes the board member who is interested in the decisional process and was pressing for "consideration," yet who, theoretically, might be largely ignored because he represents no significant subgroup or was not in the hyperactive careerist cadre. It distinguishes also, on the other hand, the board member who, in theory, had to be taken into consideration because of his organizational status, but who is not highly interested or pressing for decisional involvement.

The individual items in our decisional analysis (Table 15.3) begin to reveal differences in the reference-group status of board

TABLE 15.3

SPECIFIC COMPONENTS IN THE DECISIONAL STATUS OF BOARD MEMBERS*

Components	*Democrats*	*Republicans*
High organizational awareness	59%	50%
High communicative involvement	59	54
Considerable demand for involvement in decisions	53	78
Ideologically orthodox	76	82
Representative of important political support groups	88	77
Aspire to a political career	88	64

* Each percentage is a proportion of all board members.

members. Over 50 per cent of the board demonstrated considerable awareness and communicative involvement in the organizational pattern. Similarly, over 50 per cent demanded involvement, with the demand being particularly high among Republicans. The overwhelming number of board members revealed that they were orthodox, represented important elements in the coalition, and were career aspirants.

Striking gradations in decisional status emerge as we continue to look at these criteria, however. Only 29 per cent of the Democratic board members met all six criteria; the same was true of only 10 per cent of the Republican board members. On the other hand, from 20 to 25 per cent of both parties' boards consisted of leaders who were ideologically orthodox and represented important subgroups, but who did not demand more involvement in decision-making. The analysis is further complicated by the finding that three-fourths of those who did not demand more decisional status perceived the board as already holding considerable decisional power. These complex patterns of variables suggest the basic decisional model used in Table 15.4.

Roughly one-fifth of the executive boards were at the "center of power." They felt they had power, were satisfied, had high awareness, were gregarious communicators, ideologically orthodox, career aspiring, and represented important subgroups

TABLE 15.4

DECISIONAL MODEL: CONCENTRIC CIRCLES OF DECISIONAL RELEVANCE (Board Members)

	Democrats	*Republicans*
"Inner decisional circle"	24%	18%
"Power malcontents" (influential organizational status)	29	32
Highly aware and involved	24	14
Less aware and involved	5	18
"Power deprived" (important organizational status)	12	9
Highly aware and involved	6	0
Less aware and involved	6	9
"Outer decisional circle"	36	41
High demand but organizational status not influential	12	36
Low demand for more involvement and organizational status not influential	18	5
Unconcerned about loss of power	6	0

(such as unions, Negroes, the business-managerial class, etc.). This was the working minority with whom the chairman obviously did and must consult. But it is equally obvious that a second group must have been on the chairman's mind a great deal, a group we shall call "the power malcontents." This is a group which admitted the board had some power, but they claimed it was not enough; a group whose demand for involvement was backed up with considerable force. They were not ideological deviants, they were careerists, and they were leaders or representatives of important subcoalitions. Though their level of awareness and extent of communicative contacts varied, they could not be ignored. Together with the "inner circle," they totalled a 53 per cent Democratic majority and a bare 50 per cent Republican minority. If to this is added a group of board members disgruntled at the lack of power, but also ideologically conformist, aspiring, and leaders of important "blocs" of supporters, then three-fifths of all board members were included. This, then, was the leadership cadre in the "decisional reference group" of the chairman. They demanded involvement, were organizationally involved, and constituted an important "impact clientele" whose support was vital and whose veto could be disastrous for the chairman.

This analysis of the decisional relationships of the chairman and the boards suggests four major theoretical orientations. One is that even among upper-echelon leadership cadres there are "anomists," leaders unconcerned about power, or holding organizational status not advantageous for making power demands. In our sample this group was a sizeable one-third or two-fifths. Secondly, it is important to note that, as operationalized here, the effective decisional group was large in size, coinciding probably with a 60 per cent majority. Third, there was considerable "potential disaffection" among these top-echelon leaders, whether they had power or felt they were without power. This may be very relevant to the high turnover of district chairmen. And finally, this was not a tightly monolithic decisional oligarchy. Analysis of those in the decisional reference group reveals that they were not an inbred, exclusive communicating cabal. They interacted diffusely in the hierarchy; they represented different subcoalitional interests, they were also individuals with self-motivating and separable career patterns and aspirations. The suggestion is implicit in the data on power perceptions, decisional statuses in the organization, involvement patterns, and demand levels, that the exercise of decision-making had to be in a very pragmatic sense broadly based, deconcentrated, and reciprocally deferential, if the chairman was to achieve the consent he needed.

The chairman's decision-making power must be understood in relation to his capacity to mobilize organizational support. He must, and did in fact, function with a realistic "calculus of support" as well as a "calculus of potential revolt." That is, he had to keep his eye constantly on the degree of support he had among the precinct leaders, who, after all, selected him in district convention. In addition to this organizational support calculus he had to be self-conscious about his "electoral support calculus," the extent of probable support for him and his organization among the various subsectors of the population from which he drew his "loyal" supporters as well as "weak" identifiers. One way to attempt an analysis of this support potential in relation to the decision-making power of the chairman, and the impact of his decisions on the organization, is to look carefully at the board members as individuals who represented subcoalitional interests and who maintained liaison with precinct leaders, as in fact some of them did much more than the chairman. Given this image of the board as individuals with a mobilization linkage function, we can then ask, "What proportions of precinct leaders and of electorate supporters were, or were not, involved in, or linked to, the decisional process through the board members who were, or were not, themselves involved in district-level decision-making?[1] For example, as explained in Chapter 4, our subcoalitional image of the Democratic party revealed that 19 per cent of the precinct leaders were Negro union members, 4 per cent were Irish union members, 7 per cent were business and professional whites, etc. Similarly, 32 per cent of the Republican precinct cadre consisted of business-managerial whites, 6 per cent were Negro union members, etc. Since these precinct cadre interests had "representatives" on the executive boards, it is proper, theoretically, to conceive of board members as surrogates or mobilizers of precinct organizational support groups. The same type of analysis is theoretically feasible for support groups of the electorate. In Table 15.5 this theoretical calculus of potential support is attempted.

The "inner decisional circle" in both parties fell short of the organizational and electoral support the chairman needed. In the Republican party the inner circle was strikingly unrepresentative, including only 26 per cent of precinct leadership subgroups

[1] Another approach to this, which analyzes precinct leaders and their relationships to the district-level decision-making process directly, will be presented subsequently.

TABLE 15.5

CALCULUS OF SUBCOALITIONAL ORGANIZATIONAL AND ELECTORAL SUPPORT BY CONCENTRIC CIRCLES OF DECISIONAL INVOLVEMENT OF BOARD MEMBERS IN DISTRICT-LEVEL DECISION-MAKING

	Democrats			*Republicans*		
Board members included in	*Precinct leaders mobilized*	*Loyal supporters mobilized*	*Weak supporters mobilized*	*Precinct leaders mobilized*	*Loyal supporters mobilized*	*Weak supporters mobilized*
"Inner decisional circle"	43%	30%	30%	26%	20%	12%
"Power malcontents"	31	31	34	40	36	25
"Power deprived"	14	9	12	6	6	6
"Outer decisional circle"	11	30	24	28	38	57

and 20 per cent of the loyal supporters groups. At least the second concentric circle had to be considered very critical if the chairman was to maintain adequate organizational support—a group of board members who did have some power but were disaffected, even though loyal to the organization. The addition of this group gave the chairman a 66 to 74 per cent majority. It left him, however, 25 to 33 per cent of the precinct leaders with no organizational liaison with district level decision-making. These precinct leaders in the two outer decisional circles came from subcoalitional groups of some size and importance. On the Democratic side, precinct leaders with no organizational power linkage included, for example, the nonunion Poles, the blue-collar workers of southern origin, and nonunion Negro leaders. Republican precinct leaders theoretically excluded from district-level decisional power comprised a particularly large group of white labor union members as well as nonlabor blue-collar workers.

The meaning of these data is that despite the power concentration preferences of the chairman or the oligarchic predispositions of his immediate confrères, decision-making at the district level of the hierarchy, though it may appear to have been the prerogative of a small numerical minority, cannot be so narrowly conceived. There was, first of all, the demand for involvement by board members who had the right to be consulted. The apathy level of the board was at the 40 per cent level, true, but not at the 90 per cent level. Second, the organizational support calculus of the chairman required that he come to terms with at least the malcontents on his board. Otherwise he would alienate, and cut himself off from, a majority of the subcoalitions which make up his precinct cadre. Third, the electoral support calculus required Republican chairmen, unless they wished to consider only their loyal supporters, to come to terms with the power-deprived contingent among board members also. Finally, though extensive consultation by the chairman seemed vital, important subcoalitional sectors of the organization seemed excluded from decision-making and liaison with decision makers, either because subgroup leaders were apathetic and did not demand involvement, because their organizational status was not influential, or because their leaders were not orthodox.

This theory of organizational decision-making in the political party, therefore, commits one to a broad conception of its function in the structure. It suggests that the decision makers in a party had to "take into consideration" a fairly large group of board members and precinct leaders if support mobilization was to be maximized. In the presence of high demand as well as subcoalitional heterogeneity, decision-making seemed to be theoretically a relatively diffuse process.

Whether this image is borne out by empirical reality—whether the chairman must indeed consult widely in order to maintain organizational support—rests largely on the decisional involvement interests and demands of the precinct leaders. It is one thing to assume that precinct leaders will defect from a chairman who does not consult their board representatives. It is another matter to test this probability directly by analysis of the power orientations of precinct leaders. Such a direct test of the theory is now attempted.

DISTRICT DECISIONAL INVOLVEMENT OF PRECINCT LEADERS

Precinct leaders had radically different perceptions about the amount of authority they had in running the district organizations. Over one-third in both parties reported they had very little or nothing to say, while 35 per cent of the Democrats and 15 per cent of the Republicans claimed they had "a great deal" to say. (Table 15.6). Democratic leaders in the aggregate appeared more concerned that they be permitted an important decisional role than did Republican leaders. And yet all our meas-

TABLE 15.6

POWER PERCEPTIONS OF PRECINCT LEADERS

	Democrats	*Republicans*
Aggregate distributions ("How much say do you believe precinct leaders generally have?")		
Very little	36%	39%
Some	7	24
A fair amount	18	17
A great deal	35	15
Not ascertainable	4	4
Measures of perceptual disagreement within each district organization		
Percentage of all precinct leaders (by district) who had violently opposed perceptions	73	41
Percentage of all person-to-person perceptual relationships which were noncongruent in any sense	66	60
Percentage of all perceptual relationships which were extremely noncongruent	23	13
Number of perceptual relationships examined by districts	3,394	3,591

ures of perceptual congruence indicate that the Democrats were more confused and in greater disagreement than the Republicans. Almost three-fourths of the Democratic precinct leaders, if examined as separable clusters of leadership in each district, had violent perceptual differences, split between those who reported "very little" to say, and those who felt they had "a great deal." Only 41 per cent of the Republicans disagreed in this way. If we examine the universe of perceptual relationships, each leader's perception in relation to each other leader's perception, by district (with one 3,000 such units of observation for each party), we get a lower measure of noncongruence, but the Democratic percentage was considerably higher.

Although we held constant in this analysis the type of district in which the leader lived and worked, there were no doubt other environmental and personal factors which conditioned the precinct leader's frame of reference for our question, and which were relevant to understanding his response. On the other hand, from the district leaders' viewpoint, certain factors must enter an analysis of whether the precinct leader was in the "decisional reference group," and whether, in fact, a particular precinct leader must be "taken into consideration." The precinct leader who implied he had "a great deal to say" might, in fact, not have a very influential status.

There are many components of organizational decision-making status. We have operationalized a few for our purposes, based on the twin notions of the interest clientele and the impact clientele. Among these components are: high organizational awareness (possessed by 50 per cent and 36 per cent of the Democratic and Republican precinct leaders, respectively); frequent communicative contact with the district level (73 per cent D, 59 per cent R); demand for more involvement (45 per cent D, 56 per cent R); top career mobility status (43 per cent D, 30 per cent R); representation of key political support subcoalitions (85 per cent D, 74 per cent R); ideological nonextremism (96 per cent D, 94 per cent R, although the completely consistent orthodox on all ideological positions were much lower, 46 per cent D and 22 per cent R); and leadership of an electorally sure or doubtful area (79 per cent D, 52 per cent R).

In pressing the analysis beyond subjective power perceptions, it is necessary to distinguish perceptions of present power from demand for power. Not all precinct leaders who said they had no power possessed a genuine interest in power (Table 15.7). It is immediately clear that the decisional apathy level was high among Republicans, one-fourth of whom were not pressing for

TABLE 15.7

PERCEPTIONS OF DEMAND FOR POWER AND PRESENT POWER

	Democrats	*Republicans*
Report precinct leaders have a say:		
Do not want more power	42%	20%
Do want more power	14	14
Report precinct leaders do not have a say:		
Do want more power	31	42
Do not want more power	13	24
	100%	100%

involvement. On the other hand, 42 per cent of the Republicans and 31 per cent of the Democrats may have been frustrated by power deprivations.

Various other screening analyses with objective criteria suggest the complexity of the decisional role. Thus, of those who said they were not consulted, three-fourths had high organizational awareness scores, whereas 5 per cent of those who said they had a considerable influence were low in organizational awareness. Further, of those who claimed to be excluded from district decision-making, large proportions had career mobility status in the organization—25 per cent Democrats, 31 per cent Republicans. Yet, 31 per cent of the Republicans and 7 per cent of the Democrats who claimed they did have something to say revealed in their communication relationships virtually no contact with district leaders; and 60 per cent of those who felt little involved revealed in their communication patterns that they did interact frequently with district leaders.

Combining the five key criteria leads to the distributions of precinct leader decisional status found in Table 15.8. This is based on perceptions of power, demand for power, communication patterns, organizational knowledge, and career status. A careful examination of the distinctions and distributions reveals that a rather large "minority" of 48 per cent of Democratic precinct leaders and a small minority (19 per cent) of Republican leaders (Groups A, B, and C) could be considered as involved at the district level. But if a top career status is considered a vital criterion (longevity of experience, mobility in the organization, and aspiration for higher status), then the effective decisional reference group of the district chairman became more constricted, comprising from 6 to 12 per cent of the precinct leaders. To sum-

TABLE 15.8

DECISIONAL STATUS OF PRECINCT LEADERS IN RELATION TO DISTRICT-LEVEL DECISION-MAKING PROCESSES (BASED ON FIVE CRITERIA)

	Democrats	*Republicans*
A. Inner circle (have power, are satisfied, aware, communicate frequently, and are top organizational mobiles)	12%	6%
B. Secondary circle (fulfill all criteria but have lower career status)		
Informal influentials	13	1
Nonmobile career status	10	5
C. Power malcontents (fulfill most of criteria, except career status which is lower, but are dissatisfied with power status, though they maintain they have power and reveal evidence of being involved)	13	7
D. Power deprived (do not have power and are dissatisfied with status)	32	49
E. Outer circle (have no power and are apathetic)	18	32

marize in another way, 50 per cent (D) and 81 per cent (R) of precinct leaders (Groups D and E) seemed effectively excluded, by objective and subjective criteria, from district-level decision-making. They seemed relatively ignorant of what went on in the organization, had atrophied or nonexistent communication lines, poor career status, and may have been apathetic about their decisional role.

Subtle pressures existed within the structure, however, which might, theoretically, lead the chairman to broaden the base of decisional consultation among precinct leaders. First, of course, was the fact that he needed their support for re-election at the next district convention. Second, he could not mobilize majority support unless he went beyond the circle of contented leaders involved. He had to work with and generate support from the malcontents (and from the deprived, in the Republican structure) and/or the outer circle of apathetics, if he was to gain a theoretical majority. Third, among the deprived there was a small contingent of precinct leaders who seemed very aware and in communicative contact with activity in the structure. To ignore these leaders might be impossible. In a sense, therefore, the district chairman was in a quandary. He was under pressure to consult those who had power but sought more as well as those who were deprived, even though many of these were uninformed about organizational affairs.

The chairman operated theoretically in an atmosphere of decisional friction and pressure. Examination of the two inner circles of decision-making (Groups A and B) reveals the group was not monolithic and like-minded. Table 15.9 shows distributions of precinct leaders in the inner circles.

If one is really interested in determining whether the district chairman must listen to the "inner circle" precinct leaders, certain factors are relevant. The chairman may have discounted the claims of a precinct leader to be heard because he was too unorthodox in his positions on issues, or came from a subcoalitional category of secondary importance (business, professional Democrats or blue-collar labor union Republicans) or because he was

TABLE 15.9

DISTRIBUTIONS OF PRECINCT LEADERS IN THE INNER CIRCLES

Inner circles (Groups A and B)	*Democrats*	*Republicans*
Ideological orthodoxy questionable	24%	65%
Represent "deviant" social categories	7	29
Are leaders of precincts "lost" to the party	16	35
Cumulative percentage whose organizational-decisional claims are questionable	38	71

a leader in a precinct hopelessly lost to the enemy. Such criteria determined the power vulnerability of precinct leaders and their right to pre-eminence in decisional matters.

By the same token those who, at first glance, might seem to be outside the chairman's decisional reference group (precinct leaders of Groups D and E) may have been leaders who could not be completely ignored. In Table 15.10 we find the distributions for the power-deprived precinct leaders (those who claimed they had no power, but who demanded a say). It would seem, then, that this group of leaders who wanted more say could not be ignored easily. Close to half of them had a solid foundation for their decisional demands.

The chairman's theoretical dilemma is obvious. Certain leaders of the inner circles who were close to decision-making had a poor organizational and demand status (from 40 to 70 per cent). On the other hand, certain leaders who wanted power, but did

TABLE 15.10

DISTRIBUTIONS OF POWER-DEPRIVED PRECINCT LEADERS

	Democrats	*Republicans*
Ideologically orthodox	66%	78%
Represent major social subcoalitions	65	90
Are leaders of precincts *not* "lost" to the party	64	56
Cumulative percentage whose organizational-decisional claims are strong	44	49

not have it, had an excellent organizational and demand status (from 45 to 50 per cent). Theoretically, this suggests that, on the basis of "demand" and "status," close to 50 per cent of all Republican precinct leaders and slightly over 60 per cent of Democratic leaders had to be consulted by the district chairman, because they could be conceptualized as relevant, in terms of interest or impact, to the decisions he must make. Before accepting this interpretation, however, further analysis is needed.

We must return to the theoretical "calculus" of organizational and electoral votes a chairman needed to maintain his leadership position. In discussing the chairman's relationship to the board members, we demonstrated that if he consulted only with the "inner circle" of the board he would lose contact with, and support from, certain key blocs of precinct leaders for whom the excluded board members might act as surrogates. This depends, however, as we said, on the expectation of and demand for decisional involvement by such blocs of precinct leaders. In order to present evidence on the necessity of the chairman to consult widely with board members, as well as to distinguish precinct leader subcoalitions by themselves, the data on the decisional statuses of precinct leaders by subcoalitional category are presented in Table 15.11.

The district inner circles of both parties, from the viewpoint of the involvement of precinct leaders, revealed greatly varying complexions. High proportions of labor union members and those with Polish nationality origin probably had the greatest decisional influence in the Democratic party, 46 and 53 per cent, respectively. The Negroes, the Irish, and nonlabor elements were much less represented in the decisional "elite." But in the Republican party, Negroes and nonlabor whites, particularly those with "deviant" nationality backgrounds, fared even worse—only 1 out of 20 of the precinct leaders from these groups demonstrated inner-circle status. In the Republican party the elements with highest relative influence were the whites, particularly those in white-collar and business-managerial occupations. In both parties there was no subcoalitional category with a low percentage

TABLE 15.11

DECISIONAL STATUS AND DEMAND PERSPECTIVES OF PRECINCT LEADERS BY SUBCOALITIONAL CATEGORY

Democrats	*A.* *Percentage of category classified as highly involved—two inner circles*	*B.* *Percentage of category excluded from A who wanted more to say about district decision-making*	*Number of cases*
Negroes	22%	96%	32
Poles	53	14	15
Irish	12	47	17
All labor	46	30	92
Nonlabor	19	54	32
Republicans			
Business-managerial	16	88	44
Nonlabor white, other white collar, Northwestern European	24	46	17
Labor whites	15	55	34
Negroes	5	56	19
Nonlabor white, nationality deviants	5	50	21

of inner-circle representatives which did not have a high proportion of precinct leaders asking for more influence.

The Democratic Negroes had a particularly high percentage (95 per cent) asking for more say in district affairs. The Republican business-managerial group was almost as high (88 per cent). This suggests that the district chairman, if he was at all sensitive to activity at the base of his organization, should, theoretically, have felt a need to refer back to large numbers of precinct leaders who felt excluded from district decision-making, whether these groups were included in the district executive board inner circle or not. Perhaps only the nonunion Poles might have been de-emphasized, for example, in Democratic circles, and the nonlabor blue-collar workers among Republicans. Their numbers were small in party leadership positions and their demands for involvement minimal. Otherwise there appeared to be great pressure from sizeable proportions of all significant groups.

The findings are, thus far, two: (1) a minority of precinct leaders seemed to be actually involved in district decision-making; (2) a large majority of precinct leaders seemed to want involvement, and on some criterion seemed entitled to be "taken into consideration" by the district chairman. Whether this theoretical image of power diffusion, an image which suggests that the chairman must "share" his decisional influence with a large number of precinct leaders, is realistic depends finally on three factors: What is required for the chairman to have a majority? How aware is he of the demand for involvement by the malcontents and deprived? Under what conditions is his organizational coalition viable without involving some of those leaders who seek consideration?

The manner in which a chairman cumulates a majority in a party structure is a complex bit of organizational calculus. The possible components which might enter into his varying coalitions are summarized in Table 15.12. Here it is seen, first, that the chairmen did maintain some communicative contact with a majority of precinct leaders, based on an analysis of precinct leaders' discussions of their patterns of interactions. Some 53 per cent of the Republican and 67 per cent of the Democratic leaders indicated they had some communication at the district level. In a sense this represented the bare bones of an actual existing majority. One notices, secondly, however, that if these were the chairmen's majorities, they were made up of leaders with varying degrees of interest, orthodoxy, organizational significance, and demand. Thus, 5 per cent of the Democratic communicating majority were apathetics and another 14 per cent were the malcontents and deprived who had a low level of orthodoxy and questionable organizational status. The respective Republican percentages of these two groups were 18 per cent apathetics and 20 per cent malcontents and deprived with questionable status.

TABLE 15.12

ALTERNATIVES FACING THE CHAIRMAN IN THE CUMULATION OF A COALITIONAL MAJORITY AMONG PRECINCT LEADERS

Possible coalitional elements	*Proportions of all precinct leaders*			
	Democrat		*Republican*	
Top careerist inner circle	12%		6%	
Residue of inner circles	24		6	
Outer circle apathetics with whom chairman has contact, and who are orthodox	1		9	
Residue of outer circle in contact with chairman	4		8	
Malcontents and deprived with whom chairman has contact and who are organizationally important and orthodox	12		4	
Residue of malcontents and deprived with whom chairman has contact	14		20	
The effective, communicating majority in contact with chairman	67		53	
Residue of malcontents and deprived with whom chairman has no contact	20		32	
Organizationally important		12		15
Organizational status questionable		8		17
Residue of outer circle apathetics with whom chairman has no contact	11		13	
Organizationally important		9		5
Organizational status questionable		2		8
	98		98	

Thus, the communicating majorities were tenuous; the chairmen could not rely on them. Third, the chairmen were out of contact with a group of malcontents and deprived leaders who were organizationally important—12 per cent Democrats and 17 per cent Republicans, to say nothing of the apathetics, who despite their disinterest were orthodox and organizationally important.

Not only were these leaders demanding more involvement, but they had a right to expect it—they were orthodox liberals or conservatives, held positions in key competitive precincts, and represented important subcoalitional groups. Yet, they were out of contact with the chairmen. If any of the elements in the chairmen's communicating majority coalition had defected—and this would have required a move on the part of only a small percentage of malcontents or deprived—an opposition coalition could have been forged against the chairmen.

Summarized another way, the chairmen appeared to have a safe central core of 12 per cent Republican and 36 per cent Democratic. The rest were disinterested, unhappy about their power status, or out of contact with the chairmen. The chairmen seemed to be maintaining contact with leaders who were not orthodox and not important cogs in the interest-group subcoalitional structure of the party (18 per cent D, 28 per cent R), while the chairmen were remote from orthodox and important precinct leaders (21 per cent D, 22 per cent R). Further, they had, in their communicating majorities, leaders who were critical and somewhat hostile (26 per cent D, 24 per cent R), while the chairmen were removed from some leaders who were satisfied with their status (11 per cent D, 13 per cent R). The elements for "revolution" existed, therefore, in such a situation, and serious questions can be raised about the viability of the structure as an aggregation of subcoalitional interest groups. The limited and varying degree of subcoalitional loyalty to the party, demonstrated in Chapter 4, as well as the high turnover in district chairmen in both parties, suggests that the chairmen's efforts to maintain a viable structure, under these conditions of limited communication and relatively high demand for involvement, were not altogether successful!

Specific documentation can be offered for the statement that precinct leaders who seemed to be excluded from "the chairman's majority," but would have liked a say and were disaffected, were, indeed, leaders of important subcoalitional elements. Such excluded precinct leaders on the Democratic side were a Negro labor union officer, an Irish labor union officer, several Negro labor union members, as well as nonlabor Negroes and several white labor union members with central European nationality origins. On the Republican side those excluded represented the following groups: several from the business-managerial sector, English and German leaders with white-collar occupations, several nonlabor union Negroes. In attempting to calculate the impact of such exclusion one should bear in mind the examples of the proportions of party strength for these subcoalitions among the party's loyal supporters given in Table 15.13. Now, of course, precinct leaders representing these groups were both included and excluded from the decisional reference group of the chairmen. Only a potential and partial loss of support, therefore, was involved in the exclusion of such leaders who demanded involvement. The actual calculus of loss would require a complex analysis of many variables. Nevertheless, the potential for disaffection and defection existed, both within the party struc-

TABLE 15.13
Proportions of Party Strength Among Subcoalitions

	Percentages of all loyal supporters	
	Democrats	*Republicans*
Negro		
Labor	13%	2%
Nonlabor	15	7
Irish		
Labor	4	–
Nonlabor	5	–
Other labor		
Whites	29	12
Central Europeans	4	–
Business-managerial	–	22
English white-collar	–	9
German white-collar	–	10

ture and in the electorate. And it was this potential which was relevant to the chairmen's personal power status as well as to the competitive and integrative viability of the party structure as it sought to optimize its electoral support.

The assessment of consequences for the noninvolvement of precinct leaders is complex. One test would be an analysis of task performance in terms of decisional status. Does it really make any difference whether precinct leaders are involved, and do those in the outer circle perform as efficiently as those in the inner circle? Our data suggest that it may make a difference (Table 15.14).[2] The Democrats particularly were a group whose task performance seemed related to decisional status. Those who felt they were involved were also those who did the best job, while those who sensed they were not consulted, or were unconcerned about "power," were less efficient. The Republican findings, however, were not as convincing, and perhaps suggest another pattern—the malcontents (who "had some say" but felt it was inadequate) were the least efficient of the whole group. The Republican apathetics ranked second in level of inefficiency.

TABLE 15.14

THE RELATIONSHIP BETWEEN PRECINCT LEADERS' DECISIONAL INVOLVEMENT STATUS AND PRECINCT TASK PERFORMANCE

	Democrats			*Republicans*		
Decisional status	*Two most efficient categories*	*Least efficient category*	*Number of cases*	*Two most efficient categories*	*Least efficient category*	*Number of cases*
"Inner circles"	89%	2%	54	65%	27%	26
"Power malcontents"	72	0	18	42	53	19
"Power deprived"	56	14	36	59	17	59
Apathetics	55	40	20	52	30	33

[2] This analysis of the factors related to efficiency is explored more thoroughly in the next chapter.

The decision-making relationships in the party structure cannot be considered irrelevant to task efficiency. The precinct leader who felt involved was also the leader who got the work done. But there were also large percentages of precinct leaders who had a fairly high level of task performance even though they perceived themselves as out of the decisional power structure. Involvement was not critical for them, apparently; other orientations and motivations supported their party activity. The district leader could not, however, ignore the fact that there might be a relationship for some between their perceptions of decisional involvement and task productivity. While he could not consult all precinct leaders, if he were shrewd and concerned with maximization of grass-roots activities, he would involve those leaders most critical for organizational success, as well as for his own longevity as chairman.

This leads to a final consideration: the distribution of precinct leaders with decisional involvement perceptions by the type of precinct they lead. One would expect, if involvement is related to organizational viability and success, that those precinct leaders in "marginal" precincts would be relatively involved. This we did find in the Democratic party, 60 per cent of the precinct leaders in marginal precincts felt they had some power, compared to 56 per cent in the sure Democratic precincts and only 34 per cent in the sure Republican precincts. But we found the opposite to be true in the Republican structure—only 21 per cent of Republican leaders in "marginal" districts felt they had decisional power, compared to 38 per cent in the sure Democratic precincts and 31 per cent in the sure Republican precincts. The level of Republican involvement in all types of precincts was lower, but it appears that the competitive areas were particularly excluded. Of Republicans in marginal districts who were excluded, the overwhelming majority were discontented, and only 7 per cent performed tasks at the top level of their efficiency, while 55 per cent performed tasks at the lowest levels of efficiency. When we thus pinpoint the areas critical for party success, the factor of decisional involvement and its possible impact on the work attitudes of precinct leaders is of dramatic significance. In terms of aggregate analysis, 12 per cent of the total of Republican leaders functioned in marginal precincts, were excluded from district decisions, and were very poor in task performance. The proportion of leaders for the Democrats on the same criteria was 3 per cent.

We have presented in this section an analysis of decision-making viewed primarily from the district organizational perspective. The Democratic and Republican parties seemed to differ considerably as decisional structures in certain respects. In both parties we found a minority of precinct leaders actually feeling that they had some say in district party decisions—48 per cent for the Democrats, 19 per cent for the Republicans. Those who believed they were consulted and were satisfied were a smaller subgroup—35 per cent of the Democrats, 12 per cent of the Republicans. Many precinct leaders apparently were excluded from district-level decisions completely, though this was much more prevalent in the Republican organization.

On the other hand, as pointed out previously, precinct leaders, too, were making decisions at the grass roots which were vitally important to the party. Most chairmen admitted that they were unable to maintain direct contact with their precinct leaders and were self-conscious about this deficiency. We can ask this theoretical question: How many precinct leaders, despite the absence of constant contact with district leaders, could still be conceived as making their decisions with the district leader as their reference group? Again a high degree of local autonomy in decision-making became evident. In order to answer this question, we looked at those precinct leaders who were indeed making action decisions at the precinct level, and then utilized some other measures to see whether the precinct leader would probably have the image of the district's interests, demands, and welfare in his mind, or whether he would make decisions on his own. The factors considered most relevant in answering this question were whether he aspired to move upward in the party hierarchy, and whether he felt involved or excluded by the district "inner circle." We hypothesized that the precinct leader who aspired and who had no bitter feelings of power deprivation would be most likely to refer back to the district level in making precinct decisions. Operationalized in this way, we identified 30 per cent Democratic precinct leaders and 13 per cent Republicans who conceivably might not operate autonomously. In a subsequent analysis it was revealed that 95 per cent of these leaders did in fact maintain formal communication contacts with district leadership.

The meaning of these data is clear. There is much empirical evidence that the vast majority of local precinct leaders were "little oligarchs," running their operations alone or with "friends and neighbors," with limited contact and involvement in district-level operations, and with limited reasons for self-consciously adjusting their work patterns and plans to perceived district-level demands. Though their communication patterns reveal that many did interact from time to time with ward, district, and other precinct leaders, they had a relatively secure status and limited reasons for even taking the district leaders' desires into consideration. On the other hand, the district leaders continued to represent the organization formally, making decisions they felt were imperative, such as patronage, finance, strategy, etc. The district leader was not a tyrant, he could not be. He did, in fact, consult most of his executive board and a small circle of career-oriented precinct leaders. His reference group was much larger if he was concerned with remaining in power and developing the organization. But his tasks were too great to permit him to actually contact his precinct leadership reference group. He sought to maintain harmony at the district level among the competing leadership sectors. He hoped to build a viable coalition and secure the support of the "power apathetics" in a crisis. But his personal position was unstable. And while he was making decisions at the district level which only a minority of precinct leaders really cared or could know about, his precinct leaders were making decisions at the local level of which he could not know and perhaps could not afford to care about. Thus a "polarity" in party decision-making processes emerges, autonomization at the precinct level, and exclusivity at the district level. The system cannot function as a bureaucracy, or even as a neat pyramidal hierarchy. Power and deference are reciprocal, as are noninvolvement and organizational ignorance—the essential elements of a stratarchical, polarized structural system.

CHAPTER 16

THE DETERMINANTS OF ORGANIZATIONAL VIABILITY

The complexity of party structural relations is suggested by the foregoing discussion of the party as a task group, as a communication network, and as a decisional subsystem. The patterns of action, information flow, and group involvement are in fact polylithic. The proportion of Democratic precinct leaders who fell into the top efficiency group, felt involved, had cosmopolitan communication patterns, and high morale was 16 per cent (the Republican proportion was 3 per cent). At the other extreme, the proportion of Democratic leaders who were utterly inefficient, uninvolved, isolates in their communication patterns, and with low morale or were apathetic was 4 per cent (the Republican proportion was 5 per cent). Between these extremes lay the 80–90 per cent of the leaders with varying patterns of task performance, interaction relationships, and morale.

The 12 district organizations varied considerably also on these dimensions. Table 16.1 reveals few districts which ranked consistently high or low on all structural variables, although Districts A and L did represent polar types. In Districts A and L the following contrasting conditions appeared among precinct leaders:

Precinct leaders	*District A*	*District L*
Who felt involved	72%	10%
Who were satisfied	67	24
Who had a cosmopolitan communication pattern	89	2

Precinct leaders	*District A*	*District L*
Who engaged in personal canvassing	50	27
Who were organizationally aware	83	41

One other district was similar to A, two others similar to L. The presence of several other types of party structure between these two extremes revealed a divergence in pattern. First, there was the "low involvement–high efficiency" structure recalling the mythological boss-and-machine days (Districts H and J). Second, and opposite to the first, the "high participation-low efficiency" structure (particularly B). Third, the organization with relatively high participation, communication, and task performance, but low morale (D and E). Fourth, the organization which enigmatically possessed high morale but ranked rather low on other criteria (G). Fifth, we found a district where the sense of involvement was relatively high, but with low morale, poor communication, and poor task performance—another enigma (F). To generalize on the basis of these patterns is tempting, but generally unwarranted. The only generalization permissible is

TABLE 16.1

District Organizational Types by Rank order, for Selected Criteria

(Based on Distributions for Precinct Leaders)

Criteria	*Range*	*District rank orders*											
		A	*B*	*C*	*D*	*E*	*F*	*G*	*H*	*I*	*J*	*K*	*L*
High percentage of decisional involvement	72–10%	1	2	3	4	5	6	7	8	9	10	11	12
High morale	76–14	3	1	4	9	7	10	2	7	5	11	6	12
Cosmopolitan communication patterns	89– 2	1	4	6	5	3	10	9	11	7	2	8	12
Efficiency: percentage engaging in canvassing	60–18	3	9	5	6	4	10	7	1	7	2	12	11

that, contrary to probable expectation, we have found structures with high involvement in decision-making in which the level of task performance was excellent; similarly, we have also found structures with low involvement and poor morale where the level of task performance was excellent. This rich variety of structural pattern types, often not fitting any expected model, suggests that such organizational properties as morale and productivity are dependent on personal perspectives as well as organizational conditions.

One of the most elusive organizational properties to explain is "morale," a concept with many meanings. In the present sense it means the extent to which the individual leader was satisfied with the general level of precinct leader involvement in the district. Approximately 45 per cent of the Democratic precinct leaders had low "morale" as thus defined, while 50 per cent of the Republicans could be so classified. Among the district organizations, two had excellent morale (one-fifth or less of the leaders expressing dissatisfaction), while three were very low in morale (two-thirds or more of the leaders expressing dissatisfaction).

Three factors seemed prominently associated with morale: the subcoalitional status of the individual, his ideological orthodoxy, and whether he felt personally involved in decisions in the district. The extreme differences in morale by subcoalitional status are seen in Table 16.2. Similarly, the differences between those were ideologically orthodox and unorthodox can be demonstrated as in Table 16.3.

These data suggest that certain subcategories of leaders sensed that they did or did not "belong." The Polish Democrats were well satisfied, as were the liberals; the Negroes and conservative-moderate Democrats were not. The middle-level white-collar Republicans were much more satisfied than the Negro Republicans or the more wealthy business and managerial group. The conservative Republicans had much higher morale than the moderate-liberal Republicans.

But these subcategories differed in important respects. One

TABLE 16.2

DIFFERENCES IN MORALE BY SUBCOALITIONAL STATUS

	Percentage with high morale
Democrats	
Poles	93%
Irish	59
Negroes	25
Republicans	
Nonlabor whites	65
Negroes	47
Business—managerial group	23

TABLE 16.3

DISTRIBUTION OF MORALE BY IDEOLOGICAL ORTHODOXY

	Percentage with high morale
Democrats	
Liberals	63%
Moderates	33
Republicans	
Conservatives	58
Moderates	37
Both parties	
Extreme unorthodox	26

way, with significant consequences for morale, was the extent to which they felt they were *in fact* consulted in district decision-making operations. Although of all precinct leaders less than 40 per cent of those who said they were consulted were in fact satisfied, for certain of our subgroups involvement feelings were critical for morale. None of our Democratic Negro leaders, for instance, who felt that they were not consulted had good morale, while 44 per cent who were consulted had high morale. Similarly, 80 per cent of the Republican business-managerial class who felt consulted had high morale, whereas only 6 per cent of those who felt they had no say had good morale. And the moderate and unorthodox partisans in both parties revealed higher morale if they were involved, as the distributions in Table 16.4 reveal. For certain groups, however, controlling for ideological orthodoxy seemed more important than involvement. This was particularly true for the White Republican blue-collar "deviants." Of those who were orthodox conservatives, 67 per cent had high morale, while the liberals among these were a particularly unhappy group (only 35 per cent satisfied). Similarly, the nonliberal Negroes were unhappy—only 5 per cent were satisfied with their decisional status in the Republican party.

TABLE 16.4

DIFFERENCES IN MORALE BY DECISIONAL INVOLVEMENT

	Percentage with high morale
Democrats	
Liberals	
Involved	76%
Not involved	29
Nonliberals	
Involved	70
Not involved	28
Republicans	
Moderates and liberals	
Involved	65
Not involved	24

Many other variables were investigated, but none proved as helpful as these. For example, we had hypothesized that extensiveness of communication contacts in the hierarchy would be related to morale. But we discovered that those whom we classified as "isolates" actually were less discontented than the precinct leaders who had wider and more frequent interactions. Again, we had expected that those leaders working in precincts lost to the opposition would have the lowest morale, but the differences were not great in the Republican party (60 per cent disaffected compared to 53 per cent) and the hypothesis was incorrect for the Democrats.

On the basis of our data, the interaction of subcoalitional status, ideological position, and decisional involvement assisted most in explaining the phenomenon of organizational morale. In certain subgroups their status in the party seemed to produce contentment, (the Polish Democrats, for example); in other subgroups their low morale seemed attributable to feelings of decisional exclusion (the Republican business-managerial class, for example); in still others, involvement was no help, and as long as they perceived themselves as ideologically unorthodox, large numbers of members apparently continued to be discontented (many of the Republican blue-collar white "deviants," for example). Thus, the organizational problem is not easily solved. An "open recruitment" structure, as found in a party, cannot increase morale for all those disaffected merely by strengthening and widening consultative relationships.

A second organizational dimension is "loyalty," devotion to the party's goals, leadership, and methods of operation. This, as much as "morale," is a structural property crucial to the party's viability as a collaborative team. One test of party loyalty used throughout this analysis was the extent to which the leadership would condone split-ticket balloting. As reported previously by this test, the level of leadership loyalty was relatively low—50 per cent in the Democratic party and 27 per cent in the Republican party were loyal. Perhaps, as a rigorous test, this places loyalty at too low a level, but it does relate the concept of "loyalty" meaningfully to the crucial task of the party, garnering votes for all of its candidates at election time. We will use this operational concept of loyalty in exploring the organizational and personal conditions explaining it.

Morale as well as involvement was closely related to loyalty in the Democratic party. About one-third of the high morale and decisionally involved Democrats were in favor of splitting the ballot, while over 70 per cent of those with low morale, and not involved, revealed such "disloyalty." Other explanatory variables had no such power, with the possible exception of ideological orthodoxy. Only 38 per cent of the liberals, but 63 per cent of the nonliberals among Democratic leaders endorsed ticket-splitting. Since involved liberals had high morale in the Democratic party, this connection of variables is a natural derivative.

But neither morale nor decisional involvement produced loyalty in the Republican leadership cadre. In fact, 70 per cent of those satisfied with their involvement status were "disloyal," and 75 per cent of those with low morale were "disloyal"—virtually the same percentages. Two other factors seemed more important: the breadth of communicative contacts and orthodox conservative ideology. Only 44 per cent of the conservatives in contrast to 82 per cent of the liberals were in favor of ticket-splitting. Furthermore, among conservatives there was one communication pattern which significantly reduced the amount of disloyalty—the cosmopolitan pattern, in which a precinct leader interacted frequently at the local level as well as the district, county, or state level (Table 16.5). The cosmopolitan conservatives were overwhelmingly loyal, only 13 per cent expressing approval of ticket-splitting. But 75 per cent of the more isolated

TABLE 16.5

THE IMPORTANCE OF IDEOLOGICAL ORTHODOXY AND COMMUNICATIVE RELATIONSHIPS FOR REPUBLICAN "LOYALTY" AMONG PRECINCT LEADERS

	Ticket-splitting approved	*Ticket-splitting condemned*	*Number of cases*
Conservatives			
Cosmopolitan communication patterns	13%	87%	16%
More localist and isolated communication patterns	75	25	16
Moderates and liberals			
Cosmopolitan communication patterns	74	26	23
More localist and isolated communication patterns	84	16	80

conservatives were disloyal, a percentage virtually identical with the norm for the total Republican group. Cosmopolitan communication patterns, however, produced only a slight reduction in disloyalty among Republican moderates and liberals. The isolates were extremely disloyal, true, but 74 per cent of the cosmopolitan moderates revealed disloyal predispositions. There seems to be no question that ideological orthodoxy and cosmopolitan information networks converged to produce the only significant reduction in Republican disloyalty. The Democrats, more loyal generally, could increase loyalty predispositions by both ideological orthodoxy (liberalism) and satisfaction among leaders as to their consultative role in the party.

The third basic organizational dimension is task efficiency or productivity (the level of precinct leader performance of a variety of campaign tasks), described earlier in detail. An efficiency score was calculated for each precinct leader, and four categories of efficiency identified on the basis of the interview responses. In general, we found approximately 70 per cent of the Democratic leaders in the upper two efficiency categories (26 per cent in the top category) and 56 per cent of the Republican leaders in the upper two categories (11 per cent in the top category). We have examined a variety of hypotheses in order to understand these differential levels of task performance.

Certain *organizational* conditions were undoubtedly of considerable importance to precinct leader efficiency. "Deviant" subgroups for example, revealed low performance levels, particularly the Negro Republicans (only 22 per cent of whom were in the top two efficiency categories), and so did the white-collar and business-professional Democrats (48 per cent of whom were efficient). In addition we discovered, as expected, that lone-operator precinct leaders (who ran the precinct without help) were strikingly inactive, as contrasted to the enterprisers (who had many helpers, held many meetings of workers, and gave personal direction to precinct work). The distributions are given in Table 16.6. Obviously a leader needs associates if he is to man-

TABLE 16.6

VOTE-GETTING ACTIVITY OF PRECINCT LEADERS BY ORGANIZATIONAL STYLE

	Percentage in highest two efficiency categories		*Percentage engaging in canvassing*	
	Democrats	*Republicans*	*Democrats*	*Republicans*
Lone operators	8%	28%	7%	24%
Marginals	70	68	32	38
Enterprisers	97	97	57	55

age a precinct effectively. But since the existence of an organization is his own responsibility, this factor is functionally interlinked with the problem of efficiency itself. Inefficiency in organizational work produces subsequent inefficiency in productivity.

A third organizational condition is the communication system in the party structure. Two types of communication pattern were related to efficiency in both parties, the cosmopolitans and the localists (the latter category consisted of leaders who interacted frequently but only within the district, and primarily at the ward and precinct level). Table 16.7 presents the distributions. In this connection related data reveal that communication with other leaders and workers at the base of the organization is critical for efficiency. The elitist with contacts only at the apex of the structure was much less likely to be performing precinct tasks, 30 per cent in effect doing no work at all. And the isolates were largely ineffective—80 per cent or more being relatively inert. Furthermore, in the communication patterns of those "deviant" groups who seemed inefficient, this factor was again important. The white-collar and business and professional Democrats with cosmopolitan and localist communication patterns were 70 per cent efficient, compared to 11 per cent for those who had less inclusive interactions or were isolated. The Negroes and blue-collar white "deviants" among Republican leaders were similarly more efficient if they had

TABLE 16.7
COMMUNICATION PATTERNS AND CAMPAIGN EFFICIENCY
(Precinct leaders)

Democrats	*Top two efficiency levels*	*Lowest efficiency level*	*Number of cases*
Cosmopolitans	80%	2%	81
Elitists	48	29	21
Localists	80	4	25
Isolates	8	84	12
Republicans			
Cosmopolitans	77	13	40
Elitists	37	30	27
Localists	64	19	54
Isolates	14	82	22

extensive and localist communication patterns—the former group included 48 per cent as efficient, the latter group only 8 per cent.

Decisional involvement is a fourth organizational variable with considerable relevance, particularly for the Democrats. There was no difference in efficiency for the total body of Republican precinct leaders among those who felt involved or not involved. But Democratic leaders who saw themselves involved or consulted in district organization decisions revealed a high efficiency score—85 per cent in the two top efficiency categories, while only 56 per cent were efficient among the uninvolved. And, again, among the white-collar and business and professional Democrats, whose efficiency was the lowest, generally, among Democrats, 80 per cent of those who felt involved revealed a high efficiency rating as compared to 41 per cent who were not involved.

Four *personal variables* concerning the perspectives of precinct leaders also have relevance for efficiency in task performance. The four which we found to have explanatory possibilities were party loyalty, morale, ideological orthodoxy, and career aspiration. A summary of the relation of these variables to efficiency is presented in Table 16.8.

TABLE 16.8

PERSONAL PERSPECTIVES AND ORIENTATIONS IN RELATION TO EFFICIENCY
(Precinct leaders)

Personal variables	*Percentages in upper two efficiency categories*		*Number of cases*	
	Democrats	*Republicans*	*D*	*R*
Loyal to the party	81%	72%	68	36
Not loyal to the party	59	50	70	104
High morale	79	58	74	59
Low morale	61	55	54	78
Ideologically orthodox	63 (liberals)	78 (conservatives)	63	32
Moderates and unorthodox	75	49	75	111
Aspire to party career	90	67	70	89
Do not aspire to party career	48	34	68	54

Liberals were relatively inefficient in both parties, but the difference in the importance of ideology was most striking in the Republican party. Generally, the orthodox conservatives were the most efficient, 78 per cent falling into upper efficiency categories, while only 49 per cent of the moderate and liberal Republicans seemed to perform well at their campaign tasks. These factors of ideological orthodoxy and party loyalty were two personal orientations conducive to efficiency among the Republicans. Ideological position seemed much less relevant among the Democrats, just as morale seemed irrelevant for Republicans. Career aspiration, however, was a most important personal orientation in both parties. In fact, the largest differences in efficiency were found when we compared aspirers with nonaspirers (a 42-point spread for Democrats, a 33-point spread for Republicans). It appears that the precinct leader who hoped to move upward in the hierarchy was inclined to bend every effort to perform his precinct tasks.

These factors do not operate with similar effectiveness, how-

TABLE 16.9
CAREER ASPIRATION AND EFFICIENCY AMONG REPUBLICAN PRECINCT LEADERS

Republicans	*Percentage in top two efficiency categories*
Negroes	
Aspire	29%
Do not aspire	0
Whites	
Aspire	78
Do not aspire	40

ever, for all subgroups of party leaders. Loyalty, for example, appeared to be a powerful motivational force for Democratic Negroes. They divided almost equally on the question of loyalty, with 94 per cent efficient loyal Negroes compared to 53 per cent of the nonloyal. But loyalty was not a discriminating factor for white-collar and business and professional Democrats: 50 per cent of both loyalists and the nonloyalists were efficient. Somewhat the same type of finding emerges from a look at the meaning of career aspiration among Republicans. Aspiration appeared to be relatively meaningless for Republican Negroes, but for the whites it was very relevant to efficiency. Aspiring Democratic Negroes revealed 90 per cent efficiency, however, as compared to 50 per cent of the nonaspiring; and white Democrats who aspired were 88 per cent efficient, compared to 48 per cent of the nonaspiring whites. This lack of connection between aspiration and efficiency among Republican Negroes suggests that either career aspirations were perceived by these Negroes as empty dreams, or that efficiency was not the route to a Republican party career for a Negro.

Efficiency can be maximized in both parties with proper organizational conditions *and* the development of certain personal perspectives (Table 16.10). Those who were not decisionally involved but had career aspirations produced at higher levels of efficiency than those who were involved but did not aspire

TABLE 16.10

EFFICIENCY MAXIMIZATION BY COMBINING ORGANIZATIONAL CONDITIONS AND PERSONAL PERSPECTIVES
(Precinct leaders)

Combinations of criteria	*Percentages in upper two efficiency categories*		*Number of cases*	
	Democrats	*Republicans*	*D*	*R*
Decisional involvement				
Aspiration high	94%	60%	47	30
Aspiration low	68	47	25	15
No decisional involvement				
Aspiration high	83	79	23	47
Aspiration low	33	33	33	45
Communication good				
Aspiration high	91	81	58	49
Aspiration low	62	89	35	18
Communication poor				
Aspiration high	83	50	12	36
Aspiration low	33	9	33	37
Communication good				
Party loyalty high	91	91	54	23
Party loyalty low	67	82	39	45
Communication poor				
Party loyalty high	38	38	13	13
Party loyalty low	50	25	32	59

(sets A and B in Table 16.10). Or, if we look at those who had very limited communication contacts in the hierarchy, aspiration did help somewhat among the Republicans, but produced a strikingly high efficiency among the Democrats (sets C and D). Party loyalty was less useful among those with limited communication contacts, yet did seem to result in more efficiency among those with extensive contacts (sets E and F). In fact, a combination of party loyalty and good communication produced maximal efficiency for the Republicans, while all four variables combined produced maximal efficiency for the Democrats.

To identify these factors in terms of primary significance is difficult. They seemed to carry differential impacts for specific subgroups. When combined, it was possible to increase precinct leader efficiency, but only up to a certain point. An illustration of this can be presented for the liberal Democrats who appeared to be the least efficient ideological subgroup among the Democrats (63 per cent generally fell in the upper two efficiency levels). If we isolate those liberals with extensive communication contacts, the percentage who were efficient increases to 77 per cent. If we add the factor of aspiration to the analysis, we find 92 per cent of the liberals efficient. Add a third factor, decisional involvement, and we find 96 per cent of the liberals (who had extensive communication patterns, career aspirations, and were decisionally involved) to be efficient. But the increment is not pronounced by the utilization of additional factors. Aspiration alone produces 85 per cent efficiency. Actually, the data suggest that we have a constellation of factors operating in unison. Thus, 40 per cent of the liberal Democrats who aspired also had extensive communication and felt decisionally involved, another 32 per cent exhibited only one or none of these maximizing characteristics. The convergence, therefore, of factors conducing to efficiency makes isolation of *the* critical factor virtually impossible.

The importance for efficiency of a factor, such as aspiration, can be seen if we examine those leaders who were lone operators and marginals, that is, whose organizational style and context seemed to preclude efficiency because they had virtually no helpers, held no precinct meetings, and gave no direction to precinct activities. These, as noted previously, had very low levels of task performance. However, 45 per cent of the Republican lone operators who aspired were found in our top efficiency categories while *none* of those who did not aspire were efficient. Similarly, there was a 50 percentage-point efficiency differential for aspiring Democratic lone operators and marginals (combined because the small number of cases of lone operators prevented separate analysis).

Finally, one *environmental* factor contributing to efficiency should be mentioned—the political status of the precinct. As Table 16.11 indicates, we found the efficiency level lowest in those precincts lost to the opposition, although the Republicans also performed as poorly in competitive precincts. Yet, at least

TABLE 16.11

PRECINCT POLITICAL STATUS, PERSONAL ASPIRATION, AND TASK PERFORMANCE

(Precinct leaders)

Democrats	*Highest efficiency category*	*Second highest*	*Third highest*	*Lowest efficiency category*	*Number of cases*
In competitive precincts	37%	33%	17%	13%	30
In sure Democratic precincts	25	53	15	8	79
In sure Republican precincts	17	28	21	34	29
Republicans					
In competitive precincts	5	44	26	26	39
In sure Democratic precincts	9	40	16	35	69
In sure Republican precincts	20	51	6	23	35
Democrats in sure Republican precincts					
Aspire	25	42	17	17	12
Do not aspire	12	18	23	47	17
Republicans in sure Democratic precincts					
Aspire	12	54	7	27	52
Do not aspire	0	0	40	60	17

one-third of the precinct leaders seemed to be inert in lost precincts. But if we isolate again those leaders in the lost precincts who had career aspirations, as in Table 16.11, we find that even under such futile environmental conditions aspiration induced efficiency. Thus two-thirds of Republican and Democratic aspirers in lost precincts seemed to work fairly well at campaign tasks. The really hopeless leaders were the nonaspirers in lost precincts, 80 per cent of the Democrats did practically nothing, and 100 per cent of the Republicans were very inactive. Aspiration, therefore, seems to be a clue to the rejuvenation of party fortunes in one-party areas.

IMPACT OF DECISIONAL INVOLVEMENT ON PERSONAL PERSPECTIVES

In connection with an analysis of the factors which help explain certain organizationally meaningful properties such as "morale," "loyalty," and "efficiency," a final discussion of the relevance of organizational conditions for leaders' personal perspectives is necessary. Without presenting the data in complete detail, a few major findings can be highlighted.

Communication patterns seem particularly important for the analysis of the Republican organization, as indicated in an earlier section. Conservative ideology appears to be intimately associated with "cosmopolitan" and "elitist" patterns of interaction. Further, those who had a narrow content focus in communication contacts were unable to articulate their role perceptions, or to demonstrate an awareness of the party's goal orientation. In addition, Republican "cosmopolitans" were the only group to reveal decisive party loyalty predispositions. These findings as to the relevance of communication for personal perspectives were not true for the Democrats. The level and frequency of communication in the Democratic party were not as important to these types of personal perspectives.

Decisional involvement, however, is an organizational condition particularly significant for an understanding of Democratic leadership perspectives, and to a limited extent, for Republicans also (Table 16.12). A careful look at the motivations of party leaders in relation to whether they were (or felt) involved in organizational decision-making reveals interesting differences.

The involved Democrats were without exception motivated, in contrast to those not involved, 38 per cent of whom would "miss nothing" if they had to drop out of party work. The involved were interested much more in the "social fun" of politics (80 per cent to 46 per cent). They were also somewhat

TABLE 16.12

THE RELATIONSHIPS BETWEEN DECISIONAL INVOLVEMENT AND PERSONAL PERSPECTIVES
(Precinct leaders)

Personal perspectives	*Democrats*		*Republicans*	
	Involved	*Not involved*	*Involved*	*Not involved*
Motivations				
Social contacts	80%	46%	35%	55%
Ideological and philosophical	6	9	22	22
Personal gain	14	7	24	3
No motivation articulated	0	38	19	20
Goal orientations				
Power seen as goal	88	66	58	50
Issue implementation	12	13	30	40
No goal articulated	0	21	12	10
Role perceptions				
Vote-mobilizer	49	48	45	45
Ideological mentor	18	20	18	30
Economic-social welfare promoter	33	11	10	18
No role perceived	0	21	27	7
Number of cases	72	56	46	91

more inclined to be concerned with personal gain, and somewhat less inclined to be ideologically interested. The differences among Republicans were not great, and not in the same direction. Whereas the involved Republicans were also more highly motivated by personal gain, they were less interested in "social fun." Involvement did not mean they were less ready to drop out of politics. In terms of motivation, therefore, involvement was more critical for the Democrats, but it by no means resulted in an issue-oriented concern about party activity.

Involved Democrats were, with no exception in the sample, able to explain their conceptions of the party's goals, and to perceive their role as leader as one with some meaning. They were also more self-consciously alerted to the power-maximization objectives of the party. This was only slightly true for the Republicans. Republican leaders who were involved actually showed less ability to explain party goals and their own role than the uninvolved! This demonstrates again that decisional involvement seemed rather irrelevant in developing Republican leadership perspectives. But for the Democrats, involvement was a critical and discriminating organizational variable.

Finally, for both parties, decisional involvement seemed significantly related to the democratic or anti-democratic political value orientations of leaders. In an earlier chapter we explained the nature of this index and the finding that 10 and 11 per cent of our Democratic and Republican leaders, respectively, revealed in their responses considerable evidence of anti-democratic value positions, and another 17 per cent (D) and 38 per cent (R) gave slight, though not convincing, evidence of anti-democratic orientations. If we now relate these data to the level of decisional involvement of our leadership groups, we find clear evidence of the relevance of this organizational dimension (Table 16.13).

The fact that nine-tenths of the Democratic leaders who felt involved in organizational decisions revealed no evidence of anti-democratic attitudes, while only half of the noninvolved gave such evidence, is not without importance. The differences

TABLE 16.13
VALUES POSITION AND INVOLVEMENT IN DECISION-MAKING

	Positive democratic values position	*Same evidence of an anti-democratic values position*	*Number of cases*
Democrats			
Involved in decision-making	89%	11%	72
Not involved	52	48	56
Republicans			
Involved in decision-making	61	39	46
Not involved	46	54	91

among Republicans, although not as large, also lay in the same direction. Whether the *fact of involvement* was the primary contribution is certainly not demonstrable here. But the inference seems at least permissible that self-perception of decisional involvement was one important aspect. Our analysis of communication contacts indicated, further, that those with limited contacts were more likely to be anti-democratic than those with extensive contacts. Thus, although the "authoritarian" type of leader may have been inclined to see himself excluded from party affairs, this explanation is not completely satisfactory. Our evidence strongly indicated one of two explanations: that organizational practices may have influenced value orientations, or that the type of leaders who were consulted in the party were those who were "democratic" in orientation. Whatever interpretation is accepted, the data imply important party differences in the "democratic" viewpoints of those who felt involved in the decision-making machinery of the parties.

CONCLUSIONS: THE CONTINUING STRUCTURAL CRISIS OF THE PARTIES

The party is indeed a paradoxical system of interaction with structural strengths and weaknesses. Major concerns for the viability of the party as a structural system of action can be deduced from the foregoing analysis. First among emerging characteristics to be noted is the realization that the party is a pluralized and diffuse control system. Not only is it apparent that the large majority of board members in district organizations had to be taken into consideration by the district chairman in making his decisions, but the majority of precinct leaders demanded consultation as well. Only 13 per cent of Democratic and 24 per cent of the Republican precinct leaders were not concerned about power. Over two-thirds of those who felt excluded in both parties demanded to be included. The inner circle of both parties was highly pluralized in composition—24 per cent of the Democratic inner circle was not ideologically orthodox, and the same was true of 65 per cent of the Republican inner circle. Similarly, the inner circle included 7 per cent and 29 per cent of the "deviant" social categories (Democrats and Republicans, respectively). This was therefore a dynamically, potentially conflicting control system. The Democratic Negroes were a case in point: only 22 per cent were in the inner circle, 96 per cent wanted more say. On the Republican side, the business-managerial class had only 16 per cent in the inner circle, 88 per cent wanted more say. The potential for disaffection was considerable and the system seemed to be pluralized in terms of both power and conflict.

A second structural characteristic is the patterned confusion in communication relationships. There is no recognized communication flow as in a bureaucratic system. From 24 (D) to 31 per cent (R) of the precinct leaders revealed nonpyramid patterns and another 18 (D) to 32 per cent (R) were localists or completely isolated. "Organizational uncertainty," to a great extent, must prevail in such a context. In fact, our data revealed that in the vital matter of communicating strategy, those who did communicate with district and county leaders were actually more ignorant of the strategy than those who were remote from such contacts. That the party is a communicating subsystem is amply revealed by the analysis, but whether communication processes contribute effectively to the structural viability of the party can be seriously questioned. A large proportion of the "social group deviants" seemed to interact only at the local level or were isolated: 57 per cent of the Democratic business and professional subcoalition, for example, 52 per cent of the Republican white working-class leaders, and 40 per cent of the Republican Negroes. Morale in such groups, particularly among the moderates and ideologically unorthodox, was low, and party loyalty was something less than enthusiastic for 50 per cent or more of the leaders in the two parties. The integrative force of the communication process is lost, therefore, for many leaders, and the party becomes a "limited indoctrination system" so far as communication of power goals and tactical operations is concerned.

A third characteristic to be noted is that of "issue deliberation avoidance." A minority of precinct leaders, 15 per cent, indicated that they ever discussed broad questions of party issues and goals, a proportion which held true even for those precinct leaders who had elite-level contacts. Interestingly enough, in both parties, those precinct leaders who did indicate that they discussed broader questions of policy were the ideologically unorthodox or nonconformist leaders! Only one-third of our board members revealed that they ever discussed ideological questions with other leaders and, more importantly, 65 per cent of the board members said they never participated in the organization of issue conferences, even though they recognized that at the grass-roots level workers were more interested in issues than candidates. Add to this information the small percentages of precinct leaders who were ideologically motivated (15 per cent), or who saw their role in ideological terms (at the most 23 per cent), and one finds corroboration for the interpretation that issue conflicts are diluted, stabilized, or neutralized.

Fourth, the autonomy and self-executing character of precinct operations is blatantly apparent. By the most careful analysis, it appears that fully 70 per cent of the Democratic precinct leaders made decisions indifferent to district leadership desires. The percentage for Republicans can be placed at 87 per cent.

This is re-enforced by the admission of district leaders that their preoccupation with the problems of harmony and utilitarian decisions of power and patronage at the district level precluded meeting with, recruiting, training, or directing precinct activists. A surprising amount of activity was noted at the local precinct level: 82 (R) to 90 per cent (D) of the precinct leaders were active in some way in campaigns, and 69 (R) to 91 per cent (D) were active in some way between elections. But only a small minority of leaders were in a state of organizational preparation which would permit them to be effective, and only 17 (D) to 25 per cent (R) performed the three most critical campaign tasks. Further, the patterns of campaign activity were often strange indeed. This chaos and incoherence in task performance attests to the pluralized control character of the structure, the inadequacy of communication lines, and the free interplay of individual motivational orientations of precinct leaders.

This leads us to a fifth observation—"the pre-eminence of the career aspiration ethic." One might well wonder why a precinct leader should seek a career in a party thus structured. Yet, 51 per cent of Democratic precinct leaders and 62 per cent of Republicans did aspire. This is particularly surprising, perhaps, in the minority Republican party whose chances for power in elections in the Detroit area were so limited. Nevertheless, it is a fact of significant implications, for it is one of the most important considerations in understanding how the structure holds together, even at the minimal level of cohesion suggested by our analysis. Most significant, for both parties, is that "career aspiration" was a major "cutting variable" for analysis of the structure: those who aspired produced at a higher level of efficiency than those who did not. For example, 45 per cent of the aspiring Republican lone operators (with no workers to help them) performed at a relatively high efficiency level, while *none* of the nonaspiring lone operators did. Again, 66 per cent of the aspiring Republicans in sure Democratic precincts performed well, while none of those who did not aspire, and worked in such precincts, was efficient. For all Democratic precinct leaders career aspiration made a great difference—90 per cent of the aspirers as against 48 per cent of the nonaspirers were efficient.

Thus, in the face of organizational confusion, conflict, and incoherence, aspiration for a party career, or for personal preferment in party politics, seemed to be a dominant drive with discriminating consequences, and a drive which seemed to be reenforced by the system. It is interesting that 65 (D) to 67 per cent (R) of those precinct leaders who felt "involved" in district-level operations did aspire to a career, at percentages roughly 20 per cent higher than for those not involved. Similarly, 62 (D) to 73 per cent (R) of those with extensive communicative contacts were aspirers, at percentages 15 (R) to 35 per cent (D) higher than those with localist or isolated communicative patterns. Communication and involvement patterns, therefore, seem to accentuate the career-aspiration ethic of the party structure.

Sixth, and finally, integrating structural relationships enhance the phenomenon of "motivational displacement" or "motivational reorientation." In an earlier chapter we analyzed developmental patterns of leadership motivation, and demonstrated that the leader moved from an earlier noninstrumentalist motivation to one highly defined in terms of personal success and personal satisfaction. In the analysis of organizational conditions we now find that involvement in the organization seems to bring with it an alteration in motivation. Utilizing that particular category of leaders who were admittedly in politics for "personal gain," we find twice as many of this type among those who were involved in the Democratic party, and eight times as many among those who were involved in the Republican party. With actually a slight diminution in noninstrumentalist (ideological or philosophical) explanations for being active among the involved precinct leaders, we see, then, a possible cumulative motivational reorientation among precinct leaders coincident with their greater attachment to, and participation in, organizational affairs.

One should not conclude from this that the impact of organization is, in normative terms, unfortunate. Our analysis has demonstrated that as the precinct leader became attached to, and integrated with, the party structure, he revealed a variety of behavior patterns which can only be construed as "beneficial" to the party. He became more loyal (70 per cent of the involved Democrats, 87 per cent of the cosmopolitan conservatives in the Republican party). His morale increased by 40 to 50 percentage points. He became more preoccupied with "democratic values" (89 per cent of involved Democrats compared to 52 per cent of the noninvolved; 61 per cent of the involved Republicans, compared to 46 per cent of the noninvolved). And the precinct leader who was involved and has extensive communication contacts *was* more likely to be motivated.

Although these salutary consequences of interaction in the party structure are significant to party viability, the impact of the structural conditions on a career-aspiration emphasis and on instrumentalist motivation cannot be denied. In a real sense, we are brought full circle to our basic paradox. In a structural, highly explosive, coalitional system, with an open recruitment strategy, like the party, viability is difficult to attain. Yet, viability at a minimal level is, indeed, attained. The consequences of "good organization" are many, among them heightened efficiency, better morale, greater loyalty. Better organization apparently can help the party to maximize its power drive, though cohesion, consensus, and coherence remain remote objectives. But the by-products of "better organization" are not to be concealed. Above all, the utilization of the party structure as an instrumentality for personal success and private need, though socially certainly comprehensible, may in fact proliferate and reenforce those very conditions which have diffused the meaning of the party in the past, and which the party must overcome if it is to be an effective ideological mechanism in the modern political system.

PART IV

THE PUBLIC AND THE PARTIES: FUNCTIONAL RELATIONSHIPS

INTRODUCTION

Party structures do not exist in a vacuum. In a very real sense, it is difficult even to conceive of the party as an organizational system without taking cognizance of its close interlocking with the social substrata. In the words of Charles Merriam, 40 years ago, in his discussion of "the nature and function of party":

> . . . what looks like a vast power of a party leader, or boss, will upon more careful analysis be found to be the visible part of a larger process not at first seen because of its being below the surface of things. Deep down in the social and economic interests of the society, hidden in its social and political psychology, lie the habits, tendencies and forces which condition the action of the party. . . .[1]

Yet, while the party is a part of the social process which underlies it, "the party is not merely a reflection of the general process."[2] "The party also performs another general function which may be defined as that of the intermediary, the buffer, the adjuster, between society and the individual."[3]

This is a central functional relationship to be explicated in a political system, for the party has a functional duality—it serves as the "reflector" and the "adjuster" of social forces, group interests, and individual acts. If we are to grasp the meaning of party, it is necessary to analyze the consequences of the party

[1] *The American Party System*, p. 386.
[2] *Ibid.*
[3] *Ibid.*, p. 399.

as "organization" for individual and group behavior in the system, while recognizing, at the same time, that the party as "organization" is indistinguishable theoretically from "the system." For analytical purposes, in this chapter, however, we shall conceptualize the party "organization" as a separate subsystem of action and seek to assess its impact on "the public." In reality the two are components of one process.

Much has been written about the functions of parties, but little empirical analysis supports generalization. Merriam saw five specific functions in 1922: selection of governmental personnel, formulation of public policies, conductors or critics of government, political education, intermediation between individual and government.[4] In addition, he utilized a central theoretical vantage point of the parties as "aggregations or groups of persons reflecting certain interests, either general or special."[5] Since Merriam's time the major discussions of the functions of party, although elaborating a functional theory in greater detail, have added little that is new in theoretical insight. The need is not, therefore, for more taxonomic functional schemes, but for specification of theories in "operational" terms, and the assembling of evidence by which these hypothetical images of party function can be tested. By utilizing our interview data for the Detroit area party structures and for the Detroit area population, we attempt to test those theories which hypothesize a functional relationship between party leadership activity and the behavior patterns of the adult public.[6]

The functional outcomes which we test have three types of contextual relevance and two types of functional valence. Any set of data can be interpreted as fulfilling needs for the party structure, for the individual citizen, and for the political system generally. That is, if public behavior is perceived as

[4] *Ibid.*, p. 391.
[5] *Ibid.*, p. 390.
[6] It should be recalled here that our cross-section sample of the Detroit area population was drawn to fall within the six congressional districts and the 87 precincts which were also the focal points for our study of party structure.

being influenced (or uninfluenced) by party behavior, this can be construed as satisfying (or not satisfying) requisite personal, party, or system needs. Thus any set of findings may have positive or negative valences, as viewed from three contexts of relevance. This suggests, of course, that a finding may be construed as functional to personal needs but dysfunctional to party and system needs, or, more probably, functional to party needs and dysfunctional to system needs. These interpretive differences in contextual relevance will be referred to as we proceed with this analysis.

CHAPTER 17

POLITICAL RECRUITMENT AND CITIZEN PARTICIPATION

One central question often posed in an open, democratic society such as ours with relatively porous party structures is: Does the party organizational effort, in its contact with the public, have value in the development of attitudes predisposing citizens favorably toward accepting activist and leadership positions with the party structure? We have noted the almost desperate conditions of turnover among the activist cadre of the party. We are also aware of the universal impression that most adults are skeptical, to say the least, of involvement in party activity. To what extent is "recruitment alienation" the consequence of party behavior?

Four questions, used in a cross-section survey, provide us with a basis for answering this:

	Percentage of total adult sample
1. If you had a son who was thinking of going into politics, would you encourage him, discourage him, or say nothing?	
Encourage him	13%
Discourage him	28
Say nothing	55

2. If you wanted to take a greater part in community affairs, do you think the best way to do this would be to work through the political parties and their organizations, or through other types of groups? (Only used with those who had voted at some time in the past.)

Through parties	25%
Through other groups	57
Through *both* parties and other groups	2
Neither, don't know, not ascertained	16

3. Do you think it is easy or hard for a person who wants to, to become a worker for a political party?

Easy	54%
Hard	28
Don't know, not ascertained	18

4. If a man has ability and is ambitious, how good a chance does he have to become an important leader in a political party?

Very good chances	19%
Good chances	35
Fair chances	28
Not good chances	7
Don't know, not ascertained	11

Since the important immediate consideration was how much of this variation in responses was due to contact with political parties, we separated those in the cross-section who had been personally exposed to some type of party contact. Interview items used to make this selection were: had they ever worked for the party, in 1956 or previously; did they belong to and attend party or political clubs; did they ever go to the party for advice or help; did they personally know Republican or Democratic precinct leaders, or other party campaign personnel; had they ever met party candidates for office; had they been personally contacted by party representatives at the home, or by phone; had their fathers ever been active in party politics; had they ever been personally contacted by party personnel for financial contributions; and had they ever received literature from the parties. The latter two indicators were given a lower weight than the other nine items. All respondents were classified by number of exposures, type of exposures, and time period of exposure. In the total sample we found 17 per cent highly exposed to party, 39 per cent moderately or somewhat exposed, and 44 per cent not exposed.

Exposure to the majority party (the Democrats) is clearly related to predispositions and attitudes conducive to party activism (Table 17.1), but the relationship may actually be inverse for the minority party (the Republicans—Table 17.2). Over 50 per cent of the most highly exposed Democrats would work for the parties, and would encourage their sons to enter politics, while those less exposed revealed much less "recruitment interest." The differences in the perceptions of the party as an exclusive system are not as significant, and also do not seem to be as relevant. Thus, 71 per cent of those only slightly exposed to the party saw it as a structure easy to enter and move upward in, but, despite this, less than two-fifths revealed an interest in party activism for themselves or their sons.

The Republicans and independents were much less influenced by party exposure. In fact, the data suggest that among such respondents those highly exposed to parties were least interested in party activism. Thus, only 10 per cent of the Republicans who were highly exposed would encourage their sons to enter politics, while 32 per cent of those with no exposure to the party would encourage their sons to enter politics! Similarly, those Republicans not exposed to party were actually more interested

TABLE 17.1

PARTY EXPOSURE AND ATTITUDES TOWARD BECOMING A PARTY ACTIVIST
(For Those in the Cross-section Who Consider Themselves Democrats)

	High exposure 1956, and before	*High exposure 1956 only*	*Moderate exposure*	*Slight exposure*	*No exposure*	
Democrats only					*But father was active*	*Father not active*
Would encourage son to enter politics	54%	43%	30%	31%	19%	17%
Would work through parties	58	50	45	39	26	35
Do not consider parties exclusive	73	67	58	71	43	58
Number of cases	26	40	84	65	42	151

TABLE 17.2

PARTY EXPOSURE AND RECRUITMENT ATTITUDES OF REPUBLICANS AND INDEPENDENTS

	High exposure 1956, and before	*High exposure 1956 only*	*Moderate exposure*	*Slight exposure*	*No exposure*	
					But father was active	*Father not active*
Republicans						
Would encourage son to enter politics	10%	23%	19%	39%	9%	32%
Would work through parties	20	8	23	29	9	24
Do not consider parties exclusive	100	65	58	73	53	66
Independents						
Would encourage son to enter politics	*	37	26	40	13	17
Would work through parties	*	21	16	24	7	20
Do not consider parties exclusive	*	95	85	68	80	75
Number of cases						
Republicans	20	26	52	33	32	73
Independents	*	19	34	25	15	64

* Too few cases for analysis.

in working for the party than those highly exposed. The independents presented no more consistent picture, and exposure to the parties does not explain differentials in their recruitment enthusiasm.

The relevance of party exposure as a critical factor is supported when this analysis is combined with exposure to television. Each repondent was classified as a television fan, a moderate user, or as unexposed to TV for political purposes, on the basis of a series of detailed questions about the specific extent of their TV viewing during the national conventions and the campaign. There is very little evidence that television exposure contributes to a party recruitment interest, as Table 17.3 reveals. Only under

TABLE 17.3

PARTY RECRUITMENT INTEREST AND TELEVISION EXPOSURE

	Two categories of high party exposure				*No party exposure*			
Would encourage son to enter politics	*High TV exposure*		*Moderate and low TV exposure*		*High TV exposure*		*Moderate and low TV exposure*	
Democrats	48%	(44)*	46%	(22)*	15%	(82)*	20%	(69)*
Republicans	17	(29)	18	(17)	40	(50)	13	(23)
Independents	25	(21)	38	(10)	21	(38)	12	(41)

* Number of cases.

conditions of low party exposure does television viewing seem to be important for promotion of recruitment interest, and then only for Republicans and independents.

For Democrats the key question is, of course, what types of people are potential recruitees of the party *as a result of exposure to the party structure?* Table 17.4 shows different proportions of socio-economic categories "influenced" by exposure to the party. Party contact for predisposed Democrats resulted in a reservoir of recruitees who were more predominantly in the white-collar or skilled-worker classes (55 per cent compared to

TABLE 17.4

CHARACTERISTICS (SOCIAL AND IDEOLOGICAL) AMONG RESPONDENTS WITH FAVORABLE RECRUITMENT ATTITUDES, HIGHLY EXPOSED AND NOT EXPOSED TO THE PARTY STRUCTURE—DEMOCRATS ONLY

	Favorable recruitment attitudes	
	Highly exposed to party	*Not exposed to party*
Occupational class		
Professional-managerial	29%	4%
Other white collar	13	19
Skilled workers	13	4
Semi- and unskilled	19	50
Not in labor force	26	23
Educational level		
Elementary school or less	30	50
High school	47	38
College, university	23	12
Ideological position		
Consistent liberals	19	15
Tend to be liberal	55	58
Not liberal	26	27
Number of cases	31	26

Note: These are based on the question: Would you encourage your son to enter politics?

27 per cent for those not exposed), and with a higher educational level (70 per cent high school or college, compared to 50 per cent for those not exposed to the party).

The functional consequences of Democratic party efforts in terms of recruitment may, thus, be considerable. The net impact of the party contact patterns seems to be that the unskilled and lower working classes were relatively discouraged from entering party work if they had been exposed to the party, while the skilled workers and white-collar class were encouraged. Further, a potentially better educated and skilled group of party workers may be available. While this may be heartening for the party leadership, it may be dysfunctional to the interests of the lower-middle and working class, and in the long run this condition may not be functional in the Democratic party's contact with the lower classes.

Party exposure does not seem to attract the more ideologically committed. The fact that 26 per cent of those who had been exposed to the Democratic party, and who revealed no antipathy to a party career for their sons, were conservatives (virtually the same percentage as for those not exposed to the party), speaks eloquently about the ideological content of party recruitment efforts. This finding is also indicative of the perceptions of these recruitees of ideological conditions obtaining in the Democratic party, and carries significant implication for the ideological structure of the Democratic party of the future. In an "open" structural system such as the Democratic party, with these conditions obtaining, a solid conservative minority in the party cadre seems certainly assured.

The nature of political leadership in the precinct is presumably related to the development of favorable recruitment attitudes among citizens who identify with the political parties. To test this theory of the impact of one element in the political environment, we examined particularly the attitudinal patterns of two subgroups, Negroes and union members. The conditions of precinct political life under which these respondents lived is of value in assessing the relevance of party leadership for the development of potential recruitment interest. Among Negroes in the sample, 42 per cent (47 per cent of those who voted) said that if they engaged in more political activity they would work through political parties. Among union members the percentage was 36 per cent (or 40 per cent of those who voted). If environment is important, we can hypothesize that Negroes living in effectively led and *Negro-led* precincts would be more favorable to party work than those living in ineffectively Negro-led precincts or in white-led precincts. And in the same vein, theoretically, the type of union leadership might properly be an important factor in the development of attitudes toward party work among union members.

The type of precinct leadership does indeed seem to be relevant, but not always in the direction one might expect (Tables 17.5 and 17.6). Four-fifths of the Negroes living in efficiently led Negro precincts had the greatest enthusiasm for party activity. But as efficiency declined, their enthusiasm also dwindled. And if their party did not have a Negro leader, but the opposition did, their enthusiasm dropped to a low point—only 23 per cent among Democratic identifiers. Yet, except in this latter case, their attitude toward party work was more favorable, even under white leadership, than that of white respondents in white *or* Negro-led precincts.

Paradoxically, union members did not respond well to the precinct leadership of union officers. They supported the idea of party work most favorably in precincts led by efficient union members who were not officers, suggesting perhaps a type of rebellion against union leadership. Even more striking is their high enthusiasm for party activity in precincts not led by union people: 67 per cent of Democrats and independents were enthusiastic in such precincts, compared to about 25 per cent in union officer precincts, and 20 per cent in inefficiently led union member precincts. In the Detroit area, therefore, for Democratic identifiers, at least, it appears that the type of precinct leadership and the efficiency of the precinct organization, resulting as they did in public contacts and exposure, were highly relevant to the content of the public's perception of party work and its willingness to consider the possibility of embarking on a party career.

THE PARTY AS A POTENTIAL CHANNEL FOR CITIZEN ACTION

The conviction that parties are intermediate action mechanisms for the public is a strong component in modern democratic theory. This image implies at least three meanings: that the party is seen by the public as acting on its behalf in the policy-making process, that through the party citizens can be informed about the world of politics, and that the public can utilize the party as

TABLE 17.5

THE IMPACT OF NEGRO LEADERSHIP IN 21 PRECINCTS ON RECRUITMENT ATTITUDES AMONG NEGROES AND WHITES

	Negro Democratic Identifiers—favorable to party work	*All Negroes —favorable*	*Negro independents*	*All white respondents*
Precincts led by Negroes in one's own party				
Very efficiently led	79%	58%	33%	24%
Moderate efficiency	59			
Low efficiency	42			
Precincts led by Negroes in opposition party only	23	40		
Precincts led by *white* leaders in both parties	*	39	*	25

Note: Each percentage is the proportion in each precinct category (in the left column) who responded that they preferred to work through parties if they became more politically active. Respondents who had never voted were excluded from this analysis.

* Too few cases for analysis.

TABLE 17.6

THE IMPACT OF WHITE LABOR UNION LEADERSHIP IN SELECTED (DETROIT AND DEARBORN) DEMOCRATIC PARTY PRECINCTS ON THE RECRUITMENT ATTITUDES OF WHITE UNION AND NONUNION MEMBERS (Democratic Identifiers and Independents only)

	Union members favorable	*Nonunion members favorable*
8 precincts led by *union officers*		
Most efficiently led	23%	22%
Least efficiently led	27	6
10 precincts led by *union members* but not union officers		
Most efficiently led	52	19 (Most and Least efficiently led combined)
Least efficiently led	20	
13 precincts not led by union members or officers	67	6

Note: Analysis the same as in Table 17.5, but restricted to Democratic identifiers and independents of Detroit and Dearborn and other cities.

a channel for its complaints and demands. As a demand channel citizens are visualized going to party leaders with their requests for action about personal, neighborhood, or community problems. And, indeed, 58 per cent of the Democratic and 38 per cent of the Republican precinct leaders revealed that they did give advice and assistance to members of the public. But only 1 per cent of the adult sample reported they had consulted precinct leaders in connection with complaints about local governmental action or inaction. While our question was not likely to discover all the demands or requests made upon all types of party leaders by the public in an area such as Detroit, the evidence suggests that a relatively small percentage of the public did avail itself of the party apparatus for demand purposes.

The functional query to be explored here is slightly different: Is the party contact effort with the public related to the development of orientations toward making political demands *and* toward using the party structure to implement these demands? The citizen most likely to go to the party for help or for action must be in a "state of activism readiness." The state of readiness by which we can identify the potential, if not actual, user of the party as a channel for action, includes several components. First, the individual must be predisposed, and willing, to engage in political action beyond the act of voting. If he sees no advantage to political activity beyond voting, or if he feels he has satisfied all of his citizen obligations by voting, he is not likely to be oriented toward the party, or any other apparatus, for demand purposes. Second, he must have some awareness of the decision-making system, more than just a general awareness about "government," "the city hall," or "Washington, D. C." The probability is that the more specific his understanding about where decisions are made, the more likely he is to be a potential activist. Third, for purposes of investigating our specific query, he should have some confidence that parties or party leaders are relevant to his political needs. That is, he must recognize parties as useful for action, not merely accept them (as our democratic mythology has indoctrinated him), as a generalized value in a democratic society. Parties must mean more to him than vague institutions somehow linked to the democratic dogma. And fourth, he must have some knowledge about the party, whether it has leaders and where those leaders are, so that if he chooses to become active he can make contact with the party apparatus.

These four components—inclination toward activism, decision-making awareness, cognizance of party relevance, and knowledge of party apparatus—define the conditions under which the potential users of the party as a demand channel can be identified. These four conditions are operationalized in our study of the Detroit public. The distributions for the entire sample by the questions used are:

Should do other things in the political area besides voting	42%
Awareness of specific governmental decision-making centers	52%
Sees parties as relevant for getting things done	16%
Knows that precinct party leaders exist in neighborhood	29%

If we combine the responses for each person in the sample, using the four specified criteria, we find differential levels of "readiness" for utilization of the party as an action channel. Only 3 per cent of the adult sample fulfilled all four criteria. Another 15 per cent did not satisfy one or two of the criteria, but did know that precinct leaders existed whom they could consult. Just slightly less than one-fifth, therefore, were conceivable as being in a state of readiness for action through parties. At the other end of the continuum are 22 per cent of respondents who fulfilled none of the criteria: they had no inclinations for action, no awareness of decision-making, no realization of the relevance of parties, and no "operational knowledge" about the party apparatus or leadership in their vicinities. The 60 per cent in the intermediate range of the continuum were in various stages of readiness: they had activist inclinations but no knowledge, nonactivist predispositions but no awareness that parties might be relevant, knowledge of the party but no inclination to be active, or no confidence about the action possibilities of parties.

Our primary concern is with the functional role parties may play in the development of states of readiness for action. Viewing the four components separately, we see that contact with the party in the variety of ways indicated earlier (10 in all) was efficacious. It must be emphasized that the party-exposure categories were initially constructed without reference to the motivation or volition of the respondent, and at least five of the items used in determining exposure were "passive" in the sense that the respondent was contacted by the party rather than representing overt action on his part in seeking out the party. The exposure index was thus motivationally "neutral" and at least partially nonvolitional.

There was a consistent coincidence between exposure to the party and party-activist orientations (Table 17.7). Those who were exposed to the party were inclined to be active, were decisionally aware, saw parties as relevant (except for the Republicans, who revealed no differences in this respect), and had knowledge about precinct leaders. This held true for Democrats,

TABLE 17.7

"Impact" of Party Contact on Citizen Action Orientations (Adult Public)

	High exposure 1956 and before	*High exposure 1956*	*Moderate exposure*	*No exposure*
Are inclined to be active				
Democrats	65%	43%	45%	34%
Republicans	55	50	40	34
Independents	53	56	50	25
Specific awareness of decision-making				
Democrats	63	68	42	38
Republicans	80	50	48	47
Independents	58	79	38	45
See parties as relevant to action				
Democrats	27	33	17	20
Republicans	15	4	13	16
Independents	16	11	6	3
Know that party precinct leaders exist in the neighborhood				
Democrats	92	88	40	2
Republicans	70	69	23	12
Independents	42	37	38	3
Number of cases				
Democrats	26	40	84	151
Republicans	20	26	52	73
Independents	19	19	34	64

Republicans, and independents. The "potential-activism" differentials between those highly exposed and not exposed to the party were considerable and consistent. If one contrasts high and non-exposure percentages for each component the range for the Democrats was 7–90 per cent, for the Republicans, 0–58 per cent, and for the independents, 13–39 per cent.

Two major interpretations of these data are, of course, possible: either the parties were naturally seeking out, or in contact with, the potential activists, or party contact did have a functional impact on the public, making it more ready for action, aware of the action relevance of parties, and knowledgeable about parties. The latter theory gains considerable support here, primarily because of the general decline in activism orientation *as party exposure declines.* Further, from a logical standpoint, knowledge about the existence of precinct leadership seems to be an *after-the-fact* outcome of party contact. The unsystematic and promiscuous contact patterns of the party personnel, alluded to in previous chapters, as well as "get out the vote" drives to involve the most apathetic, lead to skepticism about the theory that parties subconsciously seek out only potential activists. No doubt party personnel do, to some extent, contact members of the public whom they see as potential activists, but our awareness of the inefficiency with which the parties go about their tasks places such a theory in jeopardy. More plausible is the theory that party exposure triggers an interest in "the political game" for many citizens. This leads, in turn, to other types of activities, such as the discussion of political issues and processes, and, over time, with repeated exposure to party through the mass media, a state of readiness develops for engagement in politics through parties as the demand channels. The fact that those respondents who were exposed to the parties before 1956, as well as in 1956, revealed the highest degree of sensitivity to political action—over 50 per cent inclined to be active—re-enforces this theory of party operation in the total context of the individual's action orientation.

Combining the data for each individual respondent to determine how many of the components of potential activism he fulfilled reveals further confirmation of our interpretations (Table 17.8). Virtually all who satisfied the minimal perspectivist requirements for utilizing the party as an action channel were highly exposed to parties: 29 and 13 per cent of those in the highest exposure categories, and only 1 per cent in the no-

TABLE 17.8

COMPOSITE ANALYSIS OF DEGREE OF POTENTIAL ACTIVISM—BY PARTY EXPOSURE

	High exposure 1956 and before		*High exposure 1956*		*Moderate exposure*		*No exposure*	
Completely oriented toward party as channel for action								
Democrats	42%	20%	13%	7%	0%	0%	0%	1%
Republicans	10		0		0		3	
Independents	0		6		0		0	
Oriented favorably toward party, but some question about activism inclinations								
Democrats	19	9	18	6	1	1	1	1
Republicans	0		0		0		0	
Independents	5		0		0		0	
Only partially oriented, but do have knowledge of precinct leaders								
Democrats	32	42	58	55	37	33	1	3
Republicans	60		70		23		9	
Independents	37		33		38		4	
Poorly oriented—no knowledge of party								
Democrats	8	27	13	30	46	51	68	62
Republicans	30		24		64		57	
Independents	48		61		36		56	
No evidence at all of activism orientation								
Democrats	0	3	0	2	12	15	31	33
Republicans	0		8		13		30	
Independents	11		0		26		42	

exposure category. On the other hand, only 3 per cent of those highly exposed to parties could not meet any of the requirements, while fully one-third of those not exposed were completely disoriented toward utilization of the party as a demand channel. The limiting effect of party contacts can be seen from the high proportions of those widely exposed to parties who were only partially or poorly oriented toward party activism. Nevertheless, the data reveal that where readiness for party activism existed, the party contact did seem consequential. Whether the party seeks out potential activists or vice versa, or whether the party does develop an interest in activism, the correspondence of these two phenomena is striking.

Citizens who were clearly ready to use the party as a demand channel revealed certain important characteristics (Table 17.9) (Restricted to those who fulfilled all or almost all of the criteria used.) They saw party conflict in issue terms, were highly interested in public affairs, and were fairly well informed. They were also somewhat more liberal on each of the issue questions used in the study, but the differences were not great. One-fourth of them had already used the party as a medium for action, compared to only 1 per cent of the total sample. Over 60 per cent were in blue-collar occupations, which compares favorably with the 67 per cent in the total sample with blue-collar occupations, and exceeded our expectations. Though relatively few in number, these potential users of the political party for advice, information, protest, and demand purposes appeared to be "political literates" from the lower-middle and lower classes, one-fourth of whom were Negroes. Their characteristics indicate that if, in modern times, the party does become a meaningful intermediate channel between the citizen and his government, it will be a link for those social classes with a changing status and increasing demands in American society and the political system. Whether the number of potential activists increases, and whether this potential becomes actuality, seems to be functionally related to the behavior of the party.

TABLE 17.9

CHARACTERISTICS OF THE POTENTIAL PARTY ACTIVISTS (COMPARED TO THE TOTAL SAMPLE)

	Were uninformed on issues	*Had used the party already*	*Negro*	*Blue-collar*		*Said there were important issues in the campaign*	*High level of interest in public affairs*			*Liberalism*		*Number of cases*
				Skilled	*Semi, and unskilled*		*Foreign*	*National*	*Local*	*Medical Aid*	*Civil rights*	
Potential activists	4%	24%	24%	37%	24%	81%	29%	54%	70%	69%	70%	37
Total sample	8	1	16	33	34	54	19	32	44	62	54	854

CHAPTER 18

POLITICAL INTEREST, VOTING, AND PARTISAN LOYALTY

The strength of a modern democratic system relies greatly on the extent and depth of the public sector's interest in public affairs, its awareness of the existence and meaning of political conflict, and its engagement in interpersonal discourse about politics. Although few members of the public may be potential recruits for the party labor force, and few may see the need to utilize the party actively as a demand channel, a level of intellectual involvement with political matters is necessary for a considerable segment if government is to be more than an elitist phenomenon. In the Detroit area, which is fairly typical of metropolitan publics, from one-fifth to three-fifths of the public was politically engaged, depending on the criteria used. Asked how interested they were in public affairs at various levels, 19 per cent said they were very interested in foreign affairs, 32 per cent in national domestic affairs, and 44 per cent in local governmental affairs. Asked whether they felt that the parties stood for the same things or different things, 54 per cent indicated that the parties differed, the same proportion who saw important issues in the national campaign. Yet only 47 per cent said that it made any difference to them "whether the Republican or Democratic party is in control of the government."

In exploring the functional relationships of parties to the level of public interest and awareness of politics, we are primarily concerned with four different dimensions: the general degree of interest in political affairs, the extent to which elections are seen as personally relevant for the individual's welfare, the perception of parties and campaigns as conflictual structures or processes, and the extent to which the individual citizen implements or manifests his political interest by participating in the political communication process. In the latter case we are interested in whether politics is discussed with others, as well as the degree of exposure to the major medium of politics—television. In the analysis we will again look at the different levels of political interest for population subgroups, ranging from high exposure to party organization efforts to those not exposed at all. While many factors are no doubt interlinked with individual political interest patterns, we are primarily asking the question: Does exposure to the party organization seem to have effect on any of the four aspects or components of the public's political interest?

Democrats and Republicans exposed to the party organization revealed a greater general interest in public affairs (Table 18.1). Those not exposed were consistently lower in interest. The differences between the two extreme exposure groups were great, particularly in the areas of national and local affairs—differences of 25 and 35 per cent for the Democrats, and 17 to 26 per cent for the Republicans. High party exposure was also associated with a high interest in *all three* areas of public affairs by the same individual.

But the independents did not reveal this pattern. In fact, those who were only moderately exposed to parties seemed to have the highest levels of interest. This is particularly noticeable in the national affairs area, where only 26 per cent of those highly exposed to the parties were "very interested," while 44 per cent of those only moderately exposed were "very interested." The interpretation of this is difficult, but clearly party contacts had a different meaning for independents than for the avowed partisans.

Our data raise serious questions concerning the function of parties in conveying to the public the meaning of party conflict

TABLE 18.1

THE PUBLIC'S INTEREST IN POLITICAL AFFAIRS BY PARTY EXPOSURE

Type of interest (Percentage "very interested")	*Most highly exposed*	*Moderately exposed*	*Not exposed*
Foreign affairs			
Democrats	34%	21%	10%
Republicans	28	18	24
Independents	24	27	18
National affairs			
Democrats	55	31	19
Republicans	48	31	31
Independents	26	44	25
Local affairs			
Democrats	62	45	37
Republicans	63	41	37
Independents	42	53	39
"Very interested" in all three levels			
Democrats	24	17	4
Republicans	17	9	14
Independents	21	19	16
Number of cases			
Democrats	66	149	193
Republicans	46	85	105
Independents	38	59	79

(Table 18.2). On the one hand, those exposed to party were more certain that the campaign was conflictual in issue terms, with a differential of 11 to 32 per cent between the exposure subgroups. But the Democrats who were exposed revealed no distinctive awareness that the parties differed basically in principle, although slight differences were found among Republicans and independents who were exposed. This is particularly significant in light of our previous analysis of party leadership echelons which revealed significant ideological differences between the two cadres of leaders. For instance, only 28 per cent

TABLE 18.2

THE ROLE OF PARTY CONTACT IN ALERTING THE PUBLIC TO THE MEANING OF PARTY CONFLICT

	High exposure to parties	*Moderate exposure*	*No exposure*
Were important campaign issues in last election			
Democrats	73%	51%	41%
Republicans	65	59	54
Independents	74	75	48
Parties stand for different things			
Democrats	73	64	72
Republicans	59	48	52
Independents	40	34	30
Does "make a difference to you whether the Republican or Democratic party is in control of the government"			
Democrats	45	56	61
Republicans	57	52	62
Independents	29	10	22

of the Republican leaders were liberal on the governmental medical aid proposal, while 76 per cent of the Democratic leaders were liberal. Yet the Democratic party in its contacts seemed either unable to communicate these differences, or it was unwilling to accentuate their differences. This latter probability may indeed be the subtle strategy of the majority party in an area such as Detroit, as it seeks to maximize its support.

The major finding is that party exposure seems completely unrelated to the public's perception of the personal consequences of party turnover in government. Among the self-declared partisans in the sample, party exposure seemed conducive to personal indifference on party changeover. Thus, only 45 per cent of the Democrats highly exposed to party felt that party control made a difference. This signifies a significant breakdown in party communication and suggests, in conjunction with our other data, that party contact may make it clear that campaign issues divide the parties, but that party positions themselves are such that election outcomes are ideologically and materially irrelevant for the voter. For large numbers of those in contact with parties, therefore, although they were highly interested in politics and aware of the existence of conflict, election results were not vital. This finding may be reassuring for the stability of the system, but it may also be linked to public apathy and party difficulties in arousing the vote.

The data reveal that people who are exposed to parties are more likely to discuss politics with friends and associates. Close to two-thirds of the Democrats and Republicans said they "usually" discussed politics with a friend, while only 30 per cent of those not exposed were involved in this way (the norm for all adults was 42 per cent). The same is somewhat, though less strikingly, true for television exposure. Approximately 50 per cent of respondents not exposed to the parties were television fans for political information purposes, compared to about 65 per cent of those who had the highest exposure to parties. Yet the differences lay in the expected direction, and suggest again that exposure to party activity produces, or is related to, a higher interest in, and active discussion of, political questions. Finally, significant differences were found by combining an interest in political affairs and discussion of them. This, in a sense, is the real test of political interest. One-half of the partisan-oriented respondents who were exposed to party contacts were both generally interested and active discussants of politics; less than 20 per cent of those not exposed to the parties met this critical test of political interest.

The evidence points clearly to a definite functional relationship between party activity and a general interest by the public in politics, an awareness by the public of the issue-competitive nature of the campaign, and active engagement by the individual in the discussion of political matters. The evidence is much less convincing on these points for independents than for self-classified Democrats and Republicans. Although, paradoxically, the parties did not seem to be able to create a personal concern about election outcomes and party control, the fact that parties, by organizational efforts, had some impact on developing or sustaining the public's interest in and alertness to public affairs is a matter of great importance. Only 27 per cent of the Detroit area public discussed politics regularly and revealed a high interest in one area of public affairs—either foreign, national, or local—yet 75 per cent of these citizens had had some contact with political parties. Though it is hazardous to leap to causal conclusions from these data, the consistency of the differences suggests that party activity may be functionally consequential to sustaining, if not creating, public interest in politics.

THE ROLE OF THE PARTY IN MAXIMIZING VOTING PARTICIPATION

Voting can be construed as a behavioral continuation or implementation of an interest in politics. We have noted the relationship between party activity and the degree of political interest of those exposed to parties; we would expect, therefore, those not exposed to parties to include a larger proportion of nonvoters, particularly since so much of the party's emphasis is on voting. The earlier analysis of the party as an efficiency structure revealed great variations in the degree of organizational attention to vote-mobilization, but that "getting out the vote" has such a large significance that everyone brought into contact with party personnel should at least be aware of his voting responsibilities and power. The precinct leaders differed greatly in campaign task performance: from 11 (R) to 26 per cent (D) were extremely active, while 10 to 14 per cent did nothing. Yet the campaign and the vote have such a critical focus that the public's contact with the parties should presumably enhance voting turnout.

To test this proposition, we looked first at the individuals in the sample who had never voted (representing about 14 per cent of the total sample). As Table 18.3 reveals, none of those highly exposed to the parties were chronic nonvoters. In contrast,

TABLE 18.3

PARTY EXPOSURE AND THE EXTENT OF NONVOTING IN THE ADULT PUBLIC

Criteria	*Highest exposure to parties 1956 and before*	*High exposure 1956 only*	*Some ex-posure*	*Very little or no exposure*
Have never voted				
Democrats	0%	0%	11%	25%
Republicans	0	8	7	14
Independents	*	0	12	30
Nonvoters in 1956				
Democrats	0	10	21	38
Republicans	0	15	16	26
Independents	*	0	22	42
1952 Nonvoters eligible to vote in 1952 who were nonvoters in 1956 (Democrats only)	0	7	9	13
	($N = 18$)	($N = 27$)	($N = 91$)	($N = 83$)

* Too few cases for analysis.

25 per cent of the Democrats not exposed to the parties had never voted, 14 per cent of the Republicans, and 30 per cent of the independents. A progressive increase in nonvoting appears as party exposure is decreased.

Similarly, in the 1956 election alone, we find that none of those most consistently exposed to the parties failed to vote, while from 26 to 42 per cent of those not exposed stayed home. A special analysis was made of the 254 nonvoters in 1952 who were eligible and old enough to vote. The analysis was confined to the Democrats, since there were too few cases of Republican 1952 nonvoters. But for these Democrats the case is again clear: as party exposure increased, nonvoting vanished. Or, to cite the data directly, party exposure meant a 13 per cent increment in voting participation, if such contact was consistent and repetitive.

A related aspect of voting participation is the "time of voting decision," that is *when* the voter makes up his mind to vote, as distinguished from *whether* he makes up his mind to vote. Respondents were asked to tell when in 1956 they had decided, before the national conventions, during the conventions, or at various chronological periods of the campaign, including the time "just before you voted." For the entire sample, 17 per cent said their minds were always made up, and another 37 per cent decided by the time the campaign began, a total of 54 per cent who made an early decision. The Republican norm was higher in 1956, 81 per cent having made up their minds by the time the campaign began. The question here is: Does exposure to the party organization tend to be related to an early, or a late, voting decision? Our data suggest two contrasting answers, one for each of the parties (there was no discernible pattern for independents). Those who called themselves Democrats tended to be early deciders if they were not exposed to the party, while the Republicans who had no party contact tended to be late deciders, relatively, as the following data in summary form indicate:

	High exposure to party	*Some exposure*	*No exposure*
Democrats deciding early	57%	70%	77%
Republicans deciding early	96%	85%	71%

Caution is necessary before deciding that the party contact produced any result. In fact, for those whose only contact with the party was in 1956, early decision suggests that party contact was irrelevant, and that the party was exerting itself with individuals who had already made up their minds. If this interpretation is correct, the Democratic organization wasted its time on fewer individuals than the Republicans, 85–96 per cent of whom had already made up their minds. A second, alternative, explanation is, of course, that the two party organizations' efforts had different consequences—the Democrats, by their contacts, forcing individuals to reconsider decisions (and thus become "late deciders"), the Republican organization reinforcing early decisions and forcing few to reconsider (resulting in a higher proportion of "early deciders"). A third theory would suggest that party contact for some late deciders can actually be dysfunctional to the party's interest, producing indecision and even party deviancy.

The evidence as to the net influence of party exposure on late deciders is somewhat ironic, suggesting, indeed, that some party contact may be dysfunctional. We examined the voting patterns of early and late deciders among committed Democrats, by party exposure (there were too few cases of highly exposed Republican late deciders to do this for Republican partisans), with the results given in Table 18.4. Clearly, those who were

TABLE 18.4

VOTING PATTERNS OF EARLY AND LATE DECIDERS, BY PARTY EXPOSURE

Early deciders	*High exposure to party*	*No exposure to party*
Voted straight Democratic	82%	77%
Split for Republicans	18	23
Number of cases	35	78
Late deciders		
Voted straight Democratic	44	64
Split for Republicans	56	36
Number of cases	25	28

early deciders and exposed to the party organization tended to have their party loyalty re-enforced, and were more likely to vote the straight ticket (82 per cent compared to 77 per cent). But the late deciders who were contacted by the party (in some cases by both parties) were more inclined to split their ballots (56 per cent compared to 36 per cent of those not exposed). Thus, the committed partisan, not canvassed by the party or otherwise exposed to party influence directly, was more likely to vote straight than if he were exposed to party influences. It should be noted, however, that this late decider who chose outside the party orbit of influence was not as "regular" as the early decider outside the party orbit of influence (64 to 77 per cent).

A combination of interpretations would probably be defensible: the parties waste efforts on committed individuals, the parties re-enforce early commitments to vote, and the parties force re-evaluations of decisions tentatively made before the campaign and reconsidered during the campaign. Early decisions plus party contact is the situation most conducive to party regularity; late decisions and party contact are least conducive to party regularity in voting.

In sum, party exposure, combined no doubt with other influences and interlinked with them, seems to be related to high voting participation. Chronic nonvoters were not found among those highly exposed to party contact. But party campaign contact efforts may be personally disruptive for the voting decision-making processes of many citizens. This suggests that party efforts before campaigns begin, resulting in early voting commitments, and activities leading to strong identifications may be important under certain electoral circumstances if the party wishes to minimize the losses resulting from campaign conflict.

THE MAINTENANCE AND DEVELOPMENT OF PARTISAN LOYALTIES

The psychological commitment of citizens to a political party is a phenomenon many times documented by political analysis. There can be no doubt that the long-range force of party identification has been one major factor in determining the equilibrium of the party system. The latent implication in the empirical study of party commitment is that to some extent loyalty to "party" is induced or re-enforced over time by the behavior of the party. Although presumably some citizens are, traditionally, habitual Republicans or Democrats irrespective of the party's leadership and organizational activity, and despite no personal contact with the party, one can hypothesize that, for most citizens, contact is relevant for strength of identification. Theoretically, contact can weaken the enthusiasm of some for their party and heighten the enthusiasm of others.

We are interested in exploring whether party contacts and

exposure are indeed relevant and, if so, the direction of the influence. A previous analysis tested the importance of party organization by looking at the strength of identification of those Democrats and Republicans residing in precincts with varying degrees of party organizational strength. We found then that, particularly for the Republicans, residence in precincts where the Republican local organization was strong relative to the Democratic organization resulted in a higher proportion of strong Republican identifiers. Other community forces besides "party" seemed to support the political loyalty of the numerically stronger Democrats.[1]

In the present analysis we are interested in attitudinal and behavioral evidence of party commitment. The respondents in our adult cross-section were asked: "Would you call yourself a strong (R or D) or not very strong (R or D)?" In the same context we asked a separate question with other attitudinal implications: "Do you consider yourself a loyal (R or D)?" Both questions were used to test for different or similar patterns of response, and thereby explore whether the phraseology evoked different meanings in the minds of our cross-section. To some extent the use of "strong" and "loyal" did have different meanings. Thus, 47 per cent of our sample said they were "loyal," but only 41 per cent claimed to be "strong" partisans. The distributions of those who called themselves Republicans or Democrats is given in Table 18.5. The two ways of approaching party affiliation are apparently different in meaning, since about 25 per cent of both groups considered themselves "loyal" *or* "strong" but not both, and the use of the word "loyal" evoked greater proportions of identifiers than did the word "strong." The Republicans who were considerably less committed to their party were particularly "weak" in party identification if loyalty and strength of commitment are combined, 32 per cent, as compared to 49 per cent for the Democrats.

[1] Daniel Katz and Samuel J. Eldersveld, "The Impact of Local Political Activity Upon the Electorate," *Public Opinion Quarterly*, Vol. 25 (Spring 1961), pp. 18–19.

TABLE 18.5

PERCENTAGES OF CROSS-SECTION CONSIDERING THEMSELVES STRONG OR LOYAL PARTY SUPPORTERS

	Loyal and strong	*Loyal but not strong*	*Strong, but not loyal*	*Neither loyal nor strong*	*Number of cases*
Democrats	49%	17%	10%	24%	410
Republicans	32	18	7	43	234

Using these attitudinal approaches to the problem, we probed to determine if exposure to the party organization is relevant for political loyalties. Table 18.6 reveals the evidence as much more convincing for the Republicans in Detroit than for the Democrats. Republicans who had for some time been highly exposed to their party were twice as likely to be "loyal and strong"; in addition, 60 per cent were "strong" Republicans, compared to only 36 per cent who were not exposed to party. The Democrats who had been highly exposed over a period of

TABLE 18.6

THE RELATIONSHIP BETWEEN EXPOSURE TO PARTY AND PARTY LOYALTY

	High exposure 1956 and before	*High exposure 1956 only*	*Moderate exposure*	*No exposure*
Democrats				
"Loyal" *and* "strong"	61%	53%	42%	52%
"Loyal" only	61	64	68	66
"Strong" only	75	69	45	64
Republicans				
"Loyal" *and* "strong"	55	50	27	27
"Loyal" only	55	58	45	50
"Strong" only	60	50	34	36
Number of cases				
Democrats	28	38	148	196
Republicans	20	26	85	103

time to the party revealed only a 10 per cent differential in party commitment, as "loyal and strong" or "strong." It is interesting to note that exposure to party seemed completely unrelated to a sense of party "loyalty"; that is, those exposed to parties were somewhat more likely to say they were "strong" partisans, but were *not* more likely to say they were "loyal" partisans. This suggests either that "loyalty" to party has no meaningful referent, or that party contact develops a "strength of attachment," an intensity, but that for many this does not imply a genuine fidelity to the party as a symbol, program, structure, or leadership group.

A second way to approach the existence of party commitment is by asking behavioral questions. We particularly inquired about the respondent's voting behavior in the 1956 election for President, governor, and congressman to see how many voted straight and how many split their ballots. In the total sample equal proportions (58 per cent) of Democrats and Republicans voted in 1956 *and* voted a straight party ticket for these offices. Calculated another way, 16 per cent of those who called themselves Democrats split their ballots in 1956 (26 per cent were nonvoters), compared to 24 per cent of the Republicans (19 per cent were nonvoters).

Analysis of the relationship between party contact and splitting the ballot discloses some interesting results. The Republican organization seemed to be able to influence its partisans to vote straight: only 15 per cent of those Republican voters highly exposed to the party were splitters, while 33 per cent of those not exposed were splitters. However, this was not so among Democratic voters: 31 per cent of those highly exposed were splitters (overwhelmingly splitting their ballots for Eisenhower), while a similar proportion of 27 per cent of those not exposed were splitters. Thus, there was the slightest tendency for Democratic party contact to be conducive to splitting the ballot. It must quickly be added, however, that if we define behavioral loyalty to the party as voting *and* voting a straight ballot for the party, those exposed to the party were most loyal. The distributions are as given in Table 18.7. Thus, the evidence of behavioral disloyalty among Democrats who were in contact with the party was primarily in splitting, while for those not highly exposed it was both nonvoting and splitting the ballot. Among Republicans, party contact seemed functional to both behavioral types of party fidelity.

The third test of party commitment is both attitudinal and behavioral. The basic question to be posed is: To what extent do those who consider themselves "loyal" or "strong" party supporters actually demonstrate consistent and persistent party support? For this purpose we used the voting behavior of respondents in 1956 (whether they split ballots for President, governor, or congressman), and their voting behavior in 1952 and 1956 (whether they switched their vote in those presidential elections).

TABLE 18.7

Party Exposure, Straight-Ticket Voting, and Nonvoting

	Highly exposed 1956 and before	*Highly exposed 1956 only*	*Moderately exposed*	*Not exposed*
Voted *and* voted a straight ticket				
Democrats	69%	69%	69%	47%
Republicans	85	85	51	50
Nonvoters only				
Democrats	0	10	21	38
Republicans	0	15	16	26

The data convincingly demonstrate again for both parties that contact with the organization is functional for the maintenance of party loyalty and its implementation in voting regularity (Table 18.8).[2] It is clear that those most exposed to the party in 1956 and before were the consistent regulars. And, further,

[2] Proportions were calculated in two ways: (1) the percentage of all respondents in each party contact category who were regulars, and (2) the percentage of the loyal or strong party supporters in each category of party contact who were regulars.

TABLE 18.8

THE ROLE OF PARTIES IN BEHAVIORAL AND ATTITUDINAL LOYALTY

	Highly exposed 1956 and before	*Highly exposed 1956 only*	*Moderately exposed*	*Slightly exposed*	*No exposure*
All respondents					
"Loyal" or "strong" *and* voted straight ticket in 1956					
Democrats	61%	61%	56%	45%	44%
Republicans	55	50	31	30	36
"Loyal" or "strong" *and* were regulars in 1952 and 1956					
Democrats	56	58	46	43	35
Republicans	61	57	33	34	38
Those who considered themselves "loyal" and "strong"					
Voted straight in 1956					
Democrats	81	77	77	67	56
Republicans	92	87	67	50	61
Did not switch from 1952 to 1956					
Democrats	67	67	56	56	39
Republicans	92	87	63	50	57

Note: Each percentage is a proportion of each party exposure category.

it appears that party contact produced greater loyalty, but was *not* more functional, so far as splitting the ballot was concerned, for maintaining party regularity from 1952 to 1956. To calculate the relevance of party contact again it is necessary to note the percentage differences between those highly exposed and not exposed to the party organization. The largest differentials for the Democrats were 28 and 21 per cent in maintaining support for Adlai Stevenson from 1952 to 1956. The largest differential for the Republicans was 35 per cent, again in maintaining support for Eisenhower among the loyal Republicans from 1952 to 1956. It is thus manifest that exposure to the variety of party activities is significantly related not only to strength of identification, but also to behavioral regularity, with the Republicans, particularly, revealing differential patterns by party contact.

One final analytical note. We probed for detail on whether our respondents felt that the opinions of certain types of public leaders were important in helping them make voting decisions. Evaluations of party leaders' opinions were included in this query, 16 per cent of all respondents replying that party leaders' opinions were very important, but the parties differed strikingly in the pattern of responses. The Democrats who had been highly exposed placed relatively great emphasis on the party leaders, 38 per cent saying that leaders' opinions were "very important" in contrast to the normal 16 per cent among those unexposed. The Republicans were generally more cynical, and those highly exposed to the parties tended to be slightly more cynical than the others, only 10 per cent of the most highly exposed felt that party leaders' opinions were very important, compared to 18 per cent of those completely removed from party contact. Thus, though both parties by their activities appear to induce more party commitment and voting regularity, esteem for the views of the party leadership seems to be irrelevant for the Republicans but important for the Democrats.

CHAPTER 19

IDEOLOGY AND ELECTORAL BEHAVIOR

In the preceding analyses we have presented data suggesting a clear functional relationship between exposure to the party and the public's interest in political matters, its awareness of issue conflict (and lack of it) in campaigns, and its record of voting participation. But the political party has a particular goal superseding these objectives. The most critical task for its own survival is the mobilization of electoral support for candidates. From a system-functional standpoint this task can be conceptualized as that of mobilizing "meaningful" electoral support for candidates, that is, electoral support which is ideologically congruent with the party's positions and tenets. Three specific questions are to be asked of the data, each question of progressive importance to the party and the system: (1) Does party organizational effort produce votes for party candidates? (2) Does party contact result in the attraction of members ideologically sympathetic to the party's position? (3) Does party effort produce voting support among those most ideologically supportive of the party's position on issues? Phrased simply, from a pragmatic viewpoint, the party is interested in votes for its candidates, but in a larger, theoretical, sense it must be interested in "ideological" votes. In assessing the importance of the party effort it is necessary to determine the balance of "ideological votes" mobilized by Party A and Party B, separately and together, and to determine whether party effort is of pragmatic importance, has ideological significance, or both.

The evidence that party effort is utilitarian in mobilizing

votes for candidates cannot be disputed. In earlier sections we discovered that those members of the public who had never voted (though eligible to vote) were not individuals highly exposed to the parties. In addition, we discovered that party contact was related to straight-ticket voting as well as to persistent party support over time. In an altogether separate analysis it was shown that those precincts with strong Democratic leadership and weak Republican leadership, produced a vote for Stevenson in 1956 which was 5 percentage points above expectation, while precincts in which the Republican leadership was definitely stronger produced a Stevenson vote 5 percentage points below expectation. Further support for these findings is shown by continuing with the type of analysis used in this chapter (Table 19.1). The turnout differential was 22 per cent for Democrats

TABLE 19.1

The Party Vote Turnout By Degrees of Party Exposure (Presidential Vote, 1956)

	High exposure	*Moderate exposure*	*No exposure*
Democratic identifiers supporting Stevenson	70%	68%	48%
Republican identifiers supporting Eisenhower	87	86	71
Independents supporting either candidate	84	79	57

highly exposed to the party organization; the differential was 16 per cent for Republican identifiers exposed to the party; and the combined parties turnout differential of independents who were contacted by the parties was 27 per cent.

In seeking to determine how ideologically supportive these votes mobilized by party effort are, it is first necessary to understand the ideological orientation of all those exposed or not exposed to the party. Again, it must be emphasized that these data are to be interpreted in the light of our findings about the ideologically distinctive nature of party leadership, the Democratic leaders liberal on medical aid, foreign aid, and civil rights, the Republican leaders conservative on these issues. Using the identical questions with members of the public, we found, not large, but consistent differences for those members of the public contacted by or exposed to the parties in contrast to those not exposed (Table 19.2).

A striking aspect of these data is that ideological differences were so slight. Thus, 65 per cent of Democrats exposed to the party were clearly liberal, but 56 per cent of those not exposed were also liberal. There were considerably more Democrats who split ideologically among the unexposed, but otherwise the party did not seem to be very efficacious in producing liberal identifiers.

TABLE 19.2

IDEOLOGICAL ORIENTATION OF THE PUBLIC BY DEGREE OF PARTY EXPOSURE

Democratic identifiers	*High exposure*	*Moderate exposure*	*No exposure*
Consistent liberals	31%	21%	22%
Tend to be liberal	34	38	34
Split ideologically	6	8	20
Tend to be conservative	24	29	20
Consistent conservatives	5	4	4
Republican identifiers			
Consistent conservatives	16	13	7
Tend to be conservative	22	16	26
Split ideologically	13	19	15
Tend to be liberal	33	33	31
Consistent liberals	16	18	21
Independents			
Consistent liberals	29	19	20
Tend to be liberal	31	16	22
Split ideologically	0	12	28
Tend to be conservative	29	40	26
Consistent conservatives	9	13	4

On the Republican side the same was true, for only 38 per cent of those exposed to the party were clearly conservatives, which is a mere 5 per cent greater than those not exposed. Ironically, the independents exposed to party influence showed the greatest differential—60 per cent of those exposed were liberals compared to 42 per cent of those not exposed.

It might properly be questioned whether party contact was at all influential ideologically. Accepting this for the moment, we can reverse the analysis and ask: How much of the party contact effort was expended on liberals and conservatives? The data suggest either very limited impact on individuals ideologically, or indiscriminate types of mobilization efforts by the parties, seeking votes wherever they were to be found regardless of the ideological position of the voters. This latter possibility is suggested by the following distributions resulting from a reanalysis of the data:

- Democratic liberals in the sample highly exposed to the party 19%
- Democratic conservatives ("splits") highly exposed to the party 15%
- Republican liberals and splits in the sample highly exposed to the party 23%
- Republican conservatives highly exposed to the party 29%

It appears that the Democratic party was contacting almost as large a proportion among its conservative partisans as among its liberals; the same was true for the Republican party. Of all liberals in the cross-section (about 56 per cent of the total), 22 per cent were subjected to the highest exposure by both parties. Of all conservatives in the cross-section (roughly 38 per cent of the total), 17 per cent were subjected to the highest exposure by both parties. Thus, the conservatives were disproportionately wooed by the parties in terms of their numerical importance in the population, but this attention to conservatives was not just a phenomenon of the Republican party, for it must be recalled that almost one-third of those Democratic identifiers contacted by the party were conservatives. It seems, therefore, that however one wishes to view the interrelationship between party contact and ideological positions of the adult public, party contact takes place with potential voters, many of whom may vote for the party, but on ideological grounds dysfunctional to the ideology of the majority of the party leadership.

These findings are not auspicious for exploration of our third question: Does party contact produce voting support which is ideologically most congruent with the party? Or, does party effort result in the mobilization of both conservative and liberal votes within the same party clientele? And, if the latter, in what ideological direction does the balance of vote mobilization lie?

There are two basic steps in the analysis by which this question may be answered. If we look, first, at the proportions of each party contact group who were party ideologists supporting the party's presidential candidate in 1956 (Table 19.3), we see that party contact is related to the mobilization of "ideological votes." Among Democrats, the high party-contact group included more liberals, more liberals who voted, and more liberals who voted Democratic (the differential was 23–27 per cent, depending on the particular calculation used). The Republican high exposure group also included more voting conservatives (a differential in comparison with the no-contact group of 12–18 per cent). And, particularly for the Democrats, the liberals who stayed home were out of contact with the party. It cannot be denied that there is a strong relationship between party effort and the mobilization of liberal Democratic and conservative Republican votes.

But a second, more complicated, step is necessary in assessing the total ideological effort of party vote mobilization efforts. One must determine the extent to which both Party A and Party B's efforts are related to the mobilization of noncongruent "ideological votes" for their own candidates as well as for the opposition. It is then necessary to see how the balance sheet of party

TABLE 19.3

THE MOBILIZATION OF LIBERAL AND CONSERVATIVE VOTES THROUGH PARTY ACTIVITY

	High exposure	*Moderate exposure*	*No exposure*
Democrats			
Percentage of total exposure group who were liberals and voted Democratic	49%	46%	26%
Percentage of exposure group who were liberals who did not vote	4	9	24
Percentage of all liberals in each exposure group who voted Democratic	72	76	45
Republicans			
Percentage of total exposure group who were conservatives and voted Republican	38	27	26
Percentage of exposure group who were conservatives who did not vote	2	2	7
Percentage of all conservatives in each exposure group who voted Republican	96	92	78

mobilization efforts looks. These calculations from the data are presented in Table 19.4.

Party contacts with the public are apparently functional to both the political system and to the pragmatic vote drives of the parties themselves, if the ideological position and the party votes are both utilized and considered relevant to the performance of the system. This is true, even though there are clearly considerable dysfunctional byproducts of the party organizational effort. Among Democratic identifiers highly exposed to the parties, for example, there were 14 per cent who were Republican voting

TABLE 19.4

THE RELATIONSHIP OF PARTY CONTACT EFFORTS TO THE MOBILIZATION OF VOTES WHICH ARE IDEOLOGICALLY SUPPORTIVE AND NONSUPPORTIVE

	High exposure	*No exposure*	*Net gain or loss due to party contact:*	
			For party votes	*For votes consistent with ideology*
Among Democratic identifiers				
Proportion of liberals who voted Democratic	49%	26%	+23	+23
Proportion of liberals who voted Republican	14	7	− 7	− 7
Proportion of conservatives who voted Democratic	24	25	− 1	+ 1
Proportion of conservatives who voted Republican	7	7	0	0
Total Democratic vote mobilized	73	51	Total net + 15	+17
Total inconsistency in vote and ideology	38	32		
Total consistency in vote and ideology	56	33		
Among Republican identifiers				
Proportion of conservatives who voted Republican	38	26	+12	+12
Proportion of conservatives who voted Democratic	0	0	0	0
Proportion of liberals who voted Republican	49	45	+ 4	− 4
Proportion of liberals who voted Democratic	3	6	+ 3	− 3
Total Republican vote mobilized	87	71	Total net + 19	+ 5
Total inconsistency in vote and ideology	49	45		
Total consistency in vote and ideology	41	32		

liberals, 7 per cent more than for those not exposed to party contact; among Republicans exposed to the party there were 49 per cent who were Republican voting liberals, 4 per cent higher than for those not exposed.

Yet one notices that party contact produced more party votes, and produced more *net* consistency or less *net* inconsistency between the vote and the ideological position of the voter. Thus, for Democratic identifiers in contact with the party, 38 per cent voted inconsistently with their ideology (theoretically speaking), while 56 per cent were consistent. The Republicans in Detroit, however, showed a *net* balance of inconsistency, due to the large group of liberals voting Republican. But, again, those in contact with the party showed less *net* inconsistency between the vote and ideology: 8 per cent compared to 13 per cent for those not exposed to the parties.

Party organizational effort on balance seems, therefore, to be more relevant for the pragmatic vote mobilization efforts of the parties *and* appears more functional for the system. This should not blind us, however, to the fact that party effort results in, or is related to, dysfunctional system consequences. The 38 per cent and 49 per cent inconsistency proportions among Democrats and Republicans, respectively, for those highly exposed to the parties, are significant findings in this respect. In simple terms the fact seems to be that the Republican and Democratic organizations did get out the vote, and did mobilize more liberal-Democratic and conservative-Republican votes. But in the process their efforts also seemed to induce more voting participation by ideologically oriented citizens (which may not be functional in both respects) than if the party had exerted no mobilization efforts. Indeed, if the mobilization of votes is the sole criterion for success, party effort paid off relatively well.

One interesting finding related to this analysis is the fact that Democrats had the greatest success in mobilizing liberals. Conservatives normally voted at the 75 per cent level, irrespective of party contact. The same is true for Republican liberals, but not for Democratic liberals. The distributions are as follows:

Among own party identifiers:	*High exposure*	*No exposure*
Democratic conservatives voting	92%	76%
Republican conservatives voting	96%	78%
Democratic liberals voting	94%	57%
Republican liberals voting	86%	78%

The Democrats had much greater success with liberals, in getting them out to vote and in getting them to vote Democratic (72 per cent of those contacted did vote Democratic). It is significant that 44 per cent of the Democratic liberals had no contact with the party at all. This figure is similar to the 39 per cent of the conservatives among Republican identifiers who were not contacted at all. In any event, it is clear that Republican organizational contacts were less important in getting the liberal vote to the polls than Democratic efforts.

A final observation about the behavior of independents should be noted. As seen previously, the independents exposed to party contact were considerably more liberal: 60 per cent compared to 42 per cent for those not exposed. They were also slightly more inclined to vote Democratic if contacted by the parties. Thus, those highly exposed consisted of 15 per cent more liberal voting Democrats than the nonexposed, whereas party exposure produced no large proportion of conservative voting Republicans. But the net effect of party contact on independents was great inconsistency between the vote and ideological position. Thus, while independents who were not exposed were only 18 per cent inconsistent, those highly exposed were 54 per cent inconsistent (including 31 per cent who were liberals and voted Republican, and 23 per cent who were conservatives and voted Democratic). It is clear from this that party activity was most functionally consequential for the system among party identifiers. Contact did produce party votes among independents, but the independent who voted as a result of party effort revealed considerable incongruity, theoretically, between his ideological position and his voting preference.

In concluding this analysis, it is important to emphasize

again that as the majority party in the area, the Democrats were the more active organization and thus had a higher degree of frequent interaction with the public. In our discussion of the task performance of precinct leaders we found, for example, that 44 per cent of Democrat and only 20 per cent of Republican precinct leaders were enterprisers. This is reflected in the analysis of party contacts with the public, for here again we find that of our total sample of party identifiers, 22 per cent consisted of Republicans in contact primarily with the Republican organization, while 34 per cent were Democrats primarily exposed to the Democratic organization. We did indeed find that Republican as well as Democratic organization work was related to greater turnout, party voting, ideological support, and consistency between the vote and the respondent's ideology. The differentials attributable to party contact reveal in fact that the Republican party's contact work paid off handsomely in these respects. Yet the proportionately lower frequency of public contact by the Republican organization had a significant impact for the net consequences of party work for party superiority in the Detroit area.

THE POSSIBLE CONTRIBUTION OF PARTIES TO "RATIONAL" ELECTORAL BEHAVIOR

A recurrent and growing concern of scholars of the political system is the extent to which the public exhibits "rationality" in its voting decisions. The basic question is: Can the American voter in our somewhat incoherent polity, without sharply differentiated party programs, and with tenuous and partial channels of political communication, cast a meaningful vote?

Many ways of conceptualizing the "vote" have been attempted by the theorists, ranging from those who see the vote merely as the expression of a candidate preference, as support for a party (whether leadership, symbol, or program), to those who view it as a calculated act which seeks to implement ideological or self-interest (or both) objectives. Anthony Downs has advanced one such theory which postulates "the vote" as the result of a "rational" determination of which party and candidate, compared with other parties and candidates, will probably best further the individual citizen's own interests.[1] In this theory the voter sees himself as "selecting a government" whose future acts and policies can advance or harm his interests. The "rational" voter then, aware of his own issue preferences, presumably informs himself fully about probable alternative future policies under alternative future governments, calculates his maximum utilities under each, and then votes. Presumably, also, for a voter thus oriented, if the information is too "costly," he abstains from voting, which theoretically might be the proper behavior of most voters in our system under this model.

Regardless of the criticisms of these different conceptualizations of the vote, or of different models of voting behavior, the concept of "rationality" is not superfluous. We need empirical attempts to explore the extent of rationality, in terms of various models, as well as evidence about conditions in the society most contributory to "rationality" under these alternative conceptualizations.

In any attempt to specify the components of electoral "rationality" the following must be considered of critical importance: (1) the issue preferences of the voter, (2) his perception of which party is closest to his own positions, and (3) his long-range commitment to, or identification with, a political party. The first two of these dimensions have a major (though not exclusively) *contemporary* orientation, while the latter dimension is primarily developmental or longitudinal. That is, the voter in a particular campaign faces immediate issue questions as well as candidates (and parties, with programs and manifestoes), and seeks to determine which of his issue positions are held by which candidates. But in the larger time perspective, it must be clearly understood that the voter has developed a party leaning or commitment which has structured his cognitive processes, and which may be a powerful influence on his decision-making processes. For perhaps three-fourths of all voters these three fac-

[1] *Op. cit.*

tors must be integrated into any analysis of "rationality"; for independents with no discernible party commitment, only the first two dimensions are relevant.

Utilizing these components, some apparent "rationality" and "irrationality" types can be identified (11 types have been developed for our analysis), though serious interpretive questions can be raised with any typology. A presentation of certain basic distributions of these dimensions for the Detroit sample, which are suggestive of the difficulties in interpretation, are to be found in Table 19.5. The "sophisticated-rational" voter is the individual who has a clear set of issue preferences (or ideological positions), clearly perceives which party most closely reflects these preferences, has been an identified partisan with this party, and votes for it (13 per cent of the party identifiers fulfilled these requirements). In extreme contrast to this is the "incomprehensibly irrational" voter, who fulfills all of the above conditions but votes for the wrong party (not one of the party identifiers fell into this category).

Between these two extremes lie various categories of rationality behavior, and a basis for judgment is not always clear. At the rationality end of the continuum are those individuals whose vote is consistent with their perception of which party is closest to their own position, and consistent with their party identification, but whose ideological position (from our standpoint) may not be congruent, for example, the Democrat who is consistently conservative on civil rights, medical aid, and foreign aid issues, but who sees the Democratic party as supporting his (conservative) positions, and who votes Democratic. These ideologically questionable rationality types comprised 16 per cent of the identifiers.

At the irrationality end of the continuum we might place those who (1) vote against their identification *and* party perception, even though their ideology is questionable (e.g., the conservative Democrat who sees the Democrats as closer to his position but who votes Republican); (2) vote against their identification for no apparent reason, having an unclear perception

TABLE 19.5

A SUMMARY OF SOME "RATIONALITY" DIMENSIONS AND VARIATIONS FOR THE ADULT CROSS-SECTION (WAYNE COUNTY)

	Consistent liberals	*Tend to be liberal*	*Split on ideology*	*Tend to be conservative*	*Consistent conservatives*
Percentage of cross-section in each ideological category	21%	34%	13%	25%	7%
Percentage of each ideological group which					
Sees Democratic party as closer ideologically	15	17	9	20	14
Sees Republican party as closer ideologically	23	26	18	19	31
Has conflicting or unclear perception about parties	62	57	73	61	54
Percentage of each ideological group					
Voting Democratic	41	40	22	37	22
Voting Republican	30	40	48	41	68
Not voting	29	20	30	22	10
Percentage of those in each ideological group who see the Democratic party as closer and who vote Democratic	88	76	*	74	*
Percentage of those in each ideological group who see the Republican party as closer and who vote Republican	59	76	86	74	83
Percentage of those in each ideological group who are in conflict or unclear in their perceptions of which party is closer and who do not vote	41	26	34	27	15

* Too few cases for analysis.

of which party is closer to their own issue position (e.g., the liberal Democrat whose perception of party proximity is blurred but who still votes Republican). In both these categories were found a total of 9 per cent of party identifiers.

One special problem in determining rationality concerns the nonvoters. When is their behavior to be considered "irrational"? It seems that a clear case can be made for the "rational abstainer" who is obviously in conflict so far as our three components are concerned (e.g., the Democratic liberal who sees the Republican party as closer to his issue positions, but who, after all, is a strong Democratic identifier, and who therefore does not vote). Less clear is the case of the abstainer who is uncertain about which party is closer to him, but who nevertheless is a party-committed person, or the person who does not have clear issue positions or party perceptions, but is at the same time a party identifier. These we have called "possibly rational abstainers." Finally, there seems to be no "rationality" position by which one can defend the nonvoting of a committed partisan, with clear issue position and party perceptions congruent with his party identification. These we call the "irrational abstainers." The percentages of party identifiers for each of these nonvoting subgroups were 4, 15, and 4 per cent, respectively.

The extent of rational behavior in these terms, though not completely relative, is arguable. For even if we accept the three components of ideology, perception, and identification in juxtaposition with the vote, the relative emphasis to be placed on each component is not absolutely determinable. Thus, is one to say that only the 13 per cent in the sample who conformed to all of our theoretical expectations are "rational," or would one say that the more inclusive figure of 29 per cent are rational, a figure representing those whose vote coincided with their perceptions of party ideological proximity? And those who were in conflict ideologically and perceptually but who voted their party identification—a sizeable group of 36 per cent of our identifier sample—at what level of rationality are they to be placed? These gradations in "rationality" suggest that from 13 to 65 per cent of the sample can be considered rational voters, to which at least another 4 per cent of "rational abstainers" might be added. It is not our intention to assert categorically the extent of rationality, but rather to identify the types of rationality, and to use these types in the ensuing discussion of the role of the party in contributing to rational and irrational behavior.

Our primary objective is to appraise the possible function of parties in rational electoral behavior. We return, therefore, to the major categories of party contact to see whether those members of the public exposed to the parties revealed patterns of behavior of a different order of "rationality" than those not exposed. One might well hypothesize that in the United States, particularly in metropolitan areas, the activities of parties would not be entirely conducive to rational behavior. Parties presumably do re-enforce identification, but in the campaigns their ideological positions, so we are told, are not clearly differentiated. Thus, the voter, though generally committed to a party, and re-enforced by the party in his identification, finds it difficult to bring into clear focus his own issue positions and those of the parties. On the other hand, as our organizational analysis revealed, the party leadership cadres did differ in Detroit ideologically, and though for many of these leaders their ideological role was not predominant, yet it is conceivable that to some extent these ideological differences might have permeated to those members of the public in contact with the parties.

Party effort seems related to more rationality *and* more irrationality—this is the central interpretive fact emerging from the data. Thus, 21 per cent of the Democrats highly exposed to the party revealed irrational behavior patterns, compared to only 15 per cent of those not exposed. Yet 68 per cent of all Democrats highly exposed were rational (using our first four rationality types), compared to 50 per cent for those not exposed. Among Republicans highly exposed to the party, although only 3 per cent were "very irrational," on the other hand only 13 per cent were "very rational"; further, there were only 39 per cent in the first two high rationality categories, compared to 42 per cent for those not exposed to the party.

TABLE 19.6

THE RELATIONSHIP OF PARTY CONTACT AND "RATIONAL" ELECTORAL BEHAVIOR

	High exposure		*Moderate exposure*		*No exposure*	
	D	*R*	*D*	*R*	*D*	*R*
Rationality-oriented types						
Sophisticated rational voters	19%	13%	10%	13%	10%	17%
Perception and identification rational voters	8	26	7	34	9	25
Identification only rational voters	40	46	47	36	26	27
Rational abstainers	1	5	2	6	5	3
Middle level rationality types						
Identifiers in conflict—vote perception only	0	0	1	2	3	2
Identifiers in conflict—vote identification only	3	3	3	2	4	1
Possibly rational abstainers	8	3	16	3	28	8
Questionable rationality types						
Anti-identification voters	21	0	10	1	10	3
Anti-identification and perception voters	0	3	2	1	0	1
Irrational abstainers	0	0	3	1	5	13
Number of cases	73	62	154	88	193	103

The most sophisticated and consistent "rationality" pattern is functionally related to Democratic party contacts (see Table 19.6). There is a 9 percentage-point differential favoring exposure to the Democratic party, but a 4 per cent differential among Republicans favoring no party exposure. In fact, for the Republicans, the only rationality behavior clearly related to party exposure is the pattern of voting which is consistent only with party identification—a 20 per cent differential in contrast to the no-exposure group.

Several other observations should be noted. First, at the top rationality level for those exposed to party effort one finds more Democrats proportionately than Republicans, but at lower levels one finds much more rational behavior in 1956 for Republicans.

Whereas 32 per cent of the Democrats in contact with the party were in the lower six rationality categories, only 9 per cent of the Republicans fell in these categories. For the no-exposure group the comparable percentages were 50 per cent (D) and 28 per cent (R). Second, voting in conflict with party identification occurred infrequently, and primarily among Democrats. Among highly exposed Democrats, 21 per cent voted in this manner, but no Republicans. In the no-exposure category, 13 per cent of the Democrats, and 5 per cent of the Republicans, voted thus. Third, the abstainers were inclined to be Democrats, but the clearly irrational abstainers were primarily confined to those Republicans not exposed to the party organization. Although Democratic abstention was high, particularly among those not highly exposed to the party, most of it (viewed from the voter's standpoint) may be defensible, consisting of individuals conflicting in their party ideological perceptions.

Finally, for large numbers of voters, particularly those in contact with the parties, the party was unable to articulate, for them, the party's ideological position. The Republican organization did a relatively poorer job in this respect than did the Democratic, for 64 per cent of those highly exposed to the Democratic party were unclear as to which party stood closer to them ideologically, while only 56 per cent of the Democrats not exposed were confused on the party's perception. Among Republicans, 45 per cent highly exposed to the party were not clear as to which party was closer, while only 27 per cent of those Republicans not exposed were perceptually unclear about the party's position. Of course some of these adults took refuge in party identification in order to produce a measure of rationality. Others abstained from voting. And some, particularly Democrats, voted for the opposition. (Among Democrats in some contact with the party, 20 per cent abstained or voted Republican; only 2 per cent of the Republicans responded in these ways.) There is a strong suggestion, therefore, as previously noted by theorists of voting behavior, that the parties seemed to confuse voters ideologically, even their own partisans. This may be pragmatically nonutilitarian as well as dysfunctional to the system and to the individual who seeks to make his voting decisions.

The analysis of independents who insist they have no party commitments, in rationality terms, requires different, less rigorous, criteria. Since party identification cannot be implied, ideological clarity and perception of the parties are most useful as components of rationality. It is interesting to discover that those independents highly exposed to party effort were slightly less clear as to which party was ideologically closer to them than those independents outside the party orbit: 78 per cent of the exposed group were unclear, in contrast to 76 per cent of the unexposed group. Party contact seemed to produce slightly more, almost inconsequential, "rationality" among independents. For example, 22 per cent of those independents exposed to the party voted consistently with their perceptions of party ideology, while only 16 per cent of those not contacted voted consistently with such perceptions. But perhaps of more consequence is the finding that independents who were unclear about where the parties stand, *but were contacted by the parties*, did vote, while those not contacted tended to stay home. The turnout rate of the former group was 79 per cent, of the latter group only 51 per cent. The party organization's effort, therefore, does not necessarily clarify the issues for the independent, but somehow, despite his perceptual misgivings, it does get him to the polls.

CHAPTER 20

PARTIES AND THE FOUNDATIONS OF POLITICAL CONSENSUS

No democratic political system will endure unless a large segment of the populace has a fundamental confidence in it. There are many requisite ingredients for the elusive phenomenon of public confidence. Some of the more overt manifestations of public behavior no doubt linked to such confidence have been discussed: interest in political affairs, utilization of political groups for political demands, loyalty feelings toward political parties, willingness to work actively for parties, and voting participation. There are, however, certain "foundations" which underlie these overt behaviors and expressions of support. At least three such foundations basic to public confidence in the system, and from which the above behaviors derive, are: knowledge, value acceptance, and action-oriented optimism. Unless a large segment of the populace factually comprehends the nature of the system, sees value in the peculiar way in which it operates, and is personally optimistic about the utility of working in such a system, the requisite confidence will not develop. And the "participation" which does occur, if it does, will either be tenuous or premised on system change.

In any society a variety of institutions and influences may contribute to these foundations—family, school, mass media of communication. It is also reasonable to expect that political parties may contribute to basic public confidence in the system. Despite the conflictual relationships between parties over controversial issues of the moment, they realize that they are tolerated by the system, have a preferential status in it, and probably they or their predecessors collaborated in the creation of the very system in which they now seek power. Although, probably, in all societies political parties have at one time been so frustrated in power aspiration as to seek major modifications in the system, particularly modifications affecting their own drive for power, basically they are aware that, with all its defects, the present system is preferable to some vague "new system" with which they are not familiar. In appealing to the public, therefore, the parties will communicate the basic assumption that the system is sound. And, if the parties' candidates "educate" the public at all, they will indoctrinate the public in significant details of the system in order that the public may understand the appeal of the party, as well as encourage the public to be optimistic about its chances of influencing policy through participation in the system.

We have sought to test the relevance of party effort to these three foundations by a series of questions in our adult cross-section interview, relating the pattern of responses to the respondents' exposure to party organization efforts. The first questions concerned the extent of the individual's factual *knowledge* about one aspect of the political system. We asked who his own congressman and senators were, and what were their terms of office (Table 20.1).

The public's knowledge of the critical facts of the election and representation subsystem was limited. Only 36 per cent in one sample knew the name of one or both of the United States senators from Michigan, and only 18 per cent knew who their congressman was, even though this interview was conducted shortly after the election. In addition, only 16 per cent knew the term of office of a senator, but 38 per cent knew the congressman's tenure. As indicative of the level of knowledge, these findings suggest marked system ignorance.

People in contact with the political parties were much more knowledgeable. For example, 58 per cent of those Democrats highly exposed to the parties knew who their senator and congressman were, while only 13 and 7 per cent, respectively, of

TABLE 20.1
PARTIES AND THE PUBLIC'S KNOWLEDGE OF THE CONGRESSMAN AND SENATORS

	High exposure 1956 and before		*High exposure 1956 only*		*No exposure*	
	D	*R*	*D*	*R*	*D*	*R*
Knew who his senator was	58%	55%	50%	62%	13%	26%
Knew senator's term	23	30	13	27	11	17
Knew who his congressman was	58	25	28	35	7	15
Knew congressman's term	54	60	40	39	34	34
Answered all 4 questions correctly	12	10	0	4	0	4
Answered 3 of 4 questions correctly	38	30	23	19	5	8
Number of cases	26	20	40	26	151	73

those not exposed knew their elected representatives. The Republican differences, particularly as to knowledge of the congressman, were not as great (no doubt related to the fact that all six congressmen from Wayne County were Democrats). The differences were not as great concerning knowledge about a representative's term of office, but they were consistent—differentials of 12 and 20 per cent for the Democrats and 13 and 26 per cent for the Republicans. On all questions, those unexposed to the parties were clearly the most ignorant. And if we combine the answers to all four questions, and ask for 75 per cent proficiency (correct answers on at least three questions), 50 per cent of Democrats highly exposed to the parties qualified as well informed in contrast to 5 per cent of those not exposed, 40 per cent of the exposed Republicans in contrast to 12 per cent. But the independents did not reveal the same level of political knowledge or the same relevance of party contact—only 26 per cent of those highly exposed were well informed, in contrast to 14 per cent of those not exposed. The parties had some enlightenment effect on independents, but the differential impact was much smaller.

The educational system by itself is either not a very effective communicator of political knowledge, or does not stimulate people to inform themselves about the facts of the political system. Only 12 per cent of those Democrats and Republicans with a college education, for instance, *who were not exposed to political parties*, had 75 per cent proficiency on our test. When those exposed to the parties are included, however, the percentage for all college-trained persons in the sample reaches 31 per cent. High-school-trained respondents were much lower, with comparable percentages of 10 and 14 per cent.

Party contact is probably a more significant factor in developing political system knowledge than education, although both types of experience combined at their highest levels produced the best records of knowledge (Table 20.2). For those with only an elementary-school education, party contact increased by 31 per cent the proportion with a reasonable degree of political information; for those with a high-school education, the proportion increased 14 per cent; for college-educated respondents, the proportion increased 21 per cent. Or, looking at those who scored zero on the test, party contact reduced the proportion of total ignorance among elementary-school-educated respondents by 23 per cent, among high-school-educated 12 per cent, among college-educated 23 per cent. These data point clearly to the conclusion that political system knowledge is enhanced by party effort, although large proportions of those exposed to the parties, especially with only an elementary or high-school education, are still woefully ignorant of the elements of the political system. The important fact, perhaps, is that absence of party effort meant that less than 50 per cent of college-educated adults achieved a 50 per cent score on the test of political knowledge.

The second "foundation" for public confidence and participation in the political system is awareness, or acceptance, of the value of component processes of the political system. Since parties work particularly hard prior to elections, the public's attitudes towards the campaign process interested us specifically. We asked the question: "Some people say the bitterness and hard feelings

TABLE 20.2
THE RELATIVE ROLE OF PARTY CONTACT IN DEVELOPING SYSTEM KNOWLEDGE AMONG RESPONDENTS AT ALL THREE EDUCATIONAL LEVELS

	High exposure			*No exposure*		
	Elementary school	*High school*	*College*	*Elementary school*	*High school*	*College*
Democrats						
Answered 3 of 4 questions correctly	36%	25%	50%	0%	7%	15%
Answered no question correctly	50	36	13	64	49	31
Republicans						
Answered 3 of 4 questions correctly	30	21	41	11	14	8
Answered no questions correctly	30	32	6	67	43	33
Combined Democrats and Republicans						
Answered 3 of 4 questions correctly	33	24	45	2	10	12
Answered no questions correctly	42	35	9	65	47	32
Number of cases						
Democrats	14	36	16	73	67	13
Republicans	10	19	17	18	42	12
Total	24	55	33	91	107	25

of a campaign are not worth what it accomplishes; others think what the campaign accomplished is worth the cost—which way do you feel?" Of the total sample, 59 per cent felt campaigns were of value, 25 per cent thought the opposite, and 10 per cent were undecided.

The majority confidence in political campaigns was only slightly accentuated for those highly exposed to parties, but this fact is noteworthy in itself, for one might have hypothesized the opposite. Party contact, however, did not evoke cynicism about the value of campaigns. A summary of the distributions follows:

Percentage feeling campaigns are worth while	*High exposure*	*No exposure*
Democrats	73%	56%
Republicans	65%	55%

Thus, a slight increment of confidence is seen among those in contact with the parties. We found, further, that while all those exposed to party activities had an opinion on this subject, approximately 15 per cent of those not exposed were unable to express an opinion. In addition, it is significant that nonvoters and independents had less enthusiasm for campaigns, irrespective of whether they were the target of party contacts: only 50 per cent of the nonvoters felt campaigns were worth while, and slightly less than 50 per cent of the independents had positive feelings about the campaign. Finally, a careful comparison of the attitude of "Eisenhower voters" and "Stevenson voters," among Democrats and independents, revealed that those voting for the presidential loser, Stevenson, were, if anything, more supportive of campaigns than those voting for Eisenhower. There is no evidence to support the theory that confidence about political campaigns is the product of the outcome of an immediate presidential sweepstakes. To some extent, therefore, parties seem to add an increment among their own committed partisans to the public's system confidence, rather than detract from that confidence.[1]

[1]Separate analyses made on related questions evaluating the role and activities of political parties generally produced findings substantiating this interpretation, although we continued to find more support among the majority Democrats than among the minority Republicans. For example, on the question of whether the respondent approved of the campaign activities and personal contact of the parties, those exposed to the Republican party were no less supportive than the unexposed, and the Democrats in contact with the party revealed over 25 per cent more approval. Republicans, particularly, were opposed to partisan local elections in the Detroit area: of those in close contact with the party organization only 10 per cent approved the idea, compared to 33 per cent of those not exposed. The Democrats who were exposed to the parties, however, revealed 50 per cent approval, compared to only 33 per cent of those outside the party orbit. The concept of nonpartisan elections at the local level, however, has been so fixed in many people's minds as normatively preferable in our system, that this is no valid test of the theory presented here.

The third foundation of the public's confidence in the political system is personal optimism about the role of the individual citizen in that system. This is not the same as involvement, though the optimistic citizen is more likely to participate politically. Rather, it is a belief that the citizen does have political relevance, is "taken into consideration," is represented, deferred to, or consulted. A variety of measures are useful in studying this basic dimension. We experimented with six, and present data on the three measures considered most valuable and appropriate. On all of these measures except one, over 65 per cent of the public revealed confidence in the system. The statement which evoked the most political pessimism was: "Sometimes politics and government seem so complicated that a person like me can't really understand what's going on." The fact that 61 per cent of the sample agreed with this statement should not be surprising—it has become a glib standardized reaction of even the sophisticated, and thus is probably a poor test of the level of the public's confidence in its own role. The other five measures produced opposite proportions of confidence; the most appropriate for identifying "hard-core pessimists" were:

> "People like me don't have any say about what the government does."
>
> (26 per cent agreed, 69 per cent disagreed, 2 per cent didn't know)
>
> "Public officials really care about what people like me think."
>
> (71 per cent agreed, 19 per cent disagreed, 6 per cent didn't know)

These two statements, one stated optimistically, the other pessimistically, evoked responses from all but a small segment of the public, produced similar proportions of pessimism, and are concerned with the basic individual-to-government relationship which is the heart of the democratic system.

Nonvoting is interlinked with political pessimism. We found, for both of these measures, that the voters reflected a normal pattern of approximately 21–22 per cent pessimism, while 52 per cent of the nonvoters felt that "people like me don't have any say," and 30 per cent felt that public officials did not "really care about what people like me think." This distinction must be kept in mind when we look at the role of party contact in promoting public confidence, since it will be recalled that nonvoting was most prevalent among those not exposed to party activity.

TABLE 20.3

POLITICAL PESSIMISM AND EXPOSURE TO PARTIES

	High exposure	*No exposure*
"People like me don't have any say about what the government does"		
Democrats	18%	45%
Republicans	13	18
Democratic voters only	15	31
Republican voters only	15	15
"Public officials don't really care about what people like me think"		
Democrats	15	28
Republicans	11	18
Democratic voters only	10	26
Republican voters only	12	23

The party organizations were "contributing" to citizen political optimism by inducing voting participation and by influencing the voter's orientation toward his role in the political system. This was more true of the Democrats than of the Republicans —the Democratic differentials for voters, between those exposed and not exposed, are 16 and 13 per cent, respectively, on the two questions. The Republicans had only a slight "effect" on the orientation of voters as revealed in differentials on the second question, but the differences are all in a direction suggesting that party contact is relevant.[2] (Only 8 per cent of the most highly exposed group of Democrats were political pessimists on the first

[2] The independents revealed no consistent differences resulting from party contact. On the first statement there was a 17 per cent differential, suggesting party contact was relevant, but on the second statement the exact reverse was true.

statement, and none on the second statement.) Party contact appears, therefore, to fortify and accentuate public confidence by making the citizen feel that he has some importance in our complex political system.

Cynical feelings about the role of the individual are clearly related to the social-class status and educational background of American citizens. The second statement, for example, revealed these proportions of pessimism among Republicans and Democrats, by educational level:

	Pessimism
Elementary education	34%
High school	22
College	7

College-educated adults may not have had much specific knowledge about the system, but they were personally optimistic about their role in it! The influence of party contact on responses to this statement shows, however, that elementary and high-school education was not an irrevocable barrier to confidence in the political system. Those with an elementary-school education who had been exposed to the parties were still not as enthusiastic, relatively, as to whether they "had any say," but they did, on the

TABLE 20.4

EDUCATIONAL LEVEL, EXPOSURE TO PARTY, AND CONFIDENCE IN PARTY SYSTEM

	High exposure			*No exposure*		
All Democrats and Republicans (Voters and nonvoters)	*Elementary school*	*High school*	*College*	*Elementary school*	*High school*	*College*
"Public officials don't care about what people like me think"	17%	12%	12%	38%	27%	0%
"People like me don't have any say about what the government does"	35	13	9	42	33	0

other hand, feel much less cynical about public officials. High-school-educated adults whom the parties had contacted also revealed consistently higher political optimism. Only the college-educated became more negative about the system and their role in it as "a result of" party contacts. The proportions are minimal, but the differences are consistent. This highly interesting finding suggests that parties may actually alienate from the system some of the more intelligent and educated members of a society. At least some college graduates may regress into pessimism as a reaction to party contact experiences!

If a political system requires these basic elements for public confidence—knowledge, belief, and personal optimism—the Detroit study suggests that parties may be efficacious in strengthening the system. Factual knowledge about the political system was woefully inadequate; belief in the value of such subprocesses as political campaigns was rather high; and feelings of personal optimism about the role of the individual in our system were shared by a large majority. But, in each case, we found that those adults who had been exposed to the party organization's efforts were much more knowledgeable, more frequently believers in the system, and felt personally optimistic about the political status of the individual in our society. While other institutions certainly play critical roles, the data presented here empirically demonstrate that the party's efforts may not only supplement such institutions (as schools) but may, for some adults, in fact help to overcome the inadequacies of our schools in stimulating public confidence in the political order.

CHAPTER 21

THE FUNCTIONAL CONVERGENCE OF SOCIAL FORCES: THE IMPACT OF PARTY EFFORT, INTEREST-GROUP LEADERSHIP, AND TELEVISION

Parties are not the only institutionalized action systems in politics, nor are individual citizens subjected solely to party influences or exposed solely to party activities. Other politically salient groups have goals in political affairs which lead them to purposive, or more subtle, acts seeking to mobilize or influence the public. And the mass communication media to which much of the public is continuously exposed carries much information, opinion, and interpretation about political affairs. The crucial question here is not whether these groups and media exert influence on the public, a probability which can be safely hypothesized, but whether these nonparty forces supplement or replace party organizational effort in performing the functions operationalized in the preceding sections. Party leadership and organizational effort, as demonstrated in the foregoing analysis, are linked functionally with patterns of public attitudes and behavior. But, as we have seen, parties do not stand alone in the political forum. Other influences operate simultaneously with the party. Does a convergence of influence mean that parties become less important functionally as labor unions, or Negro political groups, and television extend the scope of their political activities? Do these influences detract from the functional importance of parties, or do parties adapt, even perhaps exploit, social forces? In any event, however juxtaposed, do parties and interest groups collaborate to produce a joint functional impact or outcome? This is the first basic query. A second and related question concerns the functional *direction* or *valence* of the activities of parties, other political interest groups, and the mass media. That is, does interest-group leadership, and do the mass media, work *with* or *against* party effort? Conceivably, parties might labor to produce outcomes which maximize the party's viability, coherence, and goal attainment as an organizational system (for example, encouraging loyalty, campaign work, and straight-ticket voting), while interest-group leadership might function to produce outcomes not pragmatically functional for the party's goals. Further, a mass communication medium such as television might break down party loyalty, discourage straight-ticket voting, or develop attitudes cynical about working through the party system. Or, to state the problem differently, television may conceivably fulfill political system needs and goals (development of interest in public affairs, rational consistency in voting behavior, consensual support for the political system), while party effort may be less system functional and more party functional. The possibility must always be recognized, of course, that party and TV may work together to maximize both party needs and system goals. These two fundamental queries, whether party effort is less relevant functionally than the effort of other politically interested social groups or of the mass media, and whether the functional direction of party effort is the same as, or different from, the functional direction of other influences, will be explored in this concluding analysis.

UNION AND NEGRO LEADERSHIP IN THE PARTY STRUCTURE: FUNCTIONAL CONSEQUENCES

Party leaders have social structural backgrounds, predispositions, and goal orientations which make them more than "party men." In fact, one can theorize that, in a real sense, they are representatives in the party hierarchy for socio-political movements. In the Democratic party's Detroit area precinct leadership, for example, 17 per cent were labor union officers and another 56 per cent were union members; 23 per cent were Negroes. In the Republican party precinct structure, 30 per cent were union members (with only one union officer); 16 per cent were Negroes. Although other social groups had leadership representatives in the party hierarchies, as indicated in the coalitional analysis of the parties presented earlier, these two types of sociopolitical leadership subgroups will be primarily utilized here to demonstrate how party and social-group leadership mesh, and the functional results.

It will be recalled that these leadership subgroups exhibited different patterns of behavior in each party. The Negro Democratic leaders, though relatively excluded from decisional involvement in the party, and demanding almost to a man, more involvement, were fairly loyal to the Democratic party, felt the parties differed substantially in what they stood for, were basically liberal on national issues, and had high records of efficiency (50 per cent asserting that they and their organizational supporters in the precinct engaged in house-to-house canvassing in the campaign). The Negro Republican leaders, almost completely excluded from decisional circles and less demanding (although 56 per cent wished more involvement), seemed less motivated, tended to feel that the parties did not differ basically, were less liberal, and had an extremely poor efficiency record (only 17 per cent engaged in house-to-house canvassing).

The labor union members in the Democratic precinct cadre were very involved in the decisional elite, consequently were less demanding of more involvement, had cosmopolitan communication patterns, felt the two parties differed basically in what they stood for, were generally liberals ideologically (although 40 per cent took moderate and conservative positions on foreign aid and civil rights), but were not overwhelmingly committed to the party (67 per cent, for example, approved of splitting the ballot). Their efficiency record was not outstanding: 36 per cent engaged in house-to-house canvassing, compared to the 27 per cent norm for all nonunion members. The labor union officers, however, had an outstanding experience record: 70 per cent had canvassed. In contrast, the Republican precinct leaders who were labor union members were fairly well excluded from the inner decisional circles of the Republican party, thus demanded much more involvement, had less extensive communication patterns, were less inclined to see the parties as differing in their stands (56 per cent compared to 82 per cent for the union members among the Democratic precinct leaders), were not very "loyal" to the Republican party (two-thirds also approved splitting the ballot), and were much less liberal than the Democrats except on the civil rights issue. Their efficiency record was somewhat lower than for their Democratic counterparts (only 26 per cent had canvassed), but this compared favorably with the record of nonunion leaders of the Republican party, 24 per cent of whom canvassed.

Bearing in mind our concern with the functions of party leadership, the major query is: What are the consequences for the party and the system of the existence of such leadership subgroups within the two party structures? These leaders have affiliational and status associations with political interest groups, they have differential patterns of perspective and work habits, and the public has differential degrees of exposure to such leadership. How do Negroes and whites respond to effective and ineffective Negro precinct leadership? How do union members and nonunion members respond to effective and ineffective union precinct leadership? Is such leadership functional or dysfunctional to the party system and the political order?

We isolated those individuals, whites and Negroes, who were residents of precincts led by Negro Democratic and Republican precinct leaders, as well as those Negroes residing in precincts led by whites. The comparison of their attitudes and behavior on a variety of selected variables, as presented in Table 21.1 is interesting.

Exploitation by the party of particular social-group leadership in certain geographical areas seems to be both functional and dysfunctional to the party. Negro Democrats and Republicans

TABLE 21.1

The Relationship Between Negro Precinct Leadership and the Public's Behavior

Norm for all respondents		*Negro Democrats in Negro Democratic-led precincts N = 61*	*Negro Democrats in white-led precincts N = 29*	*Negro Republicans in Negro Republican-led precincts N = 15*	*Negro Republicans in white-led precincts N = 15*	*Whites in Negro-led precincts N = 33*
76%	Voting participation 1956	84%	79%	80%	73%	67%
51	Consider self "strong" partisan	59	59	47	47	38
77	Straight voting	90	83	*	*	91
11	Voted for opposite party's presidential candidate	0	14	7	7	17
54	Parties differ in what they stand for	74	89	53	33	48
47	Personally makes a difference which party wins election	67	76	47	53	55
24	Willing to work through the parties	56	36	38	43	27
	Party leaders' opinions ranked as					
16	Very important	20	24	31	14	19
41	Not important	42	44	46	79	50
18	Most important (of all leaders)	12	24	31	0	23
21	Highly exposed to party effort	20	7	20	13	48
59	Highly exposed to television	62	76	53	73	67

*Too few cases for analysis.

turned out to vote at a higher rate under Negro leadership (80 per cent or better), but at the same time whites living in Negro-led precincts had a relatively poor participation record (67 per cent). The party also seemed to gain more straight-ticket voting in Negro-led precincts (90 per cent as compared to 83 per cent for the Negro Democrats generally), and there was less defection for the opposite party's presidential candidates (among Democrats). But, again, the whites in Negro-led precincts, who were not very loyal partisans from the outset (only 38 per cent consider themselves "strong" partisans), show more capacity for irregular voting. Finally, Negro Democrats and Republicans were more exposed to the party effort and susceptible to party influence in those precincts where Negroes were in charge. Thus, the Negro Democrats seemed to be more willing to work with or through the parties (although this observation is countered by subsequent evidence), while it had no such effect among Negro Republicans. The whites in Negro-led precincts were, however, despite considerable party contact, relatively negative about working for the party. Thus, while maximizing its vote turnout and voting regularity, and possibly mobilizing a cadre of workers for the party *among Negroes*, the party, by cannily placing Negroes in leadership positions, may develop voting irregularity, weak party identification, and withdrawal from party involvement *among whites*. Since their number is fewer, however, in such geographical areas, these effects represent pragmatic gains for the party.

From a system-functional standpoint, the consequences of party and social group leadership interaction were mixed. Voting turnout was increased, as was exposure to party influence. But fewer Negroes saw the parties as differing in their stands when the precinct was Negro-led, and even fewer saw the results of the election as personally relevant. Further, it is interesting to note that Negroes in Negro-led precincts were less likely to be exposed to television as a source of political information and influence, but were, at the same time, more exposed to party efforts. This suggests that the competitive and deliberative aspects of the political process are somewhat diminished for such Negroes, while their party and social group loyalties become closely intermeshed. Their perceptions and cognitions of the campaign process thus may be primarily social-group-oriented, not party-oriented.

Efficient task-oriented Negro leadership accentuates even more some of the behavioral effects noted above. By dividing Democratic respondents into two groups, those residing in precincts led by efficient Negro Democratic precinct leaders and those residing in precincts inefficiently led by Negroes, the distributions in Table 21.2 emerge. The effective Negro precinct leader in the Democratic party was obviously one who maximized the party's vote, stemmed the tide of political deviationism, and developed a clientele highly supportive of the party organization. Curiously again, however, his supporters were much less exposed to political television.

Dividing the Negro respondents living in the effectively

TABLE 21.2

DEMOCRATIC IDENTIFIERS (NEGROES)

	Residing in precincts led by efficient Negro Democrats $N = 45$	*Residing in precincts led by inefficient Negro Democrats* $N = 16$
Voting	87%	75%
Supporting Eisenhower	0	31
Voting straight ticket	100	58
Willing to work through party	65	31
Having strong identifications	69	31
Highly exposed to parties	22	13
Highly exposed to television	51	94
Feeling the parties differ basically	76	69
Feeling the election personally makes a difference	62	81

Negro-led Democratic precincts into two groups, those most exposed to the Democratic party organization and those not exposed at all, we see the "consequences" of the party effort for those most likely to be influenced by it.

TABLE 21.3

DEMOCRATIC IDENTIFIERS (NEGROES) RESIDING IN PRECINCTS LED BY THE MOST EFFICIENT NEGRO DEMOCRATIC LEADERS

	Most exposed to party organization	*Not exposed*
Voting 1956	95%	85%
Strongly identified with the party	68	82
Willing to work through the party	58	75
Highly exposed to television	68	45
Who feel the parties differ basically	73	85
Who feel the election personally makes a difference	58	70

As the Negro is drawn into contact with the effective Negro precinct leader in the Democratic party, the chances that he will not vote practically disappear. He continues to be a regular "organization-partisan" voter, but he is less loyal or "strong" than the Negro not exposed to the party, shows less enthusiasm about working in the party, is somewhat less certain about party issue differences, and more ready to question the personal relevance of party control for him. The conclusion is inescapable that the effective Negro Democratic leader may gain Democratic votes among Negroes, but he does not necessarily maximize party loyalty among his clientele. While retaining his party leadership status through vote production, he may actually produce dysfunctional attitude patterns among his constituents, Negro and white, attitudes that minimize the ideological significance of party conflict, and alienate the Negro, as well as the white, from participation in the party process.

Union members and officers who are party leaders have been highly acclaimed as effective vote-producers, particularly in the Democratic party. Our analysis of this cadre of Democratic precinct leaders did indeed reveal that the union officers, at least, had high records of efficiency. Seventy per cent canvassed, compared to 36 per cent of union members who led Democratic precincts and 27 per cent for nonunion Democratic leaders. By analyzing the Democratic respondents who resided in these precincts, both union and nonunion, and by further distinguishing those in contact with the party organization and those not in contact, we can test this proposition empirically (Table 21.4).[1]

The functional role of union leaders in the Democratic party is a myth in many respects, as the data on these selected variables indicate. Although union officers who were Democratic leaders had high vote turnout for those members of the public whom they contacted (87 per cent—a figure not shown in the tables[2]), the record for the most effective union member leadership in Democratic precincts is not highest among union members themselves. Actually, union members in nonunion-led precincts had a better participation record, and union leaders performed better in mobilizing the nonunion vote than the union vote! Further, the split ballot among union and nonunion adults in effectively union-led precincts was abnormally high—29 and 30 per cent. In the same vein, it should be observed that strong party identification was not associated with exposure to effective union party leadership.

The role of union leadership in making citizens aware of the personal relevance of party conflict also raises many questions. Only 29 per cent (the lowest in all these categories) of indi-

[1] This analysis was made in the Detroit and Dearborn sections of the sample only, and exclusively for Democratic union leaders and Democratic members of the cross-section. There were too few Republicans to permit adequate control over the analysis.

[2] A separate analysis of union officers by effectiveness of leadership and party contact was not possible because there were too few cases in the sample. This figure of 87 per cent is the proportion of union and nonunion members, Democrats *and* independents, with high party exposure, voting in 1956 in precincts led by union officers.

TABLE 21.4

THE RELATIONSHIP BETWEEN UNION PRECINCT LEADERSHIP AND THE BEHAVIOR OF A CROSS-SECTION OF DEMOCRATS

	Union members in precincts effectively led by union Democratic leaders		*Union members in precincts ineffectively led by union Democratic leaders*		*Union members in precincts not led by union members in the Democratic party*	*Nonunion adults in precincts led effectively by union members in the Democratic party*		*Nonunion members in precincts not led by union members in the Democratic party*
	Highest party contact	*No party contact*	*Highest party contact*	*No party contact*		*Highest party contact*	*No party contact*	
Voted in 1956	79%	56%	81%	61%	83%	85%	62%	67%
Split or voted straight Republican	29	0	13	11	17	30	8	28
Strong Democratic party identification	46	75	31	78	50	45	54	50
Willing to work through parties	58	13	44	6	56	30	8	11
Believe parties differ basically	58	69	31	78	33	65	62	44
Believe it makes a difference which party controls the government	29	75	38	72	61	40	38	39
Number of cases	24	16	16	18	18	20	13	18

viduals in contact with the most effective union party leaders hold the belief that party control is important to their personal lives. Yet 75 per cent of union members not exposed to this leadership felt a personal relevance. This same relationship was also found among those Negroes exposed to the most effective Negro precinct leadership. On the other hand, union members (but not nonunion people) who were in contact with union party leadership were more willing to work with or for the party organization (the reverse of the finding in the analysis of the effect of Negro leadership). But even on this matter union members who resided in precincts *not* led by union people manifested as high a willingness to work for the parties (56 compared to 58 per cent).

One must conclude from these exploratory data that, contrary to the role of Negro leadership, even from a *pragmatic* vote-mobilization standpoint, union leadership is not as functional to the party as one might expect. And from a system-process standpoint, union party leadership, as in the case of Negro party leadership, may actually have dysfunctional outcomes, muting party differences, encouraging party disloyalty and irregularity, and making it more difficult for the member of the public exposed to such leadership to see the personal relevance and utility of *party* conflict.

THE FUNCTIONAL INTERPLAY OF PARTY EFFORT AND EXPOSURE TO TELEVISION: CONGRUENCE OR CONFLICT?

There is a widely held belief today that television has replaced the precinct leader as the mobilizer of political support and the conditioner of political perspectives. Thus, V. O. Key wrote that "the doorbell ringers have lost their function of mobilizing the vote to the public relations expert."[3] Others have questioned the utility of party organization. And, despite the findings presented in detail earlier in this section, the question is indeed still appropriate, How much of the variance in behavior which we

[3] *Politics, Parties, and Pressure Groups*, pp. 375–76.

discovered, and attributed to exposure to party organization efforts, disappears when we classify respondents also on the basis of exposure to political television?[4] Is party contact still clearly visible as an important factor? And, if television exposure reveals functional differences in behavior and attitude, are these differences in the same direction as those found to be related to party contact?

There is no doubt that television is associated with high interest in public affairs. The following evidence of this for foreign affairs, for example, appeared among the sample:

	High exposure to TV	*Low exposure to TV*
Very interested in foreign affairs		
Democrats	17%	10%
Republicans	24	20
Independents	31	12

Television by itself, however, was not as related to high interest in public affairs as party effort and television combined (see Table 21.5). Those respondents who had no party contact but were highly exposed to television revealed some increased interest in public affairs, from 6 to 11 per cent for the Democrats and from 13 to 22 per cent for the Republicans. But even though television could "stimulate" political interest among politically isolated individuals, it could not raise the level substantially. When one looks at those who revealed an interest in public affairs *and* were actively involved in the discussion of political issues, the role of party contact can be seen as critical, particularly for the Democrats, although substantial differences

[4] We used five questions to determine exposure to television (see appendix questions 1, 2, 3, 3a, 3c), relating to frequency of watching the two conventions of the parties, frequency of exposure to campaign television, and selectivity by party of television watching. Dividing our respondents into "high" and "low" exposure, 59 per cent were in the former category and 41 per cent in the latter.

TABLE 21.5

THE JOINT "IMPACT" OF PARTY AND TELEVISION ON THE POLITICAL INTEREST OF THE PUBLIC

	High exposure to TV		*Low exposure to TV*	
	High party contact	*No party contact*	*High party contact*	*No party contact*
Very interested in foreign affairs				
Democrats	41%	11%	18%	6%
Republicans	34	22	18	13
Independents	29	24	14	11
Very interested in national affairs				
Democrats	61	20	41	22
Republicans	59	36	29	17
Independents	33	21	14	20
Interested in one area of public affairs *and* discuss with friends				
Democrats	50	13	45	13
Republicans	62	30	29	9
Independents	33	17	14	11

existed for the Republicans and independents also. It is significant that of the Democrats and Republicans there was at least a 30 per cent increase in political interest among those highly exposed to television when they *also* had been highly exposed to party organization efforts.

The role of both party contact and television in getting out the vote is striking. In 1956 nonvoting was virtually nonexistent among Republicans, Democrats, and independents who had been exposed to the parties, whether or not they had been television followers. But except for the independents, television was important for those isolated from the parties. Thus, only 20 per cent of such isolated Democrats failed to vote when exposed

TABLE 21.6

PARTIES AND TELEVISION: GETTING OUT THE VOTE

	High TV exposure		*Low TV exposure*	
	High party contact	*No party contact*	*High party contact*	*No party contact*
Nonvoters 1956				
Democrats	0%	20%	0%	36%
Republicans	3	6	6	13
Independents	4	41	7	31
Split the ballot				
Democrats	35	24	16	18
Republicans	4	33	13	13
Independents	35	53	43	48
Decided early				
Democrats	51	76	68	78
Republicans	100	78	87	69
Independents	64	47	*	81

* Too few cases for analysis.

to television, but 36 per cent failed to vote when completely isolated from both television and the party. On the other hand, both television and party contact seemed functionally related to split-ticket voting among the Democrats. Among Republicans and independents, television was related to split-ticket voting for those not exposed to the party organization. Finally, it is interesting to see that television and party both conduced to delayed voting decisions among the Democrats, but not among the Republicans. This may, of course, be a peculiarity of the 1956 election, or it may reflect the different types of individuals contacted by the parties (the Democrats concentrating more on late deciders), although the latter suggests a canniness and discrimination in party campaign strategy which our analysis of the party leadership does not substantiate.

It seems clear that party and television operate in complementary fashion to stimulate an active interest in politics and to get out the vote, although exposure to both may not lead to the highest party regularity. This is not to say that *causation* has been established, since, as mentioned previously, the interested citizens and the voting public may be the ones inclined to be in contact with the party and exposed to television. (The fact that 70 per cent of the public in 1956 consisted of voters not highly exposed to either institutional force might belie this assumption.) But our major inquiry here concerns functional interrelationships suggestive of causal connections. When we find that 17 per cent of the Democrats highly exposed to television were very interested in foreign affairs, and that 41 per cent of these were very interested when also highly exposed to the parties, we can assert a probability of functional relatedness while not proving "causal flow." Similarly, we found that 23 per cent of Republicans highly exposed to television split their ballots, but of those who were also highly exposed to the party, only 4 per cent split their ballots, suggesting again the complementary effect of two forces on the individual, although again not demonstrating causality. Certainly it can be said that when individuals, by self-exposure or unwitting exposure, find themselves subjected to the political influences of both party and television, they are very likely to emerge as voters and citizens interested in political affairs.

Citizens who are interested enough in politics to be highly exposed to politics through television may be nonvoters (20 per cent of the Democrats, 15 per cent of the Republicans, and 30 per cent of the independents). Contact with the parties reduced percentages of nonvoting among these television fans to 0, 3, and 4. This is highly suggestive of a clear functional relationship between party effort and voting participation.

How does the party interrelate with television in the development or reenforcement of party loyalties and identification? As indicated above, split-ticket voting seemed to be increased by both forces among Democrats. Among Republicans who did not have any contact with the parties, television increased split-ticket voting. We asked respondents whether they considered themselves to be "strong" partisans, and again found that Democrats in contact with their party have been less loyal if highly exposed to television, which operates, in this sense, as a "countervailing force." Yet it appears that television cannot be considered exclusively responsible for this development among Democrats, for Democratic party contact also reduced the proportion of loyalty among television fans. More important, perhaps, is the fact that television was associated with an increase in party loyalty among both Republicans and Democrats who were isolated from their party organizations.

TABLE 21.7

Parties and Television: Partisanship

	High TV exposure		*Low TV exposure*	
	High party contact	*No party contact*	*High party contact*	*No party contact*
"Strong" Democrats	64%	71%	86%	61%
"Strong" Republicans	60	40	47	35

One of the most disturbing sets of findings concerns the relation of party and television to the citizen's perception of party conflict and his evaluation of its meaning for him. Both forces seem to maximize an awareness of the existence of campaign issues, but uncertainty as to the personal relevance of this conflict also seems to be associated with these forces. For those with no party contact, television emphasized the personal importance of the election outcome. Further, it seems that exposure to the party among television fans resulted in a decreased sense of the importance of the election. It is significant that the highest percentages of awareness (62 and 80 per cent) are for those respondents highly exposed to TV but with no party contact! Television thus seems to be more functional than the parties

TABLE 21.8

PARTIES AND TELEVISION: RELEVANCE OF CAMPAIGN ISSUES

	High TV exposure		*Low TV exposure*	
	High party contact	*No party contact*	*High party contact*	*No party contact*
Aware of campaign issues				
Democrats	77%	50%	64%	36%
Republicans	76	66	47	39
Feel it makes a difference which party controls the government				
Democrats	39	62	59	58
Republicans	66	80	41	52

are themselves *to the party task* (assuming this to be the development of an awareness of the personal importance of the voting act), and to the *political system goal* (assuming that one such system goal might be the quickening of the citizen's perception that party conflict is meaningful).

Underlying these considerations is the basic question of ideological and voting consistency. Party effort together with the influence of television did tend to contribute to such consistency, although the record is mixed. In both parties the organization's efforts seemed conducive to ideology—vote consistency among those highly exposed to television, and among Democrats with low TV exposure levels. But this was not so for Republicans not highly exposed to television: the party contact did not maximize consistency under these circumstances. On the other hand, television played a consistency role only among Democrats outside the party orbit, and for Republicans it was a medium re-enforcing the party's efforts. With such findings it is difficult to ascribe with much confidence a significant role to television. Party effort seemed to play a somewhat more important role in promoting behavioral consistency but was ineffectual among Republicans who were not TV fans.

TABLE 21.9

PARTIES AND TELEVISION: IDEOLOGICAL AND VOTING CONSISTENCY

	High TV exposure		*Low TV exposure*	
	High party contact	*No party contact*	*High party contact*	*No party contact*
Democrats who "tend liberal" and vote Democratic	64%	61%	64%	50%
Republicans who "tend conservative" and vote Republican	44	27	29	35

It is interesting to note the nonvoting records of liberals and conservatives in this connection (Table 21.10). Again, television did little to stimulate liberals to vote, but party contact seemed to be critical. This was only true for Republicans who were not exposed to television, however. Neither medium exerted a major role in the mobilization of conservative votes, but the Democratic party effort seemed rather important in the mobilization of liberal votes.

We now turn to the fundamental question of the functional relationship of party and TV in relation to the foundations of political consensus. As discussed previously, at least three major components of public confidence in the system need careful ex-

TABLE 21.10

PARTIES AND TELEVISION: NONVOTING RECORDS

	High TV exposure		*Low TV exposure*	
	High party contact	*No party contact*	*High party contact*	*No party contact*
Democrats: liberals not voting	2%	26%	8%	22%
Republicans: conservatives not voting	3	3	0	12

ploration: knowledge, beliefs, and optimism. The data suggest that both party and television exposure combine to enhance the citizen's knowledge about the system, although Democrats and Republicans with no exposure to the parties cannot be assisted very much by television. The only decent levels of information occurred among those exposed to both party and television. For example, among Democrats highly exposed to television, only 20 per cent were well informed, but this percentage moved

TABLE 21.11

THE ROLES OF TV AND PARTY IN RE-ENFORCING SUPPORT IN THE POLITICAL SYSTEM

	High TV exposure		*Low TV exposure*	
	High party contact	*No party contact*	*High party contact*	*No party contact*
Knowledge of the system				
Answered 3 or 4 of the knowledge items correctly				
Democrats	45%	6%	9%	3%
Republicans	34	12	24	13
Belief				
Believe campaigns have value				
Democrats	70	60	50	51
Republicans	76	58	41	48
Willing to work through parties				
Democrats	50	42	59	22
Republicans	11	22	19	17
Optimism				
Feels he has no say				
Democrats	23	28	9	65
Republicans	7	12	24	30
Feels public officials don't care				
Democrats	14	26	18	30
Republicans	3	20	24	13

up to 45 per cent for those highly exposed to the party. (For Republicans in a similar context, the percentages are 20 and 34 per cent.)

Second, television seems more effective than party in conveying to the public the value of the political campaign. Those not exposed to television became, if anything, more cynical about campaigns as they were contacted by, or exposed to, the party organization. Among Republicans, particularly, high television exposure developed support for the idea of the political campaign.

But television functions differently in promoting support for party involvement. Among those highly exposed to the parties (and thus presumably constituting a potential cadre of party workers), television actually discouraged the undertaking of party work. For Republicans highly exposed to television, party contact was also dysfunctional in this sense. Extremely small proportions of Republicans who had been exposed to the party were willing to work for the parties (11 and 19 per cent), and high television exposure may result in less willingness. At least 50 per cent of the Democrats exposed to the parties were willing to work for them, but again television decreased this enthusiasm.

Third, the citizen has more confidence in his own political action status if he has some exposure to the party, or high exposure to television. This was particularly true for the Democrats. Party contact among those Democrats not highly exposed to television was functional to political optimism (56 per cent fewer reporting they had "no say" in the political system). Television was similarly effective among Democrats out of touch with the party, but the differential is at the 40 per cent level. The Republicans were much less affected by either party effort or television, but the highest percentages of optimism (93 and 97 per cent) are found for Republicans highly exposed to both television and the party.

The functional congruence of party and television seems in most respects clearly substantiated. Both forces converge to stimulate political interest, voting participation, awareness of political issues, the maintenance of public knowledge about the political system, and optimistic feelings about the individual's role in that system. A by-product of these outcomes may be more "independence" in voting behavior (split-ticket voting), more deliberation in voting decisions, and some weakening in party identification and loyalty. The functional direction of television and party also diverges in certain respects. Television has much more utility in alerting the citizen to the relevance of the election to his own personal interest, while parties are less effective. Television plays an unimportant role in the stimulation of consistency between ideological positions and the vote, and, if anything, tends to discourage citizens from working actively through the parties.

Party effort emerges from this analysis as a critical force, related to the shaping of the citizen's political attitudes and influencing his behavior. We have found repeatedly that even those with high exposure to television (presumably the most politically alert and concerned sector of the citizenry), if also exposed to the party organization's efforts, reveal distinctive patterns of perspective. They reveal more interest in politics, more discussion about politics, better voting records (though not necessarily increased partisan regularity in voting) more awareness of campaign issues, more behavioral consistency between ideology and the vote, more political knowledge, more support for the value of political campaigns, more optimism about the individual's political action role in the system. This does not mean that we have demonstrated a positive causal interconnection between party and public behavior. A multiplicity of forces operate upon the individual citizen, and no doubt many citizens exhibited a number of these behaviors prior to the party's influence. Nor is this to eulogize the accomplishments of the parties, for this would ignore the fact that approximately 50 per cent of the citizens *highly exposed to the parties* were woefully uninformed about the political facts of life, about 30 per cent did not think campaigns were very valuable, 15 per cent were pessimistic about the individual's place in the system, 30 per cent were not aware of the existence of campaign issues or that parties "stand for different things," and 50 per cent were not certain that the election outcome was very relevant personally. In the light of such findings, one may well be critical of the party's efforts. But it cannot be denied that the party as a political force, ineffective and inadequate as much of its leadership and organization is, has not been superseded by other political influences or institutions. The party is functionally relevant to the public's behavior and attitudes, both in the utilitarian sense of achieving party goals, and in the broader sense of contributing meaning, coherence, and support for the political system and society of which it is one significant part. The party effort may touch only a minority of the body politic, and undoubtedly leaves many of this minority indifferent or even hostile to the party process. But for the large residue of the public exposed to the party organization, the party effort is clearly functional to political interest, involvement, and consensual support for the political system.

CHAPTER 22

SYNTHESIS: THE POLITICAL PARTY AS A DYNAMIC STRUCTURE IN DEMOCRATIC SOCIETY

A simple and lucid interpretation of the findings from our study, fitted into a neat theoretical image of the political party, is not only difficult but may be, in one sense, contrary to reality. We have not sought to oversimplify, or to eliminate empirical discoveries which might clash with theoretical expectation. There are many uniformities in our data; there are also many irregularities which do not blend smoothly with the central tendencies of the analysis. But this is of the nature of the phenomenon. Parties are fascinating, complex, human groups. While attempting, therefore, to synthesize majority patterns, we must realize that our knowledge of the party is still not complete. Empirical research of the party, when it does not settle for superficial simplicity, will gradually replace intuition and impression as the authoritative basis for knowledge.

We have investigated the nature of parties in one great metropolitan setting, the Detroit area. This is an area, like other metropolitan settings, of tremendous social and economic heterogeneity and transformation. Its ethnic-group diversity is almost incredible, its Negro concentration unrivaled, its occupational and income variations extreme, and its social and residential mobility patterns profuse. Within this social complex political conflict is maximal, between interest group protagonists, between ideological forces, and between the Republican and Democratic parties. The contest for political control is continuous and intense, for nonpartisan municipal offices, county offices, state and congressional power positions. While the Democratic party appears to hold a clear (though not necessarily permanent or "natural") majority, this is not so for many communities in the area. Both parties engage in perpetual conflict, for they know that a 5 to 10 percentage-point variation in the Detroit area vote spells the margin of state control, whether for the governorship, the United States senatorship, or the Presidency. In this setting of extreme social change and continual political warfare, the party structures are immersed. As city and area political structures, their patterns of leadership, organization, and functional performance must be understood as reciprocals of the society and community with which they are inextricably linked. The parties are acted upon by this environment; they, in turn, act upon it.

THE GENERAL EMPIRICAL IMAGE OF THE PARTY

In the foregoing analysis we have seen that the party is a complex intermediate organization in American metropolitan society. It is a mass organization, attracting and recruiting activists and followers from the lowest social classes, from minority racial and ethnic groups, and from those with established and traditional social status. The party is led, not by a "blue-ribbon" social elite class, but by a diverse aggregation of careerists from all segments of the social spectrum. It is, in fact, somewhat astonishing to see the party of the "left" co-opting leadership from conservative social groups, while the party of "conservatism" seeks leadership among groups recently risen in social and political status. The political party penetrates deeply into the social structure, fulfilling social and political functions for those whom it attracts, and to whom it appeals. The party is a critical social institution for many Americans, serving a number of personal-social needs, performing important functions of mediation between the citizen and his government. This is not to say that the party is a "master institution," as some writers would have us believe. Leadership is too diverse for it to be a monolithic and disciplined structure. Efficiency in the performance of party tasks is too marginal for the party to function as an effective "machine." Subcoalitional factionalism is too realistic for absolutist party loyalties to emerge. Control processes are too entropic to permit an elite-dominated hierarchy. A large proportion of the public in our study (approximately 60 per cent) was almost completely unexposed to the party structure, with the result that party impact is severely restricted.

Nevertheless, the party does perform important tasks in the system. It does recruit leadership which is reasonably realistic, goal-oriented, ideologically distinctive, competitive, and oriented to democratic values. It does contribute to citizen interest in public affairs, to party loyalty, to "getting out the vote," and to the confidence of the citizen in the political system. And the party does adapt more realistically to its environment than might be expected. In sum, the party is no "master institution" but a minimal-efficiency structure, closely linked to the social and economic milieu in which it functions, interacting with and influencing the American public as well as exerting a profound impact on many activists willing to take positions within its echelons. Though performing social and political tasks at a marginal level, the party is at any time capable of expanding the scope and intensity of its role in the American system, for the modern party in the American metropolis has the potential for tremendous social, ideological, and political power.

Throughout this analysis we have emphasized that the party is not a neatly pyramided bureaucracy, an elite class, or an oligarchy. Theories of the ruling class, or of oligarchy, disguise more reality about the party than they disclose. In lieu of such theories we have developed, and empirically explored, four theoretical constructs which together bring us much closer to the meaning of party. The party is an open, clientele-oriented structure, permeable at its base as well as its apex, highly preoccupied with the recruitment of "deviant" social categories, and willing to provide mobility and access for these categories into the major operational and decisional centers of the structure. The party is also a "stratarchical" control structure, rather than an elitist command structure. Power is devolved and proliferated to echelon commands, decision-making is autonomized at the lower reaches of the structure, and deference is not exclusively upward, but reciprocal. In addition, the party structure must be visualized as a tenuous alliance of socio-economic subcoalitions with varying degrees of subgroup cohesion, identification, and interaction, subcoalitions which exist in a mutually exploitative relationship to the party, and with varying potentials for disloyalty and disaffection. Finally, we see the party, not as a singular body of elitists, but as an aggregate of career classes performing differential structural functions, yet not molded into a hierarchy of subelites whose power prerogatives and structural status are closely determined by a top leadership group. Patterns of career aspiration and mobility do indeed exist, but there are too many self-generating forces, and too much organizational incoherence, for career destinies to be determined by an "elite center."

The evidence documenting these images of the party, though not overwhelming or complete, is highly supportive. The frustration of the top-echelon leaders is itself eloquent testimony. To a man they decried the tenuousness of their control, the absence of sanctions, the absence of patronage, the virtually impossible task of maintaining harmony, their own recognized expendability. The social composition of the party elites also supports our theory, for it is not a leadership which is socially congruent or extremely unrepresentative of the party "mass." In a genuine sense, "the elite" consists of hierarchical representatives of social interests whose loyalty to the subcoalitions may often be so strong that one wonders whether party decision-making is not in effect a bargaining process among subgroups in the structure. Similarly, the ideological unorthodoxy of those at the apex seriously undermines the concept of oligarchy. Thus, 30 per cent of the Democratic board members were "conservatives," and one-third of the Republican chairmen and board members were "liberals." Among precinct leaders whom we considered to belong in the district organizations' "inner circles," 24 per cent of the Democrats and 65 per cent of the Republicans did not conform ideologically with the major ideological directions of those at the top echelon of the party structure.

Our data do not support the theory of the party as directed by a handful of leaders, maintaining themselves in power by self-consciously recruiting and indoctrinating new careerists with elite perspectives. At most, 38 per cent of our precinct leaders were elite recruits, and only one-tenth of these revealed organizational mobility. This is not to deny that career tenure and mobility, as well as group involvement over time, produce patterns of attitudes and behavior which appear conformist. But the extensiveness of nonconformity, the heterogeneity of perspectives, the diversity and confusion in role-perceptions, despite career mobility and extensive involvement, strongly indicate that group conformity is not elite-induced. Communication with the upper-echelon leaders may, in fact, result in relatively extreme ignorance about the operational strategy of the party; conversely, the lone operator at the base of the structure, isolated from elite associations, may produce at a relatively high level of organizational efficiency. Personal motivations, career aspiration, and communicative interaction with like-minded activists, whether at the elite level or not, are the critical factors for explaining the behavior of the precinct leader. This is no bureaucratic institution by which norms, values, ideology, and operational regulations are transmitted. Nor is this an oligarchical system exploiting the activists for leadership ends. It is an open, stratarchical, subcoalitional, and pluralized leadership structure.

THE SOCIOLOGICAL CHARACTER OF THE PARTY

The political party is as significant a social group as it is a political group. It is a social action system of "interdependent activity," to use Herbert Simon's phrase. It is not merely an individuated aggregate of leaders and activists, each of whom acts and thinks independently. Our analysis reveals that citizens join the party, and maintain or improve their leadership status in it, to fulfill basic motivational drives and needs. Over 50 per cent admitted to personally instrumental satisfactions. They perceive the party as a group meaningful for personal ends. Further, ideological analysis indicates clearly that, while the leadership is again not completely congruent in positions on all issues, the party structure may be characterized as a group in ideological terms—the Republican structure predominantly conservative, the Democratic structure strongly liberal. This convergence of attitudinal positions is a group phenomenon; it does not occur by chance. Again, the communicative patterns are diffuse, yet we could classify as "isolates" only 6 per cent of the Democratic precinct leaders and 15 per cent of the Republican precinct leaders. The party is an interacting network of activists, 80 to 90 per cent of whom engaged in some type of tasks relevant to the group goal, which the majority saw, manifestly or latently, as that of winning power. Thus, although these are not tightly-knit "machines," or even self-consciously collaborative "teams," they are structures of interacting, moderately goal-oriented, ideologically distinctive, strongly motivated sets of leaders, a majority of whom are aware of the group, their status in it, its opportunities for them, and their task responsibilities.

The party fulfills social functions even as it is a group for political purpose. As one district chairman put it, "Many people are in party work to improve their own lot, socially or economically." This is true at the base, as well as at the apex, of the structure, for 63 per cent of the Democratic precinct leaders and 47 per cent of the Republicans admitted that they would miss social contacts and friendships most if they had to drop out of politics. The fact that 80 per cent of the precinct leaders engaged in some type of social activities in their precincts, or were advisors to their constituents on personal problems, further corroborates the heavy emphasis on social interaction. And it is not irrelevant, in this connection, to point out that 40 per cent of our top leadership cadres revealed upward economic mobility during the course of their party careers. Add to this the tremendous aspiration pressure in both parties at all echelons, 57 per cent of the precinct leaders alone looking forward to position advancement, as well as the fact that 17 per cent had already demonstrated organizational mobility. Such findings indicate that the party is utilitarian for the fulfillment of social functions and needs. The demands for social recognition, social status, social intercourse are clearly demands which the party is perceived as gratifying for a large number of activists.

As a group in the social system party cohesion is explicable in terms of the fulfillment of these personal-social needs. The ordinary activist sees the party as motivationally satisfying and instrumental. As in other groups, he seeks to implement his career mobility aspirations, and through communicative contacts becomes more conscious of the meaning of the group for him. Finally, he strives for involvement in decision-making at the various levels of the structure: 34 per cent (R) and 56 per cent (D) of precinct leaders did feel involved, and two-thirds of the remainder wished to be taken into consideration. It is factors such as these which help explain "maintenance dynamic" of the political party. They may be more important than party goal orientation, role-perception, ideological conviction, or party loyalty, although these factors are not to be overlooked as important for significant minorities of activists. This is not to say that party activists are totally oblivious to "power." It *is* meant to imply, however, that if social rewards and social functions were eliminated from the party process—if social-group mobility were restricted, career aspirations discouraged, social contact minimized, and the possibility of involvement frustrated—few party activists would be left to perform the chores which lead a party to power.

The party structure has a considerable impact on its leaders, influencing the attitudes and values of those activists most highly involved in, and interacting with, other leaders in the group. First, the party affects their motivational expectation. Over two-thirds of the precinct leaders changed their motive for party work after they entered the party, the great majority becoming more concerned with satisfaction of personalized demands. Similarly, the Democrats who were involved revealed up to 40 per cent more interest in personal gain and social contact than those not involved; 24 per cent of the Republicans were interested in personal gain, compared to 3 per cent of those not involved. Second, the party seems to impress on those leaders most highly integrated a sharper awareness of the power-winning goal of the party, particularly among Democratic leaders: 88 per cent of those involved saw the party's goal as power, compared to 66 per cent of those not involved. Third, the party induces greater loyalty among the leaders who are in close contact with the organization. Decisional involvement results in a 40 per cent differential in party loyalty: only one-third of the involved revealed disloyal tendencies, while 70 per cent of the uninvolved revealed them. Similarly, extensive communicative contacts combined with ideological orthodoxy produce a striking pattern of Republican party loyalty: the orthodox cosmopolitans were 87 per cent loyal, while the unorthodox isolates were 25 per cent loyal.

A fourth evidence of the impact of group involvement relates to career aspirations, which develop as a result of integration with the party group. In both parties two-thirds of the involved precinct leaders desired to move upward in the structure, while only 40 per cent (D) and 50 per cent (R) of those who felt they had been excluded from group decision-making were thus motivated. Fifth, there is a moderate relationship between cosmopolitan communication patterns and ideological orthodoxy. Thus, 1 per cent of the cosmopolitan Democrats were conservative, while 20 per cent of those with more limited contacts were conservative; further, only 12 per cent of the Republican localists and isolates were conservative, while 48 per cent of the Republican cosmopolitans were conservative. Sixth, there is no question but that involvement with the group results in greater efficiency in task performance. We have presented a vast array of data to test for factors related to efficiency. It is sufficient to present one small finding: over 80 per cent of the "isolates" in both parties were at the lowest efficiency level, while only 2 per cent of the Democratic cosmopolitans and 13 per cent of the Republican cosmopolitans were extremely inefficient leaders. Finally, we probed the relationship between leader involvement and leader value orientations. Although this analysis was admittedly highly exploratory and incomplete, it was interesting to discover that the highly involved leader in both parties revealed a more positive "democratic" structure of values.

With such data it appears that group processes and relationships have indisputable influence on the individual leader, if he is interacting with other leaders in the structure. To a limited extent, the group subtly indoctrinates its cadres. One senses that the particular techniques and interaction relationships by which this impact occurs differ for the two parties, but whatever the difference in mechanisms, there is a flow of influence. The involved, aspiring, cosmopolitan, high-morale party activist exhibits attitude and behavior patterns distinguishing him markedly from the isolated, nonmobile, nonaspiring, or apathetic "regular."

Critical for our analysis was the realization that there is not *one* Democratic party structure and *one* Republican party structure. In a real sense ours was a study of two county structures, 12 district structures, and 174 precinct structures. In presenting the findings we noted radical differences in leadership behavior from one structure to the next. Why should only 35 per cent of the Democratic leaders in one district be manifestly conscious of power as the party goal, as against 86 per cent of the leaders in another district? Why should only 40 per cent of the leaders in District Z be liberal on civil rights issues, compared to 89 per cent in District X? Six per cent of the Republican leaders were liberal on the medical aid issue in District A, while 55 per cent were liberal in District B. Fifty per cent of the Republican leaders in one district were ideologically motivated for party work, whereas none were so motivated in an adjoining district. And, in terms of organizational dimensions it is significant to note that one finds 67 per cent of the leaders satisfied with their involvement in decision-making in one district, while only 24 per cent were satisfied in an adjacent district. These are examples of the tremendous differences in structural types. We are in no position to explain satisfactorily why these differences exist. It seems highly probable that particular structures develop over time in a geographical area, with particularized political norms, ideological perspectives, operational codes, and patterns of organizational relationships. Party structures are not fixed in a rigid mold, but do, apparently, evolve their own political culture and *Weltanschauung*.

It seems clear, in fact, even from this single empirical analysis, that these structures are not static or closed. They reveal a high degree of dynamic interaction with the social environment within which they recruit and function. Throughout the study, we found this to be more true of the Democratic than the Republican structures, but both parties are aware of the environment and seek to exploit it. This tendency was documented in the promiscuity with which leadership is recruited, and in the competitive recruitment from "deviant" social categories. It must be recalled, in this connection, that 30 per cent of the Republican precinct cadre were union members, 10 per cent were Negro blue-collar, 13 per cent were Irish and Poles; on the Democratic side 10 per cent were in business and managerial professions, 15 per cent were German and English, 7 per cent had incomes over $15,000. We found adaptation manifest in the occupational diversity of the personal political associates of the leaders: over 30 per cent of the Republican leaders had blue-collar political associates; 31 per cent of Democratic leaders had white-collar political associates who held business and managerial occupations. This tendency is also reflected in the social composition of the top elite nucleus: 30 per cent of the Republican executive board members were blue-collar; 47 per cent of the Democratic executive board members were business and managerial. Upward hierarchical mobility for precinct leaders seems more difficult for certain social categories in the Republican party (notably Catholics and unskilled workers), yet the heterogeneous composition of the middle and top leadership cadres in both parties attests to the relative absence of social exclusiveness in structure. Finally, although we found some striking evidence of "nonrealism" in the leadership of both parties (particularly in comprehension of the social bases for the public's political behavior), we could only properly classify one-fifth of the precinct leaders as clearly out of touch with social reality and ignorant of the social adaptation role.

The party must, therefore, be perceived as in a state of continual, dynamic interaction with its social and political environment. The party is a competitive, constant, social-renewal group, if it is at all success-minded. Aside from the findings concerning promiscuity of recruitment and social adaptiveness of the leadership cadres, other empirical discoveries are relevant to this image. For example, the party leadership *is* continuously renewed—almost 50 per cent of our precinct leaders had less than four years' experience, and 22 per cent entered party work in the campaign year of 1956, when our study began. In the middle-level cadre, 10 per cent of the board members had less than four years' experience in the party. Further, the intergenerational overlap in career origins of party leaders assures a continual rejuvenation, with the 30 per cent of the leadership who began party work 20 or more years earlier providing continuity. "Renewal" takes place at the top of the structure also. So far as we could determine, half of the district chairmen had occupied their positions four years or less. And by 1960, four years after our study, only one-third still held power.

The potential renewal capacity of the party is suggested by some of our findings concerning the nature of party leadership and activity in precincts which were marginal, sure for the party, and lost for the party. In competitive precincts both parties recruit heavily from social categories presumably in the opposition camp—57 per cent of the Republican and 83 per cent of the Democratic precinct leaders in marginal precincts came from such "deviant" social categories. Yet, wisely or not, these leaders in marginal precincts are not all middle-of-the-road moderates.

For example, on the medical aid issue none of the Republican leaders in marginal precincts was liberal, while 80 per cent of the Democrats were. On the other hand, the parties are not completely status-minded, disillusioned structures in lost precincts. Interesting in this connection is the fact that 75 per cent of the Republican leaders in precincts lost to the Democrats aspired to a party career, and two-thirds of these aspirants were performing at the highest levels of efficiency in precinct tasks. This discovery suggests one reason for considerable electoral change in our system. Dynamism may characterize party leadership even in the most hopeless precincts. Adaptation to the social environment is a natural pragmatic strategy—if the party is indeed oriented toward success. It is the continuous revolution and turnover in party leadership, the urge to mobilize support in the face of ridiculous odds, and the social adaptive conditions of the party operation (quickly learned, if not instinctive, with the politician imbued with a drive for personal and/or group power), which stamp the party as a distinctive socio-political institution in a state of dynamic equilibrium.

THE IMPLICATIONS OF PARTY FUNCTIONAL ANALYSIS

There is no doubt that the party effort is restricted, judging by reports from the public about its contacts with the party organization. Approximately 60 per cent of the cross-section reported very little or no exposure to party efforts. Yet, since one-fourth to one-third of those not exposed to the parties infrequently or never vote, the party contact record may not be quite so dismal. If we exclude the 12 per cent in our sample who had never voted, though eligible, we find close to 50 per cent of the metropolitan voting public had been contacted in some way by the party organization.

Upon examination of the types of party contact, however, we find that the party effort, while multidirectional, does not operate on the principle of the allocation of most effective resources. Three-fourths of our sample reported that they had received party literature at their homes, but only 8 per cent said they had been personally canvassed at home; 7 per cent recalled being telephoned by party workers, and the same percentage remembered positively that they were contacted by the party on election day. Similar proportions recalled being asked for campaign contributions (16 per cent), meeting party candidates (16 per cent), knowing precinct leaders personally (8 per cent), or taking an active part in campaign work (13 per cent). Yet much larger proportions of the public approved of being contacted by the parties—37 and 38 per cent, respectively, saying they would not resent being asked for money by party workers, or would not object to personal contacts at the home. It appears that the parties are still bent on contacting the public through the mailbox, when there is a high probability of success through personal contact. Further, the parties do not cumulate their contact techniques, for only 17 per cent of our respondents revealed they had been exposed to three or more of these types of party effort. The Democrats, in one sense, are the most disadvantaged by attrition in party organizational work. Exactly 50 per cent of the metropolitan area voters not exposed to the parties were Democratic identifiers, while 31 per cent called themselves Republicans, and 19 per cent said they were independents.

Party effort with the public does have returns, however, and in many respects serves party interests significantly. The functional relationships explored in this connection do not demonstrate a clear "causal flow," but the findings are highly suggestive of one. We find, for example, that as party exposure increases, nonvoting systematically decreases. There were no nonvoters among any members of the cross-section who had been highly exposed to the party effort. Strong party identification is much more likely to be found among those exposed to the party effort, particularly among Republicans—60 per cent of the exposed being strong Republicans compared to 36 per cent of those not at all exposed to the party. Straight-ticket voting is also found to be clearly associated with party exposure in both parties (a 22 per cent differential for the Democrats, a 35 per cent differential for the Republicans). And, for the Democrats, exposure to the party seems significantly associated with attitudes favorable to working for the party, 50 per cent of those highly exposed were agreeable, while only 17 per cent of those not exposed would have worked for the Democratic party. Party effort seems, therefore, to be functional for self-serving ends and for the maintenance of the party as a viable electoral support group.

The consequences of party effort, however, in certain respects, have side effects which are dysfunctional to the goals the party seeks to implement. One example of this occurs in the apparent delay of voting decisions by Democratic identifiers. As exposure to party contact increases, larger proportions of these Democratic identifiers are "late deciders" (23 per cent of those not exposed, 30 per cent of those moderately exposed, 43 per cent of those highly exposed). Further, the "late deciders" highly exposed are more likely to split their ballots than are those outside the party contact effort. This suggests that those exposed to the party effort are more "deliberative" in their calculations about voting (among the majority Democrats). Exposure to party may trigger, or be associated with, other types of exposure. The result is ambivalence, indecision, and for some, more independence in the voting decision.

Another example of dysfunctional side effects from party effort is the case of the efficient Negro leader of a precinct which is heavily Negro in composition. Theoretically, parties place "dominant interest" leaders in such positions to maximize the vote among Negroes. And our data reveal that this tactic does hold value for vote mobilization, since 95 per cent of those Negroes exposed to efficient Negro leaders in the Democratic party did vote (and voted a straight ticket), while only 85 per cent of those not exposed voted. But it is interesting to note that Negroes highly exposed to efficient Negro precinct leaders are also less likely to be strongly identified with the Democratic party (68 to 82 per cent), to see the parties as differing basically in principle, and to be willing to work for the political party

(58 per cent compared to 75 per cent). This suggests that Negro leaders as subcoalitional representatives may actually stimulate more interest in, and loyalty to, the Negro political movement than the particular political party with which they identify. This may be termed the "Trojan horse effect."

Another outcome related to this type of party leadership situation might be called the "rebel reaction effect." We find, for example, that white respondents living in Negro-led precincts, whether Republican or Democratic, reveal a very weak sense of party identification, a greater inclination to split their ballots, and an unwillingness to work for the political parties. The "rebel reaction effect" was also found among certain types of citizens residing in precincts led by union officers or union members. Thus, union members of our cross-section in contact with efficient precinct leaders, who were also union officers or members, had a high proportion of split-ticket voting (29 per cent) and a low proportion with strong party identification (46 per cent). Union members not exposed to party contact, or residing in precincts not efficiently led by union leaders, actually had less split-ticket voting (11 per cent at the most), and were more loyal to the party (75 per cent for those not exposed to union party leadership). In fact, union members in precincts *not led* by union party leaders had a slightly higher voting turnout and less split-ticket voting. Further, nonunion adults living in precincts led by union party leaders, and highly exposed to the party effort in these precincts, may also be rebelling, since only 30 per cent were willing to work for the party (compared to 58 per cent for all Democrats highly exposed to the party). Whether these consequences are manifestations of "rebel reaction" or "Trojan horse" phenomena, it seems clear that the utilization of interest-group leadership by the party may, under some circumstances, result in alienation, even among those members of the public who presumably will be mobilized and attracted to the party by such utilitarian strategies.

A special case concerns the so-called independents. The parties spend less time and effort on these adults, apparently, since only 12 per cent of the independents were highly exposed to the parties, compared to close to 18 per cent of the partisan identifiers. In one sense this is unwise, because party effort does seem functional to the voting turnout of independents: none of those highly exposed were nonvoters, in contrast to 12 per cent of those moderately exposed, and 30 per cent of those never exposed. But party effort has no noticeable effect on independents in other important functional respects. It does not stimulate them to be more interested in public affairs, it does not interest them in political action, and it does not convince them that they would enjoy working for the parties. The true independent, apparently, is much more influenced by other stimuli and forces in his political environment. Yet, since the majority of metropolitan independents are liberals, and since party effort is clearly associated with increased turnout of independents, from a self-interest standpoint the parties cannot afford to ignore them, and might well increase efforts to mobilize the independent vote.

Both parties are in a serious quandary, in American metropolitan society, on the question of appealing to the public in strong ideological terms. Our data reveal, in startling fashion, the paradoxical state of the public's ideological perceptions of the parties. Over 60 per cent of the consistent liberals had conflicting or unclear perceptions of the parties' ideological positions, and 23 per cent felt that the Republican party was closer to their own position. Similarly, 54 per cent of the consistent conservatives were in conflict or unclear, and 14 per cent felt that the Democratic party was closer. In such a context, it is pragmatically feasible for the parties to contact the public with ideological appeals only if this technique will maximize voting support. Our data reveal that party effort does in fact achieve mobilization of ideologically committed partisans. For, even with the minimal ideological effort currently expended by parties, we found that liberals can be brought to the polls to vote Democratic (72 per cent in the high-exposure group and 45 per cent in the no-exposure group), while conservatives can be brought by party effort to the polls to vote Republican through party effort (96 per cent in the high-exposure group but only 78 per cent in the no-exposure group). Only 2 and 4 per cent of the conservatives and liberals, respectively, who were exposed to the parties did not vote. On the other hand, under the present conditions of unclear ideological appeals by the parties, both parties lose some of their own ideologues to the opposition. For the Democrats in Detroit this was particularly true in 1956, since 14 per cent of those highly exposed to the party effort were liberal Democrats who voted Republican (compared to 7 per cent of those unexposed). Why do the parties not carry more straightforward ideological appeals to the public?

There appear to be three major reasons for muting the ideological appeal. First, of course, is the ideological distribution of the public in the metropolitan area—32 per cent conservatives, 55 per cent liberals, 13 per cent ambivalent or unsure of their ideological position. Thus, mobilization of the conservative vote exclusively would not lead to power. Second, there is the fact that both parties find within their public support sectors large proportions of citizens whose ideology may be at odds with the ideological direction of the party but who are, nevertheless, party identifiers. Thus, 4 per cent of the Democratic identifiers were consistent conservatives and 25 per cent tended to be conservative; but 19 per cent of the Republican identifiers were consistent liberals and 31 per cent tended to be liberal. Third, the parties cannot be sure that, given a clear-cut ideological appeal, voters would decide in congruence with their ideological positions. Our data bear out this anxiety, but only to a limited extent, for we find among those liberals *who saw the Democratic party as ideologically closer* to their positions, only 2 per cent voted Republican and 10 per cent did not vote. And, among those conservatives *who saw the Republican party as closer* to their positions, only 2 per cent voted Democratic, while 15 per cent did not vote. None of those respondents who voted for the "wrong" party, however, had been exposed to concerted party efforts.

The first and second explanations seem to be more defensible than the third, but they are also powerful deterrents to an ideological appeal, particularly for the Republican party, if its strategy is to appeal to conservatives exclusively. It is in this context that one must comprehend the low saliency of ideology in leadership perspectives and party appeals. The implications of this analysis help us understand why only 10 per cent of precinct leaders were ideologically motivated and why only one-third of top-echelon leaders emphasized issue strategy in the specification of their organizational tasks. Two-thirds of the Republican leaders were consistent conservatives, but they did not appeal exclusively to conservatives. Three-fourths of Democratic leaders were liberals, but they did not appeal exclusively to liberals. And this utilitarian strategy seems to pay off handsomely, for 61 per cent of the conservatives who identified with the Democratic party stayed in the party and voted Democratic, while 80 per cent of the Republican liberals stayed in the Republican party and voted Republican. Of greater significance for our analysis, however, is the fact that the ideologically quiescent appeal of the party, through its precinct leaders and workers, contributes to this result. We find that of those Democratic conservatives highly exposed to the party, 80 per cent remained loyal in their voting behavior, compared to 70 per cent of those unexposed. More striking is the finding that of those Republican liberals highly exposed to the party, 93 per cent voted Republican, while only 67 per cent of those not exposed voted Republican. Although the parties can mobilize ideologically consistent votes, from a pragmatic standpoint they are also successful, through party organizational effort, in maintaining the voting loyalty of those in their public support groups whose ideological position would seem to dictate other behavior. Given the ideological distributions in the public and among the party identifiers, this seems to be a party strategy of high self-serving utility, despite its system-dysfunctional connotations.

The outcome of the party effort for the political system is important to bear in mind in assessing the role of the party organization. We have seen how party effort is associated with increased voting turnout, strengthening party identifications and loyalties, and developing attitudes favorable to working for the party operation. In addition, our analysis revealed that exposure to the party results in a greater interest in foreign affairs, national domestic affairs, and local public affairs. This is particularly noticeable even for those highly exposed to television as a source of political information. Thus, among Democrats and Republicans who were constant viewers of television, those highly exposed to the party were much more interested in "national affairs" (61 and 59 per cent) than were those not exposed to the party (20 and 36 per cent). It cannot be argued, therefore, that TV has replaced the party in stimulating the public's interest in politics.

In strengthening the foundations for political consensus, the party effort is also functional to the system. Among Democrats and Republicans highly exposed to the parties, approximately one-third had a reasonably adequate factual knowledge about the political system, while less than 10 per cent of those unexposed were adequately informed. Further, those in contact with the parties are more likely to recognize the value of political campaigns and to be optimistic about their own political action roles in the system. It is important in this connection to note again that this party outcome is true even among those highly exposed to television. For example, among Republicans and Democrats who were TV fans, those with high exposure to the party organization were much less cynical about the role of the citizen in the political system, only 14 and 3 per cent, respectively, saying that "public officials don't care" about the ordinary citizen, while 26 and 20 per cent of those not exposed to parties (but highly exposed to TV) gave this response. It is also significant that the impact of party holds true, and is in fact particularly noticeable, when we control for the educational level of our respondents. Thus, for example, those with an elementary-school education only were most pessimistic about politics ordinarily, 34 per cent saying "public officials don't care," while only 22 per cent of those with a high-school education felt that way. But those with an elementary education who were also highly exposed to the parties had a different set of interpretations about politics, only 17 per cent revealing a pessimistic political orientation.

We do not mean to exaggerate the functional impact of the parties; we are concerned with functional direction and functional potential. Certainly, the limited exposure of a large proportion of the public to the party organization suggests caution in assessing the parties' role in the system. And certainly, also, our data reveal that large numbers of citizens exposed to the parties are not interested in politics, are not knowledgeable about politics, and are not optimistic about the citizen's role in the political system. Finally, we realize that there are certain functions which parties are supposed to perform that we have not been able to assess adequately, such as the selection of candidates for party office and the control of elected representatives once they are in office. (We actually found very little indication that the party organizations, as organizations, were heavily involved with these matters, primarily because of the direct primary system for nominating candidates; but our data were too sparse to speak authoritatively on these functional problems.)

Despite reservations, there is clear evidence that if the party organizations choose to act, and when they act, they do produce outcomes which will maximize, and even make more rational, the participation of the ordinary citizen in the political process. This, after all, together with the maximization of the party goal of winning or keeping power, is the major theoretical perspective from which we must view the nature of the party in the democratic society. Parties which serve no functions requisite to their own maintenance or to the meaningful involvement of the public in political affairs, will, in democratic societies, disappear, or take on new forms. From our analysis, there can be no prediction that parties in metropolitan areas such as Detroit will disappear.

The party in the American metropolis is a dynamic social and political structure. To use a phrase from Franz Neumann, it seeks to "translate social power into political power." As does any dynamic institution, it faces recurring crises and strains, due to the dynamism of internal pressures and the dynamism of external threats. We have referred frequently to the empirical actuality of these strains—the problems associated with motivational diversity and displacement among the activist cadre, the goal and role uncertainty and misperception of sizeable minorities in the structures, the career-aspiration and decisional-involvement pressures of those at the base of the party, the questionable party loyalty of some of the socio-economic subcoalitions in the organization, and the tolerance of operational autonomy and inefficiency on the part of lower-level activists. While these stresses do indeed exist, they do not signify the demise of party, for the party is an amazingly adaptive social and political subsystem. It relies on its leaders after all, in whose perceptions and beliefs, actions and interactions, and continuous contact with the public rests the fate of the party.

We conclude as we began, with the theory of Charles Merriam, who wrote 40 years ago:

> Of great significance in the political party are its leaders, its magnetic centers of personal interest and enthusiasm . . . all leaders from the smallest voting unit to the largest. . . . These key men carry much weight with their fellows, and their enthusiasm, lukewarmness or defection is of great significance. Often their personal judgment or advice is more effective than any other single consideration in determining party allegiance in their immediate circles of acquaintance. Numbers of their fellow voters follow them closely. . . . When these leaders weaken or desert or divide or are indifferent, their party group is shaken and disaster is near. But if their interest is keen and their enthusiasm runs high, the effect is clearly evident in the party strength in the vicnity.[1]

[1] *The American Party System*, pp. 32–34.

APPENDIX A

CROSS-SECTION INTERVIEW SCHEDULE

Appendix A, Cross-Section Interview Schedule

Detroit Area Study
Survey Research Center
Project 843

University of Michigan
Winter, 1957

A STUDY OF POLITICAL PARTICIPATION

Interviewer ______________________ Date __________ Sample No. ____

LISTING BOXES

TO SELECT RESPONDENT, USE SELECTION BOX ON INSIDE FRONT PAGE OF COVER SHEET

LIST ALL ADULTS IN THE DWELLING UNIT

Relationship to Head	Age	Sex	Marital Status	Adult No.	Check Resp.

LIST ALL MINORS IN DU

Relationship to Head	Age	Sex

SCHEDULE OF QUESTIONS

1. One of the things we are interested in is just how much attention you paid to the last election campaign. For example, when the Democratic political convention was on TV last August and Stevenson was nominated, did you watch all or just about all of this convention, more than half of it, about half of it, less than half of it, or none or almost none of it? (SHOW CARD I)

1.All or just about all	2.More than half	3.About half	4.Less than half	5.None or almost none

- 2 -

2. When the Republican political convention was on TV and Eisenhower was nominated, did you watch all or just about all of this convention, more than half of it, about half of it, less than half of it, or none or almost none of it? (SHOW CARD I)

1.All or just about all	2.More than half	3.About half	4. Less than half	5.None or almost none

3. After the conventions were over, how frequently did you watch political programs or speeches on television? (SHOW CARD II)

1.Everyday	2.Almost everyday	3.Once or twice a week
4.A few times a month	5.Once a month	6.A few times a year
7.Less often	8.Never	

(IF EVER)

3a. Did you watch TV more at the start of the campaign, more towards the end, or about the same through the campaign?

1.Start	2.End	3.Same

(IF MORE AT START OR END) 3b. Why was that? ____________

____

____

____

3c. Were the programs you watched mostly Republican, or mostly Democratic, or did you watch them both about the same?

1.Rep	2.Dem	3.Same

4. Aside from Sunday, what newspapers do you read regularly? (CHECK BELOW FOR EACH PAPER REPORTED)

Paper Usually Read	If Reads X	Supports
Detroit Free Press	____	____
Detroit News	____	____
Detroit Times	____	____
(Other) ____	____	____

Reads no paper

(ASK FOR EACH PAPER READ) 4a. Can you tell me if this paper supported (1) Eisenhower, or (2) Stevenson, or was it (3) neutral? (RECORD ABOVE)

- 3 -

5. Do you think that during the last campaign the newspapers gave one party a better break than the other or did they treat both parties about the same?

[1.One party got a break] [2.Treated both parties the same]

(IF ONE PARTY GOT A BREAK) 5a. Which papers gave which party a break?

____

____

6. Did you happen to read anything in any magazine during the campaign about the election?

[1.Yes] [2.No]

(IF YES) 6a. Which magazine? _______________

____

7. Would you say that for information about politics and elections you rely mostly on newspapers, or radio, or television, or magazines?

[1.Papers] [2.Radio] [3.TV] [4.Magazines]

8. Do you think that the Democratic and Republican parties stand for the same things or for different things?

[1.Same] [2.Different]

(IF DIFFERENT) 8a. What do you feel the Republican Party stands for?

____

____

____

____

____

8b. What do you feel the Democratic Party stands for?

____

____

____

____

9. All in all, does it make any difference to you whether the Republican or the Democratic Party is in control of the government?

[1.Yes] [2.No]

(IF YES) 9a. How is that? ______________________

____

____

____

10. Generally speaking, then, do you usually think of yourself as a Republican, a Democrat, or what?

[1.Rep] [2.Dem] Other (SPECIFY) ______

(IF REP OR DEM)

10a. Do you consider yourself a loyal (R or D)?

[1.Yes] [2.No]

10b. Why do you feel this way? ______________________

____

____

____

____

(IF YES TO Q10a.) 10c. Under what conditions would you consider leaving your party? ______________________

____

____

____

10d. All in all, then, would you call yourself a strong (R or D) or a not very strong (R or D)?

[1.Strong] [2.Not very strong]

(IF NOT REP OR DEM)

10e. Do you consider yourself closer to the Republican or the Democratic party?

[1.Rep] [2.Dem] [3.Neither]

10f. Why do you feel this way? ______________________

____

____

11. Not all people were able to vote in this last election, of course. How about you, did you vote in the election last November? [1.Yes] [2.No]

(IF NO: DID NOT VOTE)

11a. Were you registered to vote in this last election? [1.Yes] [2.No]

(IF YES) 11b. How did it happen that you didn't vote?

____

____

____

____

(IF NO) 11c. Why was that? [Not American citizen]

(Other reasons) __________________________

____

____

(IF R NEVER VOTES, SKIP TO Q18.)

(IF YES: DID VOTE)

11d. At what point in the last campaign did you make up your mind how you were going to vote? Was it: before the conventions, during the conventions, in the first half of the campaign, in the last half of the campaign, or just before you voted?

[1.Before conven.] [2.During conven.] [3.First of campaign] [4.Last of campaign]

[5.Just before voting] [6.R's mind always made up]

(DO NOT ASK IF #6 CHECKED ABOVE) 11e. How was it that you made up your mind at that particular time?

____

____

____

____

- - - - - - - - - - - - - - -(continued)- - - - - - - - - - - - -

- 6 -

(IF YES: DID VOTE) (Cont'd)

11f. Do you remember approximately what time of day it was when you voted?

[1.Yes] [2.No]

(IF YES) 11g. How did you happen to vote at that time?

____

____

11h. Did you vote for Eisenhower or Stevenson in this election?

[1.Eisenhower] [2.Stevenson] Other ____________

11i. In this election in Michigan, Cobo ran against Williams for governor. Did you vote for Cobo or Williams?

[1.Cobo] [2.Williams] Other ____________

11j. (IF R VOTED EISENHOWER-WILLIAMS, OR STEVENSON-COBO IN 1956) I see that you split your ticket in voting for president and governor. Why did you do that? ____________

____

____

____

____

11k. Whom did you vote for for congressman from this congressional district in the last election--the Republican or the Democrat?

[1.Rep] [2.Dem] Other ____________

11l. (IF R VOTED EISENHOWER-DEMOCRAT, OR STEVENSON-REPUBLICAN) Why did you split your ticket in voting for president and congressman? ____________

____

____

____

12. (IF R IS AT LEAST 25 YEARS OLD) Now in 1952, the first time Stevenson ran against Eisenhower, do you remember for sure whether or not you voted?

[1.Voted] [2.Did not vote] [3.Don't remember]

(IF VOTED IN 1952)

12a. Did you vote for Eisenhower or Stevenson?

[1.Eisenhower] [2.Stevenson] Other ________

12b. (IF SWITCHED VOTE BETWEEN 1952 AND 1956) I see that you changed your vote between 1952 and 1956. What was it that made you change? (BE SPECIFIC)

____

____

____

13. (IF R IS AT LEAST 29 YEARS OLD) Eight years ago, in 1948, you remember that Dewey ran against Truman. Not many people voted that year, but do you remember for sure whether or not you voted in that election?

[1.Voted] [2.Did not vote] [3.Don't remember]

(IF VOTED) 13a. Who did you vote for?

[1.Dewey] [2.Truman]

Other ________

14. Since you have been eligible to vote, how many of the state and local elections that are held in years between the presidential elections have you voted in? (SHOW CARD I)

[1.All or just about all] [2.More than half] [3.About half] [4.Less than half] [5.None or almost none]

(IF NEVER VOTED IN THESE ELECTIONS) 14a. How is it that you have never voted in these elections?

____

____

____

____

____

(ASK ONLY IF R HAS EVER VOTED)

15. Do you believe a citizen pretty well lives up to his responsibilities if he votes, or do you feel that there are other things as well that he should do in the political area?

[1.Vote] [2.Other things]

(IF OTHER THINGS) 15a. What other things do you have in mind?

____

____

____

16. If you wanted to take a greater part in community affairs, do you think the best way to do this would be to work through the political parties and their organizations, or through other types of groups?

[1.Parties] [2.Other groups]

16a. Why do you feel this way? ______________

____

____

____

____

(IF #2 CHECKED ABOVE AND "OTHER GROUPS" NOT SPECIFIED)
16b. What sorts of groups would you work through?

____

____

17. Here are some opinions which we have found important to people in helping them to make up their minds on voting.
Taking each one separately, would you say that to you it is: (1) very important, (2) somewhat important, or (3) not very important?

CARD III	Rating
a. The opinion of close friends	____
b. The opinion of family members	____
c. The opinion of religious leaders	____
d. The opinion of union leaders	____
e. The opinion of employers and business leaders	____
f. The opinion of nationality or racial group leaders	____
g. The opinion of leaders of a political party	____

17a. Which one of the opinions on this card do you think is most important? ____________

- 9 -

18. Now, about political activity in this neighborhood, did either of the two parties send mail to your home or distribute handouts or other literature?

[1.Yes] [2.No]

(IF YES)

18a. Which party did this? [1.Rep] [2.Dem] [3.Both]

18b. What did you do with the literature you received? Did you (1) throw it away without looking at it, or did you just (2) look it over, or did you (3) read it carefully? (ASCERTAIN FOR EACH PARTY INVOLVED) ________

19. In the last campaign both parties asked people to contribute money. In some neighborhoods they went door-to-door, or sent appeals in the mail. Were you or was anyone in your family asked to contribute money to support the campaign?

[1.Yes] [2.No]

(IF YES)

19a. Which party did this? [1.Rep] [2.Dem] [3.Both]

19b. How were you asked? (ASK FOR EACH PARTY INVOLVED) ________

20. Did you or anyone in your family give any money to either party during the campaign?

[1.Yes] [2.No]

(IF YES) 20a. Who gave money and to which party? ________

21. How do you feel about being asked to contribute money to political parties?

- 10 -

22. As far as you know, did either of the two parties send a person around to your house to talk with members of your family about politics? [1.Yes] [2.No]

(IF YES)

22a. Which party did this? [1.Rep] [2.Dem] [3.Both]

22b. What was the purpose of the visit? (ASK FOR EACH PARTY INVOLVED)

____

____

23. Did anyone from either of the two parties call you or any member of your family on the phone during the campaign? [1.Yes] [2.No]

(IF YES)

23a. Which party did this? [1.Rep] [2.Dem] [3.Both]

23b. What was the purpose of the phone call(s)? (ASK FOR EACH PARTY INVOLVED) ______________________________

____

(IF ELECTION DAY ACTIVITIES NOT MENTIONED ABOVE)

24. Did either of the two parties contact you at your home (or where you work) on election day itself? [1.Yes] [2.No]

(IF YES) 24a. Which party did this? [1.Rep] [2.Dem] [3.Both]

25. During the campaign, did you meet any candidates [1.Yes] [2.No]

(IF YES)

25a. Who was he (were they)? ______________________________

____

25b. Where did you see him (them)? ______________________________

____

____

- 11 -

26. Did either of the two parties do anything in this neighborhood during the campaign which we haven't mentioned?

[1.Yes] [2.No]

(IF YES)

26a. What was this? ______________________

____

____

26b. Which party did it? [1.Rep] [2.Dem] [3.Both]

27. How do you feel about being contacted by a party worker or candidate during an election? (GET DETAILED RESPONSE)

____

____

____

____

(ASK IF ANY POLITICAL ACTIVITY IN AREA)

28. All in all, then, which party would you say did the most to win voters for their ticket in this neighborhood?

[1.Rep] [2.Dem] [3.Both] [4.Neither]

29. Would you say that in this neighborhood most of the political activity centered around the race for the presidency, the governorship, congress, or another contest? (IF OTHER, SPECIFY).

____

30. Aside from the political party people, did anybody contact you about voting or registration before the election?

[1.Yes] [2.No]

(IF YES)

30a. What people were these? That is, were they from a special group or organization, or what?

____

____

____

30b. What did they contact you about?

____

____

____

- 12 -

31. How about you? Have you ever done any sort of political work or activity?

(IF YES) [1.Yes] [2.No]

31a. When was that? ______________________________

31b. What did you do? ______________________________

31c. What do you feel is the greatest satisfaction you receive from political activity?

____

32. Here is a list of the different kinds of clubs and organizations that are found in greater Detroit (SHOW CARD IV). Which of these kinds of groups do you belong to? (X BELOW)

[None]

X If Member	Card IV	X If Member	Card IV (cont'd)
____	Labor unions	____	Sport teams
____	A church	____	Professional groups
____	Church-connected groups	____	Political groups
____	Fraternal lodges	____	Improvement assoc's.
____	Veteran's organizations	____	Women's clubs
____	Business, civic groups	____	Charitable groups
____	PTA	____	Other groups
____	Neighborhood clubs, centers		
____	Nationality groups		

(ASK FOR EACH GROUP CHECKED)

32a. What is the name of this group? (GET SPECIFIC NAME, E.G., UAW-CIO, NOT JUST CIO; RECORD BELOW)

32a Organization Name	32b Attendance	32c Interest	32d Vote	32e Import	32f Issue	32g Agree

(DO NOT ASK OF CHURCH) 32b. Would you say that you attend: (1) most of the meetings of this group, (2) about half, (3) just a few meetings or (4) none? (RECORD IN COLUMN 32b, ABOVE)

32c. How important is this group to you? That is, are you: (1) strongly interested in it, (2) somewhat interested, or (3) not very interested in it? (RECORD IN COL. 32c, ABOVE)

32d. Should a member of this group vote (1) Republican, (2) Democratic, or (3) doesn't it make any difference to the group how a member votes? (RECORD IN COL. 32d, ABOVE)

(IF REPUBLICAN OR DEMOCRATIC) 32e. Is it (1) pretty important that a member of this group vote that way, or is it (2) not really important? (RECORD IN COL. 32e, ABOVE)

32f. Are there any political problems or issues that this group takes a stand on? (RECORD IN COL. 32f, ABOVE,IF YES OR NO)

(IF YES) 32g. Do you generally (1) agree, or (2) disagree with most of the positions taken by this group? (RECORD IN COL. 32g, ABOVE)

(IF R BELONGS TO ANY GROUP)

32h. Are you on a committee or do you hold any office in this (any of these) organizations? [1.Yes] [2.No]

(IF YES AND R IN MORE THAN ONE GROUP) 32i. Which organization is that? ____________________

- 14 -

(IF R IS A MARRIED WOMAN)

33. Is your husband a member of a labor union? [1.Yes] [2.No]

(IF YES) 33a. Is his union in the UAW, another CIO union, the AFL, or what?

[1.UAW] [2.Other CIO] [3.AFL] Other ______

34. Do you think that labor union members, as a group, should or should not take a stand on political issues?

[1.Should] [2.Should not]

(ASK IF R IS A UNION MEMBER) 34a. Do you feel that you yourself should or should not support the position of union leaders on political matters?

[1.Should] [2.Should not]

(ASK ONLY OF WHITES)

35. Do you believe that people of the same nationality background, as a group, should or should not take a stand on political issues?

[1.Should] [2.Should not]

(IF SHOULD) 35a. Do you consider yourself to be a member of a nationality group?

[1.Yes] [2.No]

(ASK ONLY OF NEGROES)

36. Do you think that Negroes, as a group, should or should not take a stand on political issues?

[1.Should] [2.Should not]

36a. Do you feel that you yourself should or should not support the position of Negro leaders on political matters?

[1.Should] [2.Should not]

37. Are there any groups or organizations that you feel you have nothing in common with and generally disagree with on political matters?

[1.Yes] [2.No]

(IF YES) 37a. Which groups are these? ______

38\. Apart from organizations and clubs, some people get together every once in a while to visit, or play cards, or do something else. How often do you usually get together with any of your relatives other than those living at home with you? (SHOW CARD II)

[1.Everyday] [2.Almost everyday] [3.Once or twice a week]

[4.A few times a month] [5.Once a month] [6.A few times a year]

[7.Less often] [8.Never]

38a. Including your own family members who live here and your other relatives, with which of your relatives do you sometimes discuss politics? (RECORD RELATIONSHIP BELOW)

[None]

Relationship	Vote

(IF ANY, ASK FOR EACH) 38b. Did this person vote for (1) Eisenhower or (2) Stevenson in the last election? (RECORD ABOVE)

39\. How about your neighbors, how often do you usually get together with any of your neighbors? (SHOW CARD II)

[1.Everyday] [2.Almost everyday] [3.Once or twice a week]

[4.A few times a month] [5.Once a month] [6.A few times a year]

[7.Less often] [8.Never]

(IF EVER) 39a. Do you sometimes discuss politics with your neighbors?

[1.Yes] [2.No]

39b. In general, would you say that the people in your neighborhood keep pretty much to themselves, or do they get together quite a bit?

[1.Keep to selves] [2.Get together]

- 16 -

39c. Are the people in this neighborhood pretty much alike or different? That is, are they in about the same kinds of jobs, racial and social groups, and so forth, or are they pretty different?

[1.Alike] [2.Different]

(IF DIFFERENT) 39d. In what ways are they different? ________

____

____

____

____

39e. Do you think that most of the people in this neighborhood tend to vote strongly Republican, Republican, fifty-fifty, Democratic, or strongly Democratic?

[1.SR] [2.R] [3.50-50] [4.D] [5.SD] [9.Don't Know]

39f. In the last election, did most of your neighbors vote for Eisenhower, or Stevenson, or were they pretty evenly divided?

[1.Eisenhower] [2.Stevenson] [3.Divided]

40. How often do you usually get together outside of work with any people you (or your husband) works with? (SHOW CARD II)

[1.Everyday] [2.Almost everyday] [3.Once or twice a week]

[4.A few times a month] [5.Once a month] [6.A few times a year]

[7.Less often] [8.Never]

(IF R IS EMPLOYED)

40a. Do you sometimes discuss politics with the people you work with?

[1.Yes] [2.No]

40b. In the last election, did most of the people you work with vote for Eisenhower, Stevenson, or were they pretty evenly divided?

[1.Eisenhower] [2.Stevenson] [3.Divided]

- 17 -

41. And how often do you usually get together with any other friends who are not neighbors or fellow workers? (SHOW CARD II)

[1.Everyday] [2.Almost everyday] [3.Once or twice a week]

[4.A few times a month] [5.Once a month] [6.A few times a year]

[7.Less often] [8.Never]

(IF EVER)

41a. Do you sometimes discuss politics with these friends?

[1.Yes] [2.No]

41b. In the last election, did most of these friends vote for Eisenhower, or Stevenson, or were they pretty evenly divided?

[1.Eisenhower] [2.Stevenson] [3.Divided]

42. Now, think of your three best friends, whether or not they are neighbors. What are their occupations? (IF FRIEND IS HOUSEWIFE- GET FRIEND'S HUSBAND'S OCCUPATION; ALSO, NOTE "HW")

	Friend's Occupation	Discuss	Vote
1.	______	______	______
2.	______	______	______
3.	______	______	______

(ASK FOR EACH FRIEND)

42a. Do you usually discuss politics with this person? (RECORD ABOVE)

42b. Was this person for (1) Eisenhower or for (2) Stevenson in the last election? (RECORD ABOVE)

- 18 -

43. Did you find that among your relatives, friends, (people you work with), and members of the groups you belong to that many people disagreed with you on voting in the last election?

1.Yes 2.No

(IF YES) 43a. In what ways did they disagree with you? ______

______

______

______

43b. How did you feel about this? ______

______

______

44. Who, if anyone, would you go to if you had a complaint about trash in the alleys, or poor street conditions, or something like that in the neighborhood?

______

45. Are there leaders or delegates in this precinct who represent the Republican or the Democratic parties?

1.Yes 2.No 3.Don't know

(IF YES) 45a. Who is he (are they) and which party(ies) does he(do they) represent?

______

______

45b. Do you know this person (these people)personally? ______

45c. Have you, or anyone in your family, ever gone to a precinct leader for information, advice, or for help in getting something done?

1.Yes 2.No

(IF YES) 45d. What sorts of things were these? ______

______

______

- 19 -

46. Do you know anyone (else) who was active in your neighborhood in connection with the national elections last fall?

[1.Yes] [2.No]

(IF YES) 46a. Did these people work directly for one of the political parties or did they work for some other group?

[1.Party] [2.Other group]

(IF OTHER GROUP) 46b. What organizations did they work for?

___

47. If you had a son who was thinking of going into politics, would you encourage him, discourage him, or say nothing?

[1.Encour.] [2.Discour.] [3.Say nothing]

(Other) ___

47a. Why do you feel this way? ___

___

___

___

48. Do you think it is easy or hard for a person who wants to, to become a worker for a political party?

[1.Easy] [2.Hard]

48a. Why do you feel this way? ___

___

___

___

49. If a man has ability and is ambitious, how good a chance does he have to become an important leader in a political party--are his chances very good, good, fair, or not good?

[1.Very] [2.Good] [3.Fair] [4.Not]

49a. Why do you feel this way? ___

___

___

___

- 20 -

50. Just what in your opinion is the type of candidate for president you would like to see run next time? (IF NAME GIVEN, ASK: Why would he be a good choice?)

51. Do you think there were any important issues in the last campaign?

[1.Yes] [2.No]

(IF YES) 51a. What were they?

52. Do you remember whether or not you were worried or concerned about the Suez Canal crisis during the last campaign?

[1.Worried] [2.Not worried] [3.Don't remember]

52a. Do you yourself know of anyone who changed his vote because of the Suez crisis?

[1.Yes] [2.No]

(IF YES) 52b. What kind of a change was that?

53. During the campaign, do you remember what Stevenson said about the hydrogen bomb tests?

[1.Yes] [2.No]

(IF YES) 53a. What did he say?

53b. Did you agree or disagree with him?

[1.Agree] [2.Disagree]

54. Here are some questions about your viewpoint on current issues. Of course, different things are important to different people, so we don't expect everyone to have an opinion about all of these. First, how do you feel about the statement that "The government ought to help people get doctors and hospital care at low cost." Do you think the government should do this or not, or don't you have an opinion on this? (SHOW CARD V)

1.Agree strongly	2.Agree	3.Can't decide	4.Disagree	5.Disagree strongly	9.No opinion

(IF OPINION)

54a. On this question of the government helping people get doctors and hospital care at low cost, is the government going too far, doing less than it should, or what? (SHOW CARD VI)

1.Going too far	2.About right	3.Doing less than it should	9.Don't know

54b. Are the Republicans, or the Democrats closer to what you want on this issue, or are they about the same?

1.Rep	2.Dem	3.Same	9.Don't know

(INTERVIEWER: DID R MENTION "SOCIALIZED MEDICINE" OR SOCIALISM"?)

1.Yes	2.No

55. How about this statement? "The United States should give help to foreign countries even if they are not as much against communism as we are." Do you think the government should do this or not, or don't you have an opinion? (SHOW CARD V)

1.Agree strongly	2.Agree	3.Can't decide	4.Disagree	5.Disagree strongly	9.No opinion

(IF OPINION)

55a. On the question of the United States giving help to countries that are not as much against communism as we are, is the government going too far, doing less than it should, or what? (SHOW CARD VI)

1.Going too far	2.About right	3.Doing less than it should	9.Don't know

55b. Are the Republicans, or the Democrats closer to what you want on this issue, or are they about the same?

1.Rep	2.Dem	3.Same	9.Don't know

56. How about this: "The government in Washington should stay out of the question of whether white and colored children go to the same school." Do you think the government should do this or not, or don't you have an opinion on this? (SHOW CARD V)

1.Agree strongly	2.Agree	3.Can't decide	4.Disagree	5.Disagree strongly	9.No opinion

(IF OPINION)

56a. On this question of the white and colored children going to school together, is the government going too far, doing less than it should, or what? (SHOW CARD VI)

1.Going too far	2.About right	3.Doing less than it should	9.Don't know

56b. Are the Republicans, or the Democrats closer to what you want on this issue, or are they about the same?

1.Rep	2.Dem	3.Same	9.Don't know

56c. Do you yourself know of anyone changed his vote because of the parties' stands on school segregation?

1.Yes	2.No

(IF YES) 56d. What kind of a change was that? ____________

57. And this statement: "The government should try to end the draft as soon as possible." Do you think the government should do this or not, or don't you have an opinion on this? (SHOW CARD V)

1.Agree strongly	2.Agree	3.Can't decide	4.Disagree	5.Disagree strongly	6.No opinion

(IF OPINION)

57a. On this question of ending the draft, is the government going too far, doing less than it should, or what? (SHOW CARD VI)

1.Going too far	2.About right	3.Doing less than it should	9.Don't know

57b. Are the Republicans or the Democrats closer to what you want on this issue, or are they about the same?

1.Rep	2.Dem	3.Same	9.Don't know

- 23 -

58. All in all, would you say you are very interested, fairly interested, or not interested in foreign affairs?

[1.Very] [2.Fairly] [3.Not]

58a. ...in things that happen in Washington--that is, national affairs?

[1.Very] [2.Fairly] [3.Not]

58b. ...and how interested are you in things that happen right here in Wayne County and the Detroit area; that is, in local affairs?

[1.Very] [2.Fairly] [3.Not]

59. We want to know what you think are the good and the bad points of both Eisenhower and Stevenson--first what do you feel are Eisenhower's major good and bad points? (GET GOOD AND BAD POINTS)

____

____

____

59a. Did your opinion of Eisenhower change in the last few months before the election?

[1.Yes] [2.No]

(IF YES) 59b. In what way? ____________________

____

____

____

59c. What do you think Eisenhower is really like? ____________________

____

____

____

- 24 -

60. How about Stevenson--what are his major good and bad points? (GET BOTH)

60a. Did your opinion of Stevenson change in the last few months before the election?

1.Yes | 2.No

(IF YES) 60b. In what way?

60c. What do you think Stevenson is really like?

61. What would you say are the major good and bad points of Governor Williams? (GET BOTH)

62. Here are some things people tell us when we interview them. Please tell me if you agree or disagree with them. I'll read them one at a time. First, People like me don't have any say about what the government does.

1.Agree | 2.Disagree

62a. Even when you know your party doesn't have any chance to win, it is important to vote.

1.Agree | 2.Disagree

62b. So many other people vote that it doesn't matter much whether I vote or not.

1.Agree | 2.Disagree

62c. Sometimes politics and government seem so complicated that a person like me can't really understand what's going on.

[1.Agree] [2.Disagree]

62d. Many local elections aren't important enough to bother with.

[1.Agree] [2.Disagree]

62e. Public officials really care about what people like me think.

[1.Agree] [2.Disagree]

63. Now here are some statements that some people make about political parties. Please tell me whether you generally agree or disagree with these. First, the Republican party is the party of the rich.

[1.Agree] [2.Disagree]

63a. The Democratic Party is controlled by the labor unions?

[1.Agree] [2.Disagree]

63b. The Democratic Party is the party of war.

[1.Agree] [2.Disagree]

63c. The Republican Party is the party of depressions.

[1.Agree] [2.Disagree]

64. Some people think <u>non-partisan</u> local elections give better government than a party system does; others feel that a party system is better. Which do you think is better for local government?

[1.Non-partisan] [2.Party system]

64a. Why do you feel this way? ____________________

____

____

____

65. Are political parties <u>run now the way they used to be</u>, or do you feel there have been pretty <u>big changes</u> in the way parties are run?

[1.No changes] [2.Changes]

652. Why do you feel this way? ____________________

____

____

____

____

- 26 -

66. Some people say that the bitterness and hard feelings of a campaign are not worth what it accomplishes; other think what the campaign accomplishes is worth the cost. Which way do you feel?

[1.Bitterness] [2.Campaign worth cost]

66a. Why do you feel this way? ____________________

____

____

____

67. Do you happen to know the names of the United States senators from Michigan?

(1) ____________________ (2) ____________________ [9.Don't know]

67a. How long is the term of office for a United States senator?

__________years

68. Do you know who the congressman from this district is?

____________________ [9.Don't know]

68a. How long is the term of office for a congressman? __________years

69. Do you know who John Feikens is? [1.Yes] [2.No]

(IF YES) 69a. Who is he? __________ ____________________

70. Do you know who Neil Staebler is? [1.Yes] [2.No]

(IF YES) 70a. Who is he? ____________________

71. Of course, a large community like the Detroit area is made up of many kinds of groups. If you had to place yourself in one of these groups, would you say you are in the:

[1.Upper class] [2.Middle class] [3.Working class] [4.Lower class]

71a. Would you say that you were average (CLASS SELECTED) or in the upper part of this group?

[1.Average] [2.Upper]

CENSUS DATA

(BY OBSERVATION OR FROM LISTING BOX)

1. Is this dwelling unit in:

[1.A structure with eight or more dwelling units] [2.A structure with two to seven dwelling units] [3.A single family dwelling unit]

2. Race of respondent: [1.white] [2.Negro] [3.Other] ________ (SPECIFY)

3. Sex: [1.Male] [2.Female]

4. Age: ____________ years

5. Relationship to Head: [1.Head] [2.Wife] (Other) ____________

6. Marital Status: [1.M] [2.S] [3.D] [4.Sep] [5.Wid]

(IF EVER MARRIED)

6a. How long have you been married? ________ years

6b. How many children have you had altogether? ____

7. What was the highest grade of school you completed? ________________

8. Do you have a religious preference? [1.Yes] [2.No]

(IF YES)

8a. What is your religious preference?

[Catholic] [Protestant] [Jewish] Other ____________ (SPECIFY)

(IF PROTESTANT) 8b. What religious denomination is that?

____

9. About how often do you usually attend religious services?

[1.Once a week or more] [2.Twice a month] [3.Once a month] [4.A few times a year or less] [0.Never]

10. How long have you lived in the Detroit area? (IF NEEDED) The "Detroit area" is any place in Wayne, Macomb or Oakland Counties.

____

(IF NOT ENTIRE LIFE)

10a. Where did you live most of your life before you came here?

________________ (TOWN) ________________ (STATE)

10b. Where were you born?

________________ (TOWN) ________________ (STATE)

- 28 -

11. Have you ever lived on a farm? [1.Yes] [2.No]

(IF YES)
11a. Where ______________________ (STATE)
11b. Between what ages? ____________ to ______________

12. Do you own this home, are you buying, or do you rent?

[1.Owns] [2.Buying] [3.Renting] [4.Other] ____________________ (SPECIFY)

13. How many other houses or apartments have you lived in here in the Detroit area?

____

(IF ANY)
13a. How long have you lived at this address? ______________

13b. Did you own the last place you lived before you moved here, or were you in an apartment, renting a house, or what?

[1.Own] (Other) ________________________________

____

13c. What was the address of the last place you lived? (GET INTERSECTION OF TWO NEAREST STREETS IF ADDRESS UNKNOWN)

____
(STREET) (CITY OR TOWNSHIP)

13d. About how many years did you live at this address? __________

14. Would you say you are satisfied, more or less satisfied, or not satisfied with the neighborhood you are in now?

[1.Satisfied] [2.More or less satisfied] [3.Not satisfied]

14a. Why would you say you feel this way? ______________________________

____

____

____

____

15. Do you plan to move from this neighborhood within the next year or so?

[1.Yes] [2.No]

(IF YES)

15a. Will you probably move to a neighborhood in Detroit, in the Detroit suburbs, or to a place outside the Detroit area?

[1.Detroit] [2.Suburbs] [3.Outside]

15b. Why do you plan to move to this new neighborhood and not some other neighborhood?

____

____

____

16. Do you have a telephone here at home? [1.Yes] [2.No]

(IF YES)

16a. How many telephones do you have here at home, counting any extensions you may have?

____

16b. Do you have any wall plugs for telephones? [1.Yes] [2.No]

(IF YES) 16c. How many telephone wall plugs do you have?

____

16d. Altogether, about how many local calls are usually made from your telephone in a day? (GET A SPECIFIC NUMBER)

____

16e. And about how often are out of town or long distance calls made from your telephone--say to places more than twenty-five miles from here? (CARD II)

[1.Everyday] [2.Almost everyday] [3.Once or twice a week]

[4.A few times a month] [5.Once a month] [6.A few times a year]

[7.Less often] [8.Never]

16f. Do you have a party line or a private line? [1.Party] [2.Private]

(IF PARTY LINE)

16g. What is the reason you have a party line rather rather than private line service?

____

____

____

16h. If private lines were available, would you get a private line within the next twelve months?

[1.Yes] [2.No]

(IF NO TELE-PHONE)

16i. Do you plan to take telephone service in the next twelve months?

[1.Yes] [2.No]

16j. Where do you usually go to make a telephone call when you are home and need to call someone, to a neighbors, to a coin telephone or where?

[1.Neighbors] [2.Coin Telephone] Other ______

(DO NOT ASK OF NEGROES)

17. What is the original nationality of your family on your father's side?

______

18. Was your father born in the United States? [1.Yes] [2.No]

19. What was your father's usual occupation while you were growing up? (BE SPECIFIC

______

20. What was your father's political preference? That is, did he consider himself a Republican, a Democrat, or what?

[1.Republican] [2.Democrat] 3.Other ______ (SPECIFY)

21. Would you say your father was very active in politics, quite active, or not active in politics?

[1.Very] [2.Quite] [3.Not]

22. What is your occupation? (IF NEEDED) That is, what sort of work do you do?

______ (E.G., LATHE OPERATOR, STOCK CLERK, HOUSEWIFE) [Retired] [Unemployed]

(IF RETIRED OF UNEMPLOYED)

22a. What kind of work did you do when you were working?

______

22b. What kind of business was that in?

______ (E.G., STEEL MILL, GROCERY STORE)

(IF EMPLOYED)

22b. What kind of business is that in?

______

22c. Do you work for yourself or someone else?

[Self] [Someone else]

23. What job did you have when you first got out of school?

______

- 31 -

24. What was your total family income in 1956, considering all sources such as rents, profits, wages, interest and so on? (CARD VII)

0.Under $1000	1.$1000-1999	2.$2000-2999	3.$3000-3999	4.$4000-4999
5.$5000-5999	6.$6000-6999	7.$7000-7999	8.$8000-9999	9.$10,000-14,999
	&.$15,000 or more			

24a. Was all of your family income from salaries and wages, or was part of it from other sources?

1.All 2.Part

(DO NOT ASK IN ONE ADULT HOUSELOLDS)

24b. How much of your total family income was the income of the head of the family?

____

(DO NOT ASK IN LONG INTERVIEW)

25. In general, do you consider yourself a Republican, a Democrat, or what?

____

____

____

CENSUS DATA ABOUT OTHER ADULTS IN DWELLING UNIT

(ENTER FROM LISTING BOX)

3. Sex: [1.Male] [2.Female]

4. Age: ____________ years

5. Relationship to head: [1.Head] [2.Wife] Other ______________

6. Marital status: [1.M] [2.S] [3.D] [4.Sep] [5.Wid]

7. What was the highest grade of school he (she) completed? ______________

8. Does he (she) have a religious preference? [1.Yes] [2.No]

(IF YES) 8a. What is his (her) religious preference?

[Catholic] [Protestant] [Jewish] Other ______________

(IF PROTESTANT) 8b. What denomination? ______________

9. About how often does he (she) usually attend religious services?

[1.Once a week or more] [2.Twice a month] [3.Once a month] [4.A few times a year or less] [0.Never]

10. How long has he (she) lived in the Detroit area? ______________

(IF NOT ENTIRE LIFE) 10a. Where did he (she) live most of his (her) life before he (she) came here?

______________ (TOWN) ________ (STATE)

10b. Where was he (she) born?

______________ (TOWN) ________ (STATE)

11. Has he (she) ever lived on a farm? [1.Yes] [2.No]

(IF YES) 11a. Where? ______________ (STATE)

11b. Between what ages? ________ to ________

22. What is his (her) occupation? (BE SPECIFIC)

______________ [Retired] [Unemployed]

(IF RETIRED OR UNEMPLOYED) 22a. What kind of work did he (she) do when he (she) was working?

____

22b. What kind of business is (was) that in? ______________

22c. Is (was) this person self-employed? [1.Yes] [2.No]

23. Did he (she) have an income last year apart from what you have already reported in your total family income?

[1.Yes] [2.No]

(IF YES) 23a. What was his (her) total income in 1956? (CARD VII) ______

24. In general, does he (she) consider himself (herself) to be a Republican, a Democrat, or what?

____

APPENDIX B

PRECINCT LEADER INTERVIEW SCHEDULE

SCHEDULE OF QUESTIONS

1. Let's start with some questions about your background in politics. What was the first campaign in which you were a party worker? ______

(IF NOT LAST CAMPAIGN)

1a. Have you worked for the party fairly continuously since then? [1.Yes] [2.No]

(IF NO) 1b. Between what years were you not working for the party? ______ to ______

2. What first led you to become active as a party worker? ______

(IF NOT CLEAR) 2a. How was it you became active at that time? ______

3. Before you actually got into party work, how did you first develop an interest in political matters? ______

4. We have found that party organizations in the different districts vary quite a bit. In this district, what is the next party organizational level between you here in the precinct and district headquarters? ______

- 2 -

5. Here is a list of different party positions (SHOW CARD I). Which of these do you now hold? [None] [Some (RECORD BELOW)]

CARD I	✓ If Now Holds	✓ If Previously Held	
a. Precinct delegate to county convention	____	____	a.
b. Ward (area or zone) party official (specify below)	____	____	b.
c. City or township party official (specify below)	____	____	c.
d. County party official (specify below)	____	____	d.
e. Congressional district party official (specify below)	____	____	e.
f. Delegate to state convention	____	____	f.
g. Other state party official (specify below)	____	____	g.
h. Delegate or alternate to national convention	____	____	h.
i. Others: Citizens for Eisenhower, Young Democrats, etc. (specify below)	____	____	i.

SPECIFIC POSITIONS: ______________________________

____

5a. Which of these have you previously held? [None] [Some (RECORD ABOVE)]

(IF EVER PRECINCT DELEGATE) 5b. How did you happen to run for precinct delegate? ______________________________

____

____

____

6. Some precinct leaders keep records or files on the people in their precinct to aid in campaign activities. Did you have such records for the last campaign? [1.Yes] [2.No]

(IF YES)

6a. In these records did you have information about <u>all</u> the people in your precinct who supported your party, ...about <u>most</u> of these people, ... or about <u>a few</u> of your party's supporters in this precinct? [1.All] [2.Most] [3.A few]

6b. In addition to the supporters of your own party, how about the independents? Did you have information about <u>all</u>, ... <u>most</u>, ... or <u>a few</u> of the independents in this precinct? [1.All] [2.Most] [3.A few]

6c. From your records could you tell just who was registered and who wasn't? [1.Yes] [2.No]

(IF YES) 6d. Was your information on registration checked with the city or township clerk's records during the last campaign? [1.Yes] [2.No]

6d. Did you use these records on election day? [1.Yes] [2.No]

(IF YES) 6e. How did you use them? ______________________________

____

- 3 -

7. What helpers did you have in your precinct work in the last campaign? (GET NUMBER AND ROLE, e.g., wife, 3 neighbors, 2 union stewards)

____

(IF ANY HELPERS)

7a. How many of these people helped you right through the campaign? (GET NUMBER) ________

7b. Were all of these helpers from your <u>own</u> precinct, or did you <u>share</u> workers from other precincts, or were <u>none</u> of your helpers from your own precinct?

| 1.Own | | 2.Share | | 3.None |

(IF OWN WORKERS OR SHARE)

7c. About how many meetings did you have with just your own precinct workers during the campaign? (GET NUMBER) ________

7d. Were there other ways in which you directed the activities of your own workers?

| 1.Yes | | 2.No |

(IF YES) 7e. What were they? ________

____

(IF SHARED WORKERS) 7f. You mentioned that you shared workers with other precincts. How was the work of these people directed? That is, were there regular meetings, phone calls, or what? ________

____

8. With respect to campaign activities, one type of campaign work is the registration drive. Have you done anything in this precinct in order to register voters?

| 1.Yes | | 2.No |

(IF YES)

8a. What did you do? ________

____

____

(IF HELPERS MENTIONED EARLIER) 8b. Were any party workers in this precinct besides you involved in this?

| 1.Yes | | 2.No |

(IF YES) 8c. About how many? (GET NUMBER) ________

- 4 -

9. What other kinds of party work did you do in this precinct during the last campaign? ____________________

(IF NEEDED) 9a. Specifically, what did you do? ____________________

10. About what percentage of the eligible voters in your precinct were <u>registered</u> to vote in the last election? __________

11. And about what percentage of those who were registered <u>actually</u> voted in the last election? __________

12. In the last campaign, did any of your party's state or national candidates—including congressional candidates—visit your precinct or neighborhood personally to meet voters?

[1.Yes] [2.No]

(IF YES) 12a. Which ones? ____________________

13. In connection with party work, how much direct contact have you had with your party's leaders at the state level? (SHOW CARD II)

[1.Often] [2.Frequently] [3.Rarely] [4.Never]

CARD II

1. Often -- throughout the year
2. Frequently during the campaign, but rarely at other times
3. On rare occasions--at conventions, party meetings, etc.
4. Never

(IF EVER) 13a. What sorts of things did you discuss? (BE SPECIFIC) ____________________

(IF NOT MENTIONED) 13b. Did you discuss campaign techniques?

[1.Yes] [2.No]

- 5 -

14. How much direct contact have you had with your party's leaders at the Wayne County level? (SHOW CARD II)

1.Often | 2.Frequently | 3.Rarely | 4.Never

(IF EVER) 14a. What sorts of things did you discuss? (BE SPECIFIC)

______

______

______

______

(IF NOT MENTIONED) 14b. Did you discuss campaign techniques?

1.Yes | 2.No

15. How much direct contact have you had with your party's leaders at the congressional district level? (SHOW CARD II)

1.Often | 2.Frequently | 3.Rarely | 4.Never

(IF EVER) 15a. What sorts of things did you discuss? (BE SPECIFIC)

______

______

______

______

(IF NOT MENTIONED) 15b. Did you discuss campaign techniques?

1.Yes | 2.No

16. And how much direct contact have you had with your party's leaders at the (LEVEL BETWEEN PRECINCT AND DISTRICT)? (SHOW CARD II)

1.Often | 2.Frequently | 3.Rarely | 4.Never

(IF EVER) 16a. What sorts of things did you discuss? (BE SPECIFIC)

______

______

______

______

(IF NOT MENTIONED) 16b. Did you discuss campaign techniques?

1.Yes | 2.No

17. If you were to name your party's most influential leaders in Wayne County, who would you name? ______________________________

____

17a. In what ways are they influential? ______________________

____

____

18. How much say do you believe precinct delegates generally have in running your party's district organization: very little, ... some, ... a fair amount, ... or a great deal?

[1.Very little] [2.Some] [3.Fair amount] [4.A great deal]

18a. Do you think that precinct delegates generally should have more say than they do in running the party's district organization, ... is it about right now, ... or should they have less say?

[1.More] [2.About right] [3.Less]

19. In your opinion, was there a fairly clear plan for your party in Wayne County for the types of activities to be followed during the campaign?

[1.Yes] [2.No]

(IF YES) 19a. How were you informed about this plan? ______________________

____

____

____

(IF NOT MENTIONED) 19b. Did you ever have meetings of precinct leaders to discuss this plan? [1.Yes] [2.No]

20. During the last campaign, about how many meetings of precinct leaders like yourself were there in this district? (GET NUMBER) ______________

- 7 -

21\. Are there any party activities that go on in your district between elections, such as dances, outings, political rallies, and so forth?

[1.Yes] [2.No]

(IF YES) 21a. What are they? ____________________

____

____

21b. What part have you taken in these activities? ____________________

____

22\. Apart from elections and getting out the vote, have you ever given advice or help to the people in your precinct?

[1.Yes] [2.No]

(IF YES) 22a. What did you do? ____________________

____

____

____

23\. Aside from your routine duties, what do you consider to be your most important job or task as a precinct leader? ____________________

____

____

____

24\. What are your plans for party work in future campaigns? That is, will you probably be more active, continue about the same, or be less active?

[1.More] [2.Same] [3.Less]

24a. If you had the opportunity to take an even more responsible position in the party than you now have, would you take it?

[1.Yes] [2.No]

- 8 -

25. Sometimes it seems that one or two key individuals, or perhaps a small group, have a lot to say in a neighborhood and get things done. Do you feel that there are people like this who are important in your precinct? 1.Yes 2.No

(IF YES)

25a. Are these people leaders in other groups? 1.Yes 2.No

(IF YES) 25b. What groups? __________

(IF NO) 25c. Why do they seem to be important? __________

25d. In the last election, did you ever turn to these people for help in your own precinct work? 1.Yes 2.No

26. Along this line, have you received suggestions from leaders or groups outside the party about your work for the party? 1.Yes 2.No

(IF YES)

26a. What sorts of suggestions did you get? __________

26b. From what kinds of groups or people did you get these suggestions? __________

27. One of our aims in this study is to learn more about why people become active politically. What do you feel are the satisfactions and rewards that the average party worker gets out of his political activities? __________

28. If you had to drop out of political activity tomorrow, what things would you miss the most from such work?

____

____

____

29. On this card (SHOW CARD III) are a number of reasons that are often given for why people become active in party work. Taking each reason separately, in explaining why you became active would you say that it is (1) very important, (2) somewhat important, or (3) not very important?

CARD III	Rating
a. I had a personal friendship for a candidate	_____
b. Political work is part of my way of life	_____
c. I am strongly attached to my political party	_____
d. I enjoy the friendships and social contacts I have with other workers	_____
e. I like the fun and excitement of the campaign contest	_____
f. I am trying to build a personal position in politics	_____
g. I see campaign work as a way of influencing the policies of government	_____
h. I like the feeling of being close to people who are doing important things	_____
i. Party work helps me make business contacts	_____
j. Party work helps me fulfill my sense of community obligation	_____
k. Party work gives me a feeling of recognition in my community	_____

29a. Which one of the reasons on this card do you think best explains why you became active?

____

30. From your own observations would you say that Republican and Democratic party workers differ at all in the kinds of rewards and satisfactions they get out of political activity?

[1.Yes] [2.No]

(IF YES) 30a. In what ways? ______________________________

____

____

____

- 10 -

31. We are also interested in getting your impression of some of the characteristics of the people in your precinct. First, which one of these three occupational groups is largest in your precinct, Professional and Business People, or Other White Collar People like salesmen and clerks, or Working Class People?

Occupational Group	✓ If Largest	Record %
Professional and Business	____	____
Other white collar	____	____
Working class	____	____

31a. About what percentage is this largest group of the total? (RECORD ABOVE)

(IF ABOVE ANSWER NOT 100%) 31b. Roughly, about what percentage are the other groups of the total? (RECORD ABOVE)

32. What are the two or three major nationality groups in this precinct?

Nationality Group	Record %	Usual Vote
____________	____	____
____________	____	____
____________	____	____

(FOR EACH GROUP)

32a. About what percentage of the precinct population are (GROUP MENTIONED)? (RECORD ABOVE)

32b. Which of the ways given on CARD IV (SHOW CARD IV) would you say these people usually vote? (RECORD ABOVE)

CARD IV

a. Strongly Republican
b. Republican
c. Fifty-fifty
d. Democratic
e. Strongly Democratic

33. In your opinion, what are the most important religious groups here--Protestant, Catholic, Jewish, or what?

Religious Group	Record %	Usual Vote
______	______	______
______	______	______

(FOR EACH GROUP)

33a. About what percentage of the precinct population are (GROUP MENTIONED)? (RECORD ABOVE)

33b. Which of the ways given on CARD IV (SHOW CARD IV) would you say these people usually vote? (RECORD ABOVE)

34. Do both Negroes and whites live in your precinct? [1. Yes] [2. No]

(IF NO, INTERVIEWER CHECK IF RESPONDENT IS [Negro] OR [White])

(IF YES)

34a. About what percentage of the total precinct population is Negro? ______

34b. Which of the ways given on Card IV do Negroes usually vote? ______

35. Roughly, what would you say is the average family's yearly income in your precinct? $______

36. Is the precinct primarily residential, industrial, or commercial and business?

[1. Residential] [2. Industrial] [3. Commercial]

37. In the last eight to ten years has this precinct changed much from residential or farm to other uses such as industrial or business? [1. Yes] [2. No]

(IF YES) 37a. What was this change? ______

______

______

______

38. About how much movement of families into or out of this precinct has occurred within the last eight or ten years--a great deal, a fair amount, little, or almost none?

[1.Great] [2.Fair] [3.Little] [4.Almost none]

(IF GREAT, FAIR, OR LITTLE MOVEMENT)

38a. Would you say this movement is increasing, has been pretty steady, or is decreasing?

[1.Increasing] [2.Steady] [3.Decreasing]

38b. Would you say that the new people moving in are about the same kind of people as those already here? That is, are they in about the same jobs, racial and social groups, and so forth?

[1.Yes] [2.No]

(IF NO)

38c. How do the newcomers differ from the older residents? ______________________

____

____

(IF NOT MENTIONED) 38d. Are any of the newcomers white persons who moved here from the South?

[1.Yes] [2.No]

(IF SOUTHERN WHITE MIGRANTS) 38e. Which of the ways given on Card IV do the Southern white migrants usually vote? ______________

39. Do people in your precinct ever have conflicts or problems in voting because they are in groups which have different views on political matters?

[1.Yes] [2.No]

(IF YES) 39a. How does this affect the way they vote? ______________

____

____

40. In which of the ways on CARD IV do the people in your precinct as a whole usually vote?

____

40a. Have the voting preferences of the people in your precinct been changing?

[1.Yes] [2.No]

(IF YES) 40b. In what way? ______________________

____

____

- 13 -

41. In the last elections, what percentage of your precinct voters voted for Eisenhower? ________________

41a. ...and what percentage voted for Williams? ________________

42. Would you say that the people in your precinct keep pretty much to themselves or do they get together quite a bit? [1.Selves] [2.Get together]

(IF GET TO-GETHER) 42a. When they got together before the election would you say that they discussed politics most of the time, some of the time, or not very often?

[1.Most] [2.Some] [3.Not often]

(IF MOST OR SOME) 42b. Do you think this had an effect on the way they voted? [1.Yes] [2.No]

43. Did your party's presidential candidate gain or loose strength in this precinct in the last election as compared to 1952?

[1.Gained] [2.About the same] [3.Lost]

43a. What events or activities in this precinct do you think were especially important in explaining this? ________________

____

____

____

43b. What events or activities outside this precinct do you think were especially important in explaining this? ________________

____

____

____

- 14 -

44. Did your party's congressional candidate in this district gain or lose strength in this precinct in the last election as compared to 1952?

[1.Gained] [2.About same] [3.Lost]

44a. What events or activities in this precinct do you think were especially important in explaining this?

____

____

____

____

44b. What events or activities outside this precinct do you think were especially important in explaining this?

____

____

____

____

45. Here is a list of different persons whose opinions are often important in helping people in general decide how to vote (SHOW CARD V). Taking each one separately, would you say that it is very important, somewhat important, or not very important?

CARD V	Rating
a. The opinion of close friends	______
b. The opinion of family members	______
c. The opinion of religious leaders	______
d. The opinion of union leaders	______
e. The opinion of employers and business leaders	______
f. The opinion of nationality or racial group leaders	______
g. The opinion of leaders of a political party	______

45a. Which one of the opinions on this card do you think is the most important?

____

46. Here is a list of the different kinds of clubs and organizations that are found in greater Detroit (SHOW CARD VI). Which of these kinds of groups do you belong to? (RECORD IN "MEMBER" COLUMN, BELOW)

CARD VI	✓If Member	✓If Officer	Record Attendance
Labor unions	____	____	____
A church	____	____	____
Church-connected groups	____	____	____
Fraternal Organization or Lodges	____	____	____
Veteran's organizations	____	____	____
Business or civic groups	____	____	____
Parent-Teachers Associations	____	____	____
Neighborhood Clubs or community centers	____	____	____
Organizations of people of the same nationality background	____	____	____
Sport teams	____	____	____
Professional groups	____	____	____
Political clubs or organizations	____	____	____
Neighborhood improvement associations	____	____	____
Women's clubs	____	____	____
Charitable and Welfare organizations	____	____	____
Other groups (SPECIFY) ________________	____	____	____
________________	____	____	____

(ASK FOR EACH GROUP CHECKED)	46a. Are you on a committee or do you hold any office in this organization? (RECORD IN "OFFICE" COLUMN, ABOVE) 46b. Would you say you attend <u>most</u> of the meetings of this group, <u>about half</u>, or <u>very few</u>? (RECORD IN "ATTENDANCE" COLUMN, ABOVE)

47. Are there any union groups, churches, business or veteran's organizations, or other groups like these that seemed to affect the way people in your precinct voted?

[1.Yes] [2.No]

(IF YES)

47a. Which ones are they?

Group	Ranking
______	______
______	______
______	______
______	______

(IF MORE THAN ONE GROUP) 47b. How would you rank these groups in order of the importance they had in affecting the way people here voted? (RANK ABOVE)

47c. In what way did these groups affect the voting of the people in your precinct? ______

______

______

______

______

47d. Did you work with the leaders of any of these groups in the last campaign? [1.Yes] [2.No]

(IF YES) 47e. What did you do? ______

48. Now, think of the three people you have worked with most closely in politics. What are their occupations? (IF FRIEND IS HOUSEWIFE, GET FRIEND'S HUSBAND'S JOB)

1. ______

2. ______

3. ______

48a. What positions or offices do they hold, if any? ______

______

______

49. With respect to your general viewpoint on current issues, how do you feel about the statement that "The government ought to help people get doctors and hospital care at low cost." Do you have an opinion on this or not?

[1.Yes] [2.No]

(IF YES) 49a. Do you think the government should do this or not? (SHOW CARD VII)

[1.Agree Strongly] [2.Agree] [3.Not sure] [4.Disagree] [5.Disagree strongly]

49b. On this question of the government helping people get doctors and hospital care at low cost, is the government going too far, doing less than it should, or what? (SHOW CARD VIII)

[1.Definitely too far] [2.A little too far] [3.About right] [4.A little less] [5.A lot less]

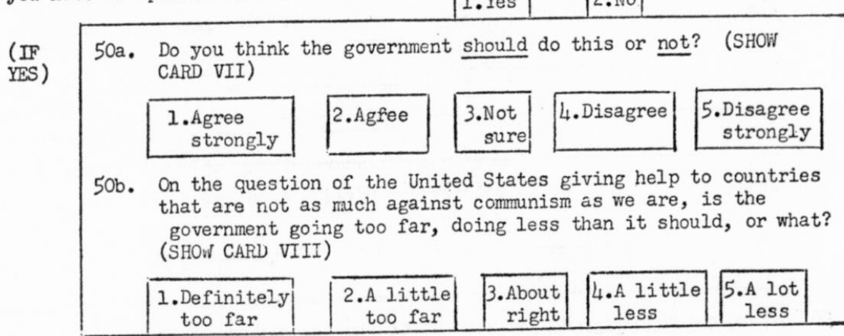

50. How about this statement: "The United States should give help to foreign countries even if they are not as much against communism as we are?" Do you have an opinion on this or not?

[1.Yes] [2.No]

(IF YES) 50a. Do you think the government should do this or not? (SHOW CARD VII)

[1.Agree strongly] [2.Agfee] [3.Not sure] [4.Disagree] [5.Disagree strongly]

50b. On the question of the United States giving help to countries that are not as much against communism as we are, is the government going too far, doing less than it should, or what? (SHOW CARD VIII)

[1.Definitely too far] [2.A little too far] [3.About right] [4.A little less] [5.A lot less]

51. The platforms of both parties were criticized as having too mild Civil Rights planks which were written to attract votes. Do you think that in the case of your party this criticism was justified?

[1.Yes] [2.No]

51a. Would you have favored a stronger plank on Civil Rights even if it meant the loss of some votes?

[1.Yes] [2.No]

52. Would you say there are important differences between the Republican and Democratic parties in what they stand for, or do you think they are pretty much the same?

[1. Different] [2. Same]

(IF DIFFERENT) 52a. What are the major differences you see? ______

53. Was there ever a time when you thought that your party's supporters would have been justified in splitting their ballots?

[1. Yes] [2. No]

(IF YES) 53a. Under what sorts of conditions would these be? ______

54. What do you particularly like about your own party? ______

55. What, if anything, would you say you dislike about your own party? ______

56. What, if anything, do you like about the opposition party? ______

57. In your opinion, what was the most important issue in the last campaign?

- 19 -

58. Some people say that politics is a "dirty game." How do you feel about this?

59. Have you ever been really disgusted with the campaign activities of anyone in your own party? [1.Yes] [2.No]

(IF YES) 59a. Without going into personalities, what types of activities were these?

60. Have you ever been really disgusted with the campaign activities of anyone in the opposition party? [1.Yes] [2.No]

(IF YES) 60a. Without going into personalities, what type of activities were these?

61. What type of candidate would you like to see your party nominate for president next time?

(IF NAME GIVEN) 61a. Why do you feel he would be a good choice?

- 20 -

CENSUS DATA

(BY OBSERVATION)

1. Race: [1.White] [2.Negro] [3.Other] ________ (SPECIFY)

2. Sex: [1.Male] [2.Female]

3. How many adults live in your home? ______

(IF NOT ASCERTAINED) 3a. How are they (is this person) related to you?

____

3b. How many persons under 21 years old live in your home? ______

(IF NOT ASCERTAINED) 3c. How are they related to you? ______

____

4. How old are you? ______

5. Are you married, single, divorced, separated, or widowed?

[1.M] [2.S] [3.D] [4.Sep.] [5.Wid.]

6. What was the highest grade of school you completed?

[0.None] [1.1-4 yrs.] [2.5-6 yrs.] [3.7yrs.] [4.8yrs.] [5.9-11 yrs.]

[6.Completed high school] [7.1-3 yrs. college] [8.Completed college] [9.Grad. work in college]

(IF COLLEGE) 6a. What college did you go to? ______

7. What is your religious preference?

[1.Catholic] [2.Protestant] [3.Jewish] [4.Other] ________ (SPECIFY)

8. About how often do you usually attend religious services?

[1.Once a week or more] [2.Twice a month] [3.Once a month] [4.A few times a year or less] [5.Never]

9. How long have you lived in the Detroit area? (IF NEEDED) The "Detroit area" is any place in Wayne, Macomb or Oakland Counties. ______________

(IF NOT ENTIRE LIFE)

9a. Where did you live most of your life before you came here?

______________ (TOWN) ______________ (STATE)

9b. Where were you born?

______________ (TOWN) ______________ (STATE)

9c. Have you ever lived on a farm? [1.Yes] [2.No]

(IF YES)

9d. Where? ______________ (STATE)

9e. Between what ages? ________ to ________

10. Do you own this home or are you renting?

[1.Owns or buying] [2.Renting] [3.Other] ______________ (SPECIFY)

11. How many other houses or apartments have you lived in here in the Detroit area?

____

(IF ANY)

11a. How long have you lived at this address? ______________

11b. What was the address of the last place you lived? (GET INTERSECTION OF TWO NEAREST STREETS IF ADDRESS UNKNOWN)

______________ (STREET) ______________ (CITY)

11c. About how many years did you live at this address? ________

12. Have you ever been overseas or traveled abroad? [1.Yes] [2.No]

(DO NOT ASK OF NEGROES)

13. What is the original nationality of your family on your father's side?

____

14. Was your father born in the United States? [1.Yes] [2.No]

15. What was your father's usual occupation while you were growing up? (BE SPECIFIC)

____

16. What was your father's political preference? That is, did he consider himself a Republican, a Democrat. or what?

[1.Republican] [2.Democrat] [3.Other] ______________ (SPECIFY)

17. Would you say your father was very active in politics, quite active, or not active in politics?

[1.Very] [2.Quite] [3.Not]

18. What do you believe your total family income will be in 1956, considering all sources such as rents, profits, wages, interest and so on? (SHOW CARD IX)

[0.Under $1000] [1.$1000-1999] [2.$2000-2999] [3.$3000-3999] [4.$4000-4999]
[5.$5000-5999] [6.$6000-6999] [7.$7000-7999] [8.$8000-9999] [9.$10,000-14999]
[&.$15,000 or more]

(DO NOT ASK IN ONE ADULT HOUSEHOLDS) 18a. How much of that will be the income of the head of the family?

____

19. What is your occupation (IF NEEDED) That is, what sort of work do you do? (BE VERY SPECIFIC)

____

[Retired] [Unemployed]

(IF RETIRED OR UNEMPLOYED) 19a. What did you do when you were working?

____

20. What was your occupation when you first became active in politics?

____

(IF RESPONDENT IS A MARRIED WOMAN) 21. What is your husband's occupation?

____

INDEX

PRINTED IN U.S.A.